VIOLATION OF DISABILITY RIGHTS

VIOLATION OF DISABILITY RIGHTS

Rohini Prasad
Sukanta Sarkar

KALPAZ

ISBN: 978-93-5128-081-1

Price: ₹ 1080

First Published, 2015

Published by

Kalpaz Publications
C-30, Satyawati Nagar,
Delhi - 110052
E-mail: kalpaz@hotmail.com Ph.: 9212142040

Laser Typesetting : Rajender Vashist, Delhi
Printed at : G. Print Process, Delhi

Cataloging in Publication Data--DK

Courtesy: D.K. Agencies (P) Ltd. <docinfo@dkagencies.com>

Baruah, R. K. (Rohini Kr.), author.

Violation of disability rights / Rohini Prasad, Sukanta Sarkar.
pages cm
Includes bibliographical references (pages) and index.
ISBN 9789351280811

1. People with disabilities--Civil rights. 2. People with disabilities--Civil rights--Asia. 3. People with disabilities--Civil rights--India. I. Sarkar, Sukanta, author. II. Title.

DDC 342.087 23

Contents

Preface

A disability is a condition or function judged to be significantly impaired relative to the usual standard of an individual or group. The term is used to refer to individual functioning, including physical impairment, sensory impairment, cognitive impairment, intellectual impairment mental illness, and various types of chronic disease. Disability is a global problem. They are found more or less in every country. Physical or mental disability is a silent crisis that not only affects the disabled persons and their families but also the social and economic development of entire society. The society has a moral responsibility to see and also to provide persons with disabilities all kinds of opportunities in order that the concerned disabled persons enjoy all human rights and fundamental freedom. Discrimination faced by disabled persons in education and in the employment sector and their continuous exclusion from the society at large, their potentialities remain untapped by the society. The United Nations declared 1981 as the International Year of Disabled Persons, in order to draw the world attention towards the plight of the disabled, recognise that disability as the first and foremost a human rights issue. Government of India already implemented various acts for the welfare of the disabled. The more familiar among them is *"The Persons with Disabilities (Equal Opportunities, Protection of Rights and Full Participation) Act, 1995"*. The PWD Act, 1995 provides for three per cent reservation in employment in the establishments of

Government of India and Public Sector Undertakings against identified posts. Section 26 of the Persons with Disabilities Act, 1995, free and compulsory education has to be provided to all children with disabilities up to the minimum age of 18 years.

In this connection, we want to place on record our deep appreciation to Prof. Ajay Pathak, Vice-Chancellor, ICFAI University, Tripura, Agartala for providing valuable inputs.

We desire to express our heartiest thank to Prof B.K. Panda, Department of Economics, Berhampur University, Odisha who despite his busy schedule and hectic academic engagements, all the time encouraged and supported us. We have also beholden to Dr N.G. Pendse, Department of Economics, Rani Durgabati University, Jabalpur who's erudite and scholarly tidbits for preparing such a vast work are still fresh in our mind. We also thanks to Dr Pradeep Kumar Pandey, Centre of Judicial Studies, Dibrugarh University, Assam; Dr Rakesh Joshi, Department of Economics, Saurashtra University, Gujarat; Dr D. Pulla Rao, Department of Economics, Andhra University; Dr Vibhuti Patel, Professor cum Director, Centre for Study of Social Exclusion and Inclusive Policy, SNDT Women's University, Mumbai; Dr WakarAmin, Department of Social Work, University of Kashmir, J and K.; Dr Shazia Manzoor, Assistant professor Department of Social Work, University of Kashmir, J and K; Dr Pallab Kanti Ghoshal, Department of Commerce, Netaji Subhas College, Udaipur, for their valuable suggestions and moral support.

We are heartily grateful to Dr Suman Kalan Chaudhury, Department of Business Administration, Berhampur University, Odisha; who always encouraged us to carry on this constructive work. Further, we express our heartily thankfulness to each and every person who directly/indirectly helped us in preparing this work.

It is hoped that this book will be very useful society in general and students of human rights/children rights in particular. Comments and suggestions are most welcomed.

Prof Rohini Prasad
Dr Sukanta Sarkar

Abbreviations

ADA	: Americans with Disabilities Act
AFDO	: Australian Federation of Disability Organisations
ANAB	: Afghan National Association of the Blind
ANAD	: Afghan National Association of the Deaf
ANED	: Academic Network of European Disability experts
APADV	: Association of the People with Visual Impairments
BDDA	: Bangladesh Disability Discrimination Act
BDO	: Block Development Officer
BLAST	: Bangladesh Legal Aid and Services Trust
BNSB	: Bangladesh National Society for the Blind
BOK	: Bank of Korea
BPHS	: Basic Package of Health Services
BPKA	: Bangladesh Protibondhi Kollyan Ain
CAR	: Central African Republic
CAT	: Convention against Torture
CBR	: Community-based Rehabilitation
CDAP	: Comprehensive Disabled Afghans Programme
CDD	: Centre for Disability in Development
CDPF	: China Disabled Persons' Federation
CDPO	: Cambodian Disabled Peoples Organisation
CIR	: Center for International Rehabilitation
CPCB	: Central Pollution Control Board

CRP	: Centre for Rehabilitation of the Paralysed
CRPD	: Convention on the Rights of Persons with Disabilities
CRS	: Commonwealth Rehabilitation Service
DAN	: Disability Action Network
DBCS	: District Blindness Control Society
DBS	: Deaf and Blind Society of Turkmenistan
DCD	: Department of Community Development
DDP's	: Disability and Development Partners
DDR	: Disarmament, Demobilisation and Reintegration
DF	: Disability Fund
DGET	: Directorate General of Employment and Training
DGHS	: Directorate General of Health Services
DPO	: Disabled People's Organisations
DRC	: Democratic Republic of the Congo
DSD	: Disability Services Division
DSP	: Disability Support Pension
DSW	: Department of Social Welfare
DSWD	: Department of Social Welfare and Development
DVFP	: Disability and Vulnerability Focal Point
DWRPD	: Department of Welfare and Rehabilitation of Persons with Disabilities
EENT	: Eyes, Ears, Nose and Throat
EFA	: Education for All
ESCAP	: Economical and Social Council for Asia and Pacific
FAPED	: Federation of the Association of People with Disabilities
FEDOMA	: Federation of Disability Organisations in Malawi
FFO	: Federation of Organisations of Disabled People
FODSWA	: Federation Organisation of the Disabled People in Swaziland
GHS	: General Health Service
GPEI	: Global Polio Eradication Initiative
HCD	: Higher Council for the Affairs of Persons with Disabilities
HKI	: Helen Keller International
HPOD	: Harvard Law School Project on Disability

HREOC : Human Rights and Equal Opportunity Commission
ICCPR : International Covenant on Civil and Political Rights
ICRC : International Committee of the Red Cross
IDA : International Disability Alliance
IDP : Internally-Displaced Person
IDRM : International Disability Rights Monitor
IHRM : Honduran Institute of Habilitation and Rehabilitation
IMF : International Monetary Fund
LARDEF : League to Support the Integration of Disabled People
LDPA : Lao Disabled People's Association
LICHO : Liberia Christian Handicapped Organisation
LLC : Local Level Committee
LNAPD : Lesotho National Association of Physically Disabled
LNFOD : National Federation of Organisations of the Disabled
LNLVIP : Lesotho National League of Visually Impaired Persons
LPHU : Lebanese Physical Handicapped Union
LSMHP : Lesotho Society of Mentally Handicapped Persons
MCDMCH : Ministry of Community Development, Mother and Child Health
MDG : Millennium Development Goal
MDT : Multiple Drug Therapy
MESVTEE : Ministry Education, Science, Vocational Training and Early Education
MLEC : Modified Leprosy Elimination Campaign
MLPA : Ministry of Legal and Parliamentary Affairs
MLSPP : Ministry of Labour and Social Protection of the Population
MMD : Ministry of Martyrs and Disabled
MOLISA : Ministry of Labour Invalids and Social Affairs
MoLSA : Ministry of Labour and Social Affairs
MSA : Ministry of Social Affairs
MSD : Ministry of Social Development

NaCSA	:	National Commission for Social Action
NADL	:	National Association of the Deaf-Lesotho
NaSSIT	:	National Social Security Insurance Trust
NCC	:	National Coordination Committee
NCCD	:	National Coordination Committee on Disability
NCCTC	:	National Cold Chain Training Centre
NCCVMRC	:	National Cold Chain and Vaccine Management Resource Centre
NCWDP	:	National Council for the Welfare of Disable Persons
NDF	:	National Development Framework
NDIS	:	National Disability Insurance Scheme
NDS	:	National Disability Survey
NFDDP	:	National Foundation for the Development of Disabled Persons
NFDN	:	National Federation of Disabled Nepal
NFOWD	:	National Forum of Organisations Working with the Disabled
NFPDN	:	National Federation of People with Disabilities in Namibia
NGO	:	Non-Governmental Organisation
NLEP	:	National Leprosy Eradication Programme
NMRC	:	National Medical Rehabilitation Centre
NORAD	:	Norwegian Agency for Development
NPSP	:	National Polio Surveillance Project
NSO	:	National Statistics Office
NUDIPU	:	National Union of Disabled Persons of Uganda
OAS	:	Organisation of American States
ODA	:	Oman Disabled Association
ODI	:	Organisation of Disabled in Iceland
OECD	:	Organisation for Economic Co-operation and Development
OPV	:	Oral Polio Vaccine
PPA	:	Participatory Poverty Assessment
PTSD	:	Post Traumatic Stress Disorder
PPI	:	Pulse Polio Immunisation
PWD	:	People with Disabilities

RCI : Rehabilitation Council of India
RESC : Revised European Social Charter
RTA : Roads and Transportation Authority
SATH : Special Attention towards Handicapped
SDG : Sustainable Development Goal
SDSC : Singapore Disability Sports Council
SLUDI : Sierra Leone Union on Disability Issues
SNE : Special Needs Education
TAC : Technical Advisory Committee
TEVET : Technical Education, Vocational and Entrepreneurship Training
THSR : Taiwan High Speed Rail
TLM : The Leprosy Mission
UAE : United Arab Emirates
UDHR : Universal Declaration of Human Rights
UKDPC : United Kingdom Disabled People's Council
UNCRPD : UN Convention on the Rights of People with Disabilities
UNESCO : United Nations Educational, Scientific and Cultural Organisation
UNHCR : United Nations High Commissioner for Refugees
UNPRPD : Nations Partnership on the Rights of People with Disabilities
UNRWA : United Nations Relief and Works Agency
UNSRPD : UN Standard Rules on the Equalisation of opportunities for persons with disabilities
UPE : Universal Primary Education
USAID : United States Agency for International Development
WHO : World Health Organisation
ZAPD : Zambia Agency for Persons with Disabilities

1

Introduction

"Childhood vaccines are one of the great triumphs of modern medicine. Indeed, parents whose children are vaccinated no longer have to worry about their child's death or disability from whooping cough, polio, diphtheria, hepatitis, or a host of other infections."

–Ezekiel Emanuel

Introduction

The Earth is unique for its atmosphere and its life's. Humans are uniquely adept at utilising systems of symbolic communication such as language and art for self-expression, the exchange of ideas, and organisation. Life has existed on Earth for billions of years, appearing shortly after the planet had cooled and liquid water became available. From the first bacteria to the amazingly complex animals we see today. Life has colonised every corner of our planet. Over the next five billion years, it will burn the last of its hydrogen, bloat up as a red giant and consume Mercury and Venus. Change has continued at a rapid pace from industrial revolution. Geologists have organised the history of the Earth into a timescale on which large chunks of time are called periods and smaller ones called epochs. Each period is separated by a major geological or palaeontological event, such as the mass extinction of the dinosaurs which occurred at the boundary between the Cretaceous period and the Paleocene epoch. Earth was able to support life only after the planet had cooled enough for a rocky crust to solidify. Once that happened, water vapour from volcanoes condensed in the atmosphere, fell as rain, and collected on the Earth's surface. Besides water vapour, volcanoes produced gases rich in the basic ingredients of life: carbon, hydrogen, oxygen, and nitrogen. Toxic gases such as ammonia and methane were common. Sexual reproduction evolved about 1.2 billion years ago, initiating a rapid increase in the pace of evolution. Sexual reproduction is a method of reproduction that combines and mixes traits from two parent organisms in order to give rise to an offspring organism. The genus Homo first appeared about 2.5 million years ago. Humans are relative newcomers to the evolutionary stage. Humans diverged from chimpanzees about 7 million years ago. About 2.5 million years ago, the first member of the genus Homo evolved, *Homo habilis.*

As time passes people are developed and technology has changes their life. Technological developments include nuclear weapons, computers, genetic engineering, and nanotechnology. Economic globalisation spurred by advances in communication and transportation technology has influenced everyday life in many parts of the world. Cultural and institutional forms such as democracy, capitalism, and environmentalism have increased influence. Major concerns and problems such as disease, war, poverty, violent radicalism, and recently, human-caused climate change have risen as the world population increases.

Who is Human?

Modern humans are the only extant members of the hominin clade. It is a branch of great apes characterised by erect posture and bipedal locomotion; manual dexterity and increased tool use; and a general trend toward larger, more complex brains and societies. Humans create complex social structures composed of many cooperating and competing groups, from families and kinship networks to states. Humans began to practice sedentary agriculture about 12,000 years ago, domesticating plants and animals, thus allowing for the growth of civilisation. Over the years, what people do in their everyday lives has dramatically changed. Different media forms serve different purposes in different individuals' everyday lives which give people the opportunities to make strategic and rational choices about what media form(s) watching television, using the internet, listening to the radio, reading newspapers or magazines, etc.

In the past, before modern technology largely alleviated the problem of economic scarcity in industrialised countries, most people spent a large portion of their time attempting to provide their basic survival needs, including water, food, and protection from the weather.

Social Problem

Social problem refers to an issue that influences and is opposed by a considerable number of individuals within a society. It is often the consequence of factors extending beyond an individual's control and local geographical environment. In some cases, a social issue is the source of a conflicting opinion on the grounds of what is perceives as a morally just personal life or societal order. Social problems brings to influential sociological findings and theories that have the ability to help us both better understand and better deal with our complex social environment. The caste system in India resulted in most of the oppressed untouchables for the past 3,000 years. The caste system was recently banned by the United Kingdom, and the United States is also planning to ban it. Inequality is another burning social problem. It is the state or quality of being unequal. It is the root of a number of social problems that occur when things such as gender, race, and age may affect the way a person is treated. Social problems in the workplace include occupational stress, theft, sexual harassment, wage inequality, gender inequality, racial inequality, healthcare disparities, and many more.

Who are Disable People?

Disability is the consequence of an impairment that may be physical, cognitive, mental, sensory, emotional, developmental, or some combination of these. An individual may qualify as disabled if they have had an impairment in the past or is seen as disabled based on a personal or group standard or norm. Such impairments may include physical, sensory, and cognitive or developmental disabilities. Mental disorders and various types of chronic disease may also qualify as disabilities. The term disability broadly describes impairment in a person's ability to function, caused by changes in various subsystems of the body, or to mental health. The degree of disability may range from mild to moderate, severe, or profound. The term disability refers to any condition that impedes the completion of daily tasks using traditional methods. National governments and global humanitarian agencies have narrowed this definition for their own purposes. A disabled person is one who has a condition called a disability that interferes with his or her ability to perform one or more activities of everyday living. For example, locomotion (indoors and going outside), getting dressed, communicating with others.

Disability is the umbrella term for impairments, activity limitations and participation restrictions, referring to the negative aspects of the interaction between an individual (with a health condition) and that individual's contextual factors (environmental and personal factors). There are over one billion people with disabilities in the world. This corresponds to about 15 per cent of the world's population. Disability is more common among women, older people and children and adults who are poor. PWDs face widespread barriers in accessing services in healthcare (including rehabilitation), education, transport and employment. Intellectual disability or mental retardation is defined as *'a condition of arrested or incomplete development of the mind, which is especially characterised by impairment of skills manifested during the developmental period, skills which contribute to the overall level of intelligence, i.e., cognitive, language, motor, and social abilities. Intellectual disability can occur with or without any other mental or physical condition'.*

The World Health Organisation defines disability as *"an umbrella term, covering impairments, activity limitations, and participation restrictions. Impairment is a problem in body function or structure; an activity limitation is a difficulty encountered by an individual in executing a task or action; while a participation restriction is a problem experienced by an individual in involvement in life situations. Disability is a complex phenomenon reflecting an interaction between features of a person's body and features of the society in which he or she lives".* United Nations Convention on the Rights of Persons with Disabilities (UNCRPD, 2006) *defines Persons with Disabilities as those who have long-term physical, mental, intellectual or sensory impairments which in interaction with various barriers may hinder their full and effective participation in society on an equal basis with others.* The Bangladesh Disability Discrimination Act, 1995 (DDA) defines *"a disabled person as someone who has a physical or mental impairment that has a substantial and long-term adverse effect on his or her ability to carry out normal day-to-day activities."* Similarly for the Americans with Disabilities Act (ADA), 1990, the term disability means *"with respect to an individual, a physical or mental impairment that substantially limits one or more of the major life activities of such an individual, a record of such impairment or being regarded as having such an impairment."*

Generally disabled person is a person with impairment who experiences disability. Disability is the result of negative interactions that take place between a person with impairment and her or his social environment. Impairment is part of a negative interaction, but it is not the cause of, nor does it justify, disability. Disability can be broken down into a number of broad sub-categories, which can include the following: (a) Physical impairments affecting movement, such as muscular dystrophy, post-polio syndrome, spina bifida and cerebral palsy; (b) Lack of or amputation of limbs or other body parts; (c) Sensory impairments, such as visual or hearing impairments; (d) Neurological impairments, such as epilepsy; (e) Cognitive impairments such as Autism or Down syndrome; and (f) Psychiatric conditions such as depression and Schizophrenia.

Persons with mental and psychosocial disabilities represent a significant proportion of the world's population. Millions of people worldwide have mental health conditions and an estimated one in four people globally will experience a mental health condition in their lifetime. Almost one million people die due to suicide every year, and it is the third leading cause of death among young people. Depression is the leading cause of years lost due to disability worldwide. Mental health problems, including alcohol abuse, are among the ten leading causes of disability in both developed and developing countries. During the 2012 United Nations Conference on Sustainable Development, Member States agreed to launch a process to develop a set of sustainable development goals (SDGs) to succeed the Millennium Development Goals (MDGs), whose achievement period concludes in 2015. The SDGs are to address all three dimensions of sustainable development (environmental, economic and social) and be coherent with and integrated into the United Nations global development agenda beyond 2015. In September 2013, at the United Nations, a 30-member Open Working Group of the

General Assembly was tasked with preparing a proposal on the SDGs. In July 2014, the Open Working Group drafted and presented to the General Assembly a proposal for sustainable development goals. The envisaged SDGs have a time horizon of 2015 to 2030.

Disability is not simply a health concern, it is a cross-sectoral issue including social welfare, education, health, employment and income generation, accessibility issues relating to transport, infrastructure and built environment, and access to water and sanitation. PWDs are equal members of the community and as such, they should participate in community-based activities in order to ensure their needs are met. Their participation in planning of disaster management and risk reduction activities throughout the decision-making process will ensure an equitable and eective programme. Disability results from a temporary or permanent impairment (physical, mental, sensory), and is further impacted by environmental, societal or cultural barriers. While emergency situations pose new challenges for all individuals, PWDs are particularly vulnerable as many times they find it especially difficult to cope when their environment and support system are dramatically altered.

The United Nations and Indigenous Persons with Disabilities

Over one billion people, or approximately 15 per cent of the world's population, have disabilities. While no global data exists regarding indigenous persons with disabilities, available statistics show that indigenous peoples are disproportionately likely to experience disability in comparison to the general population. Indigenous persons with disabilities often experience multiple discriminations and face barriers to the full enjoyment of their rights, based on their indigenous status and also on disability. The international community has recognised that special measures are required to protect the rights of the world's indigenous peoples. The first instrument that addressed their rights was the 1957 ILO Convention 107, which has been superseded by the 1989 ILO Convention 169 on Indigenous and Tribal Peoples. Over the past few decades the United Nations has increasingly engaged indigenous people through two International Decades as well as the establishment of specific entities that promote their rights within the UN system.

The Convention on the Rights of Persons with Disabilities (2006), the first legally binding disability specific human rights convention, adopted by the United Nations gives two descriptions of disability. The Preamble to the Convention states that *"Disability results from the interaction between persons with impairments and attitudinal and environmental barriers that hinder their full and effective participation in society on an equal basis with others."* Again it emphasises that *"Persons with disabilities include those who have long-term physical, mental, intellectual or sensory impairments which in interaction with various barriers may hinder their full and effective participation in society on an equal basis with others."* Both the expressions reflect a shift from a medical model to social model of disability.

Millennium Development Goals

The Millennium Development Goals (MDGs) established a unifying set of developmental objectives for the global community. Bringing together United Nations agencies, governments and civil society around eight key development issues, the MDGs foster collaborative action to reduce poverty, improve health and address educational and environmental concerns around the world's most pressing development problems. The MDGs are specifically designed to address the needs of the world's poorest citizens and the world's most marginalised populations. MDGs will not be achieved if their policies, programmes, monitoring and evaluation do not include persons with disabilities. While persons with disabilities make up ten per cent of the world's population, disability is associated with twenty per cent of global poverty according to the World Bank's findings. Currently, there are no references to persons with disabilities either in the MDGs themselves or in the accompanying body of guidelines and policies, programmes and conferences that are part of the on-going MDG efforts. In addition, the new revisions of the MDGs currently in process do not include persons with disabilities.

The international community needs urgently to act to mainstream disability in the MDG processes. This requires policy-makers and technical experts specifically tasked with the programmeming, monitoring and evaluation of current MDG programmes to begin to consider disability so that the next phase of the implementation of the MDGs will include disability as an important component of its core mission. Promoting gender equality and empowerment of women is essential to the achievement of the internationally agreed development goals, including the Millennium Development Goals. Women and girls with disabilities experience double discrimination, which places them at higher risk of gender-based violence, sexual abuse, neglect, maltreatment and exploitation. The global literacy rate is as low as one per cent for women with disabilities, according to a UNDP study.

Challenges before Disability

Disabled people are large minority groups, starved of services and mostly ignored by society, live in isolation, segregation, poverty, charity and even pity. Disability includes blindness, low vision, leprosy-cured, hearing impairment, locomotor disability, mental retardation and mental illness. Due to discrimination they don't go to public places and not free to get those rights which a normal person gets. They are deprived of education and employment. Persons with disabilities often face societal barriers and disability evokes negative perceptions and discrimination in many societies. As a result of the stigma associated with disability, persons with disabilities are generally excluded from education, employment and community life which deprives them of opportunities essential to their social development, health and well-being. Sport can help reduce the stigma and discrimination associated with disability because it can transforms community attitudes about persons with disabilities by highlighting their skills and reducing the tendency to see the disability instead of the person. Common experience reveals that persons with disabilities are more likely to be left behind or abandoned during evacuation in disasters and conflicts due to a lack of preparation and planning, as well as inaccessible facilities and services and transportation systems. Most shelters and refugee camps are not accessible and people with disabilities are many times even turned away from shelters and refugees camps due to a perception that they need complex medical services. Disruption to physical, social, economic, and environmental networks and support systems affect persons with disabilities much more than the general population.

The growing relationship between HIV/AIDS and disability is an emerging issue and cause for concern as persons with disabilities are at higher risk of exposure to HIV. Additionally, there is a growing understanding that persons living with HIV or AIDS are also at risk of becoming disabled on a permanent or episodic basis as a result of their condition. Sexual and reproductive health service providers may lack knowledge about disability issues, or have misinformed or stigmatising attitudes towards person with disabilities. Women and girls with disabilities are especially vulnerable to sexual assault or abuse. Persons with intellectual impairments and those in specialised institutions are also at particularly high risk. Around the world, children with disabilities are a large proportion of the children and persons with disabilities not enrolled in school, which results in their exclusion from vital sexual and reproductive health education that is often provided in school settings.

Conclusion

Disability is the umbrella term for impairments, activity limitations and participation restrictions, referring to the negative aspects of the interaction between an individual and that individual's contextual factors. Everyone in the world, male or female, rich or poor, educated or non-educated, married or unmarried, should have equality in human right. Intellectual disability is a global phenomenon which needs a global perspective. Everyone should have an equalised opportunity to have an access to care, education, vocation, socialisation, etc. by a global team for a global struggle. The Millennium Development Goals established a unifying set of developmental objectives for the global community. Over one billion people, or approximately 15 per cent of the world's population, have disabilities.

Selected Books

1. Baker, E., Wang, M., and Walberg, H. (1994). The effects of inclusion on learning. Educational Leadership 52, 33-35.
2. Banerji, M. and Dailey, R.A. (1995). A study of the effects of an inclusion model on students with specific learning disabilities. Journal of Learning Disabilities 28(8), 511-522.
3. Chapter 2, Attitude towards disability and people with disabilities, Retrieved from http://siteresources.worldbank.org/INDIAEXTN/Resources/295583-1171456325808/Chapter02.pdf

4. Connelly, F.M. and Clandinin, D.J. (1990). Stories of experience and narrative inquiry. Educational Researcher 19(5), 2-14.
5. D'Alonzo, B.J., Giordano, G. and Vanleeuwen, D.M. (1997). Perceptions by teachers about the benefits and liabilities of inclusion. Preventing School Failure 42(1), 4-10.
6. Educators for Inclusive Programmes: A Call for Professional Unification. Early Childhood Education Journal 25(2), 137-139.
7. Fuchs, D. and Fuchs, L. (1995). What's special about special education? Phi Delta Kappan 76, 522-530.
8. Gargiulo, R.M.; Sluder, L.C.; and Streitenberger, D. (1997). Preparing Early Childhood.
9. Giangreco, M.F. and Putnam, J.W. (1991). Supporting the education of students with severe disabilities in regular education environments. In Critical issues in the lives of people with severe disabilities, ed. M.H. Meyer, C.A. Peck, and L. Brown, 245-270. Baltimore: Paul H. Brookes.
10. Harry, B., Allen, N. and McLaughlin, M. (1995). Communication versus Compliance: African-American Parents' Involvement in Special Education. Exceptional Children 61(4), 17-21.
11. King, I. (2003). Examining middle school inclusion classrooms through the lens of learner-centreed principles. Theory into Practice 42(2), 151-157.
12. Read more at http://www.brainyquote.com/quotes/keywords/disability.html#f1hkKvt2XKJ2gupD.99.

2

Disability: Global Perspectives

"Freedom from activity is never achieved by abstaining from action. Nobody can become perfect by merely ceasing to act. In fact, nobody can ever rest from his activity even for a moment. All are helplessly forced to act. . . . A man, who renounces certain physical actions but still lets his mind dwell on the objects of his sensual desire, is deceiving himself. He can only be called a hypocrite. The truly admirable man controls his senses by the power of his will. All his actions will be disinterested. Activity is better than inertia. Act but with self-control. If you are lazy, you cannot even sustain your own body."

–Bhagavad Gita

Introduction

All people of our earth are not same. They are not getting the same facilities. Disability is a challenge in the modern world. Some people are born disabled; others become disabled as a result of an accident or disease. Disabilities range from moderate to significant and can be temporary or permanent. With the help of a supportive community, education and vocational opportunities, disabled persons can make progress. Disability affects hundreds of millions of families in developing countries. Disability rates in the population are higher among groups with lower educational level in the countries of the Organisation for Economic

Co-operation and Development (OECD). On an average, 19 per cent of less educated people have disabilities, compared to 11 per cent among the better educated. Ninety per cent of children with disabilities in developing countries do not attend school. Persons with disabilities are more likely to be victims of violence or rape, according to a 2004 British study, and less likely to obtain police intervention, legal protection or preventive care. Women and girls with disabilities are particularly vulnerable to abuse.

In developed countries, disabled people are three times more likely to be denied healthcare than other people. Barriers include stigma, discrimination, lack of adequate healthcare and rehabilitation services, and inaccessible transport, buildings and information. In developing countries the picture is even worse. Children with disabilities are less likely to start or stay in school than other children, while employment rates are 44 per cent, compared with 75 per cent for people without disabilities in OECD countries.

Estimation of Disability

Around 15 per cent of the world's population, or estimated one billion people, live with disabilities. They are the world's largest minority. This figure is increasing through population growth, medical advances and the ageing process, says the World Health Organisation. An estimated 386 million of the world's working-age people have some kind of disability, says the International Labour Organisation. Unemployment among the persons with disabilities is as high as 80 per cent in some countries. Often employers assume that persons with disabilities are unable to work. A 2004 United States survey found that only 35 per cent of working-age persons with disabilities are in fact working compared to 78 per cent of those without disabilities. Two-thirds of the unemployed respondents with disabilities said they would like to work but could not find jobs. Of the some 70 million persons with disabilities in India, only about 100,000 have succeeded in obtaining employment in industry.

Eighty per cent of persons with disabilities live in developing countries, according to the UN Development Programme (UNDP). The World Bank estimates that 20 per cent of the world's poorest people have some kind of disability, and tend to be regarded in their own communities as the most disadvantaged.

Statistics show a steady increase in these numbers. The two-way link between poverty and disability creates a vicious circle. Poor people are more at risk of acquiring a disability because of lack of access to good nutrition, healthcare, sanitation, as well as safe living and working conditions. Dr Amartya Sen pointed out in his keynote address at the World Bank's conference on disability; the poverty line for disabled people should take into account the extra expenses they incur in exercising what purchasing power they do have.

Disable People in Africa

Africa is the world's second-largest and second-most-populous continent. Africa's largest country is Algeria, and its smallest country is the Seychelles, an archipelago off the east coast. The climate of Africa ranges from tropical to subarctic on its highest peaks. Its northern half is primarily desert, or arid, while its central and southern areas contain both savanna plains and very dense jungle regions. The African Union is a 54-member federation consisting of all of Africa's states except Morocco. The union was formed, with Addis Ababa, Ethiopia, as its headquarters, on 26 June 2001. Although it has abundant natural resources, Africa remains the world's poorest and most underdeveloped continent. Poverty, illiteracy, malnutrition and inadequate water supply and sanitation, as well as poor health, affect a large proportion of the people who reside in the African continent. Africa's population has rapidly increased over the last 40 years, and consequently, it is relatively young.

Persons with disabilities face a lot of challenges and are sometimes abused both in the developed and developing countries. It was in realisation of this anomaly and the need to accord these individuals their full rights as human beings and also some special rights by reason of their circumstance that countries of the world through the instrumentality of the United Nations have developed several Instruments to affirm the rights of persons with disabilities. These rights are hinged on the universality, indivisibility, interdependence, and interrelatedness of all human rights and fundamental freedoms and the need for persons with disabilities to be guaranteed their full enjoyment without discrimination.

The number of disabled persons in the world is on the increase. The progress in technology, the efficiency of medical and surgical care and better methods of functional rehabilitation have all contributed to reducing mortality rates and to the presence of greater numbers of people with disabilities in the world today. People with disabilities in developing countries in Africa face many limitations, despite the proclamation of the UN Decade of Disabled Persons. Their human rights receive little or no respect, the general development programmes do not take into account the needs of disabled people or their participation in programmes, disabled people have little or no access to services offered to other citizens, they are unable to take decisions concerning their own future, and they are generally poor, living at the bottom of the social scale.

Disable People in North Africa

North Africa is the northernmost region of Africa. Northern Africa includes seven countries or territories; Algeria, Egypt, Libya, Morocco, Sudan, Tunisia. The distinction between North Africa and much of Sub-Saharan Africa is historically and ecologically significant because of the effective barrier created by the Sahara Desert for much of modern history. The Atlas Mountains, which extend across much of Morocco, northern Algeria and Tunisia, are part of the fold mountain system that also runs through much of Southern Europe. Sheltered valleys in the Atlas Mountains, the Nile Valley and delta, and the Mediterranean coast are the main sources of fertile farming land.

March 14 is the National Day of Persons with Disabilities in Algeria. Youngsters with disabilities face many issues related to their education and healthcare. The financial help given to their parents is also important. As for adults, it is their right to having revenue, a job, a home and access to transportation and other amenities that is highlighted. The disabled receive 4,000 DZD (it was 3,000 DZD before 2007) monthly from the government and all Algerians know this is not enough to make a decent living. It is even suppressed if the person with a disability is employed, and people below 18 are not entitled to get it. Disabled associations want this to be re-evaluated and increased to 21,000 DZD and they want it for all the disabled regardless of their age or occupation. Disabled people pay less tax on imported adapted vehicles.

Algeria, Morocco, and Tunisia were among the eighty countries that signed the Convention on the Rights of Persons with Disabilities and the Optional Protocol at a ceremony at the UN General Assembly hall in New York. The signature came after ten days of discussion of the treaty's provisions, which will give greater rights and freedoms to disabled people around the world under UN auspices. This is the first human rights convention adopted in the 21st Century, and in addition to national monitoring mechanisms, it requires the establishment of an international committee of experts including people with disabilities to monitor the treaty's implementation.

Handicap International is working in Algeria and its goal is to ensure that the needs and contributions of disabled people are recognised and included at all levels. In 1998, Handicap International began working with local and national partners to provide training and support for service providers working with people with disabilities so that they could improve the care they offered. Although legislation to protect and promote the rights of people with disabilities was introduced in 2002, there is still a long way until aspects of the legislation are meaningfully realised for people with disabilities. More recently, governments have shown willingness to further the inclusion of people with disabilities. The Convention of the Rights of Persons with Disabilities was ratified in 2009. As many suffered injuries during the war in Libya, International Medical Corps has prioritised rehabilitation services and support for the disabled. Through support from ExxonMobil, Government provides equipment and critical services for disabled Libyans through rehabilitation centres across the country and work to train local health workers including physiotherapists. Evidence and experience shows that when barriers to their inclusion are removed and persons with disabilities are empowered to participate fully in societal life, their entire community benefits. Barriers faced by persons with disabilities are a detriment to society as a whole, and accessibility is necessary to achieve progress and development for all.

Injured and disabled people are struggling to access the aid they need more than two and a half years after the start of the Syrian crisis, according to the charity Handicap International. Today, on the International Day of Persons with Disabilities, the organisation has called the crisis highly disabling and said that more needs to be done to reach the most vulnerable people. Handicap International is deeply concerned about the consequences that will result from landmines and explosive remnants of war in Syria, and is educating civilians about the risks in order to prevent accidents. Explosive weapons, including cluster munitions, have been used indiscriminately in civilian areas, and will remain a threat long after the conflict ends. According to the Cluster Munition Monitor, almost 90 per cent of cluster munition victims recorded in 2012 were killed or maimed in Syria. Handicap International is a charity working in situations of poverty and exclusion, conflict and disaster in 60 countries worldwide. Its activities include clearing landmines and unexploded ordnance, educating communities about the risks, supporting survivors by providing artificial limbs and rehabilitation, and campaigning for their rights.

The Libyan government passed a law in 1981 which *"identified the mentally and physically retarded and disabled."* The law set out to provide housing, home care, education, prosthetic limbs, and rehabilitation to disabled persons. In addition, under the law, the government would confer tax reductions and financial assistance to those living with a disability, not including the Social Security fund provided by the government to provide relief to the disabled. The government also set out to facilitate access to public transportation for those with a physical or mental disability. The FIIAPP International and Ibero-American Foundation Administration and Public Policy mobilised two years ago to Tunisia about 20 experts in labour and school enrollment for disabled people, among other issues. They have trained 36 educational professionals and 48 labour consultants. The twinning project under the name of *'Support for socio-economic integration of people with disabilities'*, has helped to improve the educational level and to establish a model of inclusive education of children with disabilities in regular education centres and to enhance access to employment for this group.

There are a good number of references to Tunisian NGOs working for persons with disabilities and DPOs (organisations run by persons with disabilities, especially membership-based organisations of persons with disabilities run by themselves), which seem to have been consulted in the production of report. However, it is not clear which of those NGOs are genuine DPOs governed by persons with disabilities. While it seems that Tunisia has made many efforts to improve its legislation related to persons with disabilities, one can see still a very strong presence of the medical model approach (many references to prevention, definition of persons with disabilities, the article on the right to health, the predominance of doctors on the regional disability commissions). There is also a strong preference for specialised solutions (transport, school, etc.) and much less focus on ensuring full accessibility of mainstream services, notwithstanding a quite comprehensive accessibility strategy.

Disabled people make up 5.12 per cent of Morocco's population, according to a 2004 government survey. This vulnerable section of society encounters major obstacles on a daily basis. Disabled people struggle to live in an environment where everything has been designed without consideration of their infirmities. The government is reportedly working to change the situation. Minister for Social Development, Family and Solidarity Nouzha Skalli has often publicly stressed the need to develop new legislation to reinforce progress made in expanding rights for disabled people. Skalli has called for the establishment of an integrated and global legislative framework which addresses the gaps and inadequacies of the current laws. The government's goal is to provide 45 per cent of disabled people with access to education by 2009. Through the creation of 200 integrated classes each year, officials hope to see that percentage rise to 75 per cent in 2012. Efforts are also under way to find solutions to counter discrimination in the workplace. *"Our ambition is to reserve seven per cent of posts for disabled people, by law,"* says Minister Skalli. New laws are also planned to guarantee disabled people's rights to medical care and to provide training to more clinical psychologists, occupational therapists and hearing aid specialists.

Sudan has enacted two specific instruments in favour of disabled persons: the Act on Welfare and Rehabilitation of Disabled Persons, 1984 and a Law Concerning the Privilege of War Disabled, 1998. A disability provision is also included in the 1998 Constitution of the Republic of Sudan, while the 1992 General Education Act provides for equal opportunity in education for people with disabilities. Article 12 of the Act on the Welfare and Rehabilitation of Disabled Persons of 1984 provides for the establishment of a fund for the welfare and rehabilitation of disabled persons to finance the activities undertaken in this field.

It also provides for the setting up of a National Council to lay down general policy for the welfare of disabled persons and supervise regional councils in Sudan. The Act makes provision for measures to promote employment for disabled persons. Article 11 of the 1998 Constitution of the Republic of Sudan lays down general principles of justice and social solidarity, including specific mention of people with disabilities. Article 3 of Labour Act 1997 states that: every person desiring recruitment and capable to work is entitled to get registered for this purpose.

Recently, Sudan opted for institutional arrangements to promote social integration of disabled persons. The Government has established an Office on Disability where most probably under the Ministry of Social Planning. It is with participants from governmental and non-governmental organisations and the private sector. The Government of Sudan has established a Production Plant for people with disabilities, with the assistance of the Islamic Rehabilitation Agency, UNDP. It aims to provide employment for qualified disabled persons in a number of trades. After effective lobbying by disabled people's organisations, the Government decided that all children with disabilities would be entitled to free education from 2002. In Sudan, there are various special institutions catering to persons with disabilities. Rejaf Education Centre for the Blind, Al-Nour Institute, the Project for the Rehabilitation of Blind People and Sudanese National Association of the Blind provide training for persons with disabilities. Measures to guarantee the right of people with disabilities to compete for jobs on an equal basis with other workers are provided through the Act of 1984 on the Welfare and Rehabilitation of Disabled Persons that established a fund for the welfare and rehabilitation of disabled persons. Sudan's geography and history of conflict has made it difficult for disabled people to access healthcare and rehabilitation. They are often hidden away. With no rights to either an education or employment, they often depend on begging to survive. In Sudan people with disabilities are often neglected, excluded from community life, have no access to social services and are often hidden away by families who considered them a problem.

There are more than 2.2 million people with visual disabilities living in Egypt most of which suffer from poverty, lack of accessibilities, ineffective educational techniques and governmental negligence. They still have hope in life and challenge their physical disabilities along with the disabilities created by the society. People facing physical challenges have been suffering for a long time discrimination and lack of accessibilities. Individuals having partial or complete loss of sight are not the least among them. The person with visual disability faces a lot of social problems. Inaccessibility of streets is another hardship that visually impaired people have to cope with. In most developed countries, sidewalks are designed to help people with visual disabilities to walk confidently without worrying to step over any obstacles or to be run-over by a vehicle. Egyptian governments throughout the years tackled the problem with successive deliberate mistakes and negligence that made the lives of the visually impaired even harder. According to the Egyptian law concerning higher education, students with visual disabilities are not allowed to be enrolled in sciences majors and they are also restricted to specified majors in the non-sciences sector. Though many non-governmental organisations work with the visually disabled people for so long, many of them failed to offer real support and medical improvement because they have focused on the financial support.

In Egypt, there are two major causes of impairments - *economic* and *social*. As a developing country Egypt suffers from widespread poverty. This is associated with unsanitary living conditions, lack of access to safe drinking water, and inadequate means of garbage disposal. Another major cause of impairment is malnutrition. Because of the poor economic income generated in rural and lower-class urban areas, malnutrition is very common. It affects mostly women and children, which puts them at a great disadvantage to fall victims of impairment. Social causes are also implicated in high levels of impairment. One is endogamous marriage. Although there is some debate over the accuracy of the figures it has been suggested that they account for 67 per cent of the total number of people with impairments. High fertility rates also contribute to the impairment of women and children.

In Egypt basic compulsory free education is guaranteed by the constitution to all Egyptian children within the age from 6-13 years. Its duration is nine years and is divided into two stages: First stage (Primary) is six years duration and Second stage

(Preparatory) is three years duration. The declaration of the Rights of Intellectually Disabled Persons adopted in 1971, secured the rights of the disabled. Its first statement declares: *"The mentally retarded person has to the maximum degree of feasibility, the same rights as other human beings, which includes the right to educational, medical, and economic security, as well as rights corresponding to particular needs in the medical and educational fields and a decent standard of living."* The second declaration states *"disabled persons have the rights to respect for their human dignity"*. Social Rehabilitation Law No. 39 stated: *Every disabled citizen has the right to benefit from rehabilitation services... Any trained disabled person should be given a license to enroll at manpower offices to enjoy the right provided for him under the provision of medical fitness in case of public services because of his defect, as indicated in the rehabilitation certificate.* In 1975, the quota of disabled was increased from two per cent to five per cent of workers in any business with over 60 employees whether in public or private sector. As a result of the UN declaration and worldwide awareness, Egypt responded to the challenge and President Mubarak declared 1988-1999 the Decade for the Protection and the Welfare of the Egyptian Child, coinciding with the adoption of the Convention on the Rights of the Child in 1989.

Disable People in West Africa

West Africa is the westernmost sub-region of the African. Islam is the predominant religion of the West African interior and the far west coast of the continent; and was introduced to the region by traders in the ninth century. Islam is the religion of the regions biggest ethnic groups by population. West Africans primarily speak Niger–Congo languages, belonging mostly. The Economic Community of West African States, founded by the 1975 Treaty of Lagos, is an organisation of West African states which aims to promote the region's economy. West Africa is inhabited by West Africans, and in line with the current membership of the Economic Community of West African States. The UN definition of Western Africa includes the following 16 countries: Benin, Burkina Faso, Cape Verde, Cote d'Ivoire, Gambia, Ghana, Guinea, Guinea-Bissau, Liberia, Mali, Mauritania, Niger, Nigeria, Senegal, Sierra Leone, and Togo.

Mali's disabled have access to some free healthcare options, and are supported by a number of associations and charities, but what they really want is to find work and contribute to the national economy. While the World Health Organisation estimates ten per cent of the Malian population is disabled, the percentage is much higher because of road traffic accidents and illnesses left untreated. Most of the employment progress has taken place in the public sector. Government ministries practice positive discrimination to hire people with disabilities, encouraging disabled people to take the entrance exam for civil servant employment. The Ministry of Social Affairs has been particularly proactive in hiring people with disabilities. The government has signed the International Labour Organisation Convention on Decent Work, which addresses employment rights of disabled people; and Mali is the seventh African country to sign the Convention on the Rights of Persons with Disabilities.

Handicap International is working in Mali from long ago. The conflict forced Handicap International to temporarily suspend its operations in Mali. Teams had been distributing food in the north of the country since summer 2012 in response to the food crisis in the region. More than 18 months since fighting broke out between rebel forces and the Malian army, the situation in Mali has yet to return to normal and civilian lives are still at risk. In Diabaly, the 17 members of Handicap International's weapons clearance team start work as the sun rises. Handicap International teams have been carrying out weapons risk education with communities and displaced people in the north of Mali since summer 2012.

Sierra Leone remains among the poorest countries in the world although extremely rich in natural resources (diamonds, gold and other minerals) and with considerable agricultural potential. The proportion of the population below the poverty line is estimated at 70 per cent and some 26 per cent is classified as extremely poor. Among disabled and non-disabled alike, most Sierra Leoneans count primarily on family and friends for social and economic support. The extended family in many low income countries is an important source of support and help for members traditionally seen as vulnerable. This highlights the necessity of ensuring the inclusion of families and communities when designing programmes and policies. People with disabilities are making ten per cent of the population mainly because of the civil war that devastated the country for a decade. People with disabilities have for years been silent and sidelined. But this is slowly but surely changing the voice of persons with disabilities and their rights has been amplified in a new law on disabilities ensuring inclusion on all fronts, in the country's development and political plans.

The Sierra Leone government in July 2009 ratified the UN Convention on the Rights of Persons with Disabilities and is currently working on national legislation to ensure compliance. President of the Sierra Leone Union on Disability Issues (SLUDI) has, in an exclusive interview with Concord Times, called on the government to speedily implement the free healthcare package as stipulated in the 2011 Persons with Disability Act. Part V, section 17(1) of the Act provides that, *"Every person with disability shall be provided with free medical services in public health institutions"*. Despite the Act making such a provision, the government is yet to fully implement the free healthcare services for persons with disability. Disabled persons are among the most vulnerable people in society and that government should do all in its powers to ensure they access free healthcare service, thus calling for the establishment of a Medical Board as also stipulated in the 2011 Act. Aside the call for the provision of free healthcare services for persons with disability, the 2011 Act among others demanded that government should provide free education to all disabled persons across the country. Government has established the National Commission for Persons with Disability; a commission charged with the responsibility to champion the cause of disabled persons.

Handicap International is work to improve the lives of people with disabilities by promoting their social inclusion and by helping to make care and support services more accessible. In 1996, Handicap International launched activities to support victims of the civil war. Today, projects promote better access to jobs and education for people with disabilities and support care providers to recognise and understand the needs of disabled people so that the services they offer are more accessible. They also support the inclusion of people with disabilities in decision-making processes by helping them to access opportunities to contribute to policy development, strategies and advocacy initiatives. It also works to reduce mortality rates and improve the health of mothers and young children. They are working to improve access to mother and child health services in order to reduce the risks of children developing impairments and to make sure there is early intervention in cases where impairments are diagnosed detected.

Eleven years of civil war have left approximately 40,000 people dead, two million people displaced and thousands of individuals amputated and injured. The war toll is even higher if one considers the indirect impact on people who did not have access to health services and nutrition during the conflict. This in turn led to an increase in mortality, morbidity and disability. The conflict ended in 2002, when a peace agreement was signed in Accra, Ghana, between the government and rebel factions. A general census conducted in 2004 estimated that there were nearly 130,000 people with disabilities in Sierra Leone, with a prevalence of 2.4 per cent of the total population. The 2004 Census data indicate that about 30 per cent of those classified as people with disabilities receive some type of assistance. The Ministry of Social Welfare is the official government administration responsible for the welfare of people with disabilities, but its resources and capabilities are very limited. In addition to the Ministry of Social Welfare, programmes in support of people with disabilities have also been established under the National Commission for Social Action (NaCSA) and the National Social Security Insurance Trust (NaSSIT). National and international NGOs continue to provide the bulk of the assistance, which has primarily focused on functional rehabilitation and psychological support services. Interventions include community-based rehabilitation projects, reinforcement of networks of rehabilitation and psychological services through hospitals and established institutions, strengthening organisations for people with disabilities and support for elaboration of a national policy for people with disabilities.

There is sufficient evidence to suggest that poverty is both a cause and consequence of disability. Poverty and disability reinforce each other, contributing to increased vulnerability and exclusion. Children with disabilities are more likely to die young, to be neglected, malnourished, uneducated, and poor. People with disabilities who are denied educational opportunities are subsequently less able to find employment, driving them deeper into poverty. During almost a decade long civil war that ended in 2002, the Sierra Leonean population experienced widespread human rights violations, affecting the majority of its population and resulting in permanent disability (physical, sensory and/or psycho-social) for many. The 2004 Census uses the World Health Organisation's general definition of a person with disabilities as, *"one who experiences any limitation in performing a daily-life activity in a manner considered normal for a person of his or her age, because of a long-term physical condition (that is, more than six months), mental condition18 or health problems."* Sierra Leone is not alone in underestimating the number of people with disabilities. Experience from other countries shows that official census estimates of the number of people with disabilities tend to under represent the prevalence of the phenomenon in the population, based on evidence seen or recorded by other organisations. The WHO estimates that in developing countries 25 per cent of the total population is adversely impacted as a result of disabilities. The cost of disability is unequally shared, as the burden of care disproportionately falls on women. Moreover, disability negatively affects family members and their ability to attend school or perform jobs and other tasks that would strengthen the social and economic environment of the household.

According to research carried out by HI in association with partners in Senegal, the disabled are less likely to have attended school, which means that around 75 per cent are illiterate. They are also more likely to need costly specialised health services yet they receive no help from the state. Moreover, only 20 per cent of the disabled population is estimated to be employed, compared to more than 50 per cent of the non-disabled population. Senegal is a signatory to the UN Convention on the Rights of Persons with Disabilities and in 2010, the National Assembly passed a law, the *'Loi d'Orientation Sociale'*, aimed at *'securing equal opportunities for the disabled and protecting them against all forms of discrimination'*. One of the law's decrees is the *'carte d'égalite de chances'*, which would provide an identity card for every disabled citizen, guaranteeing their rights, certain privileges and government support in accessing healthcare, training, employment and public services.

Nigeria is estimated to have a population of 169 million; although it is argued that the country had not had any credible census since 1816. Based on the World Report on Disability approximately 25 million Nigerians have a disability, with 3.5 million of these having very significant difficulties in social and physical functioning. These disabilities include physical and intellectual developmental conditions. In addition to stigma and negative attitudes, the most common problem associated with the poor social care situation for the disabled is the lack of recognition and financial support social agencies face in Africa, particularly in Nigeria. Due to reduced spending on social welfare, as it is believed by the government not to directly contribute to the economic growth and development of the country, social agencies are limited in the amount of human and material resources they can obtain for the successful implementation of their social programmes for the support of the disabled and/or vulnerable people in general. Approximately 25 million people are living with a disability; some are cared for by their family members, others are left homeless in terrible living conditions begging on the streets.

In West Africa, people with particular social identities and interests often organise themselves into societies and associations. In Nigeria, World Health Organisation estimates put the number of people with disability at 19 million of the country's population. This figure is too large to be excluded from the policy framework of the country. The exclusion of this group, many of whom have brought honour and laurels to the country, especially in sports and the academia, manifest, primarily, because there is no legislation protecting people with disability against discrimination. The country needs to overhaul its transportation system in order to give disabled persons access to the service. For instance, there are no standard bus stops where disabled people could commute and the 'molue'-type system does not stop for to enable the disabled person's board and disembark. Disabled persons are denied job opportunities even when they are most qualified, accentuating their preponderance in the employment market. Some people ignorantly believe that the disabled need not work because of the trouble they will go through.

Human Rights in Mauritania are generally seen as poor according to international observers, including Freedom House, the United States Department of State, and Amnesty International. Amnesty International has accused the Mauritania legal system of functioning with a complete disregard of legal procedure, fair trial, or humane imprisonment. Amnesty International also has accused the Mauritanian government of an institutionalised and continuous use of torture for decades. Women often become disabled due to their disadvantaged position in society. They tend to receive less food than males and they are weaker and more susceptible to disease. In parts of Africa and Asia, women are also disabled by female circumcision, the process of removing the clitoris and sometimes the labia in young females.

The Liberia Christian Handicapped Organisation (LICHO), which was founded on the 2nd May, 1987, is a registered non-governmental and non-political organisation with the government of Liberia, through the Ministry of Foreign Affairs. It is founded and run by a group of disabled persons with the sole aim of advocating for the protection and promotion of the right and development of the disabled, empowering and building their capacity in various vocational skills trainings for self-employment and sustainable development. LICHO will set up a general cassava farm for the training of the disabled in simple farming method, and to also establish Garie Production Center to produce Garie for the local markets and markets across the borders. This centre will serve two major purposes: Serve as the means to sustain the project and the future running of the organisation.

The process of the return to democracy embarked upon in Burkina Faso since the promulgation of the 11th June, 1991 Constitution is developing in a favourable climate and makes the implementation of the rights and responsibilities embodied in the African Charter on Human and Peoples' Rights conducive. Within the framework of its national policy of the promotion and protection of human rights, Burkina Faso has, from 2003, undertaken numerous activities the objective of which is to strengthen civil and political rights (Title 1), the progressive improvement of economic, social and cultural rights (Title 2) and the reaffirming of the specific rights enshrined by the Charter (Title 3). The rules of access and of procedure before the Courts are the same for all persons seeking justice who come before these Courts within the context of their respective competences. Any violation of the physical integrity of an individual constitutes an offence in the eyes of the Law. To ensure a better protection of the entire resident population the State has taken a certain number of measures within the context of the national security policy.

In most developing countries, including Ghana, disabled persons constitute an impoverished marginalised group, characterised by lack of access to public health, education, and other social services that would ideally support and protect people with disabilities. Economically as well as in social terms, disabled persons in developing countries are classified among the poorest of the poor. People with disabilities are often regarded as unproductive and incapable of contributing in a positive way to society, and rather seen as constituting an economic burden on the family and the society at large, which leaves them in a vicious cycle of poverty. Previously, a quota system was in effect so that employers with a certain number of employees were obliged to have a percentage of PWDs employed. However, the system was poorly monitored and has been dropped. In 2005, a national health insurance scheme was launched by the government, to enable the population access to affordable health facilities. Unless PWDs are classified as indigents, they are not entitled to exemption from paying the subscription fee, an option which according to the plan may be granted to poor people. The process of developing a policy on disability has been long and tedious. Cabinet passed the policy and the National Disability Policy Document was printed in December 2000. The bill was finally passed by parliament in June 2006. The Disability Council will be responsible for financing part of its activities.

Limited access to education, unemployment, stigmatisation, social exclusion, negative socio-cultural perception and poverty are few challenges facing Persons with Disability in Ghana. In Ghana the 2010 population and Housing Census puts the population of severely disabled persons at three per cent (737,743). This means that the population of Persons with Disability in Ghana could as well be between 15 and 20 per cent. An estimated 70 per cent of persons with disability live in rural areas and thus encounter a lot of challenges in their participation in decision-making and general access to information, resources and opportunities. Formal education for most people with disabilities is a hard nut to crack mainly because most of them are intimidated by their disability. Some families unfortunately also discriminate against members with disability. They would rather finance the education of a child without disability than one with a disability.

Disabled persons as a consequence of their disability have reduced capability of activity that causes many difficulties to life, work and studies. The impact of disability on life activities may be different and depends upon the specific context such as the environment-urban or rural and type of country- either developed or less developed and cultural/societal norms as they relate to people with disabilities. Several conventions have been established by many international organisations and countries as well, to protect the rights of the disabled. The Disability Act of Ghana 715 states that a person shall not discriminate against a prospective employee on an employee on the grounds of disability unless disability is in respect of the relevant employment. It further states in paragraph 89 that the ministry though the public employment centres, shall assist to secure jobs for persons with disability.

Disable People in Central Africa

Central Africa is a core region of the African continent which includes Burundi, the Central African Republic, Chad, the Democratic Republic of the Congo, and Rwanda. The basin of Lake Chad has historically been ecologically significant to the populations of western Central Africa, with the Lake Chad Basin Commission serving as an important supra-regional organisation in Central Africa. The main economic activities of Central Africa are farming, herding and fishing. At least 40 per cent of the rural population of northern and eastern Central Africa lives in poverty and routinely face chronic food shortages. The Rwandan Education Sector Strategic Plan (ESSP) 2006–2010, 18 states that some ten per cent of all students suffer from some form of disability. This is a significantly higher figure than the 4.7 per cent of the general population who are disabled, as suggested by the 2002 census. Rwanda's Special Needs Education (SNE) Policy reiterates this ten per cent figure and suggests this means around 175,205 learners could have some degree of disability. In Rwanda, 2008 was the first year for the government's programme to facilitate disabled students' enrolment in higher education. In that academic year, 15 blind students, six deaf students and one physically impaired student were enrolled in universities.

With the National AIDS Control Council (CNLS) and Handicap International, Rwanda's Umbrella of Persons with Disabilities in the Fight against HIV/AIDS (UPHLS) has been able to initiate some HIV sensitisation activities specifically designed for people with disabilities, including training peer educators who are able to communicate in sign language. According to the UPHLS, many challenges remain in addressing HIV among Rwanda's disabled population, including high illiteracy, no harmonised sign language and little knowledge of Braille, fear of double stigma as a result of being both HIV-positive and disabled, health workers who are unable to communicate effectively with sight or hearing-impaired patients and lack of national data on HIV/AIDS and disability. As a signatory to the UN Convention on the Rights of Persons with Disabilities (CRPD), the Government of Rwanda has confirmed its commitment to take a strategic stand on disability based on a vision which covers human rights, inclusion and empowerment of persons with disabilities. This vision recognises that an equal society is an inclusive society, where reasons for exclusion are examined and addressed. It is also one which recognises that disability is part of the human condition in every society, rich and poor. Disability is not a specialised concern but a fundamental issue of universal human rights. In Rwanda, poverty can be seen as both a cause and an effect of disability. It also had a massive genocide in 1994 during which an estimated 800,000 people were killed.

Chad offer specialist support to children when there are a combination of factors related to disability or health condition, the family's abilities to cope and the resources available to the family. In early 2013, the UNHCR estimated that there were more than half a million displaced people in Chad, this includes refugees, asylum-seekers and internally-displaced persons (IDPs). The presence of over 300,000 refugees. The majority of whom are from Sudan and the Central African Republic (CAR) weighs heavily on Chad's limited resources, as the country is one of the poorest in the world. CARE began operations in Chad in 1975, implementing both humanitarian and development programmeming, with a strong focus on meeting the needs of the refugee populations fleeing violence in their own countries. To the south, the recent political turmoil in the Central African Republic has led to a wave of people seeking refuge in Chad. According to the UNHCR, more than 6,500 people have left CAR in 2013 to escape the renewed fighting, looting and instability of this often forgotten crisis. Many of the newly-arrived refugees are elderly, sick, pregnant women, children or mentally and physically disabled people. These new arrivals are being integrated into existing camps in southern Chad, where CARE works. CARE is focusing much of its response to the refugee crisis on meeting the increasing needs of those arriving through entry points in the south. Overall, CARE's country office in Chad is now providing support to more than 58,600 refugees in southern Chad and is closely monitoring the ongoing humanitarian situation in the southeast and throughout the country.

The Leprosy Mission (TLM) works in the Guera region of the Republic of Chad. There is an increasing awareness of TLM's work among the local population. As well as working with people who are disabled due to leprosy, TLM Chad is increasingly working with people who have physical disabilities because of other causes through the distribution of walking aids, bicycles, tricycles, wheelchairs, donkeys and orthopaedic appliances. TLM Chad is encouraging the development of disabled people's organisations (DPO), whose members include those affected by leprosy, in the Guera region. TLM Chad also supports the National Leprosy Control Programme through the training and supervision of health staff. The Government of Chad is promoting long-term economic growth in order to reduce poverty and vulnerability and improve living conditions, health and education for its population. The recently updated National Strategy for Growth and Poverty Reduction embodies the government's development goals. The main priorities of the strategy and targets for investment are agriculture and rural development.

The outlook for people living with disabilities in the Democratic Republic of Congo remains bleak, despite a variety of efforts to improve their lot and bring them in from the margins of society. There are roughly 9.1 million people with disabilities, 11 per cent of the total population of 60 million. Both the elderly and people with disabilities have the right to specific protections with regards to their physical, intellectual and moral needs, says Article 49 of the constitution. The government has a duty to promote the presence of people with disabilities in the heart of national, provincial and local institutions. There are several initiatives (both public and private) to try to address the challenges faced by this community. The Democratic Republic of Congo is striving to recover from the five-year conflict of 1998-2003 which led to mass population displacement. Eastern parts of the country remain beset by violence. Handicap International has worked in the Democratic Republic of Congo since 1995. Handicap International has recently begun a new demining initiative in the provinces of Orientale and Maniema in the north of Democratic Republic of Congo, a country where they worked for nearly twenty years.

Disable People in East Africa

The geography of East Africa is often stunning and scenic. The climate of East Africa is rather atypical of equatorial regions. Because of a combination of the region's generally high altitude and the rain shadow of the westerly monsoon winds created by the Rwenzori Mountains and Ethiopian Highlands, East Africa is surprisingly cool and dry for its latitude. Several East African countries have political coups, ethnic violence and oppressive dictators. Since the end of colonialism, the region has endured the following conflicts. Kenya has enjoyed relatively stable governance. Tanzania has known stable government since independence although there are significant political and religious tensions resulting from the political union between Tanganyika and Zanzibar in 1964. Zanzibar is now a semi-autonomous state in the United Republic of Tanzania. Rwanda, Uganda, Burundi, Djibouti, as well as the Puntland and Somaliland regions, has also seen relative stability. South Sudan peacefully seceded from Sudan in 2011; six and a half years after a peace agreement ended the Second Sudanese Civil War.

Kenya acknowledges disability as a phenomenon that cuts across all spheres of society and which requires support from all sectors. Despite the lack of accurate data on the number of persons with disabilities, it is noted that persons with disabilities are not a homogeneous group but are varied in terms of the nature of their disability and their mental, physical and social needs. Persons with disability represent a critical segment. Like in most developing countries people with disabilities are a marginalised population and face problems as a result of their disability. Most have no access to education, health, employment or rehabilitation. The Republic of Kenya in Eastern Africa is bordered by Ethiopia to the north, Somalia to the east, Tanzania to the south, Uganda to the west, and Sudan to the northwest, with the Indian Ocean running along the southeast border. Disabled persons in Kenya like in most developing countries are a marginalised population and face problems as a result of their disability. Most have no access to education, health, employment or rehabilitation. Kenya acknowledges disability as a phenomenon that cuts across all spheres of society and which requires support from all sectors. The first post-independence education and manpower-training enquiry, the Ominde Commission of 1964, recognised the need for education and training in the disability sector. It recommended measures to address the Government's role in the coordination and improvement of service quality and delivery strategies and transition from school to employment world.

Applying the WHO recommended ten per cent to today's Kenyan population of approximately 36 million would indicate that there may be some three million disabled people. The Government of Kenya has adopted a number of laws and policies pertaining to people with disabilities, including their right to productive and decent work and basic services. The Persons with Disabilities Act, 2003, is a comprehensive law covering rights, rehabilitation and equal opportunities for people with disabilities. It creates the National Council of Persons with Disabilities as a statutory organ to oversee the welfare of persons with disabilities. The Ministry of Gender, Children and Social Development is the focal point for disability issues. Among its many services, the Ministry is responsible for 12 rural rehabilitation centres throughout the country and Nairobi's Industrial Rehabilitation Centre, which trains persons with disabilities for jobs. The National Rehabilitation Committee of the Department of Social Services also provides for vocational rehabilitation services. It is decentralised into 49 District Rehabilitation Centres. The National Council for Persons with Disabilities, the official arm of the government on disability issues, is under the Ministry of Gender, Children and Social Development. The Government declared 1980 the National year for persons with disabilities ahead of the 1981 United Nations International Year of the Disabled Persons. Various barriers ranging from environmental, communication, social to economic, prevent persons with disabilities from attaining acceptable quality of life.

The Persons with Disabilities Act, 2003 hereinafter referred to as PDA, prohibits all forms of discrimination against persons with disabilities which the only statute that outlaws discrimination against persons with disabilities. PDA is a fairly new Act and it has not been subject to interpretation in any courts of law in Kenya. The PDA includes provisions to prohibit discrimination on the basis of disabilities in various sectors including education, employment, health, and provision of services in both the public and private sector among others. The Kenya Society for the Blind was established long before independence in 1956 with broad objectives of promoting the welfare, education, training and employment of people who are blind. This body is established under the Kenya Society for the Blind Act. Although poverty is a sub-global problem affecting most sectors of population, persons with disabilities experience higher incidence of poverty than others. The Vocational Rehabilitation Division of the Department of Social Services under the Ministry of Gender, Sports, Culture and Social Services is responsible for 12 rural rehabilitation centres throughout the country and Nairobi's industrial rehabilitation centre, which trains persons with disabilities for jobs.

The National Development Plan (2002-2008) has provisions that focus on strengthening vocational rehabilitation centres for people with mental and physical disabilities and affirmative action in areas of employment, vocational training and education. The Council for Persons with Disabilities has an obligation under Section 13 to secure five per cent of all casual, emergency and contractual positions in employment in private and public sectors for persons with disabilities. The 2005 Draft National Policy on Persons with Disabilities indicates that *"The Persons with Disabilities Act, (2003) provides a legislative framework through which issues of access will be addressed"* Clause 11 of the Draft National Policy provides that it is of equal importance to recognise what constitute issues of access. Under the Persons with Disabilities Act, Section 18 prohibits discrimination in the admission of students with disabilities and mandates learning institutions to accommodate the needs of those students. Section 19 mandates the Council to work *"in consultation with the relevant agencies of government to make provisions in all districts for an integrated system of special and no-formal education for persons with all forms of disabilities and the establishment where possible of Braille and recorded libraries for persons with disabilities"*.

The state of persons with disabilities in Ethiopia is even more tragic and severe due to the presence of diversified pre and post-natal disabling factors (like infectious diseases, difficulties contingent to delivery, under-nutrition, malnutrition, harmful cultural practices, lack of proper child care and management, civil war and periodic drought and famine) and the absence of early primary and secondary preventive actions. In Ethiopia, some associate disability (handicap) with spiritual evil and do not let disabled persons to go out in public. This leads to families hiding disabled family members which lead to inaccurate information and statistics on disabilities. Most disabilities such as blindness, polio, hearing impairment, intellectual disability, leprosy, and the like are preventable provided the necessary measures are taken. The programme for medical rehabilitation of persons with disabilities is aimed at furnishing devices to support missing or damaged organs and to provide necessary healthcare such as physiotherapy, hydrotherapy, sound therapy and massage. The Ethiopian government announced proclamation No.101/1993, following ILO rules and regulations on the employment of persons with disabilities. The United Nations Educational, Scientific and Cultural Organisation have financed a school for children with hearing impairment. International NGOs such as Save the Children Fund, Oxfam and CBM have played a large role in disability-related assistance. Programmes focus on CBR, vocational training, awareness creation, and educational support.

Based on the World Report on Disability jointly issued by the World Bank and World Health Organisation, there are an estimated 15 million children, adults and elderly persons with disabilities in Ethiopia, representing 17.6 per cent of the population. In Ethiopia, 95 per cent of all persons with disabilities are estimated to live in poverty. Many depend on family support and begging for their livelihoods. The Government of Ethiopia has adopted and implemented a number of laws, policies and standards pertaining to people with disabilities, including their right to productive and decent work. Constitution of the Federal Democratic Republic of Ethiopia was adopted in 1995; Article 41(5) of the Constitution sets out the State's responsibility for the provision of necessary rehabilitation and support services for people with disabilities. The Federal Civil Servant Proclamation No. 515/2007 provides for special preference in the recruitment, promotion, and deployment, among others, of qualified candidates with disabilities. National Plan of Action of Persons with Disabilities (2012-2021) aims at making Ethiopia an inclusive society. It addresses the needs of persons with disabilities for comprehensive rehabilitation services, equal opportunities for education, skills training and work, as well as full participation in the life of their families, communities and the nation. At the federal level, the Ministry of Labour and Social Affairs (MoLSA) is the main governmental organ responsible for the provision of social and vocational rehabilitation of people with disabilities.

The East and Horn of Africa continue to suffer from conflict and displacement. While the number of people in the region requiring humanitarian assistance has risen significantly, access to those in need is often impeded. Some six million people of concern to UNHCR, including 1.8 million refugees and more than three million internally displaced people (IDPs), require protection and assistance in the region. The situation in Sudan remains complex. Violence in South Kordofan and Blue Nile States, as well as in parts of Darfur, has sent refugees fleeing into several neighbouring countries. In 2013, conflict between ethnic groups over mining rights, and a general breakdown in law and order in the Darfur region of Sudan, resulted in loss of life as well as displacement both internally and externally. Thousands of refugees have streamed into neighbouring eastern Chad in search of protection. In South Sudan, inter-ethnic conflict in Jonglei State has displaced thousands of people. The resurgence of a Ugandan rebel group, the Allied Democratic Forces, in the eastern areas of the Democratic Republic of the Congo (DRC), has forced some 66,000 refugees across the border into south-western Uganda. During the first eight months of 2013, some 44,000 refugees arrived in Ethiopia, mostly from Somalia, Eritrea, Sudan and South Sudan. Eritrea is host to a refugee population of some 4,000 refugees, mostly from Somalia, who has been in the country for two decades.

Tens of thousands of people disabled by shrapnel and landmines during South Sudan's two-decade-long war with Sudan and thousands more disabled through disease and accidents are struggling to find support in Africa's newest country, where proper healthcare and funding are in short supply. An estimated 50,000 people in South Sudan are physically disabled, according to the International Committee of the Red Cross (ICRC). People with disabilities are being discriminated [against at all stages] of life, at household decision-making levels and with public services.

Children with disabilities in the self-declared republic of Somaliland should be given priority in education, livelihood and health policies, child rights activists. The physical environment [access to schools and hospitals], attitudes of people and lack of public awareness and sensitisation are the real barriers to the development of these children and not their impairment. Policies on children with disabilities are not a priority in the country.

There are several thousand children living in Somaliland with physical and psychological disabilities but only very limited facilities are available to cater for their need. Somalia's infant and maternal mortality rates are among the world's highest, with the main causes of death being diarrhoeal diseases, malaria and respiratory infections. Access to basic services such as primary education, proper healthcare, and safe drinking water is still a challenge in many areas. Somaliland's constitution denies people with physical or psychological disabilities the right to run for public office. Accurate data on the number of children with disabilities in Somaliland is not available, but DAN estimates that at least ten per cent of children in the country have some form of disability.

Children with disabilities in Somaliland often suffer discrimination and ill-treatment mainly due to ignorance about their condition. One report suggested that nearly half of households surveyed had at least one member with a disability. Children with disabilities were less likely to go to school or play with other children and two in five supported the idea of tying them up and 28 per cent giving them less food. A community-based rehabilitation project carried out by Disability Action Network (DAN) a Somaliland-based organisation to support the needs of people with disabilities with physiotherapy and orthopaedic appliances have been supported by UNICEF. As a new nation, South Sudan is building some of its institutions from the very start, with core administrative structures and mechanisms of political representation beginning to emerge. The Government is still struggling to provide basic services for the majority of the population. UNHCR continues to encourage South Sudan to sign and ratify relevant international conventions and treaties related to the protection of refugees and the prevention of statelessness. The Office enjoys the support of the Commission of Refugee Affairs, in establishing an active field presence in Unity and Upper Nile states. In 2014, UNHCR's main focus in South Sudan will be to respond to the needs of Sudanese refugees in the camps. UNHCR will maintain its strategic and operational partnerships to deliver protection and assistance to refugees, returnees and IDPs in the country.

According to the Ugandan definition, disability is a condition that denies a person a normal economic and social life, which has lasted, or is expected to last, six months or more. In Uganda, epilepsy and rheumatism are classified as disabilities, although internationally they are not. Using the Ugandan definition, four per cent of the population (approximately 1,072,000) had a disability, compared to a figure of 3.3 per cent using the international definition. The numbers of disabled people are not evenly distributed throughout the country. In 1997, a new government initiative called universal primary education (UPE) was implemented, with the intent of broadening access to primary schooling, largely through reducing costs of such schooling. Its effects were dramatic. The Uganda Participatory Poverty Assessment (PPA) process is a partnership between the Government of Uganda, local governments, NGOs, academic institutions and donors. Today, disability concerns in Uganda have reached a level where they are part and parcel of the country's general concerns, which have to be addressed in national policies and programmes. A number of legal provisions, such as the Parliamentary Elections Statute 1996, the Children Statute 1996, the Local Government Act 1997, the Land Act 1998, the Uganda Communication Act 1997, the Traffic and Road Safety Act 1998, the UNISE Act 1998 and the Movement Act 1998, attempt to address the needs of disabled people. The National Union of Disabled Persons of Uganda (NUDIPU) was formed in 1987, by 17 groups of people with disabilities as an umbrella organisation to provide a united voice for the disability movement.

The Government of Uganda has adopted a number of laws and policies pertaining to people with disabilities, including their right to productive and decent work and basic services. The Persons with Disabilities Act, 2006, makes provisions for the elimination of all forms of discriminations against people with disabilities and towards equal opportunities. Also provides for a tax reduction of 15 per cent to private employers who employ ten or more persons with disabilities either as regular employees, apprentice or learner on a full time basis. The Department for Disabled Persons under the Ministry of Gender, Labour and Social Development has the primary responsibility for registration, vocational rehabilitation and coordination of employment for persons with disabilities. The Ministry of Gender, Labour and Social Development coordinates the Uganda Community Based Rehabilitation (CBR) Programme. Uganda adopted CBR in 1992 as a strategy within general community development for rehabilitation, equalisation of opportunities and social inclusion of all children and adults with disabilities.

The Ugandan Bureau of Statistics has produced various estimates of prevalence rates of disability, which significantly contrast with each other. The Northern Uganda Survey of 2004 estimated that 72 per cent of people with disabilities in the Northern Region are living in a state of chronic poverty, with men far more likely to be poor than women. The most deeply entrenched levels of social exclusion, marginalisation and discrimination are faced by people with disabilities living in the Northern Region. Many have spent their whole lives living in IDP camps. From the focus group discussions held in Gulu District, it was clear that many people with disabilities were unable to access humanitarian aid provided by mainstream agencies. The Ministry of Gender, Labour and Social Development runs community-based rehabilitation programmes in ten districts, but it is not in a position to scale up these services to cover the whole country. In principle, the Ministry of Education and Sports endorses the principles of inclusive education, yet national disabled people's organisations with the support of the President are lobbying for more special schools to be built, in the belief that such schools will provide a better education. The disability movement in Uganda is reputedly one of the most vibrant throughout Africa, and has played a key role in the promotion of disability rights throughout the continent. The National Union of Disabled People in Uganda is the national umbrella disabled people's organisation, comprising 14 national DPOs, which often cater to the needs of single impediment groups.

More than three million women and men in Tanzania, or approximately nine per cent of the population, have a disability. Tanzania has adopted and implemented a number of laws, policies and standards pertaining to people with disabilities, including their right to productive and decent work, vocational training and basic services. The 1977 Constitution and its amendments prohibit discrimination against persons with disabilities. Vocational Education and Training Act 1994 (No.1), provides a legal framework for the implementation of a flexible vocational education and training system that responds to the labour market. Disabled Persons (Employment) Regulations 1985, defines the eligibility and registration requirements for disabled persons under the Disabled Persons (Employment) Act 1982. The Ministries of Education, Justice, and Labour are responsible for enforcing the protection of rights of persons with disabilities for education, legal claims, and labour rights, respectively. Tanzania works to implement the Plan of Action for the African Decade of Persons with Disabilities. It also follows the UN Standard Rules on the Equalisation of Opportunities for Persons with Disabilities.

The major objective of the 2008 Tanzania Disability Survey was to determine the prevalence of disability in the country. The survey also intended to determine living conditions among people with disabilities, such as their experiences with the physical environment and attitudes, their main sources of income, education level, possession of assistive devices etc. Despite Tanzania's very significant effort to increase the opportunities for children to access schooling, there is still a serious under enrollment of children with disabilities. Tanzania ratified the UN Convention on the Rights of Persons with Disabilities and its Optional Protocol on November 10, 2009 and its Optional Protocol on May 12, 2008.

Disable People in Southern Africa

Southern Africa is the southernmost region of the African continent. In the UN scheme of geographic regions, five countries constitute Southern Africa. The Southern African Customs Union (SACU), created in 1969, also comprises the five countries in the UN sub region of Southern Africa. The region is distinct from the rest of Africa, with some of its main exports including platinum, diamonds, gold, and uranium. The pursuit of economic and political stability is an important part of the region's goals, as demonstrated by the SADC. In terms of economic strength, South Africa is by far the dominant power of the region. Southern Africa is home to many cultures and people.

The Disability agenda in Botswana has benefited from the interaction with the International context with special reference to the work of the United Nations which culminated in the adoption and entry in force of the 2006 Convention on the Rights of Persons with Disabilities and the recent initiatives of the African Union for the extension of the Plan of Action of the African Decade for People with Disabilities. People with Disabilities have successfully advocated for departure from the charity and medical models of disability. The medical model views disability as a disease, focusing exclusively on medical services to the individual, promoting and perpetuating exclusion from the mainstream of society. It ignores the social context of disability and the fact that it is society which creates the disabling environmental and attitudinal barriers which stand in the way of social inclusion. The Government of Botswana, a few years after attaining independence began to gauge the need for helping people with disabilities. In the early 1970s' the Government commissioned a study on different disabilities that were prevalent in the country in order to analyse the situation. The Ministry of Education was supplemented by the introduction of special education concepts while formulating education policy in 1977. These concepts have now led to the establishment of the Special Education Division, which has been set up for planning and overseeing education of people with special needs.

The 2004 Swaziland Constitution provides protection for persons with disabilities and requires Parliament to enact relevant implementing legislation. Parliament had not passed laws to prohibit discrimination against persons with disabilities in employment, or to provide access to healthcare or other state services by the end of the year. According to the 1997 census, there are 27,698 disabled persons, or three per cent of the population. 86 per cent of them live in rural areas. This is lower than the WHO estimates for Government of Swaziland, Central Statistics Office. The Government of Swaziland has consulted the disability sector in the processes to develop disability policies and/or disability inclusive policies. The Ministry of Health and Social Services has the overall responsibility for disability issues. It has a National Disability Unit that serves as the government focal point for disability issues. The Federation Organisation of the Disabled People in Swaziland (FODSWA) is an organisation. It run and managed by disabled people themselves. FODSWA is a gender sensitive organisation; it promotes gender sensitivity amongst its members. FODSWA was formed in 1993 by disabled people's organisations. The main purpose of the formation of the Federation was to build effective and efficient leadership amongst its affiliates and to act as a link between government and disabled people's organisations.

The organisation has drawn up a five-year plan on the development of women with disabilities in Swaziland.

The 1994 Constitution of Malawi explicitly and implicitly recognises the rights of disabled people in the country, with a specific sections dealing with disability issues. Malawi has signed UN Convention of the Rights of People with Disabilities on the 27th September 2007, but has yet to ratify it. In 2004, the Government of Malawi initiated a review of its 1994 Constitution by establishing the Constitution of Malawi Review Commission. The key government department for disability issues is the Ministry for Social Development and People with Disabilities, which were established through presidential directive in December, 1988. The National Policy on Equalisation of Opportunities for Persons with Disabilities was published in 2006. Its purpose is to promote the rights of people with disabilities to enable them to play a full and participatory role in society. It was drafted by the Ministry of Social Development and People with Disabilities, and was ratified by the Cabinet in November 2005. The Government under the auspices of the Malawi Council for the Handicapped, established a community-based rehabilitation (CBR) programme during the 1980s, with financial and technical support being supplied by the ILO and UNDP. This programme was reviewed in 2006 which recommended that it is more closely aligned the Malawi's Special Needs Education Policy. The Federation of Disability Organisations in Malawi (FEDOMA) is the national umbrella disabled people's organisation that was established in 1999.

Disability issues are both directly and indirectly addressed within the 1990 Mozambique Constitution. Within Mozambique, disabled people have the following constitutional rights, with Article 13 explicitly dealing with War Disability and Article 37 addressing disability issues in general. The Government of Mozambique produced its first National Policy on Disability in 1999, which was developed in close collaboration with key stakeholders working within the disability sector, including disabled people's organisations. Despite the fact that this Policy has been approved by policy-makers in 2002, it has yet to be enacted by Parliament. The Ministry of Health has primary responsibility for providing rehabilitation centres. The Ministry of Women and Social Action is responsible for coordinating psychosocial and economic reintegration activities, which includes community-based rehabilitation. Mozambique is a nation that has been ravished by war and civil strife over a protracted period, which has inevitably had a very significant detrimental impact on the quality of life of disabled people.

Angola is the arena for Disability and Development Partners (DDP's) most substantial capacity-building programme with LARDEF. It started in 2001 when DDP visited Angola to research the situation of disabled people in a conflict situation, and also with the view of finding a partner with potential for development work with disabled people. LARDEF, established in 1997 was a voluntary organisation made up of 19 founder members, war veterans and people who been disabled as a result of the conflict. LARDEF's vision 'an environment without barriers where disabled people are included in society and their rights are respected' and their determination to support and integrate disabled people in society continue to be impressive. Over the six years LARDEF has developed into a dynamic organisation, with a membership of nearly 8000 disabled people and is ever determined to fulfill its mission to represent and promote the rights, interests and participation of disabled people. Seventy per cent of the population still lives in poverty despite the post-conflict reconstruction and development programmes. Among them an estimated 1.2 million people with disabilities are probably the most disadvantaged, as they are still marginalised and excluded from social, livelihood and development opportunities and denied equality.

The transfer of Handicap International's community-based rehabilitation activities to local partners is currently underway. The network of local disabled people's organisations in three provinces (Huambo, Benguela and Huila), will receive support until the end of 2013, to ensure that they continue to go from strength to strength. Handicap International first started activities in Angola in 1984, but was forced to evacuate the country between 1989 and 1994 when fighting in the civil war was at its heaviest. In 1994, with the civil war still on-going, rehabilitation centres and prosthetics workshops were created. In 2005, a number of projects were handed over to centres operated by the national disability rehabilitation programme. The impact of Africa's longest running civil war still affects people across Angola and landmines still pose a significant danger. It is estimated that at least 500,000 Angolans are living with a disability. It is essential to strengthening the capacity and autonomy of disabled people's organisations so that they can effectively promote and protect the rights of disabled people. The Association of the People with Visual Impairments (APADV) in Benguela and the League to Support the Integration of Disabled People (LARDEF) will provide long-term coordination and technical support for the network of disabled people's organisations.

Angolan Federation of the Association of People with Disabilities (FAPED) appears in the ambit of the self-representation of the associations of disabled people at both national and international levels. It aims to coordinate the actions of its members to partner with the Angolan government in developing disability politics and including it in the national politics of development. FAPED has its office in 28, Hojiya Henda Street, in the municipal district of Rangel, Luanda. FAPED has access to the minimum conditions to perform its work, including internet and e-mail facilities. The objectives of FAPED are (a) To represent Associations of Disabled People at National level and to participate in discussions with Government about the politics linked to the people with disabilities; (b) To coordinate and organise actions to support the implementation of integral rehabilitation projects; (c) To organise and participate in National and International Forums with the purpose of promoting people with disabilities' skills at technical and scientific level; and (d) To participate in the definition of politics of social promotion of people with disabilities.

The 2001 Census, conducted by the Government of Namibia estimated that there were approximately 85,000 disabled people living within the country, this being roughly equivalent to five per cent of the total population. The Census showed that there were an equal proportion of men and women who were registered as disabled. The primary responsibility for disability issues within the Namibian Government lies with the Ministry of Health and Social Services. In 1997, the Namibian Government developed its National Disability Policy, which is underpinned by the social model of disability. The overall objective of this policy is to ensure that all disabled people are able to participate in mainstream contemporary society, by providing adequate services. The Namibian Government has passed several pieces of legislation that has direct relevance to disability issues. The National Disability Council Act 2004 makes provision for advisory body to be established, mandated to provide strategic oversight on the implementation of the National Disability Policy. It also has responsibility for commenting on any future legislation that had any direct and indirect impact on disability issues. The Ministry of Health and Social Services published its Policy on Orthopaedic Technical Services in April, 2001. The National Federation of People with Disabilities in Namibia (NFPDN) is the national umbrella disabled people's organisation in the country. Founded in 1990, the Federation has been funded by the European Commission and the Finnish Embassy. The Government of Namibia has made some progress in attempting to apply the tenets and underlying principles that underpin the UN Convention on the Rights of Persons with Disabilities.

Disabled people in Lesotho are among the most marginalised and disadvantaged groups in the country. They are often forced to be dependent on relatives or other care-takers. According to the Lesotho Demographic Survey (2001), 4.2 per cent of the population has some form of disability and about one-third of these are children under 15 years. However, due to unreliable data these statistics do not objectively present the situation, magnitude and prevalence of disability. The current education system does not cater for the needs of disabled people. School infrastructure is often not accessible to people with physical and visual impairments, for instance classrooms may still be accessed via stairs rather than ramps. The medium of communication used in schools may exclude deaf and visually impaired learners due to a lack of teachers with Braille and Sign Language skills.

Lesotho ratified the Convention on the Rights of Persons with Disabilities on 2nd December, 2008. Article 4 of the Convention calls for countries that have joined the Convention to engage in the development and implementation of policies, laws and administrative measures aimed at securing the rights of people with disabilities and to abolish laws, regulations, customs and practices that constitute discrimination towards people with disabilities. The Convention requires states that are party to it to engage in the formulation of legislative tools aimed at domesticating the Convention. To date Lesotho has not adopted any pieces of legislation that promote protection of people with disabilities and their full inclusion in the society despite the early ratification of the Convention. In their fight against discrimination, people with disabilities have established four Disabled Peoples Organisations (DPOs) and an umbrella body Lesotho National Federation of Organisations of the Disabled (LNFOD). The four DPOs are Lesotho Society of Mentally Handicapped Persons (LSMHP), Lesotho National Association of Physically Disabled (LNAPD), Lesotho National League of Visually Impaired Persons (LNLVIP), and National Association of the Deaf-Lesotho (NADL).

The Constitution of Lesotho recognises education as a directive principle of state policy under Chapter 3 of the Constitution and not as a justiciable right. However, the Child Protection and Welfare Act of 2011 and the Education Act of 2010 expressly affirm the right of children with disabilities to education. In addition, Section 4(2) (b) of the Education Act imposes an obligation on duty bearers to ensure that children with disabilities are included in the educational system. The right to education is protected under Article 24 of the United Nations Convention on the Rights of Persons with Disabilities. This provision also places an obligation on state parties not to exclude children with disabilities from free and compulsory primary education, and that the inclusion is complemented by accessibility, reasonable accommodation, and effective individualised support aimed at maximising academic and social development. There is a lack of commitment by the government in creating the necessary inclusive environment through facilities, support and capacity building programmes to fill the gaps in the educational sector.

According to the World Health Organisation estimates, about two million women and men in Zambia, or 15 per cent of the population, have a disability. The Government of Zambia has adopted a number of laws and policies pertaining to people with disabilities, including their right to productive and decent work and to basic services, workers compensation, social security, and entrepreneurship development. The 1991 Zambian Constitution, amended in 1996, contains one provision on disability relating to just and equitable social benefits and amenities suitable to the needs of disabled people. The country's Constitution is under review. The Technical Education, Vocational and Entrepreneurship Training (TEVET) Act, 1998, states that the *"special needs of people with disabilities will be taken into consideration"*.

The Citizen Economic Empowerment Commission Act, 2008, aims at empowering people with disabilities economically through start-up businesses that will employ others. The Persons with Disabilities Act, 2012, aims to domesticate and implement the UN Convention on the Rights of Persons with Disabilities while repealing the 1996 Persons with Disabilities Act. The Ministry of Community Development, Mother and Child Health (MCDMCH) are entrusted with formulating policy for people with disabilities. The Zambia Agency for Persons with Disabilities (ZAPD) has the responsibility to coordinate the implementation of the National Policy on Disability and acts as an advisory body to the Ministry. The Ministry Education, Science, Vocational Training and Early Education (MESVTEE) have responsibility for developing science and technology and for the provision of technical education and vocational training. The Technical Education, Vocational and Entrepreneurship Training Authority (TEVETA) have responsibility to improve technical education and vocational training, while linking them to the requirements of the employment sector.

The nearly two million people with disabilities in Zambia face significant barriers to HIV prevention, testing, and treatment, Human Rights Watch said in a report released today. While the Zambian government has made considerable progress scaling up its response to HIV generally, few programmes are accessible to people with disabilities and social stigma prevents their access to HIV services on an equal basis with others. People with various disabilities told Human Rights Watch that they are often viewed as a sexual and face negative attitudes about their right to marry and have children. Those responses sometimes restrict their access to HIV prevention, testing, or treatment services.

The 1982 National Disability Survey of Zimbabwe came up with a working definition of disability as *'a physical or mental condition, which makes it difficult or impossible for the person concerned to adequately fulfill his or her normal role in society. In 1996, the Disabled Persons Act of Zimbabwe expanded on this to define a disabled person as 'a person with a physical, mental or sensory disability, including a visual, hearing or speech functional disability, which gives rise to physical, cultural or social barriers inhibiting him from participating at an equal level with other members of society in activities, undertakings or fields of employment that are open to other members of society'*. According to the World Health Organisation, ten per cent of the world's populations are people living with disabilities. As such, Zimbabwe, with a population of 12 million people, should have 1.2 million people living with disabilities. However, surveys have recorded a much lower figure. The Zimbabwe InterCensal Demographic Survey of 1997 recorded a total of 218,421 people with disabilities in the country about two per cent of the total population. Of these, 56 per cent were male and 44 per cent were female.

A number of negative beliefs on the causes of disabilities persist, such as associating disability with witchcraft or maternal promiscuity. The culture in Zimbabwe is still to look at disability as a curse. The disabled are becoming increasingly marginalised, with the state and civil society neglecting their basic needs. People with disabilities are more likely to be victims of sexual abuse and rape than their non-disabled counterparts. It came out clearly that the vulnerability of people with disabilities is high, mainly due to the prevailing economic situation, cultural beliefs, and the general abuse of people with disabilities by family members, relatives and other sexual predators. Increased vulnerability was rooted in the belief that the disabled were not sexually active and less vulnerable to HIV. Stigmatisation of the disabled was highlighted by the lack of HIV/AIDS information available to them. There is a lot of illiteracy among people with disabilities. Zimbabwe's 1992 Disabled Persons Act (DPA) does not make provision for positive discrimination or affirmative action for disabled persons in the job market. In a country burdened with an 80 per cent unemployment rate and economic meltdown, employment prospects for disabled people are particularly grim. The high rate of unemployment among people with disabilities is due mainly to their lack of educational qualifications and discrimination from the employers. As has been established, many people with disabilities are denied the right to attend school.

Census 2001 was the second census to be carried out in a democratic South Africa to provide demographic and socio-economic data required to inform policy decision-making as well as ascertain the achievements made in the provision of basic services to the people. Since 1994 the government has formulated various policies to address the inequities which were embedded in the policies pursued by the apartheid regime. The policies have focused on empowering previously disadvantaged groups including women, children and disabled persons. The data collected in Census 2001 indicates that there were 22,55 ,982 people with various forms of disability. This number constituted five per cent of the total population (4,48,19,778) enumerated in the census. The comparison between disabled and non-disabled persons with regard to age, education attainment and employment indicates that disabled persons were generally older, a significant percentage (30 per cent) had no schooling and about 18 per cent were employed, compared to 35 per cent for the rest of the population. Disabled People South Africa (DPSA) noted that disabled people faced a host of discriminatory practices, including human rights abuses, which were often not brought to the fore. Attitudes and economic practices posed the greatest hindrance.

Disable People in Europe

Europe is the world's second-smallest continent by surface area, covering about two per cent of the Earth's surface and about 6.8 per cent of its land area. Europe, in particular ancient Greece, is the birthplace of Western culture. As a continent, the economy of Europe is currently the largest on Earth and it is the richest region as measured by assets under management with over $32.7 trillion compared to North America's $27.1 trillion in 2008. The European Union, an intergovernmental body composed of 28 European states, comprises the largest single economic area in the world. Eighteen European Union countries share the euro as a common currency. Since the Renaissance, Europe has had a major influence in culture, economics and social movements in the world. The culture of Europe can be described as a series of overlapping cultures; cultural mixes exist across the continent. Historically, religion in Europe has been a major influence on European art, culture, philosophy and law. The largest religion in Europe is Christianity, with 76.2 per cent.

The Academic Network of European Disability experts (ANED) were established by the European Commission in 2008 to provide scientific support and advice for its disability policy Unit. In particular, the activities of the Network will support the future development of the EU Disability Action Plan and practical implementation of the United Nations Convention on the Rights of Disabled People. The Academic Network of European Disability experts were established by the European Commission in 2008 to provide scientific support and advice for its disability policy Unit. In particular, the activities of the Network will support the future development of the EU Disability Action Plan and practical implementation of the United Nations Convention on the Rights of Disabled People.

Disable People in Northern Europe

Northern Europe is the northern part or region of Europe. It consists of the Scandinavian Peninsula, the peninsula of Jutland, the Baltic plain that lies to the east and the many islands that lie offshore from mainland northern Europe, Greenland and the main European continent. Countries in northern Europe are known to have large, developed economies and some of the highest standards of living in the world. All countries score highly on surveys measuring quality of life, such as the Human Development Index. People who have physical or functional, mental or sensory impairments have the inalienable right to be full and equal members of their societies. However, almost everywhere they are discriminated against either directly or indirectly. Direct discrimination is based on negative attitudes, prejudice, or sometimes even on discriminatory legislation. Indirect discrimination is caused by physical barriers such as stairs as the only means to get to vital locations or by the use of media that people who are visually impaired or hard of hearing cannot use without assistance. Indirect discrimination is also banned by international legal instrument and Finnish legislation. The Constitution of Finland and EU legislation prohibit any discrimination on the basis of a disability. The Convention on the Rights of Persons with Disabilities entered into force in 2009. Finland has signed the Convention and is currently in the process of revising its legislation to meet the new requirements. All Finland's development co-operation partner's countries have ratified the Convention. The promotion of the human rights of persons with disabilities belongs to the very basic commitments guiding our development co-operation.

Norwegian politicians like to portray Norway as a modern, democratic nation with equality and equal opportunities for all.

But not even in as prosperous a country as Norway, does this apply to disabled people. Norwegian Federation of Organisations of Disabled People (FFO) was founded on 21st September, 1950, and is a central co-operative body of organisations of disabled people. Fundamental to FFOs work is its belief in a society based on solidarity a society that ensures to all the right to freedom, social security and societal participation. FFO envisions a society where disabled people have equal opportunity to take part in all aspects of society, where disabled people are equal in all respects. The Norwegian Association of the Disabled is an interest organisation for disabled people. The organisation has eleven sub-organisations for people with specific disabilities, a youth branch, nine regional and three hundred local groups. The goal is full equality and participation in society for people with reduced mobility.

In Sweden 1.5 million people are disabling. In 2011, the Swedish Government launched a new strategy to guide its disability policy for the period leading up to 2016. The aim is to give people with disabilities a greater chance of participating in society on the same terms as others. Ten priority areas have been identified, three of which are given special attention: the justice system, transportation and IT. In Sweden, there is social welfare for all, but there are also special programmes designed to address the needs of people with disabilities. One important feature of the Act concerning Support and Service for Persons with Certain Functional Impairments (LSS) gives disabled people the right to personal assistance, in principle free of charge. The amount of help they receive is determined by the extent of their disabilities. People with disabilities can apply for municipal grants so they can have their accommodation modified. This may involve having doorsteps removed, support rails mounted, doorways widened, automatic door openers fitted, or special elevators installed. Such grants cover all types of disabilities, including mobility disability, impaired vision, mental disorders and allergies. The first such grant was made available on a trial basis in 1959, and was introduced formally in 1963.

Sweden is one of the states that have ratified the Convention on the Rights of Persons with Disabilities. The UN human rights conventions are legally binding for the countries that have chosen to ratify them. The aim of the Convention is to eliminate obstacles preventing people with disabilities from exercising their human rights. In June 2011, the Government adopted a five-year strategy for disability policy. It builds further on the 10-year action plan that applied in 2000-2010. The strategy is based on the United Nations Convention on the Rights of Persons with Disabilities, to which Sweden has acceded. The responsibility for individual support and service for people with disabilities lies primarily with the municipalities and county councils. This applies to measures under both the Social Services Act and the Act concerning Support and Service for Persons with Certain Functional Impairments.

The state provides financial grants to the municipalities' operations, and also in some cases to the county councils. The Assistance Compensation Act and the Assistance Compensation Ordinance contain rules on compensation to certain disabled people for the costs of personal assistance. The Swedish Agency for Disability Policy Coordination coordinates work on implementing and following up disability policy, while policy is actually implemented by agencies in most sectors of society. The National Board of Health and Welfare is responsible for all supervision and granting of permits under the Social Services Act and the Act concerning Support and Service for Persons with Certain Functional Impairments. The Swedish Institute of Assistive Technology is a national resource centre in the field of assistive technology and accessibility for people with disabilities. The Disability Delegation is a forum for discussion and mutual information between the Government and disability organisations concerning issues that are of particular interest to people with disabilities. Minister for Children and the Elderly Maria Larsson is chair of the Delegation.

In 1993, Denmark adopted an equal opportunity resolution appealing to public and private companies and institutions to apply the principle of equal rights and opportunities for disabled and non-disabled people. Although not a legally binding act, it is a parliamentary resolution strongly recommending equal treatment for people with disabilities. The Danish Disability Council is a government-funded organisation. Its role is to guide and advise the government on issues concerning disabled people and their conditions. There are a number of benefits for people with disabilities, which include financial allowances and assistance. All benefits and allowances depend on the type and degree of disability. Services and benefits for people with disabilities are financed by local authorities. The Disabled Peoples Organisation is an umbrella organisation of associations for people with disabilities. The Danish Association for the Disabled is an association for people with disabilities whose aim is to improve the living conditions for people with reduced mobility. The Danish Association for the Deaf and Blind aims to improve the living conditions for people with visual and hearing impairments. They run a number of initiatives throughout the country, including support groups. Special transport in equipped mini buses is available to people over the age of 18 with reduced mobility, but in order to qualify the person must be in a wheelchair, or need other special equipment to get around, and the equipment must be allocated by the public authorities. The Metro has been designed so that people with disabilities should be able to use it with as little assistance as possible. Parking places for people with a disability are marked with a wheelchair symbol. In Copenhagen, vehicles with a disabled parking permit may park free of charge in public parking zones.

Since 1997 the National Labour Market Authority has run a programme on employment of people with disabilities. As part of this programme, the Danish National Institute of Social Research has carried out a number of research projects about employment of people with disabilities. Most employment legislation stems from 1998. The flex job scheme created jobs with a permanent wage subsidy of 50 per cent or 65 per cent. Awarding of disability pensions became a municipal responsibility as for other maintenance benefits. The Law on disabled persons in employment also dates from 1998. It contains among other things the so-called icebreaker scheme, where a seriously disabled person with an education can be hired with a wage subsidy of 50 per cent for up to six months and in special cases up to nine months. Another scheme introduced in this law is for personal assistants.

Estonia is party to most international human rights instruments related to education and employment, including those with provisions on people with disabilities. The Constitution does not explicitly prohibit discrimination on the grounds of disability. Estonia has not yet transposed the provisions of the EU Race Equality Directive or the EU Employment Directive into national legislation. National disability policy is based on the United Nations Standard Rules on Equalisation of Opportunities for Persons with Disabilities. The Constitution guarantees the right to education for everyone, and this right is supported by the Education Act. General legislation on basic and secondary education also regulates special education. Children with special needs, including children with intellectual disabilities, have the right to study at a mainstream school in the area where they live, provided the local authorities have ensured a suitable learning environment. Estonia is one of the few countries to have specifically addressed the educational needs of people with disabilities during its EU accession process. Although Estonia recognises certain principles of inclusive education in law and policy, in practice, most children with intellectual disabilities still do not have the opportunity to receive an education in a mainstream setting. The Constitution guarantees freedom of choice in employment and special care of the State and local governments for people with disabilities. There is no specific legislation on the employment of people with disabilities.

Estonia is concerned about the increase in the number of disabled people every year. People with disabilities are granted various services and benefits to help them find and maintain work. The principle underlying the provision of welfare services is that a person needing help must get help as close to his/her residence as possible and according to his/her individual needs. People with disabilities constitute a risk group in the labour market and they account for about ten per cent of the registered unemployed. Rehabilitation service is a social service provided to improve the ability of persons to cope independently, their social integration and employment or commencement of employment. In the case of persons who are unable to work due to age, disability or special needs regarding mental health, rehabilitation service is provided to support their ability to live independently and reduce the care burden of their family members. Children's rehabilitation service is aimed at ensuring equal development opportunities at the time of attaining working age. Rehabilitation services may be provided by sole proprietors, legal persons, local government agencies or agencies administered by governmental authorities registered as providers of rehabilitation services in the register of economic activities.

In 2007, 25.6 thousand persons of working age were for the first time recognised as disabled in Lithuania. Against 2006, this number grew by more than by 25 per cent, and made 12 persons per 1000 working age population. Most (24 per cent) persons of working age were for the first time recognised as disabled due to diseases of the circulatory system. In 2007, 2.2 thousand children were for the first time recognised as disabled. Each third of them was recognised as disabled due to mental or behavioural disorders. According to the data of the Lithuanian Labour Exchange (2007), there were 12122 registered disabled unemployed persons (disabled persons, against the total number of persons 6.5 per cent). The number of employed disabled persons was 5798 (disabled persons, against the total number of persons 5.8 per cent). 1421 disabled persons participated in vocational training and retraining programmes. According to the data of the Department of Statistics to the Government of the Republic of Lithuania (2007), there were 111 special pre-primary education establishments for disabled children (3620). Pensions for incapacity to work are paid to individuals with a minimum contribution period for state social insurance. The requirements for the minimum and compulsory period of insurance for the pension for incapacity for work depend on an individual's age. Disabled people at university, college or vocational school get special financial support.

The Supreme Council of the Republic of Lithuania, following both the Basic Provisional Law of the Republic of Lithuania and the principles of humanism and justice, seeking to implement the rights of the disabled as guaranteed in international documents, and recognising that integration of the disabled into social and state life is an indicator of civilisation, adopts this Law. The Law on the Social Integration of the Disabled shall regulate the establishment of disability, medical, vocational and social rehabilitation for disabled persons, the adjustment of conditions for the disabled, as well as the development and education of the disabled, and shall establish legal, economic and organisational guarantees for the occupational, vocational and social rehabilitation of the disabled.

The Ministry of Welfare of the Republic of Latvia is the leading institution of the state administration in the areas of labour, social security and gender equality. The mission of the Ministry of

Welfare is to stabilise the condition of people in situations of social risk, to reduce the possibility of social risk. National Council for the Disabled Persons is the coordinating body for policies in the field of integration of disabled people into society. The Council was established in 1994. Members of the National Council for Disabled People are ministers and members from national level disabled people's organisations. Important national laws, policies and strategies concerning disabled people include: Law on medical and social protection of disabled persons (1992) defines the status of disabled person and establishes the main rights of disabled people. Conception 'Equal Opportunities for All' was intended to create equal opportunities for people with disabilities, promote social rehabilitation, restore working capacities, achieve education and involvement in the labour market. The State Medical Expertise Commission on Health and Working Capacities maintains a database on disability matters, including data about status (employed, unemployed), age, gender, kind of disability, severity of disability and others). The State Social Insurance Agency performs the public administration functions in the area of social insurance and social services maintains a data base on pension and social benefit receivers, amount of pensions, etc. According to data from State Medical Expertise Commission on Health and Working Capacities only 13-14 per cent of disabled people are employed. People with disabilities are recognised as a risk group subjected to poverty and social exclusion, but activities are planned using a mainstream approach. Disabled persons are mainly not treated as a separate group, there are no specific income policies for disabled and non-disabled people, with the exception that minimum level for disability pension is stated by the Law.

The Organisation of Disabled in Iceland (ODI) was founded in 1961. There are 34-member associations. Representatives of all the member associations sit on the Board of ODI. The purpose and goals of ODI may be found in ODI's constitution. There are a number of vocational training centres and sheltered workshops in operation in Iceland that opened in the 1960s to the 1980s, including Tjaldarnes, a training school for men with intellectual disabilities as well as the sheltered workshops of Bjarkaras and Laekjaras, among others. The number of disability rights organisations in operation, some of which are consulted by the Icelandic government in policy-making decisions, is an important strength, as is the number of supported employment programmes. The 2006 National Disability Survey (NDS) was the first major survey of people with disabilities. It provided a basis for the estimation of the prevalence of disability in the population and for the examination of the living circumstances and needs of people with disabilities. The first report from the NDS produced tables showing the nature, severity and cause of the disability. It also showed the age of onset by gender, age group and region. The second report focused on a broad range of characteristics of people with a disability, including education, work and important aspects of the social and physical environment. Disability is seen primarily as a personal or medical issue. The medical model has been criticised by those proposing a social model of disability. The social model of disability shifts the focus from the individual's impairments to the environment; the organisation of society; and the social, attitudinal and environmental barriers that restrict the full participation of people with a disability. The World Health Organisation advocates a biopsychosocial model of disability, which combines elements of both the medical and social models.

There are ten million disable people in Britain. The North East of England has the highest proportion of disabled people, accounting for 22 per cent of the population. The prevalence rate of disability rises with age around one in twenties children are disabled, compared to around one in five working age adults, and almost one in two people over state pension age. The United Kingdom Disabled People's Council (UKDPC) is the UK's democratic representative national organisation, which is a member of the worldwide Disabled People's Movement, through its membership of Disabled People's International. The UKDPC was set up in 1981, by disabled people, to promote their full equality and participation in United Kingdom society, to strengthen the voice of disabled people in the UK and to ensure justice and rights for all disabled people regardless of impairment.

Disable People in West Europe

Western Europe is the region comprising the westerly countries of Europe. The United Nations Statistics Division considers Western Europe to consist of just nine countries. Western Europe's significant historical events include the Renaissance, the Protestant Reformation by Martin Luther and the Counter-Reformation of the Catholic Church, the Age of Enlightenment, the French Revolution and the Industrial Revolution. There are five million disabled people living in France, two million of who are less mobile. Thirty per cent of motor disabilities are caused by accidents. Some 135,000 disabled children attend ordinary schools and 110,000 go to specialised institutions. One disabled working-age adult in three is unemployed. The budget allocated to the policy for the disabled totalled €29 billion in 2004. On the basis of a classification proposed by the World Health Organisation in 1980, revised in 1993, the concept of disability has been superseded by that of situation of disability, which is not limited to a functional handicap and impairments but takes into account the social disadvantage that results from a functional handicap or impairments, which are aggravated by the social, material, human and technical environment.

At the end of 2013, roughly 7.5 million severely disabled people were living in Germany. This was an increase of around 260,000 or 3.6 per cent compared with the end of 2011. Accordingly, 9.4 per cent of Germany's total population was severely disabled in 2013. Slightly more than half (51 per cent) of the severely disabled were men. The German Disability Council is an association of more than 40 disabled people's organisations whose overall membership represents more than 2.5 million disabled people. Member associations maintain their autonomy and represent their interests. Every member organisation has one vote in the general council. The continuity of the political and organisational work of the German Disability Council is ensured by the working committee. It consists of 12 people; at least six of them have to be people affected by disability or a chronic disease. General Equality Act (2006) applies to disabled people and other groups, it guarantees the right to non-discrimination in employment, education, access to goods and services, buying and renting property. It rules that public authorities and private business have the duty to monitor and promote equal rights, on the grounds of disability as well as age, gender, sexual orientation, race, ethnicity, religion, and belief. Federal Disability Equality Act (2002) guarantees disabled people the right to access to public places and buildings, public transport, the internet and political elections. It guarantees the right to communication, and acknowledges sign language as an official language. It also rules that the special needs of disabled women are to be respected. This law also regulates both function and tasks of the Federal Ombudsperson for People with Disabilities. In 1994 the German constitution was amended. Article 3 (3) of the Basic Law forbids discrimination on the ground of disability.

Belgium pursues an equal opportunities policy and its approach to people with disabilities and their role in Belgian society. Further legislation in 2003 outlawed discrimination of any form (including towards people with disabilities). Where a disability exists the aim is to ensure as full and as active participation as possible in everyday life. Physical barriers to participation must be removed as far as possible. People with disabilities must be given the same access to services and facilities as the able-bodied. They must be given equal opportunities in the workplace. Regional agencies exist to help the disabled and address these issues. People with disabilities and their families are regularly consulted by these agencies regarding improvements and specific local matters. About 45 years ago, Belgium issued a law for a quotum for disabled people in employment. This law was never implemented for the private sector but it was implemented in the public sector. However, the law is not followed well nor are there sanctions. Since 2003 there is an anti-discrimination law in Belgium. In this law, disability is among 13 possible grounds for discrimination. It is not expected that the anti-discrimination law will change much in the situation of disabled people. Approximately 60 per cent of people with disabilities do not work. Those who do, namely 40 per cent, mean that there is about one in every 14 employees who is disabled. The policies for disabled people are based on the conviction that employers are willing to employ disabled people but that they need assistance. Disabled people who are working may not fulfill the production requirements of the job. The European Committee of Social Rights in Strasbourg has stated that the Belgian Government doesn't provide enough support for disabled people. The verdict came after a complaint from a coalition of about 20 different disabled people's organisations and parents associations, including Onafhankelijk Leven (Independent Living Flanders) and Ensemble Vie Autonome (CIL Wallonia). In Belgium there is a structural shortage for most kinds of support for disabled people, including places in residential care institutions, day care centres and so on, but also there are waiting lists for Personal Assistance. In Wallonia and Brussels the situation is even worse. The waiting list problem has been an eyesore for Onafhankelijk Leven for many years. Parking people for indefinite time on a waiting list for Personal Assistance and support they need and are entitled to be unacceptable for the Belgian Independent Living Movement.

People with disabilities in Switzerland are better represented in the workforce than in other countries but still face more obstacles than the general population. Switzerland's first set of indicators on equality for disabled people, released by the Federal Statistics Office just ahead of the UN day, show that there are almost one million people living with some form of disability that's around one in seven of the population. Switzerland has enshrined the principle of equality for disabled people into its constitution. An anti-discrimination law has been in force since 2004. On 15th April, 2014 Switzerland ratified the UN Convention of the Rights of Persons with Disabilities as 144th signatory state. It enters into force in Switzerland in mid-May. The organisations of persons with disabilities welcome this move. Switzerland on the whole has an awareness of the difficulties facing disabled people and has legislation and facilities in place to assist. This ensures standards of access and mobility comparable to those in the EU. A national Disability Discrimination Act was put into effect on 1st January, 2004. Efforts are being made by the Federal Office for Equality of People with Disabilities to raise further awareness. Financial assistance is given to disability organisations to enable further integration of disabled people into all aspects of life. Work is also underway to make all pre-existing public buildings accessible to disabled people. New private buildings must also be constructed to be accessible, unless exempt under certain size conditions. There are seats for the use of disabled persons on public transport. For longer journeys it is advisable to pre-book to reserve the seat. There are also disabled parking spaces, outlined in yellow and displaying a wheelchair symbol. These can be used by holders of a parking authorisation card and apply throughout Switzerland. In Switzerland, disabled children can receive quality care even after their parents pass away.

Disability Concept of the Austrian Federal Government was passed on the 22nd December, 1992 under the then Federal Minister of Labour and Social Affairs, Josef Hesoun. It was drawn up by the Federal Ministry of Labour and Social Affairs in close co-operation with the Austrian associations for disabled people. Based on a comprehensive understanding of disability policy, it covers all areas of human life. An amendment to the Austrian Federal Constitution was passed in July 1997, according to which nobody may be discriminated against because of his or her disability. The Republic (the Federal Government, provinces and municipalities) aims to guarantee equal treatment of disabled and non-disabled people in all areas of daily life. Austria became a member of the European Union two years after the Disability Concept was passed. This is a fundamental programme which forms the foundation of the Austrian Disability Policy, and in order to publicise it at European level in these times of European integration, the document has also been translated into English and French. In 1977, the Federal Ministry for Social Administration drew up a concept for integration of disabled people (the rehabilitation concept) which dealt primarily with issues of rehabilitation, advice for disabled people and the principles of Sheltered Workshops. Disabled children are in principle able to attend a common day nursery, a day nursery with integration groups or a remedial or special needs nursery. Special needs nurseries on average take between eight and 15 children. The Austrian Federal Government emphasises that early detection and aid are crucial if disabled people are to be successfully integrated into society. The Austrian government intends to give disabled people the opportunity to undergo qualified, contemporary vocational training. Following the principle of integration, it gives priority to access to general training courses over special training facilities.

There are approximately 600,000 accidents in Austria each year; of these almost 5,000 are fatal and about 460,000 necessitate sick leave (with hospital treatment required in about 220,000 cases). Associated with this is not only the human suffering, which is almost impossible to quantify, but also the enormous cost to the economy, estimated at about $5,088,000 every year. The number of accidents at work has been falling slightly for some years, as a result of employee protection regulations, medical care at work, the activities of workplace inspectors and preventative measures by accident insurance companies. The medical and orthopaedic care for disabled persons does not really differ from that of any other person. One important precondition for the success of rehabilitation measures is the early recognition of disabilities: there are both private and public institutions which offer early recognition and formative support services. The Austrian Federal Government aims to achieve as high a level of integration of disabled children and young people in schools as possible. For this reason it will be necessary to create additional facilities for special needs assistance and joint teaching of disabled and non-disabled children, despite the fundamental recognition of the special needs school as a possible educational institution.

The Luxembourg National Council of Disabled People is officially represented by the association Info-Handicap, a not for profit association with 55 associations of and for persons with a disability. Other significant national organisations of disabled people include: The National Council of DP provides a complete national overview of all organisations targeting every disability (mental, physical, sensorial, etc.) and all domains of activity and support. Luxembourg has signed the United Nations Convention and the Optional Protocol. Luxembourg should strengthen responsibilities and incentives for both employers and employees in order to encourage more people to work, according to a new OECD report. This is one of the recommendations in Sickness, Disability and Work: Breaking the Barriers (Vol. 2) – Australia, Luxembourg, Spain and the United Kingdom which analysis disability policies and proposes reforms to reduce the number of people claiming benefits and help them re-enter the labour market.

By law, everyone in Luxembourg in gainful employment (employed or self-employed), or receiving replacement revenues from social security schemes, must be affiliated to the healthcare scheme. The healthcare scheme covers the incapacity for work resulting from sickness and involving suspension of earnings by providing periodic replacement payments. The scheme protects the health of the mother and that of the child by providing prenatal and postnatal maternity leave. Period replacement payments are provided in case of a significant risk to the mother's health and that of her child during pregnancy. Special parental leave for family reasons (e.g., sickness of children) are also considered.

Entitlement to disability benefits requires the beneficiary to prove a period of 12 months of insurance periods during the three years preceding the date of occurrence of the disability certified by the social security medical counsel, or the expiry of the sickness benefit. Nonetheless this period is not required if the disability is attributable to an accident of whatever nature or a professionally recognised illness, occurring during the period of affiliation. In 2006, Luxembourg participated to the study conducted by the OECD on sickness, disability and work. In 2008, the General Inspectorate of Social Security (GISS) made an evaluation of the measures regarding the professional reintegration of people with reduced work capacity. The joint committee, ministries and administrations concerned, as well as employer and trade unions, gave their appreciation of the cogency and the operation of the current procedures, by analysing the positive points and the problems encountered.

Disable People in South-East Europe

Eastern Europe is the eastern part of the European continent. There is no consensus as to the precise area it refers to, partly because the term has a wide range of geopolitical, geographical, cultural, and socioeconomic connotations. The Ural Mountains, Ural River, and the Caucasus Mountains are the geographical land border of the eastern edge of Europe. Albania has a disability legal frame. Disabled people officially are entitled to all human rights, (education, employment, health, etc.) and of the freedoms (opinion, expression, etc.) as other citizens, with whom they are equal in front of the law. The constitution stipulates that the state and the government must act in favour of disabled persons in fields of health rehabilitation, the special education, the social integration and living conditions improvement. Albanian Legislation classifies disabled persons in five categories: 1. Labour Invalids. 2. War Invalids. 3. People with development disorders (to the birth or before the age of 21 years). 4. People suffering from mental disorders. 5. Other invalids. Ministry of Education is responsible for the education of the disabled children. Ministry of Labour and Social Affair is responsible for disabled persons.

At the moment the total of people with disabilities is 75,044 in Albania, but this number includes only those who are considered as subject of payment of allowances. The real number might be significantly higher. Albania has a disability legal frame, and all the disabled people have the same rights (education, employment, health) and freedom as others citizens (Article 25 of the Constitution of Albania), but there is still a lot do in terms of their implementing. Regarding the employment situation, the Labour Code prohibits any kind of discrimination and the working hours are reduced to six hours per day. After the war in Bosnia and Herzegovina a new statutory and legislative order on the basis of the new territorial, economic-political and ideological relationship order was established. Contentious and insufficient beginning reforms on economic and social level are most strongly affecting the poorest categories of citizens and especially people with disabilities whose situation dramatically deteriorated. Most organisations unite people with multiple disabilities. Traditional organisations are better organised. They cover all organisational forms on local, regional and federal levels as well as they do in the Republika Srpska on local and republic level. Bosnia and Herzegovina ratified the Convention on the Rights of Persons with Disabilities and its Optional Protocol on 12th March, 2010. Bosnia and Herzegovina signed and ratified the UN Convention on the Rights of People with Disabilities in 2010, but has made little progress in implementing it. People with disabilities represent one of the most vulnerable and hidden groups in the country.

The Law on integration of people with disabilities, the Labour Code and the Law on the encouragement of employment are the main legislations to support employers in Bulgaria. Under Article 25 of the Law on integration of people with disabilities, employers may apply for various support schemes and grant to the Employment Agency providing they retain the disabled employee for more than three years. This includes funding schemes to adapt the working conditions, equipment and premises. Under Article 26, they may receive a bonus on their social insurance tax fee (up to 30 per cent) for the disabled worker. In Bulgaria, disabled workers are supported by various measures provided by the Law on integration of people with disabilities. Article 23 states that both the Ministry of Labour and the Employment Agency are responsible for the delivery of schemes and programmes to encourage job inclusion and to promote equal opportunities for the people with disabilities to participate on the labour market.

Article 24 states that disabled workers are entitled to specific equipment as well as to the adaptation and adjustment of their working conditions and grants are made available to that effect under Article 25. This applies to both newly employed disabled workers and existing employees that acquire a temporary or permanent disability. Employers with limited resources may be exempted from undertaking such measures. The Law on protection against discrimination is the main legislation regarding disability-based discrimination. Section I regulates various protections relating to labour rights, access to further training, promotions, harassment, redundancy. Employers will be held responsible for discrimination acts. The National Agency for people with disabilities conducts information campaigns about the employment schemes that are available as part of the Law on integration of people with disabilities. The campaigns target disabled people, employers and placement agency, social enterprises and co-operatives.

In Greece there are no complete data concerning disabled persons. EUROSTAT reports a percentage of 10.3 per cent on the general population, which is analysed to 10.6 per cent of men and 9.9 per cent of women. On the Article 22 of the Greek Constitution is based the right of disabled persons to work and the protection of their work such as work conditions, their remuneration, their promotions, their education, their training and the prohibition of discrimination against the disabled. Work is a right, protected by the State, which looks after the creation of work conditions for all citizens and for the moral and material elevation of civil and rural population. All citizens, no matter their gender or any other discrimination, are entitled to the same reward for providing work of the same value... The State provides for the social insurance of the working people, following the Law. Greek constitution has Article 21, paragraph 6 that says *"Persons with disabilities have the right to enjoy measures that ensure their autonomy, professional inclusion and participation in the social, economic and political life of the country"*. Several more articles are complementary to this one. For example, the Article 25 is the guideline for a State of Justice and protects disabled persons and Article 5A, paragraph 2 refers to electronic accessibility. It says: *"Everyone has the right to participate in the information society. Facilitation of the access to the information that is electronically available as well as their production, exchange and diffusion is a duty of the State, keeping the guarantees of Articles 9, 9a and 19"*. There are numerous provisions for the disabled in the Civil Law, referring to: Their right to undertake legal transactions; Indemnification by those who have caused the disability; judicial assistance; and Inheritance law.

In Turkey, according to Statistics Institute of Turkey figures, there are about 8.5 million people with different physical and mental disabilities which count approximately 13 per cent of the total population. Living standards of people with disabilities and quality of services offered to them take place an important role in health, education and economic development indicators of countries. Policies related to people with disabilities have developed at international level in recent years. Collecting statistics about disabled population has been given great importance with the purpose monitoring and evaluation of related policies. Since there is currently no registration system of people with disabilities, there is lack of quantitative and qualitative information about people with disabilities. According to a 2002 government study, an estimated 8.5 million disabled people live, at the time nearly 13 per cent of the population, which has since grown to 79 million people. But walking around a major city like Istanbul, one would never know. The disabled are kept sequestered at home, a source of shame for the family. A new legislative package approved by the parliament on 6th February, 2014 could improve the working conditions and rights of the nearly ten million disabled people if it is properly enforced. While experts and civil society organisations applaud the new laws, they emphasise that proper implementation and enforcement of such measures has been lacking in the past, but must be ensured in order to improve life for the disabled and their families.

Under the law, the state will subsidise the payments made to disabled workers by offering companies a five year tax reduction for each disabled employee. According to the Disabled Law of 2005, every company with more than 50 employees must hire a three per cent quota of disabled workers, while the public sector is obliged to have at least four per cent. The Ministry of Education and the Ministry of Labour and Social Security will develop vocational habilitation, rehabilitation and training programmes for the handicapped according to work and occupational analysis by the Ministry of Labour and Social Security. The Ministry of Transport is conducting a project to make airports accessible for the disabled. The major problem in all areas is the lack of mainstreaming and consequently lack of implementation. The financial support provided to the disabled and their families is an important tool to make them integrated into the society, while the increase in the employment opportunities, as a positive discrimination for the disabled, will also make them feel as individuals who are taken into consideration as full members of this society. For that, the full accessibility in the urban life is a must for the disabled to take further steps to be integrated into the society and contribute to the general welfare of the country without facing further invisible barriers in daily practices. The incentives for the establishment of protected workplaces for the mentally disabled constitute a very important step.

A major achievement has been that deaf blindness is now legally recognised as a disability in Romania and this shows a new level of support and understanding from the Government. At an international level, Romania ratified the UN Convention on the Rights of People with Disabilities in 2010 and this too has been an important step forward for the rights of disabled people. Working in Romania still has its challenges. Around 20 per cent of the populations are living in extreme poverty and 44 per cent in rural areas still making it hard to identify and reach deaf blind people. A lack of consistency and stability also makes working with the Romanian Government a challenge. There is still a long way to go in promoting the rights of disabled people and ensuring that deaf blind people can access the services that they need but progress has undoubtedly been made.

There are reportedly more than 165,000 disabled people in Moldova, roughly five per cent of the population. The disabled are among the most disadvantaged in the country and their basic rights are often neglected. The centre defends and promotes the rights of disabled persons by informing them of their legal rights, by offering *pro bono* legal assistance, by raising public awareness about problems the disabled face and by strengthening the capacity of non-governmental organisations that offer services to the disabled. The centre was founded in 2006 by people with disabilities and is located in the premises of the National Center for People with Disabilities. It offers free legal assistance to national centre patrons in exchange for free office space and access to equipment. The centre's legal team consists of two full-time lawyers and several volunteers. The government of Moldova joined with mental health and children's advocates in paving the way to end an era of isolating people with mental disabilities in institutions. The Memorandum of Understanding for Deinstitutionalisation and Community Living for People with Mental Disabilities were signed today by the Ministry of Social Protection, Family and Child, the Open Society Mental Health Initiative, the Soros Foundation-Moldova, Hope and Homes for Children, and Keystone Human Services International. By signing the memorandum, the ministry and the nongovernmental organisations are committing today to a four-year collaboration that will end the further institutionalisation of children with mental disabilities and establish models for community-based services that will replace the institutions in the long run. The Moldova Ministry of Social Protection, Family and Child has the mandate to guarantee the realisation of the provisions in the Constitution regarding the development, promotion and implementation of state policies of social protection, family and child in order to ensure the social security and increased living standards of the population.

Legal Assistance Center for Persons with Disabilities is a nongovernmental, non-profit, apolitical, public interest organisation, established on 14th July, 2006, by a group of people with disabilities. The major objectives of the Centre are: (a) achieving, defending and promoting the rights of persons with disabilities; (b) informing people with disabilities about their legal rights; and (c) raising public awareness about the problems of people with disabilities. Law on social protection of invalids in the Republic of Moldova from 1991 provides that every company, institution and organisation is required to reserve at least five per cent of the total number of jobs for people with disabilities. Employers who fail to do so must deduct to the unemployment fund a sum worth an average annual salary for each unreserved job. People with disabilities in the Republic of Moldova are forming a vulnerable group requiring the creation of conditions for their integration into society. Integration, not isolation or institutionalisation is the main objective of social policies that comply with international practices and principles. People with different forms of disability and their families form a category of disadvantaged persons compared with other population groups. Almost no building in Moldova has ramps to allow access for persons with disabilities; this is one of the main problems faced by this category of people. Although national legislation requires public authorities to provide physical infrastructure to adapt to the needs of persons with disabilities, currently there are only few public institutions adapted to the needs of these people. In addition, is being attested the lack of standards regarding the minimum means and facilities of access to public buildings and the lack of national and local ratings with respect to the need and costs of adapting infrastructure of public buildings and living space.

In Ukraine, two-thirds of working age people with disabilities is unemployed. Discrimination and stigma surrounding persons with disabilities is a legacy of the former soviet system when persons with disabilities were segregated from the society. They often had limited access to employment and social services. UNDP Ukraine in collaboration with the International Labour Organisation and the State Employment Centre has implemented the *"Social Inclusion of People with Disabilities through Access to Employment"* project. In 2009, the project's experts and a working group developed a new Model and a Methodology of Job Placement and Employment for People with Disabilities by State Employment Centres. The model uses a new approach to employing people with disabilities. To improve this situation, the UNDP, ILO and State Employment Center launched a Project in 2008 entitled: Social Inclusion of People with Disabilities through Access to Employment. The overall objective of the Project is to facilitate a proactive inclusion of people with disabilities into the open labour market in order to safeguard their equal rights and opportunities. To fulfill this task, the Project founders agreed to elaborate a new approach to establishing an effective mechanism of job placement of people with disabilities. UNDP and ILO, have one more goal with this Project: to dispel a social myth that people with disabilities would be professionally uncompetitive. Working on the elimination of employers' stereotypes and the social stigma towards people with physical, sensory and mental disabilities, UNDP and ILO have contributed to enforcing the principle of equal opportunity in Ukrainian society.

The success of the Russian Paralympic team in the recent Winter Paralympic Games and the state-of-the-art facilities built for the Games in Sochi could give the impression that today's Russia is doing a lot to integrate disabled people into society. A nationwide study conducted by Human Rights Watch of Russians with a range of disabilities revealed legitimate concerns and frustrations with both state and society. The infrastructure in Russian cities poses an insurmountable obstacle for many people with physical impairments, and it is especially hard for disabled people to find work. According to Human Rights Watch experts, most of the problems Russia faces today in caring for people with disabilities are rooted in the Soviet past. The situation has changed dramatically for Russians with disabilities since that time. Russia has ratified the United Nations 2012 Convention on the Rights of Persons with Disabilities and also launched a $5.5 billion project for its implementation. By 2015, funds will be disbursed for renovation of public buildings and redesign of sidewalks and for new buses and trains. Additionally, websites for government agencies will be updated to provide information on programmes for people with disabilities. With more than 16,000 wheelchair users, Moscow should be leading the way in developing infrastructure for Russians who have mobility challenges.

Belarus remains the only country in Europe that has not acceded to the UN Convention on the Rights of Persons with Disabilities. People with disabilities remain marginalised in Belarus. Disabled people have to deal with both physical and regulatory barriers. The main blame for this lies with the state authorities and a society that still retains the stereotypes about the people with disabilities. However, people with disabilities themselves take matters into their own hands and fight for their rights more and more often. Today they require the solidarity of Belarusians and the international community to achieve the accession of Belarus to the UN Convention. More than 512,000 people with disabilities live in Belarus. Among them, 20,000 use wheelchairs. Moreover, the annual incidence of disability increases by around 50,000. Every twentieth Belarusian is disabled, but society seems not to notice this problem. The absence of adequate infrastructure leads to all-to-familiar stories where people with disabilities rarely leave their flats. Belarus is slowly creating the necessary conditions for the disabled in the form of ramps or low-floor buses. Only 14 per cent of Belarusian disabled people of working age have a job. Belarusian authorities still have not introduced any anti-discrimination legislation and some laws violate the rights of the disabled. Western aid has been of great importance to Belarusian people with disabilities. The disability rights movement remains an important part of civil society in Belarus.

As Belarus prepares to adopt the UN Convention on the Rights of Persons with Disabilities, issues related to the rights of people with disabilities are moving up on the agendas of both Government decision-makers and members of civil society. Recently conducted consultations on the future of global development in Belarus saw the broad participation of diverse groups and sectors, and people with disabilities are strongly advocating for social inclusion and changing attitudes. In Serbia, ten per cent people are disabling. In 2003, Serbia recognised for the first time that people with disabilities are a vulnerable group requiring extra assistance, and in 2010, an employment quota system was brought into effect. This system required employers to hire at least one person with disabilities for every 20-50 employees, and to hire another person with disabilities for every 50 additional employees. Almost 3,700 people with disabilities found employment, up from only 600 in 2009. UNDP also joined the UN Global Compact to teach private sector employers how to hire people with disabilities, comply with hiring quotas, and increase workplace accessibility by installing ramps for wheelchairs or software for people with visual impairments. Efforts also exist to help people with disabilities with employment. In 2010, the Serbian Government set up the Centre for Professional Rehabilitation and Employment of Persons with Disabilities to provide vocational training, business start-up grants, and work placements in public and private organisations.

In recent years a strong tendency towards establishing standards and legal regulation has been noticed to improve the lives of people with disabilities. The basic act is the Constitution of Poland adopted on 2nd April, 1997. Constitution as the most important legal act, introduces a number of protective regulations. Article 69 of Polish Constitution has states that public authorities shall provide assistance to disabled persons to secure subsistence, adaptation to work and social communication. Constitution establishes the rights of citizens with disabilities and obligations of public authorities towards them. Another important act is the Card on the Rights of Persons with Disabilities which was established by the resolution of the Polish Parliament on 1st August, 1997. Actions taken to increase the employment of people with disabilities have been identified by the Act on Vocational and Social Rehabilitation and Employment of the Disabled established on 27th August, 1997. Polish law regulates also more specific issues. An example of such regulation is the Construction Law, which provides detailed requirements for investments. The same subject is also regulated by the Regulation of the Minister of Infrastructure about the technical conditions for buildings and their location. Obviously, the Polish Parliament remembers about special needs of people with disabilities in almost every area of human life. Government takes legal actions to promote employment of handicapped people. The most important are financial benefits offered to the employers. The Government funds parts of the salaries as well as social contribution of employees. The biggest barriers for employers are the poor infrastructure, the need for adaption the workplace, the low level of social integration and the lack of universal acceptance for disability which reflects in unfavourable reaction of employers.

The Slovak Republic has signed the United Nations Convention and the Optional Protocol. The Slovak Republic is currently aligning its legal framework with the UN Convention. Financial allowances for severe disability compensation were available for: personal assistance, purchasing and repairing aids (assistive devices), purchasing a personal motor vehicle, housing adaptation, additional expenses (special diets, hygiene or clothing, footwear and furnishing replacement, operating a personal motor vehicle, care for an assistance dog) and for caring. In Slovenia it has been estimated that between 160,000 and 170,000 people are disabled (disabled workers, children and youth with special needs, military and war disabled, and moderately, seriously or severely mentally and physically disabled persons). Legislation takes care of most of the major factors that promote the development of disability policy and regulate the social status of persons with disabilities in various areas such as independent living, accessibility, schooling, training, employment, technical aids, rehabilitation, etc. In September 2011, almost 16,400 persons with disabilities were unemployed, which is around 15 per cent of all registered unemployed persons. On the other hand, 30,400 persons with disabilities were employed (16,600 men and 13,800 women) or 3.8 per cent of all persons in employment (persons in paid employment and self-employed persons, excluding farmers). Employment rehabilitation and employment of persons with disabilities are legally regulated, there is a quota system of employing disabled persons. An important way of employing disabled persons is employment in special enterprises employing people with disabilities, which represent a special form of social economy since they employ and train disabled persons who due to disability could not get a job or keep it at employers in normal working environment.

According to Article 14 of the Constitution of the Republic of Slovenia everyone shall be guaranteed equal human rights and fundamental freedoms irrespective of personal circumstance. In the amendment of Article 14 which entered into force on 15th June, 2004 personal circumstances also include disability. The Constitution expressly underlines the equality of persons with disabilities before the law, and that nobody shall be disadvantaged on grounds of disability. Everyone shall be guaranteed equal human rights and fundamental freedoms irrespective of national origin, race, sex, language, religion, political or other conviction, material standing, birth, education, social status, disability or any other personal circumstance. The adoption of the United Nations Convention on the Rights of Persons with Disabilities, the purpose of which is to encourage the persons with disabilities to fully enjoy human rights and fundamental freedoms on an equal basis, to protect such rights and freedoms, to ensure them to persons with disabilities and encourage the respect for their dignity is expected in 2006. In 1991, Slovenia adopted the Concept of Development Strategy for Persons with Disabilities. Between 1991 and 2006 a set of regulations was adopted in the fields of education, healthcare, employment, elimination of obstacles in the environment and ensuring benefits for persons with disabilities. Various national and development programmes in different fields offer solutions essential for the living of persons with disabilities. The Government also adopted the decision to declare the International Year of Persons with Disabilities. That year was marked by a broader European-wide action addressing awareness raising and combating discrimination of persons with disabilities. A comprehensive programme of activities was organised at the national level that comprised 42 consultation sessions, conferences, public forums, round tables and presentations. There were even more events organised at the local levels. On 7th December, 2005, the Government adopted National guidelines to improve accessibility of built environment, information and communications to persons with disabilities.

In Hungary, access to inclusive education and any kind of employment for people with intellectual disabilities remains very limited. The education of children with intellectual disabilities remains highly segregated. Most of these children are educated in special schools, which, though they often provide a good quality education, do not prepare students for social inclusion or equip them with the skills they need to later access employment. Hungary has ratified most international instruments, including those with provisions on people with disabilities, but it has yet to ratify the Revised European Social Charter (RESC) or Protocol No. 12 to the European Convention on the Protection of Human Rights and Fundamental Freedoms (ECHR). The Hungarian Constitution does not include disability as a specifically prohibited ground for discrimination. However, the Act on Equal Treatment and Promotion of Equal Opportunities (Equal Treatment Act) introduces a comprehensive anti-discrimination framework, which also covers people with disabilities. Hungary has a comprehensive disability policy, the National Programme on Disability Affairs (National Disability Programme), which also addresses access to education and employment. The 2001 National Population Census indicates that there are approximately 57,000 people with intellectual disabilities in Hungary, a significant decrease from the number reported in the 1990 Census. In Hungary, many people with intellectual disabilities are placed under guardianship by the courts at age 18. Hungary's Public Education Act is the main legislation governing public education, including special education. The 2003 amendments to the act introduce an explicit prohibition on discrimination on the ground of disability, defined as lack or impediment of abilities.

The Hungarian Constitution guarantees the right to work, the right to freely choose a job or profession and the right to equal compensation for equal work without discrimination, but it does not specifically address the employment of people with disabilities. In the area of employment, two types of capacity are assessed for people with disabilities: working capacity and employment capacity. The National Medical Expert Institute conducts assessments to evaluate the working capacity of adults with intellectual disabilities. People with intellectual disabilities are heavily dependent on social welfare benefits. Most adults with intellectual disabilities do not have the required work experience to access unemployment benefits or the invalidity pension. The main Government policy on the employment of people with disabilities is described in the National Disability Programme. The programme contains a number of goals that are highly relevant to promoting the employment of people with intellectual disabilities. The Government promotes the employment of people with disabilities on the open labour market and in sheltered workplaces through the quota system, State subsidies and tax incentives. Despite these incentives, in Hungary, the vast majority of people with disabilities do not have access to any kind of employment.

Disable People in Southern Europe

Geographically, southern Europe is the southern half of the landmass of Europe. Southern Europe's most emblematic climate is that of the Mediterranean climate, which has become a typically known characteristic of the area. Those areas of Mediterranean climate present similar vegetations and landscapes throughout, including dry hills, small plains, pine forests and olive trees. Romance languages and Modern Greek are the heirs of Latin and ancient Greek, which served as the main historical languages of the Mediterranean region.

The Spanish Constitution acknowledges legal equality for all Spaniards without any discrimination on grounds of race, sex, religion, opinion or any other personal or social condition or circumstance. The Social Integration of Disabled People Act passed in 1982, is the framework document that has inspired all subsequent social policies in the field of disability. It was sanctioned shortly after the International Year of Disabled Persons and just before the approval of the UN Programme of Action concerning Disabled Persons. The Government implemented general labour reforms in both 1994 and 1997. The 1994 reforms were set in the context of an employment crisis, and included measures for increased flexibility in hiring and firing conditions as well as tougher eligibility criteria for unemployment benefits. There have been several National Action Plans for Employment developing continuously in Spain since 1995. 1992 was the Tenth Anniversary of the Programme of Action concerning Disabled Persons. It was also the year, in which the first ten years of the LISMI were assessed, leading the United Nations to propose a short-term strategy for the year 2000 with the slogans *'a society for everyone'* and *'from awareness to action'*.

In 1993, the Spanish Council of Representatives of People with Disabilities was created. It is a defense and self-advocacy platform for people with disabilities that attempt to promote their full citizenship and rights equal to other members of the community. There are a number of employment opportunities for Spanish people with disabilities which vary according to individual capacity: Occupational Centres, which aim to provide occupational therapy and personal and social adjustment for those who cannot be integrated into other schemes; Special Employment Centres, which carry out productive work and ensure remunerative employment, regularly participating in market operations; Supported Employment, which is employment in the open market with ordinary companies but with the necessary supports inside and outside the workplace provided; and Ordinary Employment, i.e., employment in normalised companies, the public sector and self-employment where most workers do not have disabilities.

While the specific issue of parenting a child with disabilities has not yet been seriously researched in Portugal, available data indicates that care responsibilities in general, within Portuguese families, are primarily ascribed to women. While Portuguese mothers of children with disability are giving up their participation in the labour force to care for their disabled child, they are entitled to only very modest financial compensation for this important social role. The legal framework for protection of equal treatment in Italy is mainly based on statute law, in the form of either acts issued by the parliament or acts having the same force and originating in a decision of the national parliament, but issued by different bodies. The key legislative provisions in order to assess the transposition in Italy of the Directives are those contained in the two Decrees enacted by the government in 2003 on the basis of the lawmaking powers delegated to government by the parliament with the omnibus act for implementation of EU law approved in 2002.

Disable People in North America

North America is a continent wholly within the Northern Hemisphere and almost wholly within the Western Hemisphere. It can also be considered a northern subcontinent of the Americas. Canada, Mexico and the United States have significant and multifaceted economic systems. The United States has the largest economy in North America, and in the world. The Pan-American Highway route in North America is the portion of a network of roads nearly 48,000 km (30,000 mi) in length which travels through the mainland nations of the Americas. Geographically the North American continent is composed of many regions and sub-regions.

Canada

About 3.8 million Canadians (13.7 per cent) reported having a disability in 2012. The percentage of Canadians with disabilities increased with age, ranging from 4.4 per cent for people 15 to 24 years to 42.5 per cent for those 75 years and over. In 2012, a greater proportion of females (14.9 per cent) reported a disability than males (12.5 per cent). This does not hold for all age groups. A similar proportion of males aged 15 to 24 (4.5 per cent) and females in the same age group (4.3 per cent) were reported having a disability. The percentage of Canadians with disabilities was lowest in Nunavut (6.9 per cent) and highest in Nova Scotia (18.8 per cent). In general, women have a higher disability rate than men, but the reverse is true among children. About 17.7 per cent of adult women have a disability, compared with just 15.4 per cent of men. Among those under 14 years of age, 4.6 per cent of boys have a disability compared with just 2.7 per cent of girls. The most common current types of disability are related to an aging population: pain, mobility and agility.

Between 2001 and 2006 the number of persons reported having a disability increased by three-quarters of a million people, reaching 4.4 million in 2006. At the same time, the non-disabled population experienced lesser growth, increasing by 3.3 per cent to reach 26.2 million people. As a result, the national disability rate increased 1.9 percentage points from its level of 12.4 per cent in 2001 to reach 14.3 per cent in 2006. Demographic shifts in the structure of the Canadian population have an effect on the disability rate. Because of the higher disability rates for older Canadians, an aging population will produce a higher overall disability rate without any change in reporting patterns. The disabled faced a number of issues through the years and in the 1970's, the Canadian Government realised the difficulties that the disabled faced. The government enacted the first law that gave the disabled specific rights. The Canadian Human Rights Act gave all Canadians equal rights on the basis of sex, race, nationality and disability. This legislature gave all Canadians the same rights under the law, which was a needed step. In 1977, to address the needs of all people the Canadian Human Rights Act was passed. It brought to light the need for all Canadian citizens to be treated equally, but it did not specifically address the needs of the disabled. In the 1970's the American government started to address the needs of the disabled, and because of this, the Canadian government also began to help the disabled.

United States

The population of people with disabilities inhabits a distinct position in the U.S. economy, both for their contributions to the marketplace and roles in government policies and programmes. People with disabilities bring unique sets of skills to the workplace, enhancing the strength and diversity of the U.S. labour market. In 2008, the federal government spent an estimated $357 billion dollars on programmes for working-age people with disabilities, representing 12 per cent of total federal outlays. Approximately 56.7 million people living in the United States had some kind of disability in 2010. The total number of people with a disability increased by 2.2 million from 54.4 million people in 2005, when disability was last measured in the SIPP, while the percentage remained statistically unchanged. Both the number and percentage with a severe disability increased over that time period. Improving the economic conditions for people with disabilities has been a focus of federal disability policy for several decades. Efforts have traditionally taken a two-prong approach: (1) to assist in reducing or eliminating the barriers to participation in the workforce, and (2) to provide cash and in-kind benefits to those who experience material hardship as a consequence of remaining barriers. People with disabilities cannot attain decent work if they do not have access to education, training and employment services and other social and development experiences that enable them to acquire employability skills.

About 56.7 million people i.e., 19 per cent of the population had a disability in 2010, according to a broad definition of disability, with more than half of them reporting the disability was severe, according to a comprehensive report on this population released by the U.S. Census Bureau. Millions of Americans use a wheelchair or a walking aid such as a cane; consequently, getting around can take a lot more effort. Nevertheless, there is some reason for optimism due to the availability of mobility products such as a wheelchair lift and handicapped vehicles like accessible vans. There are positive trends in public transportation as well. In 2007, some 98 per cent of transit buses were equipped with ramps up from just 62 per cent in 1995. Employment represents another challenge area for America's disabled population. An estimated 14.5 per cent of disabled people have been unemployed, compared to nine per cent of the general population. Another obstacle for the disabled is education. Some 28 per cent of disable people ages 25 and older have less than a high school education.

Mexico

Mexican President Felipe Calderon signed into law a measure to extend anti-discrimination protections to people with disabilities. In a ceremony at the official residence of Los Pinos, Calderon said that for the first time *"the ban on treating the disabled in a discriminatory way has been raised to the status of law."* The state will no longer adopt a paternalistic attitude toward the disabled, the President said. The law aims to acknowledge human dignity, eradicate prejudice and lack of understanding and provide equal opportunities for this sector. The measure is being channeled through the National Council for the Development and Inclusion of Disabled Persons, a federal organisation. Close to 1.7 million of the close to 113 million inhabitants of Mexico are disabled, according to official data.

Mentally and physically disabled children and adults continue to live in abusive and squalid conditions in many orphanages and mental health facilities throughout the country. A report on Nov. 30, 2012 by Disability Rights International, working with the Mexican Commission for the Defense and Promotion of Human Rights, indicates that not much has changed in Mexico ten years after a Mexican Commission for the rights of cognitively and physically challenged people conducted a similar survey. Children in Mexican institutions have been especially at risk. In the new report, government officials admitted there were no registry and no method for tracking children, leaving them potential victims of human trafficking and forced labour. A grandmother in Mexico City was unable to locate her granddaughter after she was placed in foster care at age six in 2005. Ironically, together with many other countries, Mexico ratified the 2006 U.N. Convention on the Rights of Persons with Disabilities. And yet the Mexican Commission that wrote the original report in 2000 has said that current violations in Mexico are still as serious as any this organisation has documented before.

Disable People in Central America

Central America is the central geographic region of the Americas. Central America is an area of 524,000 square kilometers (202,000 sq mi), or almost 0.1 per cent of the Earth's surface. Central America is part of the Mesoamerican Biodiversity hotspot, boasting seven per cent of the world's biodiversity. In Central America, the official language majority in six countries is Spanish and one that officially speaks English (Belize), Mayan languages constitute a language family consisting of about 26 related languages, in 1996, Guatemala formally recognised 21 languages Mayan. Central America is currently undergoing a process of political, economic and cultural transformation that started in 1907 with the creation of the Central American Court of Justice.

Panama

In December 2002, President of Panama Mireya Mocoso signed Executive Decree No. 88 modifying Law No. 42, to strengthen the foundations of equal opportunities for persons with disabilities, particularly in the area of access to work. The Law outlines a series of initiatives directed to provide equal opportunities for persons with disabilities across the country. Alba

Tejada de Rolla, Minister of Labour of Panama, has recognised on many occasions that even though Law No. 42 was approved, persons with disabilities still confront discrimination in diverse spheres of society including access to work. Until quite recently, there was virtually no accessibility for persons with disabilities in public institutions or private buildings, including places of commercial activity. This affected particularly persons using wheelchairs. Authorities of the government of Panama recognise that this situation is being improved yet there is a lot to be done.

Although many deaf people do not consider themselves to be disabled, various Panamanian disability organisations and legislation include them in the population which they serve. For this reason, the wider situation of the disability community is discussed to better understand the position of deaf Panamanians. According to the census in 2000, the total population of Panama was approximately three million; 52 thousand of those reported having disability (1.8 per cent of the total population). Deaf people report that there is still discrimination in hiring procedures and that hearing loss may prevent a deaf person from gaining employment, even if a hearing person competing for the same position is less academically and/or professionally qualified. From 1995 to 2000, various legislation (including Law 34 in 1995, Law 42 in 1999, and the Executive Order 1 of 2000) began the implementation of inclusive education for people with disabilities. Special education programmes tend to be located in the major cities of Panama because more rural areas lack the financial resources to support specialised programmes. However, financial efforts to support integration and inclusive education have been supported by Fernandez de Torrijos, the 2005–2009 Presidents' wife. Panama is one of the few countries in Latin America that provides at least some hearing-screening programmes. There are three main organisations serving people with hearing loss in Panama. The Centro Especializado de Aprendizaje, Voz, Audicion y Lenguaje (CEPAVAL) was established in 1977.

Guatemala

The situation of persons with multiple disabilities, many of them presenting mental disability, is blurred in Guatemala. These persons have been deprived of all the rights they are entitled to and their destiny is marked by inhuman loneliness. It is important to mention that the situation of persons with any disability, particularly those presenting multiple disabilities, is determined by and immersed within the circle of poverty and disability. Guatemala could be the worst place in the world to live with a disability. There is almost no government help and many people with disabilities live isolated lives hidden away from public view. An incredible 14 per cent of Guatemalans have a disability, and for most, life is very harsh. Wheelchair Basketball Team Transitions is one of the only providers of help to people with disabilities. The organisation provides special education, healthcare, rehabilitation and individually-customised wheelchairs manufactured in a workshop staffed entirely by wheelchair users. Transitions also work to change prevailing negative attitudes towards people with disabilities. Members of staff from the wheelchair workshop also form the Guatemalan Wheelchair Basketball Team. In countries like Guatemala, low income, inadequate access to health services and unsanitary and unsafe living and working conditions mean increased vulnerability to disease and injury, causing disability.

Guatemala ratified the United Nation's Convention on the Rights of Persons with Disabilities in 2009, which protects the rights and ensures the just treatment of persons with disabilities. However, Guatemala has yet to implement them because the changes are so sweeping and resources so scarce that it would take years to make the necessary changes. One of the first obstacles in addressing disability is creating an extensive and unified definition of disability. The Guatemalan government ratified the UN Convention on the Rights of Persons with Disabilities in 2009. Article 15 of the CRPD provides that persons with disabilities shall not be subjected to torture or cruel, inhuman, or degrading treatment or punishment. Furthermore, Article 16 states that persons with disabilities shall be free from exploitation, violence, and abuse. As a State Party to the CRPD, the Guatemalan government's adherence to both of these provisions is suspect, especially in light of the reported grave conditions at Federico Mora hospital. The Guatemalan government has also ratified the UN Convention against Torture (CAT). The treaty enforcement body of the CAT, the UN Committee against Torture, has established that *"each State party should prohibit, prevent and redress torture and ill-treatment in all contexts of custody or control, for example, in prisons, hospitals, schools, [and] institutions that engage in the care of children, the aged, the mentally ill or disabled."*

Honduras

Honduras is the third poorest country in the region and one of the least developed in the world. There is general agreement regarding the most appropriate disability related terminology. According to the household survey, the total population of Honduras is estimated to be 6,697,916 people. The Honduran government has not yet issued any statement in support of the creation of a United Nations Convention for the protection of the rights of people with disabilities, and it has not signed the Inter-American Convention on the Elimination of All forms of Discrimination against People with Disabilities. Honduras has several national laws that specifically protect or benefit people with disabilities. Military Junta's Decree 962, dated 7th May, 1980, which created the National Council on Comprehensive Rehabilitation to coordinate and supervise disability services. Legislative Decree 86-45, dated 11 April 1984, which proclaimed of April as the *"Day of Solidarity toward the Handicapped"*, to be observed every year. Legislative Decree 17-91, also known as the *"Promotion of Employment for People with Disabilities Act"*, dated 26 February 1991, which encouraged the integration of people with disabilities into the open labour market or other appropriate occupational alternatives. In 1987, the Training and Rehabilitation of People with Disabilities Act was passed by the legislature. Implementation of its provisions became the responsibility of the Institute for the Habilitation and Rehabilitation of People with Disabilities. However, this institute was closed for budgetary reasons, and so the goals contained in the legislation remain largely unfulfilled.

Children with disabilities suffer from physical or mental problems that limit their growth and development. The principle causes of disabilities in Honduran children are malnutrition, illness, complications at birth, and accidents. In general, children in extreme poverty are more likely to become disabled because of inadequate nutrition, unhealthy living conditions, a lack of access to healthcare, exploitative and inappropriate work, and a lack of adequate supervision. Children with disabilities are faced with discrimination and segregation, and many families are keeping their children at home due to embarrassment. A few families send their children to beg in the street. The Honduran Institute of Habilitation and Rehabilitation was established by decree No. 184-87 in 1987. The responsibilities of the Institute were transferred to the Ministry of Health in 1995 under the Integral Rehabilitation Division as part of state modernisation reforms. Chapter VIII Article 169 of the Constitution of the Republic of Honduras (1982) guarantees support and promotion of education for persons with disabilities by the nation. Chapter IV Article 142 of the Constitution of the Republic of Honduras (1982) guarantees social security to all citizens including persons with disabilities, guaranteeing the rights for security of an individual's means of financial subsistence, or the right to employment. Today, there are a greater number of public and non-profit private institutions, as well as NGO's concerned about development of the potential of persons with disabilities with an integral and participative focus.

There are 3.3 million Hondurans under 18 years of age, accounting for 44 per cent of the country's total population, according to National Institute of Statistics figures for 2009. Forty-nine per cent of Hondurans under the age of 18 are girls. The indigenous and Afro-Honduran population, of 800,000 people, constitutes ten per cent of the country's total population, according to National Institute of Statistics estimates for 2008. With regard to global child malnutrition, the target for 2015 is 10.7 per cent, which has not yet been achieved in rural areas. Various estimations suggest that there are almost 700,000 persons with disabilities living in the country, which is equivalent to ten per cent of the population. The 2002 survey recorded 177,516 persons in Honduras as having a *disability*, but the definition used was rather narrow.

Nicaragua

From 1960 to 1990, the interior regions of Nicaragua were the site of prolonged and violent political revolution. The conflicts resulted in an increased number of persons with disabilities throughout the country. Currently, disability rights are protected by Law 202; however, this law is largely unknown by many governmental offices. According to the National Institute of Statistics and Census (INEC), as of April 2004 the population of is 5,400,000, and 12.5 per cent, approximately 675,000 people, have some kind of disability. Nicaragua ratified the Organisation of American States (OAS) Inter-American Convention on the Elimination of All Forms of Discrimination Against Persons with Disabilities on 15 July 2002. The instrument was deposited with the General Secretariat of the OAS on 25 November 2002. In regard to national legislation, disability-related laws have been based on international human rights documents, including the UN Standard Rules, to which Nicaragua adheres. The Constitution of the Republic addresses the rights of persons with disabilities, as do a number of other codes and laws. At the national level, no public or private institutions keep records of discrimination against persons with disabilities in the areas of housing, employment, education or transportation. Although the Parent-Child Relationship Act, enacted in 1982, contains no special restrictions for the adoption of children by persons with disabilities, there are limitations for those people who have psychiatric disabilities and no family. The unemployment rate for persons with disabilities is unknown, it is assumed to be extremely high. Although some employment protections are available for people with disabilities in Law 185, in Law 202, and in the Constitution of the Republic, Nicaragua has no national norms or policies that specifically state that a person with disabilities cannot be discriminated against in employment on the basis of his or her disability.

The Nicaraguan society admits that in spite of its efforts made there would always be people with disabilities. The situation of disability is a problem that has been increasing during the last years due to multiple of causes leaving disabilities of considerable magnitude: armed conflict that the country lived constitutes a major factor in the increase of the disabled population. Nicaragua has continued to execute institutional rehabilitation programmes since 1958 when it had to confront an aggressive epidemic of poliomyelitis that staggered the responding capacity to the health sector, and due to these circumstances that office has been exercised by the Ministry of Health without differentiation between it and the agency for disability and rehabilitation. In 1995 Law 202 was approved, law for the Prevention, Rehabilitation and Equality of Opportunity for People with disabilities, which redefines the responsibilities of the sphere of the office, designated the National Council of Rehabilitation as the coordinating entity for the States efforts, and as a mechanism for definition and applications of the office in the subject of prevention, rehabilitation, and equality of opportunities. In 2002, Law 423 was approved, General Health Law, in which it establishes the Ministry of Health as the governing body relating to provision of medical rehabilitation services. To improve the quality of rehabilitee attention, a greater equity in the provision of services is required, expand those to accomplish a greater elevation of coverage and destine sufficient economic resources to attend the demands generated.

The Nicaraguan government does not fund any programmes for individuals with disabilities in Matagalpa. Families with disabled children face huge obstacles and often lack the means to overcome them. Many are marginalised and disproportionately affected by poverty, lacking basic services like education, employment, and even transportation.

Costa Rica

Costa Rica is not as easily accessible for people with disabilities as many wealthier countries. Laws based on international standards that promote equal opportunity and accessibility is in place, but lack of funding has led to uneven implementation and enforcement. Under Costa Rica's Equal Opportunities Law for People with Disabilities, no person may be discriminated against for their disabilities and no employer can deny work to a disabled and otherwise qualified applicant on the basis of their disability. This law, which was passed in May 1996, also requires public places and transportation to provide facilities that enable access for people with disabilities. The country has an Ombudsman who is charged with protecting the human and civil rights of citizens. The Ombudsman is appointed by Parliament and reports to Parliament, not to the government. The Ombudsman's budget comes directly from Parliament. The Ombudsman can start legal procedures on its own against anybody, public or private, including the government which happens frequently. In Costa Rica we have had and still have typical charity organisations for people with disabilities who in the 1980 have asked the public in nation-wide radio and television campaigns for money to be used for programmes for disabled people.

In 1994, as a result of pressure from the disability movement, the government created the function of the Presidential Advisor on Disability, a politically appointed position in the President's Office. A disabled person got the job. The new Costa Rican law is called *"Equal Opportunities Law for People with Disabilities"* and was enacted by Congress in May 1996. The law is based on international documents such as the Standard Rules on the Equalisation of Opportunities of Disabled People, the Inter-American Convention of Human Rights, the United Nations Children's Convention. Its philosophy consists of the principles of non-discrimination and equalisation of opportunities, defined as the process of adapting the environment, services, information, activities as well as attitudes to the needs of all people. Lobbying for the law, the drafting and consulting process, and getting it passed in Congress made the law and its implications for disabled people widely known among the general public. The media which had followed the process from the beginning informed about the law and its role in the country's social legislation. Soon after its passing, many state agencies and private organisations started training activities and requested copies of the law.

El Salvador

El Salvador is a constitutional, multiparty democracy with a population of approximately 6.1 million. The constitution provides for freedom of movement within the country, foreign travel, emigration, and repatriation, and the government generally respected these rights in practice. The government cooperated with the Office of the UN High Commissioner for Refugees and other humanitarian organisations in providing protection and assistance to internally displaced persons, refugees, returning refugees, asylum seekers, stateless persons, and other persons of concern. The country's laws provide for the granting refugee status or asylum, and the government has established a system for providing protection to refugees. The law provides protection against the expulsion or return of persons to countries where their lives or freedom would be threatened on account of their race, religion, nationality, membership in a particular social group, or political opinion.

Many argue that El Salvador has come a long way towards trying to repair its disabled past by declaring itself mine-free in

1994, implementing the 2001 National Disability Rights law and ratifying the United Nations Convention on the Rights of Persons with Disabilities in 2007. The Permanent Table of the Office of the Ombudsman for Human Rights (PDDH) and disability rights civil society organisations such as the Landmine Survivors Network have led the struggle in Central America to promote the rights of people with disabilities and guarantee them "free and equal access to services" through the construction of accessible infrastructure and much-needed legislation. The evolution of disability rights since the civil war that ended in 1992 shows two decades of struggle to reevaluate the meaning of disability, enforce legislation, and create national awareness of disability rights. It is estimated that 70,000 individuals were killed twelve-year armed conflict and another 300,000 people disabled from it.

The 1990s disability rights movement was focused on the disabilities of war survivors, and excluded the comprehensive disability awareness found in the 2007 UN Convention on Disability Rights. In 2001, the El Salvador Congress passed a law requiring the following: *"equal opportunity for people with disabilities, access to education, and the opportunity to work."* The law states that both public and private employers should hire one person with disabilities for every twenty-five workers. On 30th March, 2007, El Salvador signed the United Nations Convention on the Rights of Persons with Disabilities. On 4th October, 2007, the El Salvador National Assembly ratified the Convention, making it the eighth country to do so since the Convention opened for signature in March of 2007. On 3rd May, 2008, El Salvador officially joined the ranks of those countries bound by the laws of the Convention. The National Council for Disabled Persons (CONAIPD) is the government agency responsible for protecting the rights of persons with disabilities. The goal of the Convention on the Rights of Persons with Disabilities and its Optional Protocol, which opened for signature on 30th March, 2007, is to *"promote, protect, and ensure the full and equal enjoyment of all human rights by persons with disabilities,"* including self-determination, physical and programmematic access, personal mobility, health, education, employment, habilitation and rehabilitation, participation in political life, and equality and non-discrimination. El Salvador lacks accurate information of the number of people with disabilities, the type of disability, and other invaluable information about disabled individuals in the country.

Belize

In 2000, the government of Belize began dismantling the Disability Services Division of the Ministry of Human Development. The Disability Services Division was responsible for developing and monitoring programmes and services for people with disabilities. After disbanding the division in 2001, the government transferred responsibility for disability service provision to private companies and nongovernmental organisations. Currently, Belize has no national laws that specifically protect the rights of people with disabilities. The Constitution of Belize makes reference to the equal rights of all Belizeans. It recognises *"the principles of social justice...that there should be adequate means of livelihood for all,...and that a just system should be ensured to provide for education and health on the basis of equality,"* but it does not specifically mention people with disabilities. People with disabilities also have the right to be elected or appointed to public office. The Belizean government does not provide a Braille version of the Constitution.

The National Library Service in Belize City provides materials in alternative formats such as video and audio cassettes, for people with visual and hearing disabilities. Local television stations are owned and operated solely by private entities and do not regularly provide captioning of their programmeming. The Disability Services Division (DSD) of the Ministry of Human Development developed a national programme for the early detection of disabilities in children. There is no national policy to encourage the employment of people with disabilities by the private sector, and there is no policy requiring the national government to employ people with disabilities itself. In Belize only 25 per cent of public buildings are estimated to be accessible to people with mobility disabilities. Belize does not have a national system of transportation that is wheelchair accessible.

Disable People in South America

South America is a continent located in the Western Hemisphere, mostly in the Southern Hemisphere, with a relatively small portion in the Northern Hemisphere. Most of the population lives near the western or eastern coasts of the continent while the interior and the far south are sparsely populated. In 1494, Portugal and Spain, the two great maritime European powers of that time, on the expectation of new lands being discovered in the west, signed the Treaty of Tordesillas. During the first decade of the 21st century, South American governments have drifted to the political left, with socialist leaders being elected in Chile, Uruguay, Brazil, Argentina, Ecuador, Bolivia, Paraguay, Peru and Venezuela. Most South American countries are making an increasing use of protectionist policies, undermining a greater continental integration.

Argentina

The number of people in Argentina with disabilities is estimated to be at least three million, with some government estimates rising to seven to eight per cent of the total population. Disabled people's organisations estimate that 15 per cent of the population has some form of disability. The first break with this categorical thinking took place in the 1970s, during the military dictatorship, when disabled activists established a group called the Crippled Peronist Front, aimed at redressing disabled people's grievances and defending their rights. In 1998, people with the most diverse disabilities and their sympathisers established the Disability Rights Network (REDI). It began by pressuring the Buenos Aires Legislature to ensure that elevators be accessible to wheelchair users. An ordinance mandated that building owners replace old elevator doors with presumably safer ones, but it did not take into account the amount of space required to accommodate wheelchairs. As a result, many of the city's wheelchair users remained locked inside their homes, unable to go to work, visit relatives, or attend rehabilitation. The Argentine economic crisis of 2001–02, in which unemployment skyrocketed, proved to be a decisive moment for disabled rights activists. Unemployment and pay discrimination, not only for disabled people, is a worldwide phenomenon. Argentine disability organisations, usually led by the non-disabled, are nearly always informed by a medical perspective and have mainly focused on assistant services i.e., performing tasks and chores for disabled people rather than creating the conditions that would enable them to function autonomously.

Brazil

Disabled people in Brazil have conquered some of the rights that are ensured by law, but a lot has yet to be done to provide their full integration with society. Accessibility is one of the main rights which must be assured to every citizen, being disabled or not. Despite some improvements made to attend the share of population which declares to have a kind of disability, it can be a real challenge to live in Brazil having its rights respected. Accessibility to buildings, restaurants, universities, hotels and public places in general is still being fought by organisations and associations that defend the basic rights for the citizens' special needs. The awareness to disabled people's accessibility has heightened over the years, and projects were created to attend the demand of this part of the population which already reaches 23.9 per cent of all Brazilians. According to the official data on people with disabilities, the 2000 Census, it can perceive that 14 per cent of the populations have some kind of disability, which represents 24 million citizens - a figure quite different from 1991, where the percentage was 1.15, statistics were multiplied by twelve. The group of people with disabilities is a pioneer in some of their conquests in comparison to other groups such as afro-descendants also excluded from the Brazilian society. Amongst the Brazilians with a perception of higher degree of disability, about 33.7 per cent never attended school and on the other hand people that do not report disabilities and the ones that present them reach 15.47 per cent and 21.6 per cent respectively. The main mechanism available for labor insertion for people with disabilities is a quota policy, established in 1999.

Brazil is one of the largest countries in the region, and has a large population of people with disabilities. The country's legal framework provides multiple protections for the rights of people with disabilities including Law 7853, which criminalised discrimination based on disability. Among people with disabilities, visual impairments predominate. About 48.1 per cent had visual impairments, 8.3 per cent had mental impairments, 4.1 per cent had physical impairments, 22.9 per cent had mobility impairments, and 16.7 per cent had hearing impairments. Rates of mental disabilities, physical disabilities, and hearing disabilities were higher among men than among women. Brazil ratified the OAS Inter-American Convention on Disability on 17 July 2001 and deposited the instrument on 15 August 2001. The Brazilian diplomatic mission, in accordance with the Brazilian government, has supported the process to negotiate a UN convention on disability rights. Even though it was not part of the Commission for the Economic and Social Development of the United Nations in 1997, government and NGO delegations worked to support the extension of the Special Rapporteur's mandate. At the national level, the primary document protecting the rights of people with disabilities is the Federal Constitution of 1988. Brazilian law provides that a judicial court may find that an individual who, by reason of a mental disability, is unable to make informed decisions concerning actions of civil life may be subject to guardianship. Persons with disabilities have the right to vote like all other citizens. The Act on National Education Guidelines and Bases (Section 58 and following sections) defines special education as the education provided to people with disabilities. There are two organisations concerned with disability issues: the National Coordination Office for the Integration of People with Disabilities (CORDE) and the National Council on Disability Rights (CONADE). Both agencies report to the Special Human Rights Secretary of the President's Office.

The constitutional provisions pertaining to the protection of the disabled also include the areas of social rights (Articles 6 and 227.1), education (Articles 7.XXV, 205 and 208.III), social assistance (Article 203, clauses IV and V), labour (Article 7.XXXI and Article 37.VIII) and architectural barriers (Article 227.2 and Article 224). Law 7853/89 contains provisions on support for disabled persons and their integration into society, creates the national coordination office for social integration, creates the national coordination office for integration of disabled persons, and regulates the activities of the Public Ministry and defines crimes and issues other rules. Disabled persons have been the object of several policies under the responsibility of different sectors of the present government which points to the high priority the government attaches to this subject. In the area of technical and work training, the secretariat of vocational training under the Ministry of Labour prepared a vocational qualification project for disabled persons. The government also reported on other activities carried out to protect the rights of disabled persons: updating of the technical standards of the Brazilian Technical Standards Association (ABNT), for the purpose of eliminating barriers to disabled persons.

Uruguay

Uruguay is facing an economic and social crisis driven by a series of domestic and international factors. Since 2000, the poverty rate has risen 45 per cent, and Uruguay's Peso was depreciated in June 2002. That year the average actual salary fell an average of 10.7 per cent compared to 2001. Over 70,000 Uruguayans have migrated to foreign countries seeking employment opportunities. At the same time, efforts have been made by the government to control public spending, resulting in a continued lack of inclusion and social integration for people with disabilities. The last national census of Uruguay, completed in 1996, recorded a population of 3,163,763 with more than half the country's population concentrated in Montevideo, the capital city. People with disabilities are protected by a variety of general and specific legal documents. Internationally, Uruguay has signed and ratified a variety of instruments approved by the United Nations General Assembly and other organisations under the UN system. Uruguay signed the American Convention on Human Rights on 22nd November, 1969 and ratified it through Law 15737 on 19th April, 1985. The National Constitution can be interpreted as guaranteeing protection for some people with disabilities. The Central Executive Board (CODICEN) estimates that 2.76 per cent of students aged 6 to 16 attending public schools have a disability. The National Honorary Disability Committee (CNHD) is the agency in charge of planning and coordinating disability policy at the national level, providing recommendations to various governmental entities, coordinating activities of nonprofit institutions, and promoting awareness.

Paraguay

The Ministry of Civil Service reports there are 1,114 disabled people working in the public sector, which accounts for one per cent of the total workforce. The Law 780, Article 6 defines them as exceptional, beneficiary or deficient persons who suffer a decrease of their mental or physical ability that affects their possibilities of self-sufficiency, learning or work, due to congenital or acquired causes. At the moment an accurate number of persons with disabilities and the distribution of persons with disabilities by age categories are unknown. In December 1996, the first bill on the creation of SENADIS was presented by the disabled people's organisations. This was received by the House of

Representatives and commissions were set up to study it, but the bill was shelved. Subsequently, in October 2010, a new bill was presented to the House of Representatives which also aim to be a comprehensive law on the rights of persons with disabilities. This was prepared without the participation of disabled people's NGOs and since its origin in the House of Representatives; it was supported as the original bill. In the Senate, where bills are studied and approved, disabled people's organisations intervened and presented a proposal with modifications. This was approved by the Senate and returned to the House of Representatives for ratification or rejection. An agreement between Paraguay's Superior National Electoral Tribunal, USAID/Paraguay and Fundacion Saraki is a big step forward for the inclusion of people with disabilities in Paraguay's electoral processes. In particular, the agreement aims to ensure the participation of persons with disabilities in the upcoming municipal elections, which are scheduled for November 2015. People with disabilities, often the poorest of the poor, are frequently marginalised from political decision-making. NDI programmes work to empower people with disabilities to engage politically and become full members of society.

Bolivia

According to membership data of the Departmental Committees for People with Disabilities, there are approximately 30,000 people with disabilities, with a large concentration (66 per cent) living in the capital cities. Due to the higher level of poverty found in rural areas, these people have been forced to immigrate to urban centres in search of a better life. People with disabilities are affiliated with different organisations, including: the Christian Fraternity for the Sick and Disabled; the Federation of Integrated Wheelchair Sports, the Bolivian Federation for the Deaf; the Bolivian Association of Parents of Children and Adolescents with Mental Disabilities and the Bolivian Federation for the Deaf and Blind. All of these organisations are grouped under the umbrella organisation, the Bolivian Confederation of Persons with Disabilities. The National Committee of Persons with Disabilities, which is the executive body of Law 1678, was established on October 15, 1996.

Chile

Chile is home to over two million people with various different disabilities. 1,625,000 is old enough to work, but 90 per cent are unemployed. Nine per cent of those who do have jobs work informally or part time. Only one per cent has a proper work contract. While laws and regulations do exist to protect disabled individuals, few are adhered to, and there is a lack of sensitivity towards the prejudices affecting the group. In 1993, the United Nations approved the *"Uniform norms on equal opportunities for people with disabilities"*. The document establishes that persons with disabilities should be empowered to execute their human rights, particularly in the field of labour. Equal opportunities need to exist in order for them to obtain a productive and paid job. Ignorance is a major obstacle that prevents people with disabilities from entering the labour market and having a normal life. People with disabilities are often very careful. They know they have to take care of themselves to avoid things getting worse. The same goes for work absence. They are absent less often from work and they are very loyal. Chile has united around the common cause of raising money for disabled children annually since 1978. According to the World Health Organisation, around 15 per cent of the world's population lives with some form of disability. The figure for Chile stands at 20 per cent, owing in part to a high rate of mining and fishing accidents. In 2008, Chile ratified the U.N. Convention on the Rights of Persons with Disabilities stating that, under international law; the government must *"promote, protect and ensure the full and equal enjoyment of all human rights and fundamental freedoms by all persons with disabilities."*

The institution which replaces the National Disability Fund (FONADIS) will have regional departments in charge of implementing policies on the issue of disability throughout Chilean territory. In addition, it will have a monopoly over these issues, as it will be the only institution empowered to draft policies and to lead the programmematic implementation of initiatives aimed at benefiting disabled people. Another important challenge that the National Disability Service must face is to coordinate among the different public services to ensure fulfillment of the measures to guarantee access to people with physical disabilities, in addition to the adaptation of all communicational and educational processes, as established by law. The issue of disability is a matter of concern for both the public as well as private sectors. Along these lines, the country has developed initiatives so that the people of Chile can learn from early childhood to appreciate and to respect differences, as is the case with the disabled toys project, which was created to teach young children the importance of inclusion.

Although Chile does not have a mental health policy, the mental health vision, principles and strategies have been encapsulated in the National Mental Health Plan of 2000. The implementation of this Plan has resulted major improvements for the mental health services, including the implementation of community-based services, which are progressively offering an alternative to traditional mental healthcare that is provided by psychiatric institutions. There has also been an increase in mental healthcare provided through primary healthcare setting, which has greatly improved access to services and treatment for the population. In 2002, the Ministry of Health of Chile requested the support of WHO to disseminate the international human rights norms and standards applicable to persons with mental disorders and improve Chilean legislation on mental health and human rights. Technical support was also provided for a comprehensive review of all Chilean legislation from the perspective of the rights of persons with mental disorders, in order to elaborate a legal basis to improve current legislation.

Venezuela

The Venezuelan government is organising a series of employment fairs to increase the number of disabled people in formal employment, as part of efforts to guarantee the disabled their full rights as citizens. The employment fairs seek to connect public and private companies with disabled people looking for work, and to help companies meet the legal requirement for five per cent of employees to be people with disabilities. The requirement is part of the Law for Disabled People, passed in 2006, which aims to ensure that disabled people enjoy the *"full and autonomous exercise of his or her capacities"*. According to the National Disabled Peoples Council, it is hoped that the first round of employment fairs will result in the insertion of 1,500 disabled people in the labour market. Currently, just fewer than 20 per cent of disabled people registered with the government health programmes are in full employment. The Venezuelan government has implemented health programmes focused on disabled people's needs, and has widened access to education for this group of the population. The rights and guarantees enjoyed by disabled people are laid out in the National Constitution and the Law for Disabled People.

When President Chavez was elected in 1999, one of his main objectives was to repay a historical debt to those who were previously marginalised by former governments. Among those groups were women, indigenous communities, African Venezuelans and disabled people. The 1999 Constitution was drafted on the premise that Venezuela will only flourish if all sectors of society enjoy their full rights as citizens and participate in all aspects of social life. Following on from the constitutional recognition, the *"Law for People with Disabilities"* 2006 was passed. The law stipulates the disabled people must have access to: (a) free medical assistance; (b) better access to public transport; and (c) adequate representation in the work place. Under the law employers will have only three years to ensure that disabled people hold at least five per cent of positions in their companies. Prior to this the previous law only required two per cent and even then that only applied to companies with more than 50 employees.

Peru

It is estimated that there are a minimum of 3.5 million people with disabilities in Peru. Of this 3.5 million, one third is eligible to participate in electoral processes, which is to say that this segment of the population has the right to elect and to be elected. It is a reality that people with disabilities do not have the full opportunities to participate in political processes and to be represented in the government, a fact that makes insertion into mainstream society extremely difficult. Peru should remove significant barriers preventing people with disabilities from exercising their right to vote and other civil rights, Human Rights Watch said in a report. The failure to dismantle the obstacles is undermining Peru's leadership as one of the first countries to ratify, in 2008, the Convention on the Rights of Persons with Disabilities. Human Rights Watch also examined the barriers that people with these and other disabilities face when exercising their political rights, including the difficulty of getting identity documents essential for voting, and the absence of support mechanisms to help people with disabilities make voting decisions. On 6th December, 2012 the Peruvian Congress approved a new disability law in line with the UN Convention of the Rights of People with Disability. This was lobbied for by the Peruvian CBR consortium and organisations of people with disabilities (DPOs), whose activities in empowerment and defence of rights are supported by CBM.

Disable People in Australia

Australia is a developed country and one of the wealthiest in the world, with the world's 12th-largest economy. Australia is a wealthy country; it generates its income from various sources including mining-related exports, telecommunications, banking and manufacturing. For almost two centuries the majority of settlers, and later immigrants, came from the British Isles. As a result the people of Australia are primarily of British and/or Irish ethnic origin. A disability is any condition that restricts a person's mental, sensory or mobility functions. It could be caused by accident, trauma, genetics or disease. A disability may be temporary or permanent, total or partial, lifelong or acquired, visible or invisible. Just under one in five Australians (18.5 per cent or 4.0 million persons) reported having a disability in 2009. A further 21 per cent had a long-term health condition that did not restrict their everyday activities. The remaining 60 per cent of the Australian population had neither a disability nor a long-term health condition. Of those with a disability, 87 per cent had a specific limitation or restriction; that is, an impairment restricting their ability to perform communication, mobility or self-care activities, or a restriction associated with schooling or employment. The prevalence of disability has fallen 1.5 percentage points from 20.0 per cent in 2003 to 18.5 per cent in 2009. After removing the effects of different age structures the age standardised rate fell by 2.1 percentage points, from 19.8 per cent in 2003 to 17.7 per cent in 2009.

Fewer people with disabilities participate in the workforce than those without disabilities. More people with disabilities are unemployed than those without disabilities. The result of a lower labour force participation rate, when combined with a higher unemployment rate, is that people with disabilities are less likely to be employed than others. Participation in the workforce also varies according to the nature of the disability. The workplace participation rate for people with a psychiatric disability receiving disability support payments is only 29 per cent. When employed, people with disabilities earn lower wages, on average, than workers without disabilities. The overall levels of income earned by people with disabilities are also lower than those without disabilities. Income varies according to the type of disability. Australia has the seventh lowest employment rate for people with disabilities in the Organisation for Economic Cooperation and Development. The number of people with disabilities employed by the Commonwealth government has declined significantly over the last ten years. Some State governments have higher rates of employment of people with a disability than the Commonwealth. In Australia, someone is registered as disabled every half an hour. In Britain, it's every three minutes. In both Australia and Britain, one in five adults has a disability of some kind.

Disability varies by birthplace or immigrant group. There was a decline in the proportion of people with disability in the population who were born in Australia or New Zealand, while disability rates for those born in South Eastern Europe have increased since 2003. In 2009, 54.3 per cent of people with a disability participated in the labour force compared to 83 per cent of people without a disability. Mental health problems and mental illness are among the greatest causes of disability, diminished quality of life, and reduced productivity. People affected by mental health problems often have high levels of morbidity and mortality, experiencing poorer general health and higher rates of death from a range of causes, including suicide. The National Disability Insurance Scheme (NDIS) is a funding, support and governance mechanism that commits to providing people with a disability the opportunity to live fulfilling and active lives. The scheme provides an opportunity for evolution in disability. It offers a platform for reform, and presents an opportunity for landmark change achieved in the teeth of straitened national and international circumstances. The NDIS will secure for the government that implements it a place in history. The NDIS is not only the right thing to do, it is necessary for the future wealth of Australia's economy and society. It will make life better for people with a disability and their families while being cost effective. The scheme is underpinned by an insurance model: (a) It is based on an estimate of the reasonable and necessary support need of people with a disability; (b) It supports and funds the need in a responsible way; (c) It encourages active participation by people with a disability; and (d) It manages risk and cost escalation.

Despite enabling Commonwealth and state legislation dating back over 20 years, and a series of across jurisdictional agreements to support people with a disability, the current disability support system is underperforming and requires an overhaul. On 10th August, 2011 Prime Minister Gillard released the PC's final report, Disability Care and Support, which sets out a vision for an entirely new model for providing care and support for people with a disability. The PC recommended a new national funding system and locally coordinated support system to provide people with a disability an opportunity to live fulfilling and active lives. From the mid-1980s, most Western countries including Australia enacted legislation which sought to address issues of social injustice and discrimination against people with a disability. The legislation also embraced the conceptual shift from disability being seen as an individualised medical problem to a social problem and the failure of society to adapt and accommodate to people with disabilities. Thus the problem became one of redressing the social inclusion of people with disabilities rather than changing their individual characteristics or behaviour.

The National Disability Strategy 2010-2020 is a 10-year commitment by all levels of government to focus on supporting people living with a disability to participate in life on equal footing with all other Australians; to have the opportunity to fully realise their potential, and to feel empowered to follow their aspirations. The COAG endorsed the National Disability Strategy on 13th February, 2011 after nationwide public consultation. The National Disability Strategy adopts a nationally unified and consistent approach that has at its core the goal of improving the lived experiences of people with a disability, their families and carers. The National Disability Strategy acknowledges the importance of collaboration across government, industry and community to strengthen the disability sector, which includes recognition that people living with a disability cannot participate in and enjoy all aspects of life or be fully included, solely within the remit of the specialist disability service system. Rather, community and mainstream services need to be accessible to all and attuned to the depth of diversity in our society, which includes people with a disability. Australia has agreed through ratifying the UN CRPD that the lives of these men and women living with a disability are valued and they should be afforded full participation in society. This obligation then becomes a responsibility carried by the whole of the Australian community, not individuals with a disability.

Australia now has the potential to fundamentally change the disability experience through a funding, governance and outcome system. The NDIS is a mechanism that will bring about efficiencies, rearrange roles and change the control hierarchy to promote choice and individuality. Australia needs a transformative shift not only in the way services are funded but also in the way they are delivered. The system must be built and structured around the needs of the individual, rather than system and organisational needs. Government needs a fundamental shift of power from organisations to individuals, who will have greater control and choice not only in the type of provider they choose but in the type of service and support. The greater choice and flexibility offered by the NDIS presents enormous opportunities to empower people with a disability. Family support can be provided in a nurturing or resentful environment, or usually somewhere in between caring but struggling. While involuntary family support is sustainable for a period of time, without systemic help most people reach their limit and begin to see their role as a chore. The provision of enduring, involuntary support is a key contributor to the dependency culture and impacts on the whole family, including the person with a disability.

The family is usually the unit of primary support for a person with a disability, and as such will feel a substantial impact from the changes to the way disability care and support is funded and made available. Most disability funding is currently dispensed through non-government organisations, with much of this provided through block funding. As such, and despite providers' best intentions to put the individual at the centre, the principal customer is currently government. Services are provided within government-prescribed service definitions, thereby inhibiting individuality. For the person living with a disability, having values and a vision in life is of the utmost importance. It is even more critical in a world of individualised funding packages and person-centred support. While the individual is central to this concept, the journey can often only be taken with the help of a facilitator or partner; in this case, the support organisation. There is a large disparity in educational outcomes between Australians with a disability and those without. The National Disability Strategy highlights education as a key pillar in moving towards a more inclusive and productive Australia. Higher levels of educational attainment are linked to better employment, financial and health outcomes. State and territory government are funding has increased the proportion of students with disabilities in mainstream schools and promoted an inclusive education for all in the last ten years.

There is an opportunity for government workplaces to lead the way, setting an example for private sector employers to operate as change agents. This will be important in demonstrating to business that there is not only a responsibility on workplaces to actively facilitate employment for people with a disability, but that it is feasible and already taking place. There is opportunity to increase the availability of appropriate and affordable housing stock for people with a disability by building partnerships with developers and harnessing private capital. The National Rental Affordability Scheme is a key vehicle to attract investment in building new affordable rental properties. Other policy levers to improve the sector's capacity to offer better access to housing and accommodation include capturing the full amount of Commonwealth Rental Assistance. As well as funder, government's new role, through the NDIA, will be as regulator-facilitator, but not purchaser or prescriber. Public awareness of the extent of severe disability in Australia is low, with the extent of disability massively hidden. Society plays a fundamental role in facilitating the shift to a more equitable disability care and support system and inclusive society. The development of fellowship and connection is a critical element in achieving an inclusive Australian society where people with a disability are treated as valued and contributing citizens. In order to achieve true social inclusion and citizenhood for people with a disability, a whole-of-government approach is required.

The Labour government laid the foundations for a revolution in services for thousands of disabled people, their families and careers. DisabilityCare Australia will mean that Australians with significant and permanent disabilities will have more power to choose their support and more control over how that support is provided. The programme, gradually being rolled out across the country, is creating personal plans that put the goals and aspirations of individuals at the centre of the support they will receive. The scheme will also give Australians peace of mind that their child or loved one will get the care and support they need in the event that they have a significant and permanent disability. Australian Federation of Disability Organisations, Matthew Wright raised significant concerns about the Government's intention to push ahead with Disability Support Pension (DSP) re-assessments for people with disability under 35 years of age. The Australian Federation of Disability Organisations (AFDO) will host a Roundtable of prominent Australians to develop a new employment model for Australia that is inclusive of people with disability. Attendees include individuals from business and industry, policy commentators, futurists, innovators and leaders in both the disability and employment sectors. The Australian Federation of Disability Organisations (AFDO) has been established as the primary national voice to Government that fully represents the interests of all people with disability across Australia.

Every five years the Australian Bureau of Statistics carries out an extensive survey that gives detailed statistics on the prevalence of disabilities in the Australian community. The last (1998) Survey found that, of the total population aged between 5 and 64 years, 19 per cent (some 3.6 million people) had some form of disability. The Survey also found that an additional 3.1 million people had some sort of impairment but it was not bad enough to restrict them in their daily activities. Of the total of those who had some form of disability (i.e., the 3.6 million groups) approximately 3.2 million people experienced some sort of restriction with respect to daily activities, employment or schooling. The Commonwealth first became directly involved with providing support for people with disabilities via the introduction of the Invalid Pension in 1908. The current version of this benefit is the Disability Support Pension and, to a lesser extent, the Sickness Allowance.

During the 1940s the number of people with disabilities increased rapidly essentially due to injuries suffered during the Second World War. In response to this, the Commonwealth established the Commonwealth Rehabilitation Service (CRS) and at the same time there was an expansion of the number of sheltered workshops and accommodation services run by volunteer organisations. Through the 1960s and 1970s the Commonwealth increasingly provided funding to help these organisations provide accommodation, employment and other support services. The main Commonwealth legislation covering the rights of people with a disability is the *Disability Discrimination Act 1992* and the main Commonwealth body that is charged with protecting the rights of disabled people and advocating on their behalf is the Human Rights and Equal Opportunity Commission (HREOC). For more background on HREOC and disability rights and advocacy see the HREOC disability rights page. Another source of information on legislation, rights and advocacy can be found at the Disability Information and Resource Centre.

Disable People in Asia

Asia is the most populous continent. Its total population in 2002 was reported to be about 3,902 million, of which almost 61 per cent is rural and 38.5 per cent lives within 100 km of the coast. The coastline of Asia is 283,188 km long. Asia is divided into seven sub-regions, namely North Asia, Central Asia, West Asia, Tibetan Plateau, East Asia, South Asia and South-East Asia. Past and present climate trends and variability in Asia are generally characterised by increasing surface air temperature which is more pronounced during winter than in summer. Increasing trends have been observed across the seven sub-regions of Asia. Inter-seasonal, inter-annual and spatial variability in rainfall trend has been observed during the past few decades all across Asia. Biodiversity in Asia is being lost as a result of development activities and land degradation (especially overgrasing and deforestation), pollution, over-fishing, hunting, infrastructure development, species invasion, land-use change, climate change and the overuse of freshwater.

Poverty is a cause of disability since the poor often lack resources to prevent malnutrition, and do not have access to adequate health services that may prevent some disabilities. Poverty is a consequence of disability since people with disabilities often lack access to education, health services and income-generating activities: they are often denied their human, social and economic rights. UNESCO data reveals that a majority of disable people is unable to earn any livelihood for a variety of reasons, such as the lack of adequate education or training. Only one to two per cent of disability in developing countries receives education. There are an estimated 650 million people with disabilities in the world (may be 12 per cent of the global population) and 80 per cent of these (520 million) are concentrated in developing countries. Furthermore, 80-90 per cent of the persons with disabilities of working age are unemployed compared to 50-70 per cent in industrialised countries.

South Asia

In each South Asian country, at least ten per cent of the population lives with a disability. Disability and poverty are intricately linked. Disability causes poverty and poverty exacerbates disability people with disabilities are among the poorest and most vulnerable. A vast number of people are disabled and lack basic support such as access to social safety nets, education, health services, and gainful employment. The incidence of disability is increasing due to conflicts, disasters, malnutrition and the HIV/AIDS pandemic. The societal cost of exclusion is high with long-lasting consequences. Disabling barriers were a powerful influence on how these young South Asian people saw themselves. Young people had to deal with disables views, both from within their family and outside, suggesting that disabled people have much in common irrespective of ethnic origin.

Census 2001 has revealed that over 21 million people in India are suffering from one or the other kind of disability. This is equivalent to 2.1 per cent of the population. Among the total disabled in the country, 12.6 million are males and 9.3 million are females. In 2009, the government said there were only 6,789 disabled people in Pakistan. Two per cent of jobs in government are reserved for those with disabilities, but they must be registered. They are also entitled to free medical treatment in all federal government hospitals, rehabilitative aid and duty-free import of cars. But many are not registered and have no stable source of income, often surviving by begging on the roadsides or other public places. According to the Afghanistan Disability

Action Plan, 70 per cent of person with disabilities aged over 15 are unemployed and 73 per cent of person with disabilities aged above six do not receive any education. The war has left about 800,000 people with disabilities in the country. Most of the people with disabilities are unemployed, illiterate and have limited accesses to health facilities. Afghanistan has signed the Convention on Cluster Munitions on 3rd December, 2008 and ratified it on 8th September, 2011. Meanwhile, in 2002 Afghanistan ratified the Convention on the Prohibition of the Use, Stockpiling, Production and Transfer of Anti-Personnel Mines and on their Destruction.

Nepali society still views disability as a penance to the sins committed in previous births. The people with disabilities are treated worst as an object of pity. People with disabilities are hided as the matter of social prestigious by families is still practiced largely. In accordance with a latest study conducted by New Era's 70.1 per cent of the persons with disabilities have stigma and difficulties to live in the community with self-respect. The women with disabilities have been facing double discriminations first as a disabled person and second as a woman. In Bangladesh, nearly ten per cent people are disabling. The National Constitution of Bangladesh has numerous provisions that obligate the government to protect the rights and dignity of all citizens of the country equally and without any bias whatsoever. It also allows room for additional and/or supplementary provisions that will ensure that citizens who do not have access to all the public amenities are able to obtain such services. The government had declared about two decades back a ten per cent employment quota for persons with disabilities and orphans. But this quota has never been properly implemented due to the lack of sensitivity of employers about the potentialities of persons with disabilities, contradictory employment policies, loopholes in the system, and a lack of proper monitoring system. In Sri Lanka, disabled children are seen as a curse and it is believed people have been born with disability as a result of bad karma from a previous life.

South-East Asia

There are over one billion people with disabilities (PWD) in the world. This corresponds to about 15 per cent of the world's population. Of the WHO regions, the Southeast Asia Region has the second highest prevalence rate of moderate disability (16 per cent) and the third highest prevalence rate of severe disability

(12.9 per cent). Persons with disabilities face physical, social, economic and attitudinal barriers that exclude them from participating as fully and effectively as other members of society. Globally, efforts are being made to rectify this and to increase disabled people's ability to participate in all activities. In Southeast Asia, and throughout the world, persons with disabilities have been marginalised from the democratic and political process. The General Election Network for Disability Access (AGENDA) project aims to improve access to political and electoral opportunities for people with disabilities in Southeast Asia. The two-year project brings together local organisations from Indonesia, the Philippines, Malaysia, Vietnam, Laos, Cambodia, Myanmar and Thailand to conduct research and share best practice in ensuring access for persons with disabilities.

There are 445,006 people with disabilities registered in Malaysia as of 2012. However, as registration is voluntary, it is not reflective of the real numbers in the country. The Government has also adopted the Persons with Disabilities Act 2008 and provides social protection services in areas such as health, rehabilitation and education for children with disabilities guided by the National Policy for Persons with Disabilities and the National Plan of Action for Persons with Disabilities. Thailand's definition of disabilities is *"A person with Disabilities means an individual who is limited by function and/or ability to conduct activities in daily living and to participate in society through methods used by persons without disabilities due to visual, hearing, mobility, communication, psychological, emotional, behavioral, intellectual or learning impairment, and has special needs in order to live and participate in society as to others."* National Statistic Organisation (NSO) was report that 1.9 million or 2.9 per cent of total population are people with disabilities.

The Government of Indonesia and non-governmental organisations provide health, education and other social services for persons with disabilities. Ministry of Manpower of Indonesia has taken the initiative to implement measures to promote the placement of persons with disabilities in the work force. The major approaches Indonesia takes to prevent disabilities is through strengthening the health system and services including immunisation, nutrition programme. The Ministries of Social Affairs, Manpower, and Defense are involved in promoting employment for persons with disabilities by way of job placements and the provision of job training. In Singapore, the number of actual disabled individuals is four per cent (4 per cent) of its population and that is by the traditional approach; many of whom fall squarely within the main categories of physical impairment, vision impairment, hearing impairment and intellectual impairment. The Singapore Disability Sports Council (SDSC) is the only organisation in Singapore which reaches across all disability groups, offering a wide range of sports at both elite and non-elite levels. It is, in fact, Singapore's national disability sports organisation.

West Asia

The Kingdom of Saudi Arabia is based on the Islamic Sharia, which emphasises human rights, and particularly person with disabilities rights to live with dignity and benefit from welfare. The Kingdom has focused on person with disability since initiation of its social and economic development plans two decades ago. Several royal foundations are quite active in terms of developing infrastructure for persons with disabilities. Institutions for persons with disabilities are more prevalent in urban than rural areas, with an uneven distribution of facilities irrelative to persons with disabilities distribution. Government education policies issued in 1970 include special education programmes for persons with disabilities. The Ministry of Labour and Social Affairs has established Vocational Rehabilitation Centre for persons with disabilities. The number of disabled in the Kingdom has reached 720,000, roughly four per cent of the Saudi population, according to the Social Affairs representative in Madinah. The ministry spends a total amount of about SR 1.6 billion annually for the benefit of the disabled. The appearance of rehabilitation was formalised in Iran in 1968 with the ratification of a law to establish the Rehabilitation Organisation, affiliated with the Ministry of Labour and Social Affairs. Of course, before that time activities in this field were carried out by the military, or the Lion and Sun Society (an organisation like the Red Cross) in Iran. The process of ratification of the Convention on the Rights of People with Disabilities in Iran was met with a lot of delays.

Oman has over 60,000 people with disabilities, according to the Oman Disabled Association (ODA), out of which 11,000 are visually impaired and 15,000 are deaf. Though literacy rates for the paraplegia make up half of the total disabled people, is improving, the deaf and blind still lag behind in terms of education. In November 2006, the UAE Federal Government passed the UAE Disability Act (Federal Law No. 29/2006) to protect the rights of people with disabilities. This law stipulates that UAE nationals with disabilities have the same rights to work and occupy public positions. The UAE ratified the United Nations Convention on the Rights of Persons with Disabilities on the 19th March, 2010. Dubai Civil Aviation Authority has dedicated personalised services at Dubai Airport for passengers with disabilities, while an increasing number of public areas and hotels now have access and facilities with specially adapted rooms and facilities for people with disabilities.

There is no accurate information or studies on the situation of disabled people in Yemen. Impairments and disabilities in Yemen are due to road accidents, hereditary issues, accidents from construction work and firearms, poor medical infrastructure and medical mistakes, iodine and vitamin 'A' deficiency, poor maternal health related to malnutrition, and other environmental factors including epidemics, natural disasters, pollution, and inaccessible environments. In Yemen as in other developing societies, poverty and disability are closely linked in a vicious circle. Rehabilitation policies in Yemen are spread over a number of legal documents issued by the Ministry of Legal and Parliamentary Affairs (MLPA). The report from Handicap International and HelpAge International claims that older, disabled, and injured Syrian refugees are being doubly victimised as the three-year long civil war continues to keep them from their homes. Displacement has a severe negative impact on the daily life of disabled and injured people, who need urgent access to health services but also long-term medical, financial and social support. The lack of psychosocial or mental healthcare is a major challenge, significantly affecting the well-being of older people but also placing an additional burden on their families. Around 7.7 per cent of Jordanian households have at least one person with a disability. Women with disabilities suffer double discrimination and are more prone to sexual and physical abuse, sometimes in the form of medical intervention. Jordan ratified the UN Convention on the Rights of People with Disabilities in 2008.

Central Asia

Nearly 570,000 people in Kazakhstan face physical or mental disabilities. Without proper support, they have no opportunity to attend school, get a job or have a family. Some people in Kazakhstan suffer from mental disabilities. UNDP is also supporting a project in Astana, the capital, to develop a mobile application to better connect deaf people with emergency services. The application will allow the emergency services to immediately see the profile and location of the person requesting help. Turkmenistan was one of the first countries in the region to ratify the Convention on the Rights of Persons with Disabilities in 2008 and has a wealth of resources to ensure the full and effective participation of children with disabilities in society on an equal basis with others. The consultation provided a special opportunity to review progress towards the implementation of the Convention and further elaboration on areas such as early childhood development, inclusive education, and the importance of support for families. During the meeting the Government of Turkmenistan and UNICEF committed to work closely to implement and monitor the Convention on the Rights of Persons with Disabilities.

The Kyrgyz Republic is strongly committed to protecting the rights of disabled children. The Government of Kyrgyzstan supports the principles of social inclusion and non-discrimination against disabled children. The state also offers valuable financial contributions to disabled children and their families with more than 20 million Soms per month paid in benefits. The UN Convention on the Rights of the Child, ratified by the government of the Kyrgyz Republic, gives every child equal rights, regardless of whether or not they are disabled. Disabled children have equal rights to a family, to participate in social activities, and to an inclusive education. According to the statistics of the Ministry of Labour and Social Development, on 1st January 2007, there were 19,931 disabled children in Kyrgyzstan, approximately one per cent of the total child population. The Government of Kyrgyzstan proclaims itself to be against discrimination against disabled children and in favour of their integration into society. Overall governmental responsibility for disabled children is mainly delegated to various ministries and their governmental organisations.

In Uzbekistan, persons with disabilities are screened in two steps. Firstly, a diagnosis is given by the hospitals where each person is registered according to his/her residential addresses. Secondly, persons with disabilities receive referrals to the Medicine Labour Expert Commissions (MLEC) of their respective district, which determines the grade of disability. There are 327,199 Persons with Disabilities (January 2001), which makes up 1.33 per cent of the total population of the country. Among them, 80,711 were newly registered in 2000. The per cent of persons with disabilities to the total population increased in the 1990s, but decreased in 2000. The Constitution and other acts of the Republic of Uzbekistan regulate all the personal, social, and economic rights of persons with disabilities. The central government exercises strong authority over local governments regarding persons with disabilities welfare administration. Special organisations and enterprises (medical institutions, boarding houses, school boarding houses for persons with disabilities, etc) provide medical and social rehabilitation, social welfare and social security services. Persons with disabilities may be involved in activities of any kind, including business.

East Asia

According to the latest census, there are 82.96 million disabled people in China, accounts for 6.34 per cent of the overall population. There are various problems relating to the living conditions of these large groups of people. Proper education plays a crucial role in solving such problems. One of the biggest problems China faces related to disabled people is the education problem. Established in 1988, the China Disabled Persons' Federation is a unified organisation of/for the 85 million people with disabilities. The State Council Working Committee on Disabilities has been established to steer and coordinate disability work. It is composed of 36 members, representing ministries and social groups. In Japan, persons with disabilities experience discrimination and abuse in nearly every domain. Unfortunately, the Japanese legislation does not provide them with adequate protection. The actual Japanese Basic Law for Persons with Disabilities does neither contain provisions giving specific rights to persons with disabilities nor set obligations upon public administration services. Furthermore, 'discrimination' is neither defined nor prohibited.

Of the 92.1 million household population in Philippine, 1,443 thousand persons or 1.57 per cent had disability, based on the 2010 Census of Population and Housing. The National Council for the Welfare of Disabled Persons is responsible for the registration of persons with disabilities in collaboration with local governments, the Department of Social Welfare and Development, and other organisations. Most persons with disabilities live in poverty. The National Statistics Office conducts a population survey every five years, which includes data on disabilities. In 2007, the population of people with disabilities in Taiwan is expected to exceed one million people. According to the latest statistics from the Ministry of the Interior in 2006, there were 969,249 people who have physical or mental disabilities registered with the department, which represents 4.24 per cent of the general population. The number of people with disabilities is still rising due to aging. One in four persons with disabilities wants to work; however, the employment rate in this population is less than 50 per cent and the unemployment rate is triple (14.70 per cent) than that of the general population (4.99 per cent).

Conclusion

Around 15 per cent of the world's population, or estimated one billion people, live with disabilities. They are the world's largest minority. Unemployment among the persons with disabilities is as high as 80 per cent in some countries. Often employers assume that persons with disabilities are unable to work. The World Bank estimates that 20 per cent of the world's poorest people have some kind of disability, and tend to be regarded in their own communities as the most disadvantaged. Statistics show a steady increase in these numbers. Persons with disabilities face a lot of challenges and are sometimes abused both in the developed and developing countries. People with disabilities in developing countries in Africa face many limitations, despite the proclamation of the UN Decade of Disabled Persons. Their human rights receive little or no respect, the general development programmes do not take into account the needs of disabled people or their participation in programmes, disabled people have little or no access to services offered to other citizens, they are unable to take decisions concerning their own future, and they are generally poor, living at the bottom of the social scale.

The Academic Network of European Disability experts were established by the European Commission in 2008 to provide scientific support and advice for its disability policy Unit. In particular, the activities of the Network will support the future development of the EU Disability Action Plan and practical implementation of the United Nations Convention on the Rights of Disabled People. In Sweden 1.5 million people are disabling. The Disabled Peoples Organisation is an umbrella organisation of associations for people with disabilities in Denmark. In 2007, 25.6 thousand persons of working age were for the first time recognised as disabled in Lithuania. There are 10 million disable people in Britain. There are five million disabled people living in France, two million of who are less mobile. There are reportedly more than 165,000 disabled people in Moldova, roughly five per cent of the population. In Slovenia it has been estimated that between 160,000 and 170,000 people are disabled.

About 3.8 million Canadians (13.7 per cent) reported having a disability in 2012. About 56.7 million people i.e., 19 per cent of the population had a disability in 2010 in USA. Mentally and physically disabled children and adults in Mexico continue to live in abusive and squalid conditions in many orphanages and mental health facilities throughout the country. The situation of persons with multiple disabilities, many of them presenting mental disability, is so blurred in Guatemala. According to the household survey, the total population of Honduras is estimated to be 6,697,916 people. From 1960 to 1990, the interior regions of Nicaragua were the site of prolonged and violent political revolution. The conflicts resulted in an increased number of persons with disabilities throughout the country. Disabled people's organisations estimate that 15 per cent of the population has some form of disability in Argentina. Brazil is one of the largest countries in the region, and thus has a large population of people with disabilities i.e., 14 per cent of the populations had some kind of disability. Just under one in five Australians (18.5 per cent or 4.0 million persons) reported having a disability in 2009. In each South Asian country, at least **10** per cent of the population lives with a disability. Disability and poverty are intricately linked. Disability causes poverty and poverty exacerbates disability people with disabilities are among the poorest and most vulnerable.

Selected Books

1. Anne Digby, and David Wright (2002). *From Idiocy to Mental Deficiency: Historical Perspectives on People with Learning Disabilities,* Taylor and Francis.
2. Benedicte Ingstad and Susan Reynolds Whyte (1995). *Disability and Culture,* University of California Press.
3. Christopher M. Bell (2011). *Blackness and Disability: Critical Examinations and Cultural Interventions,* LIT Verlag Münster.
4. Colin Barnes and Geof Mercer (2010). *Exploring Disability,* Polity.
5. Dan Goodley (2010). *Disability Studies: An Interdisciplinary Introduction,* SAGE.
6. David Wright, Anne Digby, and Digby Anne (1996). *From Idiocy to Mental Deficiency: Historical Perspectives on People with Learning Disabilities,* illustrated.
7. Gary L. Albrecht, Katherine D. Seelman, and Michael Bury (2001). *Handbook of Disability Studies.* SAGE Publications.
8. Gary L. Albrecht, Katherine D. Seelman, Michael Bury (2001). *Handbook of Disability Studies,* SAGE Publications.
9. Geoffrey Dale Arnott (2011). *The Disability Support Worker,* Pearson Education Australia.
10. Graham Pullin (2009). *Design Meets Disability,* MIT Press.
11. Hayley Fitzgerald (2008). *Disability and Youth Sport,* Taylor and Francis.
12. Henri-Jacques Stiker (1999). *A History of Disability,* University of Michigan Press.
13. Jane Seale (2006). *E-Learning and Disability in Higher Education: Accessibility Research and Practice,* Taylor and Francis.
14. Karen P. DePauw, and Susan J. Gavron (2005). *Disability Sport,* Human Kinetics.
15. Lennard J. Davis (1995). *Enforcing Normalcy: Disability, Deafness, and the Body,* Verso.
16. Lennard J. Davis (2006). *The Disability Studies Reader,* Taylor and Francis.
17. Lennard J. Davis (2013). *The Disability Studies Reader,* Routledge.
18. Mairian Corker and Tom Shakespeare (2002). *Disability/ Postmodernity: Embodying Disability Theory,* Bloomsbury Academic.
19. Mairian Corker, and Tom Shakespeare (2002). *Disability - Postmodernity: Embodying Disability Theory,* Continuum Publ.

20. Martha Craven Nussbaum (2006). *Frontiers of Justice: Disability, Nationality, Species Membership*, Harvard University Press.
21. Paul K. Longmore (2003). *Why I Burned My Book and Other Essays on Disability*, Temple University Press.
22. Rob Imrie (1996). *Disability and the City: International Perspectives*, SAGE.
23. Robert McRuer and Anna Mollow (2012). *Sex and Disability*, Duke University Press.
24. Robert McRuer (2006). *Crip Theory: Cultural Signs of Queerness and Disability*, NYU Press.
25. Sharon N. Barnartt (2010). *Disability as a Fluid State*, Emerald Group Publishing.
26. Shelley Lynn Tremain (2005). *Foucault and the Government of Disability*, University of Michigan Press.
27. Simi Linton (1998). *Claiming Disability: Knowledge and Identity*, NYU Press.
28. Soren V. Randall (2006). *Learning disabilities: new research*, Nova Science Publishers.
29. Steven D. Edwards (2005). *Disability: definitions, value and identity*, Radcliffe Publishing.
30. Tobin Siebers (2008). *Disability Theory*, University of Michigan Press.
31. Tom Shakespeare (1998). *Disability Reader: Social Science Perspectives*, Bloomsbury.

3

Disable People in Asia

"Love is patient, love is kind. It does not envy, it does not boast, it is not proud. It is not rude, it is not self-seeking, it is not easily angered, it keeps no record of wrongs. Love does not delight in evil but rejoices with the truth. It always protects, always trusts, always hopes, always perseveres. Love never fails. But where there are prophecies, they will cease; where there are tongues, they will be stilled; where there is knowledge, it will pass away."

–Bible

Introduction

Asia is the most populous continent, located primarily in the eastern and northern hemispheres. It covers 8.7 per cent of the Earth's total surface area and comprises 30 per cent of its land area. Asia has extremely diverse climates and geographic features. Climates range from arctic and subarctic in Siberia to tropical in southern India and Southeast Asia. It is moist across southeast sections and dry across much of the interior. Statistics about Asian peoples include information on well-being, migration and settlement, language and culture, and population size for different Asian ethnic groups. The two primary prehistoric centres from which migrations of modern human populations over the continent took place were Southwest Asia and a region comprising the Mongolian plateaus and North China. Within historic time the aggressive expansion of particular ethnic groups has either driven weaker groups away from their territory or resulted in the newcomers' assuming control of the territory and reducing the older inhabitants to the status of ethnic minorities. Despite rapid economic growth, Asia remains home to 67 per cent of the world's hungry of over 550 million people. Because the poor spend such a large share of their income on food, they have been significantly affected by higher and more volatile food prices, which has been a setback for the region's achievement in reducing poverty. Food security, therefore, remains a pressing concern in Asia.

Asia faces five challenges as it pursues sustained economic growth, says the IMF's Finance and Development magazine: overcoming the middle-income trap, improving its institutions and governance, coping with an aging population, curbing rising inequality, and promoting financial development. The Bank of Korea (BOK), the International Monetary Fund (IMF), and the IMF Economic Review were holding a conference on *"Asia: Challenges of Stability and Growth."* The conference was hosted by the BOK and was take place in Seoul on September 26–27, 2013. Asia must navigate four big challenges in 2014 i.e., inflation, interest rates, Japan's regional role and politics, all of which could dent investors' hopes for a cheery new year. Risks are finely balanced. For each positive, a significant challenge remains. The lack of inflation is a key issue as it has been accompanied by a collapse in nominal gross domestic product growth. Disability and poverty are dynamic and intricately linked phenomena. In developed countries, a large body of empirical research shows that persons with disabilities experience inter alia comparatively lower educational attainment, lower employment and higher unemployment rates, worse living conditions, and higher poverty rates. In developing countries, the still limited body of empirical research points toward individuals with disability being often economically worse off in terms of employment and educational attainment, while at the household level, the evidence is mixed.

The World Health Organisation has defined health as *"a complete physical, mental and social well-being and not merely the absence of disease or infirmity."* The concept has more recently been extended to include health related quality of life. According to the international classification of impairments, disabilities, and handicap, impairment is concerned with physical aspects of health, disability has to do with the loss of functional capacity resulting from impaired organ, and handicap is a measure of the social and cultural consequences of an impairment or disability. The International Year of Disabled Persons in 1981 stimulated much interest worldwide in disability. UNICEF has estimated that four-fifths of the disabled people of the world live in developing countries.

Disability in South Asia

South Asia comprises the sub-Himalayan countries and, for some authorities, adjoining countries to the west and east. The South Asian Association for Regional Cooperation is an economic co-operation organisation in the region which was established in 1985. The current territories of Bangladesh, India, Sri Lanka and Pakistan form the core countries of South Asia, while Nepal, Bhutan, Afghanistan, and Maldives are generally included. The history of core South Asia begins with evidence of human activity of Homo sapiens, as long as 75,000 years ago, or with earlier hominids including Homo erectus from about 500. With the core seven countries, the area covers about 4.48 million km^2 (1.7 million mi^2), which is ten per cent of the Asian continent or 2.4 per cent of the world's land surface area. Dozens of languages are spoken in South Asia. These languages share many characteristics such as grammatical structure and vocabulary, but they are also distinctly different.

Bangladesh

Disability is a universal element in the human condition to which no one is immune. Unrecognised as a problem for development, the condition of being disabled is at the bottom of the development agenda. The comprehension on disability, throughout the history, has rested on make-belief ideas. The direct result of these stereo-typed imaging and consequential action by the society and polity on the persons with disabilities has been their neglect. Many people in Bangladesh view disability as a curse and a cause of embarrassment to the family. There have been only a few systemic interventions to raise awareness of persons with disabilities at the community level. Most of the people being guided by the social taboo, seemingly suffer from scarcity of knowledge about disability. The Ministry of Social Welfare, in association with the National Forum of Organisations

Working with the Disabled (NFOWD) initiated draft legislation on disability related issues in 1996. This legislation was formally enacted in April 2001 and is known as The Disability Welfare Act of 2001. Disability is intractably complex form of deprivation. The concept of disability has been termed as a crude political label, a probabilistic type of development problem- different from those, which are location, income or gender specific.

Access to economic opportunities for people with disabilities is really very scarce. Lack of practical experiences and vocational skills are also obstructing their access to income generation options. A majority of the people with disabilities, including those with a severe level of disability has the confidence to acquire education and engage in financially gainful contributing activities enabling them as effective contributors. The Government of the People's Republic of Bangladesh, as a member of Economical and Social Council for Asia and Pacific (ESCAP) expressed her commitment to the goal of equality of people with disabilities. The Disability Welfare Act 2001 addresses, among others, protection of rights of people with disabilities, equal opportunities for participation in education, training, employment opportunities etc. There are specific indications in the said Act to promote employment of the people with disabilities in government and other recruitment process.

Government of Bangladesh is now very conscious and become proactive on the need for appropriate policies, laws and plans for the education, training and rehabilitation of the PWDs (Persons with Disabilities). Government took initiative to establish a close coordination with Government and non Government organisations for persons with disability. Bangladesh Government has approved a National Policy in 1995 which acknowledges the constitutional and international obligation of the PWD's. The policy gives the guideline for prevention, identification, education, rehabilitation, research, and other facilities and management of national programmes for the welfare and development of the persons with disabilities. Legislation with the title of *"Protibandhi Kallayan Ayn-2001 (Disability Welfare Act-2001)"* has been enacted in 2001 for the disabled in the parliament. The draft of legislation had been prepared in consultation with the people with disabilities by National Forum of Organisations Working with the Disabled (NFOWD). The disability issue is now highlighted both by the

Government and by voluntary organisation and NGOs working in the sector of disability through different means of communications for creating positive awareness towards the disability issue. Government of Bangladesh has included issue of special education of the people with disabilities in the National Education Policy. Society for the Welfare of the intellectually disabled, Bangladesh is a National level voluntary organisation with more than 7000 members. It are running 445 Special education, integrated education and vocational classes in 51 branches throughout the country and about more than 10,000 children with intellectual disability are getting educational services through its schools and Community Based Rehabilitation Programmes.

The World Health Organisation offers guidance in determining the health environment of Bangladeshi children from birth to ten who have disabilities needing interface with education. The environment of a child born, particularly a child born in poverty, can only be called dangerous. UNICEF's report on the State of the World's Children paints a very bleak picture for a child born. The Salamanca Framework for Action (1994) was a significant milestone in the education for children with disabilities: The Statement defines and recommends the mode of service delivery (inclusion) and the timing of intervention, linked to inclusive practices. Bangladesh endorsed the Education for All (EFA) framework and is a signatory to the Salamanca Statement and Framework for Action on Special Needs Education (1994) and the Dakar Framework for Action (2000). The decade 1993-2002 was proclaimed by the United Nations Economic and Social Commission for Asia and the Pacific (ESCAP) as the Asian and Pacific Decade of Disabled Persons. In May 2003, the ESCAP adopted a resolution on promoting an inclusive, barrier-free and rights-based society for persons with disabilities in Asia and the Pacific. The United Nations Standard Rules on the Equalising of Opportunities for Persons with Disabilities was adopted by the United Nations in 1993. The Convention on the Rights of the Child (CRC), to which Bangladesh is a signatory, establishes minimum standards for every aspect of children's lives, including education. The national framework for disabilities is the Bangladesh Constitution which states *"no citizen shall, on grounds only of religion, race, caste, sex, or place of birth be subjected to any disability, liability, restriction or condition with regard to access to any place of public entertainment, or resort, or admission to any educational institution."* The Bangladesh Parliament adopted its first comprehensive disability legislation, the Bangladesh Persons with Disability Welfare Act 2001, in April of that year. Persons with multiple disabilities (more than one type of impairment) are also covered under the Act, whether the cause of the disability is congenital or a result of accident or disease, maltreatment, or other reasons. On May 7, 2002, The National Action Plan for People with Disability (PWD) was promulgated as a directive from the office of the Prime Minister. The Action Plan stipulates what needs to be done to realise the goals of the Disability Welfare Act in five areas: education, health, employment, accessibility, and transportation. The National Coordination Committee (NCC) on Disability was set up to provide a forum for open dialogue between the government and NGOs in order to promote mutual understanding and co-operation and to identify and discuss issues that impede co-operation on disability issues between the government and NGOs.

The Centre for Disability in Development (CDD) is a not for profit organisation established in 1996 to develop a more inclusive society for persons with a disability. It is estimated that 16 million people are living with a disability, receiving little or no assistance and excluded from mainstream life. CDD works in partnership with a network of over 350 organisations both nationally and internationally. Their innovative approach to disability inclusion is now being used as a model in other countries. From a government to community level, attitudes towards disabled people are changing. No longer are disabled people habitually confined to the home or as systematically neglected in education, employment, health and a vast number of other human rights as they were even 15 years ago. Disabled people have more positive roles in society and there's more support and greater opportunities to participate.

Khondoker Shahriar Shakir is a lawyer practicing in the Supreme Court of Bangladesh. Shakir has made involvement in public interest law a large part of his professional life. He has conducted public interest cases regarding disability rights, including landmark challenges to the participation of qualified persons with disabilities in examinations for the civil service and judiciary. The Bangladesh Legal Aid and Services Trust (BLAST) is a national legal services and human rights organisation that provides free legal aid from the frontlines of the formal justice system to the apex court. BLAST has long provided legal aid to persons with disabilities, including through public interest litigation, and is currently working to develop more specialised legal services to secure the rights of persons with disabilities. The Harvard Law School Project on Disability (HPOD) is a global disability law and policy centre at Harvard University founded with a mission to support the implementation of the UN Convention on the Rights of Persons with Disabilities throughout the world.

Although women with disability constitute a large proportion of the population, very little information is available about their characteristics, the constraints they face in their daily lives and the quality of life they enjoy. The government has limited programme interventions in addressing issues related with disability and for the disabled. In recent years, a number of organisations in the non-government sector have come up with programmes and projects for the benefits of the disabled. However, organisation run by the disabled dealing exclusively with disability issues is yet to emerge. Data and information on the situation of women with disabilities are limited due to lack of elaborate studies or researches on the subject. The study *'Feminine Dimension of Disability'* done by Nirafat Anam in 2002 try to reflect on the situation of the adolescent girls with disability in the country. The other noteworthy study *'Feelings: on Disability Issue in Bangladesh'* by Shahidul Haque and Shahnaz Begum tried to look into various issues that are related with the lives of the disabled persons. It appears that not yet any attitudinal study has been conducted highlighting many dimensions of the lives of the women with disabilities.

The Asian and Pacific Decade of Disabled Persons essentially called for using Community-Based Rehabilitation (CBR) as a specific strategy for implementing rehabilitation activities in the communities. The CBR approach has been increasingly accepted and in recent years medical and occupational rehabilitation services have been included in CBR. NGOs and governmental agencies have been increasingly implementing CBR programmes and projects across the country. The Centre for Rehabilitation of the Paralysed (CRP), a large NGO located in Savar, has a massive rehabilitation programme with a sophisticated logistic centre for different types of treatment and therapies. Recently, a special Tele-link system was installed to contact overseas medical experts and surgeons when necessary. The Rotary Club of Dhaka launched an institution for persons with visual impairment in 1957 with technical assistance from Helen Keller International (HKI). Two types of education systems for the visually impaired are in operation. They are the Special Education and Integrated Education systems. For the hearing impaired, the Government of Bangladesh manages seven schools throughout the country. The government undertook the National Complex for Special Education with assistance from the Norwegian Agency for Development (NORAD). At present there are 33 Special Schools for persons with hearing impairment. Seven are under government management, with a total capacity of 1,500 students. There is only one education centre at the secondary level. The Impact Foundation Bangladesh is involved in the areas of public awareness of disabilities and improving prevention and rehabilitation. Its major initiative is the building of a Floating Hospital which provides persons with disabilities in remote riverine areas general treatment and special surgical operations. The Bangladesh National Society for the Blind (BNSB), in addition to its other activities for Persons with Disabilities, has been working to prevent blindness. Since the liberation of the country in 1971, a large number of people have become disabled and vulnerable, due to the lack of proper healthcare, traffic rules and social security. These people are frequently neglected and do not have the opportunity to live with prestige and honour.

The Constitution of the People's Republic of Bangladesh guarantees human rights and equality in all respects: political, social, religious, education and employment, irrespective of race, caste, sex, ethnicity and disability. It has numerous provisions that obligate the government to protect the rights and dignity of all citizens of the country equally without any bias (Articles 10, 11, 15, 17, 19, 20, 21, 27, 29, 31, 32, 36, 38 and 39). In 2001, the Parliament of Bangladesh enacted The Disability Welfare Act (DWA) 2001 (also known as Bangladesh Protibondhi Kollyan Ain (BPKA)) whereby rights of persons with disabilities received statutory recognition for the first time in the history of country.

This act is primarily welfare-based and emphasis is given to the impairment of the individual, but not on social and environmental barriers. The National Coordination Committee on Disability (NCCD) and the National Foundation for the Development of Disabled Persons (NFDDP) were established under the Ministry of Social Welfare. In 1995, the National Policy on Disability was approved outlining guidelines for prevention, identification, education, rehabilitation, research and management of the national programme. In September 2006, the National Action Plan for persons with disability was approved by the National Coordination Committee on Disability.

Nepal

Nepal is a very diverse society with a home to more than 100 different ethnic/caste groups and distinct language, culture, religions and living in different geographic terrain, Social and power structures, institutionalised through the caste system, stratifies individuals into unequal positions from and by birth. As one of the most inequitable societies in the world, a sizeable proportion of the population is excluded and discriminated on basis of caste, class, ethnicity, gender and even geographic location. Persons with disabilities are among those who have been historically excluded from the mainstream socio-politics and economic development. Ecologically Nepal is a very diverse country with large areas of hilly and mountainous terrain. Due to this difficult terrain infrastructure tends to be very underdeveloped. Nepal is also one of the poorest countries in the world. Nepal first achieved democracy in 1990. However, the benefits of democracy did not reach the vast masses of the population particularly in rural areas, a fact which led to the Maoists insurgency which began in 1996. In 2004, the fragile beginnings of democracy were clamped down by a royal take over with the king resuming absolute power.

Acquiring accurate data on the prevalence of disability is a difficult task for different reasons, including the lack of a common understanding how to define disability and the stigma associated with it. The official data from the population census in 2001 mentions 103,795 persons with disabilities on a total population at that time of 23.1[9] million, or 0.45 per cent. In different Nepali cultures, disability is still viewed as a sin of the previous life, and hence a shame to the family, which often results in concealing the family members from society and denying them a dignified life. Lack of adequate human resources (e.g., in health and education), access to facilities and informa-tion, inaccessible infrastructure and transportation have been major obstacles in ensuring a dignified life for persons with disabilities. Interim Constitution of Nepal has established education as one of the fundamental rights of every citizen so as to live a life with dignity. The UN Convention for the Right of persons with disabilities obliges Nepal to ensure that persons with disabilities are not excluded from the general education system on the basis of disability, and particularly children with disabilities must not be excluded from free and compulsory primary education, or from secondary education. Under the obligation of international human rights treaties and the CPRD in particular, *"a State must provide persons with disabilities with the same range, quality and standard of free and affordable healthcare and programmes as provided to others without any discrimination"*. The Nepalese Social Protection and Welfare of Disabled Persons Act from 1982 have a provision of five per cent quota in employment for persons with disabilities. However, implementation and adhering to this Act is still a challenge. Where some persons with disabilities might have benefitted in the government services, not much has happened in the corporate or the development sector.

The concept of social inclusion is still not properly theorised and there is a need of fundamental research to develop the thematic meaning of social exclusion-inclusion. DFID (2005) defines *"Social exclusion-inclusion is a process by which certain groups are systematically disadvantaged because they are discriminated on the basis of their ethnicity, race, religion, sexual orientation, caste, descent, gender, age, disability, HIV status, migrant status or where they live"*. The social exclusion exhibits dynamic process and complex nature which is also the characteristic of social exclusion process of People with Disability. It persists a given set of procedures, institutions, and terms of public discourse. The extent of PWD exclusion appears to be largely dependent on the severity and type of disability and also the awareness of the society people. In Nepal, Handicap International has been present since 2000. Handicap International works primarily through partner organisations in the development of projects and activities for the physical rehabilitation and inclusion of people with disabilities into the mainstream development process. Prevention of disabilities and combating exclusion and stigmatisation of persons with disabilities are also a major focus work.

In 1976, the World Health Organisation estimated that more than ten per cent of the world's population was suffering from some kind of disability. Since 1971, a number of studies have been conducted by government institutions, NGOs and INGOs to estimate the number of disabled people in Nepal. The 1971 census, estimated 1.5 per cent of the population over ten years of age had disabilities. The Disability Sample Survey of 1980 reported a prevalence rate of disability of three per cent of the population. The 1981 census estimated that five per cent of the population had disabilities. The survey, Mental Retardation in Nepal (1989), estimated 4.9 per cent of the population had mental retardation. The Survey of the Prevalence of Deafness and Ear Diseases in Nepal (1991) put the figure of deaf children aged five years and above at 16.6 per cent in five districts. The study on Disabled People in Nepal (1995) conducted in eight districts, estimated 4.55 per cent of the population to be disabled. The Disability Survey of Kanchanpur District (1995) estimated that five per cent of people in the district were disabled. The Situation Analysis of Disability in Nepal estimates the national prevalence of disability at 1.63 per cent of the population. Mostly, non-disabled people in society consider people with disabilities as weak, feeble and a burden to society. Disabled children, especially girls with disabilities from low-caste communities, are further discriminated against and marginalised. The government has long been involved in providing for the disabled, but the level of assistance has not met the needs of the disabled. The Ministry of Women and Social Welfare is the focal point of efforts in disability affairs, but other ministries also have programmes for disabled persons. Governmental agencies working for disability include the National Planning Commission Secretariat, the Ministry of Education, the Ministry of Health, the Ministry of Finance, the Ministry of Local Development, and the Social Welfare Council.

The Nepalese constitution defines persons with disabilities as persons who are mentally or physically unable or incompetent to lead a normal life. The term includes persons whose mobility is impaired, who suffer from spinal curvature, have visually impaired in one or both eyes, have hearing impairment, are unable to speak properly, or whose hands, legs, or fingers are impaired or missing. The 1971 census referred to the Person with Disabilities population as the economically inactive population due to physical disability. This study defined persons with disabilities as those who by virtue of congenital disease, acquired diseases, or injury, are incapable of living an independent personal or social life, or engaging in gainful employment, or acquiring normal education consistent with his/her age or sex. Policies given in the Ninth Five Year Plan are priority issues for person with disabilities welfare. These are the provision of free medical, educational and vocational training services; partnership between person with disabilities-related ministries and organisations, improving person with disabilities facilities, data management, Person with disabilities employment measures, promoting production of assistive devices and the development of communication tools and media programmes.

National Federation of Disabled Nepal (NFDN) is an umbrella organisation representing the Disabled Peoples' Organisations (DPOs) working for the rights of persons with disabilities across the country. Nepal ratified the UN Convention on the Rights of persons with disabilities in December 2009 and the optional protocol in 2010. There is increasing awareness and acceptance of persons with disabilities in the society, as well as increasing access to services for persons with disabilities, though lot more can be desired. Although Nepal has many legal provisions for persons with disabilities, the implementation of these laws is very weak. The awareness and understanding of disability as a human rights and social inclusion issue is still limited. Mainstreaming a disadvantaged group needs deliberate efforts and extra initiative. It also requires a separate, dedicated funding (financing affirmative action), concrete, disaggregated monitoring indicators and a focal point responsible for follow up and support. Inclusion will not happen without deliberate effort and funding. UNICEF has a provision for an Equity Fund which can be used to finance the extra/additional initiative for mainstreaming disadvantaged groups at programme level.

The Government of Nepal has ratified the Convention of the Rights of the Child (1989), and is a signatory of the declaration Education for All (1990) and the Salamanca Declaration (1994).

These documents call for the provision of public education to all children, regardless of their physical, intellectual, emotional, social, linguistic, or other conditions. The Department of Education had taken up the challenge of initiating inclusive education. Governmental agencies such as the National Planning Commission Secretariat, the Ministry of Women, Children and Social Welfare, the Ministry of Education, the Ministry of Health, the Ministry of Finance, the Ministry of Local Development and the Social Welfare Council are working for disability in various ways. Several initiatives to provide integrated and inclusive education for children with disabilities have also been taken by charity organisations, religious institutions, local NGOs and international organisations.

The Government of Nepal and the United Nations acknowledge that, while Nepal has made important progress toward achieving universal primary education as part of its commitment to the Millennium Development Goals, children from marginalised communities, such as children with disabilities, represent a significant portion of the approximately 330,000 primary school aged children who remain out of school. Nepal has ratified a number of international human rights treaties, including the UN Convention on the Rights of Persons with Disabilities, which articulates that children with disabilities are entitled to the same rights as other children, including the right to inclusive education. Although in theory the government promotes an inclusive education policy, in practice, it supports a system of segregated resource classes designated for children with disabilities in mainstream schools and separate schools for deaf, blind and children with physical and intellectual disabilities. Despite national policies on inclusive and child-friendly schools, the government is failing to make the school environment accessible for children with disabilities, which in many cases effectively denies these children their right to education. Furthermore, schools are often inadequately staffed, have no flexible curriculum and limited teaching materials, leading to an inferior quality of education for children with disabilities, compared to other children. The Ministry of Education initiated orientations on inclusive education for district education officers, who are in turn required to organise trainings for school administrators and teachers in each district.

India

Census 2001 has revealed that over 21 million people in India as suffering from one or the other kind of disability. This is equivalent to 2.1 per cent of the population. Among the total disabled in the country, 12.6 million are males and 9.3 million are females. The number of disabled is more in rural and urban areas, such proportion of the disabled by sex in rural and urban areas. Such proportion has been reported between 57-58 per cent for males and 42-43 per cent females. The disability rate (number of disabled per 100,000 populations) for the country as whole works out to 2130. This is 2,369 in the case of males and 1,874 in the case of females. Among the five types of disabilities on which data has been collected, disability in seeing at 48.5 per cent emerges as the top category. Others in sequence are: in movement (27.9 per cent), Mental (10.3 per cent), in speech (7.5 per cent), and in hearing (5.8 per cent). The disabled by sex follow a similar pattern except for that the proportion of disabled females is higher in the category in seeing and in hearing. Across the country, the highest number of disabled has been reported from the state of Uttar Pradesh (3.6 million). Significant numbers of disabled have also been reported from the state like Bihar (1.9 million), West Bengal (1.8 million), Tamil Nadu and Maharashtra (1.6 million each). Tamil Nadu is the only state, which has a higher number of disabled females than males. Among the states, Arunachal Pradesh has the highest proportion of disabled males (66.6 per cent) and lowest proportion of female disabled.

Enhancing employment opportunities for people with disabilities is one of the main concerns of the disability sector in India. The Ministries responsible for Employment at the Central level are (1) Ministry of Labour and Employment, (2) Ministry of Personnel, Public Grievances and Pensions, (3) Ministry of Housing and Urban Poverty Alleviation, (4) Ministry of Commerce and Industry, (5) Ministry of Micro, Small and Medium Enterprises; (6) Ministry of Rural Development. Ministry of Human Resource Development is as vocational, higher and technical education falls under them and the Ministry of Social Justice and Empowerment, is the nodal Ministry for disability. Government Departments and Public Sector Undertakings (PSUs) have been an important employer of disabled people. In fact, the first Special Employment Exchange was set up way back in 1959 in Mumbai. Government of India initiated the policy of three per cent reservation in jobs for disabled people more than three decades ago in 1977. However, the reservation was only in the lower ranking jobs (C and D categories). In 1995, when The Disability Act was passed, the reservation was extended to higher ranking jobs (A and B categories) as well. The general feeling in the disability sector has been that the system of identification of jobs is very restrictive. Due to this, many disabled people have been denied job opportunities in spite of having necessary qualification and skills.

Bhutan

Bhutan is a democratic, constitutional monarchy whose king, Jigme Khesar Namgyel Wangchuck, is the head of state, with executive power vested in the cabinet, headed by Prime Minister Tshering Tobgay. The country began a gradual transition from an absolute to a democratic constitutional monarchy in 1998, culminating in its first general election for the National Assembly in 2008. In July, the country held its second general elections, in which the former opposition People's Democratic Party gained a majority of the seats in the National Assembly, resulting in the country's first democratic transfer of power to the opposition.

According to the Population and Housing Census of Bhutan, the number of disabled persons is 21,894, representing 3.4 per cent of the country's total population. This relatively low incidence of disabled people, compared to the WHO data, may be related to local definitions of disability, varying cultural perceptions of disability and the types of occupation practiced in the community. Regardless, a significant percentage of the population is living with a disability. The provision of rehabilitation services for persons with disabilities is relatively new. As in many developing countries, Bhutan's healthcare professionals are the key persons providing information and delivering medical and rehabilitation services to the disabled population. They play an influential role in determining the priorities and direction of rehabilitation services. The Royal Government of Bhutan strives to provide the opportunity for every individual citizen to develop their unique gifts to better their lives and contribute to the nation building. In order to provide equal opportunities to all citizens, Bhutan established its first specialised institute catering to the educational needs of the visually impaired in Khaling, Trashigang, in 1973 under the patronage of His Royal Highness Prince Namgyel Wangchuck. Realising the need of such enabling services for people with other forms of disabilities, the Royal Government expanded the special education programmes in 2001. A pilot programme establishing Changangkha Lower Secondary School as an integrated school providing special needs educational was initiated in 2001. In 2003, a Deaf Education Unit was established in Drukgyel Lower Secondary School.

In Bhutan, the prevalence of children with disabilities is evident from the Disability Assessment Report, 2011 which reveals that at least 21.7 per cent of children aged two to nine years have mild to severe disability. Although, numerous initiatives to create provisions for education and other support services to cater to the needs of children with special educational needs are underway, there needs to be more focused plans and strategies. Special Education is an educational programme designed for students with special educational needs, which requires additional support services in the form of trained teachers, teaching approaches, equipment and care within or outside a regular classroom. The Government places highest priority in ensuring the provision of educational services to all its citizens. In such endeavour, the government realised that the children with special educational needs require concerted efforts to improve access to quality educational services. This will enable the government to achieve its goal of 'Education for All'.

After Bhutan became signatory to ESCAP Commission on Disability in 1993 there has been increased concern for disability prevention, rehabilitation and providing equal opportunities for the disabled. The Community Based Rehabilitation (CBR) Programme was initiated in 1997 as a pilot project in Khaling, Trashigang by using the primary Health Care infrastructure. WHO initially and DANIDA in 1999 provided technical and financial support. Disability is not well defined condition and there are many terminology and conceptual difference. According to a survey from the pilot programme, the disability prevalence is 3.5 per cent. The National Population and Housing Census stated 3.4 per cent of the total population people with disabilities. From the experiences, CBR needs multi-sectoral approach. The CBR Programme will seek to address the needs of all identified disabled persons in the community. Bhutan suffers from a double burden of disease as is true for other countries in the Region. The mountainous terrain of the country, communication difficulties and predominantly sustenance agriculture as the basis of living for most of the population, ensures the able bodied population to be physically active and fit. However, NCDs such as cardiovascular diseases, cancers, chronic pulmonary diseases and diabetes mellitus are on the rise. There has been a changing trend in the life style of the urban population. Obesity as well as sedentary habits is not so uncommon.

Afghanistan

Afghanistan is one of the most mine contaminated countries in the world. It is believed that there are still about a million mines in the country, killing and maiming hundreds of people every year. Afghanistan is one of the poorest countries in the world and many people have injuries or permanent disabilities as a result of conflict. Access to health services remain limited and poor housing, a lack of access to clean drinking water and electricity affect people across the country. Although Afghan officials say access to basic health services has been extended to about 80 per cent of the population, money and transportation are two of the main problems faced by most disabled Afghans. Among the difficulties reported, disabled persons faced problems mainly regarding money for fees or medication and transportation, the absence of transportation, and far behind, the absence of medication. The government of Afghanistan pays a monthly stipend of 500 Afghanis to war disabled, which is insufficient to meet their basic needs. The International Committee of the Red Cross (ICRC) says it has donated prostheses and orthoses (artificial aids such as a brace) to over 80,000 disabled people since it launched its orthopaedic services in Afghanistan in 1988.

Ninety five per cent of children with disabilities do not attend schools due to inaccessible environment. The level of literacy rate for adults and children with disabilities is very low because of the less attention and lack of literacy education facilities in the country. There are around three million people living with various types of disability and half of them are in the working-age, but only limited number of these people has some kind of employment opportunities, while the majority of people with disabilities do not have access to job and employment in the present situation. Afghanistan is not an easy place for anyone to make a living. But for those with disabilities, it's a downright hostile environment. Tens of thousands have been maimed and disabled during decades of conflict. Jobs are scarce, and there's almost nothing that's handicapped-accessible. Women and girls with disabilities are often exposed to poverty more than boys and men with disabilities and face discrimination within the family. Women and girls with disabilities encounter all kinds of discrimination as they are exposed to greater risk of physical and sexual abuse and often are not given adequate sexual health and reproductive rights advice. Young children with disabilities require access to early intervention services, including early detection and identification (within the first five years after birth). Many people are suffering from psychological disorders blighted by decades of war. The mentally disabled face discrimination here, leaving their loved ones to bear much of the burden.

Disability is increasingly part of the lives of veterans. The types of disabilities that are related to combat injuries include physical injuries, traumatic brain injury, hearing loss, post-traumatic stress disorder, and a combination of ailments and injuries. Minor traumatic brain injury can even occur in those who were not directly hit by a blast and never lost consciousness. Kevlar helmets and body armor have helped reduce the mortality rate but cannot provide complete protection, particularly when dealing with injuries to the head, neck, and face. It is currently estimated that 3.7 per cent of the Afghan population (over 850,000 people) suffers from various forms of disability. Inclusive initiatives are still very limited while perceptions on disabilities are still very rooted in culture and traditions. Poor people with disabilities are the most vulnerable. Disabled women who are considered to be more incapable than disabled men and suffer from indifference, discrimination and isolation. There is a general lack of knowledge and capacity within families and communities to interact with and care for people with disabilities, especially the intellectually disabled. The war has left about 800,000 people with disabilities in the country. Most of the people with disabilities are unemployed, illiterate and have limited accesses to health facilities. According to the Afghanistan Disability Action Plan,

70 per cent of person with disabilities aged over 15 are unemployed and 73 per cent of person with disabilities aged above six do not receive any education.

Disability has been linked with the issue of martyrdom. War injured people have been regarded as disabled needing various services. The Ministry of Martyrs and Disabled has been tasked with responsibility to cater for the needs of all disabled people. There is a serious lack of reliable data on disability and disabled people. The fact that disability has been regarded as a war issue led to one single agency responsible for their welfare. This hindered the smooth integration of disability issues into mainstream government programmes including statistics and surveys needed for planning such programmes. The overwhelming majority of disabled and their families experience social and economic deprivation and many of their basic rights are denied by institutional structure. Poverty and unemployment are key factors for perpetuating the exclusion of disabled people, but at the same time both can be a result of disability. There are many factors which causes impairment and lead people to become disabled. The most notable in the context are war and landmine issues, given the long years of armed and political conflict in the country. The lack of awareness on disability prevention led to many new cases of impairment which could be avoided. Further, the poor medical infrastructure meant that many treatable cases have to develop into permanent impairments. Other causes of disabilities are environmental factors including epidemics; accidents; natural disasters; and pollutions by poisoning and toxic waste all lead to causing impairments. Inaccessible environments in turn lead to creating new disabilities and perpetuating existing ones. The Transitional Islamic State of Afghanistan has paid special attention to minority issues including disabled people. The government of President Karzai through the National Development Framework (NDF) has relentlessly supported the development of disability national institutions, namely, the Ministry of Martyrs and Disabled (MMD).

The long years of war has literally affected every aspect of life, but disabled people were much more affected than others due to their vulnerable position in society. Although there is no national umbrella organisation of disabled people, a growing number of disabled people organisations and groups are now emerging although at a very slow pace. This includes the Afghan National Association of the Deaf (ANAD), the Afghan National Association of the Blind (ANAB), the National Association of Disabled Women in Afghanistan (NADWA), Disabled Shura of Afghanistan (DSA). Many attempts have been made to set up a coordination mechanism for the disability sector and provide reliable data for planning. The continued political conflict in the country has resulted in limited services being available for war veterans and other disabled people. The Ministry of Martyrs and Disabled (MMD) is leading a number of other line Ministries including Ministry of Public Health (MoPH), Ministry of Education (MoE), and Ministry of Labour and Social Affairs (MoLSA) in developing internal policies targeting disabled people. Education policy has no reference to special education of disabled people including a higher education. The most comprehensive policy position on disability was drafted in early 2003 as a result of a highly political situation created by disabled war veterans.

The National Disability Survey in Afghanistan (NDSA) is the first household survey on disability that attempt to utilise the capabilities approach. This survey aims to determine the prevalence of disabilities and provide a cross-cutting overview of the situation of persons with disabilities by collecting reliable information about their needs, and promoting integration of their concerns into the programmes and policies of the government. In Afghan culture, disability is perceived differently according to gender differences, traditional or ethnic attitudes and religious motives, and even the person's economic status. They are different beliefs about persons with disabilities considered as a group or several distinct groups. Persons with disabilities are facing different prejudices and are more or less vulnerable in day-to-day life. Lack of awareness and strong cultural beliefs lead the population to consider other causes of disabilities, especially congenital ones, as shameful. Mental retardation is commonly denied and considered as a Post Traumatic Stress Disorder (PTSD) resulting from past bomb attacks children may have been exposed to. Since the end of 2001, real progress has been made by the Afghan government and people to secure peace, stability and to rehabilitate the devastated infrastructure. Despite these efforts Afghanistan remains one of the poorest and least developed countries in the world with some of the worst health statistics. Supported by the donors, WHO, UNICEF, and other development partners, the MoPH in 2002 developed a national package of health services, the Basic Package of Health Services (BPHS), which addressed the greatest health needs of the population. In 1995, UNDP set up the Comprehensive Disabled Afghans Programme (CDAP). The CDAP was designed as a comprehensive model of services for and with persons with disabilities, based on Community Based Rehabilitation in 50 districts.

In late 2003, the Afghan Task Force on Disability completed the Comprehensive National Disability Policy under the framework of the National Constitution. The vision of this Comprehensive National Disability Policy is to create a barrier-free society based on the principles of participation, integration and the equalisation of opportunities, defined by the United Nations in its World Programme of Action concerning Disabled Persons; the Standard Rules for the Equalisation of Opportunities for Disabled Persons; The Biwako Millennium Framework for Action towards an Inclusive, Barrier-free and Rights-based Society for Persons with Disabilities in the Asia and Pacific region, and more recently in the elaboration for the International Convention to Protect and Promote the Rights of Disabled Persons. The unemployment rate is estimated based on a Government survey, to be 33 per cent. The Government continues to make efforts to pursue economic development by reducing poverty and unemployment, with special attention to the needs of women and youth. Since its establishment of the interim government, Afghanistan has specified target areas in the labour and social affairs sector, including skills development in general, the Disarmament, Demobilisation and Reintegration (DDR) Programme, as well as protection of martyrs and people with disabilities.

There is a lack of attention towards disabled community in the country. The Development and Ability Organisation (DAO) was founded in 2004 to develop advocacy and awareness activities and research for people with disability throughout Afghanistan. The goal of DAO is to promote the goals of an inclusive, barrier-free and rights based society for persons with disabilities. It is to protect and promote the rights and dignity of disabled people within the framework of an Afghan

Constitution. Accordingly, disabled Afghans are entitled to the enjoyment of the full range of civil and political, and socio-economic and cultural rights declared in the Universal Declaration of Human Rights (UDHR) and UN Standard Rules on the Equalisation of opportunities for persons with disabilities (UNSRPD) and the Afghan constitution. Handicap International's goal in Afghanistan is to improve the lives of people with disabilities, particularly those that have received injuries as a result of landmine accidents. Its first activities started in 1987 when it began providing rehabilitation services for landmine victims at an orthopaedic-fitting centre in Kandahar. The rehabilitation centre now supports thousands of people each year whilst its network of volunteers works with communities to raise awareness about the danger of landmines and refer those in need to the rehabilitation centre. It currently supports people and communities in the provinces of Kandahar, Herat, Helmand and Kabul.

In October 2002, during the UNESCAP high level intergovernmental meeting, Afghanistan signed the resolution for the extension of Asian and Pacific Decade of Disabled Persons, 1993-2002, for another decade, 2003-2012. Afghanistan has signed the Convention on Cluster Munitions on 3rd December, 2008 and ratified it on 8th September, 2011. Meanwhile, in 2002 Afghanistan ratified the Convention on the Prohibition of the Use, Stockpiling, Production and Transfer of Anti-Personnel Mines and on their Destruction. But the warring factions in Afghanistan continuously use different types of mines and explosives which make it difficult for Afghanistan to get rid of these silent killers in the near future. An Indian organisation, specialising in prosthetic legs, will supply artificial limbs free of cost to 1,000 physically challenged Afghan nationals in the war-torn country. The Jaipur Foot has signed an agreement with the Afghan government to supply 1000 prosthetic legs to terror attack victims and polio sufferers. Jaipur Foot will manufacture limbs for those who have lost their legs to roadside bombings, terrorist attacks or polio disease. The Indian organisation had agreed to provide the limb free of cost. India has also planned to help the Disabled Technical Institute in Afghanistan to enable the people in Jaipur to produce artificial limbs themselves. The programme Enabling and Mobilising Afghan Disabled (EMAD) targets people with disabilities, their families, community leaders, government officials, school administrators, teachers, non-governmental organisations and disabled peoples' organisations in Kabul and Parwan provinces. The project works to strengthen and empower people with disabilities towards full participation in every aspect of life, through rehabilitation, awareness, advocacy, education as well as social and economic support.

Pakistan

Persons with disabilities are mostly unseen, unheard and uncounted persons in Pakistan. They are the most marginalised group. Persons with Disabilities face overwhelming barriers in education, skills development and daily life. Most currently offered services focus on children, with little availability for adult Persons with Disabilities. In Pakistan, no single ministry or federal department deals with, issues related to disability. There is only the ministry, responsible for social welfare, women's development and special education, which touch upon person with disabilities issues. Pakistanis believe that persons with disabilities are a social burden and a curse on the family. These beliefs lead to the misunderstanding of disability.

The systematic care of persons with disabilities was brought into focus in the 1980s with the observance of 1981 as the United Nations International Year of Disabled Persons. The need was then felt for their education, rehabilitation and cares both by government and by the private sector. A law on the employment and rehabilitation of persons with disabilities was passed in 1981. The Law is a comprehensive legislation that spells out the responsibility of the State toward the prevention of disabilities; protection of rights of persons with disabilities; and provision of medical care, education, training, employment, and rehabilitation to persons with disabilities. There are many negative attitude, cultural myths and superstitious beliefs towards Person with Disabilities. The disabled persons are generally insulted and rarely function as useful members of society. Most of the public places like shopping malls, railway stations, Hotels, and cinemas, educational institutions, in the country do not cater to the mobility and access needs of the physically disabled persons, ramps for wheel chairs are absent are the gradient is too steep for PWDs to use independently; public buses are not accessible to disabled persons.

Poverty and disability are closely linked and have detrimental impact on the level of inclusion in society and its overall development. From social perspective, both poverty, and disability are product of capitalist development. They are both socially constructed and culturally produced in a given society. Poverty leads to disability resulting in diseases and impairments. Equally true, disability leads to poverty in the sense that those with impairments will engender extra cost of living related to their specific needs. Various measures can be considered as instrumental strategies in fighting widespread poverty amongst disabled people. This primarily includes different kinds of remunerated employment schemes as well as policies, legislation and welfare provisions. Across the world, disabled people are experiencing social and economic deprivation. Poverty has been identified as principal obstacle that prevents the fulfillment of such rights and ultimately hinders development efforts, especially in developing countries. Disabled people are disempowered by the current economic situation. This essentially means that people suffer from impairments caused by poverty because of the inability of the state to provide a welfare system to its citizens, which includes medical support.

People with disabilities are the most marginalised group and face great stigmatisation in society. This may be due to the fact that independent assessments have found a significant lack of information, rules and regulations, rehabilitation centres, and specialised services for people with disabilities. The Ministry of Women's Development, Social Welfare, and Special Education has authority to formulate policies on employment and rehabilitation for people with disabilities. However, policies are then implemented at the local level, and no particular department is responsible for programmes for people with disabilities. The Pakistani government has established 46 special education schools that provide assessment, diagnostic, and special education services. The National Policy of Special Education (enacted in 1998) and National Policy for Persons with Disabilities (enacted in 2002) give oversight of special needs schools to the Ministry of Women's Development, Social Welfare, and Special Education, rather than the Ministry of Education. There is a strong association between poverty and disability.

The Pakistan Society for the Rehabilitation of the Disabled (PSRD) is a nonprofit organisation with the aims and objective to undertake activities for the welfare of people with disabilities for full integration and independence, adopt preventative measures, and to increase awareness. Facilities and activities of PSRD include the operation of an orthopedic surgical unit, an outpatient department, a physiotherapy department, an orthotics and prosthetics workshop, a high school, a vocational training unit, a vocational rehabilitation centre, computer training centre, etc. PSRD may be a valuable resource for information on disabilities related issues. Pakistan Disabled Foundation is an organisation of the peoples with disabilities of all categories, working actively in all walks of life to the maximum possible extent. Special Attention towards Handicapped (SATH) is a non-profit organisation working with disabled children who live in marginalised communities in rural and suburban area through community based rehabilitation programme. Handicapped children are often neglected in Pakistani society. STEP is a cross disability organisation, with a prime objective of empowerment of disabled persons through capacity building and advocacy. STEP is engaged in Leadership, ICT and Independent Living training of disabled persons.

The Government of Pakistan ratified the Convention on Rights of Persons with Disabilities (CRPD) in 2011, prior to which no national monitoring mechanism was established to report the status of disabled people to International CRPD Committees. Still, national and provincial governments need to design inclusive measures and formulate the relevant legislation so as to ensure the safeguarding of the rights of disabled people and to promote the Convention. The efficiency of the public education system is considered low, based on various key indicators like high dropout rates, poor quality of education, ineffective utilisation of development funds, lack of evidence-based planning, and problems related to education governance.

Maldives

The Maldives is comprised of approximately 1200 islands, around 200 of which are inhabited. Almost 40 per cent of the islands have a population of less than 500 people. These islands are scattered across an area of over 90,000 square kilometers of ocean. The Government provides a range of useful services to help persons with disabilities. The non-governmental organisations play an important role in the provision of services for persons with disabilities. Current national thinking on disability issues is guided by the draft National Disability Policy and the recently ratified United Nations Convention on the Rights of Persons with Disabilities. The first ever disability screening was undertaken in 1981. Then there were 1,390 persons with disabilities that comprised 0.9 per cent of the population. In 2000, according to the Population and Housing Census data there were 4,728 persons with disabilities. According to the preliminary report of the Disability Screening Survey undertaken by Handicap International in 2009, about 4.7 per cent were found to have severe permanent functional limitations or disabilities. The WHO estimate for persons with disabilities is between 5 to 15 per cent of the population. The 2002 survey showed disability among males (4,902) is slightly higher than females (4,314). Kurumba Maldives is a conveniently located Island for disabled guests to enjoy. The resort has a cement pathway on the inside ring of the resort and directly through the middle. This is suitable for wheelchairs. Golf Buggies are available to assist upon requests. Whilst there are no specific disabled rooms, the resort will put in a ramp for the rooms. The closes rooms are the Superior Rooms and Garden Pool Villas. The Resort team is able to provide wood or carpet to assist with access to the beach. The resort has one beach wheel chair suitable for water entry with supervision.

The Convention on the Rights of Persons with Disabilities and its Optional Protocol was adopted on 13th December, 2006 at the United Nations Headquarters in New York and was opened for signature on 30th March, 2007. The Maldives signed the CRPD on 2nd October, 2007. The purpose of the Convention is to promote, protect and ensure the full and equal enjoyment of all human rights and fundamental freedoms by all persons with disabilities, and to promote respect for their inherent dignity. The Maldives has signed-up to eight of the nine core United Nations human rights instruments. Maldives is a member of the Biwako Millennium Framework for Action towards an Inclusive, Barrier-free and Rights-based Society for Persons with Disabilities in Asia and the Pacific (BMF). The BMF is a set of policy guidelines and regional mandate adopted by 62 Governments in the Asia Pacific region in May 2003. Maldives has international commitments under the Standard Rules to attain equal opportunity for persons with disabilities. The Constitution protects the rights of persons with disabilities. According to Article 17 of the Constitution, everyone including those with mental or physical disability is entitled to the rights and freedoms included in the Constitution without discrimination of any kind. The Government submitted to the Parliament a bill on protecting the rights of persons with disabilities on 20th July, 2009. The bill submitted by the Government was proposed to establish the essential legal framework for all support and services provided to persons with disabilities. The bill on *Protecting the Rights of People with Special Needs and Providing Financial Assistance* was returned by the President to the Parliament on 5th January, 2010 for reconsideration.

Despite having ratified the Convention on the Rights of Persons with Disabilities back in April 2010, the Maldives must provide regulatory reforms ensuring against disability-based discrimination and abuse in local society, according to the International Disability Alliance (IDA). The UNHRC has already identified key issues to be taken up with the Maldives, concerning its International Covenant on Civil and Political Rights (ICCPR) commitments. The IDA also called on the government to provide healthcare services including mental and reproductive healthcare to disabled people along with other related services while ensuring the *"free and informed consent"* of the recipient. In addition, the report also called for authorities to ensure *"involuntary treatment and confinement"* were not allowed under national laws. Addressing Article 13 of the CRPD, the IDA also called for the provision to disabled people of *"effective access to justice on an equal basis with others"*. This would ensure that disabled people could serve both directly and indirectly in the country's criminal justice system, according to the recommendations.

In 2007, the Government developed a draft of the necessary policy instrument to address the rights of persons with disabilities. Draft National Disability Policy is based on the human rights-based approach rather than the previous charity approach. Persons with disabilities were consulted extensively in the formulation of the draft National Disability Policy. The Maldivian Democratic Party (MDP) *"Aneh Dhivehi Raajje"* Strategic Action Plan 2009-2013 has several policies and strategies that are related to the rights of persons with disabilities, but the required clarity and sense of purpose is lost. The Maldivian government focal agency for support and services for persons with disabilities is the Ministry of Health and Family. The Government started setting up classes for children with disabilities in 2006, with a vision to set up minimum one school in each atoll that enrolls children with special needs by 2010. Estimates are that there are about 2,250 children with disabilities. There are altogether 11 schools across the Maldives that provide education opportunity for children with disabilities. The Government provides approved essential psychotropic drugs free of charge to registered psychiatric patient.

Sri Lanka

In Sri Lanka, disabled children are seen as a curse and it is believed people have been born with disability as a result of bad karma from a previous life. As a result they are often treated appallingly. In the Batticaloa District, Hope for Children are working with MENCAFEP to try to alleviate some of the problems caused by this deep-rooted belief through their satellite centre for disabled children and their families. Handicap International provides assistance to victims of armed conflict, promoting social inclusion, and developing partnerships at all levels to implement and support national disability policies. Handicap International has been working since 2004. The predicament of people with disabilities has been exacerbated by three decades of armed conflict. Following the Tsunami in 2004, Sri Lanka suffered further extensive damage, both physically and socially. Handicap International works to reduce the impact of natural disasters on populations living in disaster prone areas in the eastern province of Batticaloa.

Disabled people are often found among the poorest of the poor and in a developing country like Sri Lanka; disabled people face discrimination at every level of society. Poverty is both a cause and consequence of disability and a majority of disabled people fined their impairment affects their chances of going to school, working for a living, enjoying family life, and participating as equals in social life. Historically, disabled people were excluded from mainstream society and development. There is an increasing recognition that development goals the United Nations Millennium Development Goals can not be met feasibly without bringing disabled people into the mainstream development process. Disability Mainstreaming is recognised at international level through the UNCRPD and various donors accept that disability must be addressed as a cross-cutting issue in all levels of development practice. There are about 1,500,000 persons with disabilities living. About 90 per cent of them live in rural areas. The root cause of disability in developing countries is considered to be poverty and the things it causes like inadequate nutrition, disease, poor drinking water, improper hygiene, accidents, armed conflicts and genetic disorders etc. Persons with disabilities find it extremely difficult to secure employment in rural as well as other areas. Lack of education, transport, vocational training and competition in the labour market are the reasons. The persons with motor and upper limb disabilities need wheel chairs, invalid tricycles, artificial limbs etc., so that they can become mobile and be useful citizens.

The legal definition of disability in Sri Lanka is that described in the Protection of the Rights of Persons with Disabilities Act. A *"person with disability means any person who, as a result of any deficiency in his physical or mental capabilities, whether congenital or not, is unable by himself to ensure for himself, wholly or partly, the necessities of life"*. The classification of types of disability used by the Ministry of Social Welfare for programme development encompasses people who have visual, speech, hearing, mobility, intellectual, and psychiatric disability and disability arising as a result of epilepsy and other causes. It also encompasses multiple disabilities, which is a combination of two or more of these various disabilities in a single individual. The civil conflict, which was ongoing for nearly two decades, left large numbers, both combatants and civilians, with injury and disability. Sri Lanka has had a tradition of paying particular attention to the education of children who have disability going back to 1912 when the first School for the Deaf and Blind was started.

The General Educational Reforms of 1997 now introduced through all levels of primary schooling are of advantage to the inclusion of children who have disability in the ordinary classroom. People who have disability are among the poorest segment of the population. Income generation is limited by lack of employment opportunity for both wage and self-employment. Employment opportunity is in turn restricted by poor access to skills development (vocational training). The majority of public buildings are inaccessible to wheelchair users and other people who have mobility disability and use walking aids. Most urban workplaces, educational and vocational training institutions and public buildings have steps at the entrance, are often multistoried and not always have lifts. The most commonly used tools and equipment by people who have mobility disability include tricycles, wheelchairs, artificial limbs and crutches and other walking aids.

Disability in West Asia

West Asia is the westernmost sub-region of Asia. It is a newer term for the area that encompasses the Middle East and the Near East. The world's earliest civilisations developed in Western Asia. Western Asia is primarily arid and semi-arid, and can be subject to drought, but it also contains vast expanses of forest and fertile valleys. Western Asia contains large areas of mountainous terrain. The population of Western Asia is over 300 million. The most populous countries in the region are Iran and Turkey, each with around 75 million people, followed by Iraq with around 32 million people. The economy of Western Asia is diverse and the region experiences high economic growth. Turkey has the largest economy in the region, followed by Saudi Arabia and Iran. The UN is the only institution that deviates from the commonly globally known definition of West Asia.

Iran

The Islamic Republic of Iran has a rich history and culture going back thousands of years. The establishment of the Persian Empire by Cyrus the Great in 559 BC marked the birth of a unified land by bringing Iranians and non-Iranians under a single ruler. A major characteristic of Iran's economy since the 1960s has been its strong dependence on oil revenues. Iran was declared an Islamic Republic in 1979 (1358) following a national referendum. The history of the disabled in Iran is quite similar to that of any other country. There was no visible ground for the development and expansion of NGOs for the disabled (DNGOs). It was not until the 1980s and the increasing presence of educated people with disabilities in society that the circumstances existed, including general and cultural awareness, to establish DNGOs which would be managed by disabled for the disabled. There is no single source of disability information. The organisations that collect information on the issue include: The Statistical Center of Iran;

Educational organisations; The Janbazan Foundation; The State Welfare Organisation; The Social Welfare and Rehabilitation University; and Non-governmental organisations.

Most public buildings are not accessible for those using wheelchairs or walking aids. Many of the buildings, including office buildings and education and training centres, have steps at their entrances and those that don't have other bar. The Government of Iran has developed a special programme for disabled war veterans. One focus of this programme has been on creating a suitable physical environment. Most members of society are not familiar with the potential of people with disabilities. Until recently, disability was considered a taboo and was kept hidden. To overcome the negative cultural attitudes toward the economic participation of people with disabilities, the State Welfare Organisation is planning to prepare a number of educational films focusing on the abilities of people with disabilities for the general public. The Islamic Republic of Iran signed the United Nations' Economic and Social Commission for Asia and the Pacific (ESCAP) Resolution 48-3 on the Asian and Pacific Decade of Disabled Persons, 1993 to 2002 (1372-1381).

Iran has not yet ratified the ILO's Vocational Rehabilitation and Employment (Disabled Persons) Convention No. 159 (1983). The only article in the Labour Law of the Islamic Republic of Iran to deal with the employment of people with disabilities is Article 119 and its addendums. The other legal case dealing with the issue of the employment of people with disabilities and the war wounded is the Bill on Supporting the Employment of the Disabled, which was passed by the cabinet in 1985 (1364). The Iranian Constitution recognises the rights of people with disabilities in the following Article: Article 29 [Welfare Rights] (1) To benefit from social security with respect to retirement, unemployment, old age, disability, absence of a guardian, and benefits relating to being stranded, accidents, health services, and medical care and treatment, provided through insurance or other means, is accepted as a universal right. The government must provide the foregoing services and financial support for every individual citizen by drawing, in accordance with the law, on the national revenues and funds obtained through public contributions.

There are three main national organisations that deal with issues related to people with disabilities: the State Welfare Organisation, the Janbazan Foundation, and the Special Education Organisation. There is currently no specific body in the country tasked with coordinating the activities of the various organisations or NGOs working on disability issues. With the approval of the Constitution of the Islamic Republic of Iran, including the provisions of Principle 29, those making policies regarding the affairs of people with disabilities decided to provide due service to special groups by establishing an organisation operating in harmony with existing efforts. There were 800 rehabilitation centres nationwide in 2001. The largest segment of these was 182 physical therapy centres that served 81,887 people. A law passed in the Parliament in 1990 (1369) established the Special Education Organisation as a government-run organisation attached to the Ministry of Education. After pre-school, this organisation is in charge of the education of the disabled pupils at the primary, secondary, and high school levels.

Officially, there are 247 NGOs dealing with disability issues. NGOs focusing on people with disabilities can be classified within three groups. First are those organisations providing vocational rehabilitation leading to employment; the second group includes organisations providing employment services to people with disabilities, such as the Qazvin Association of the Disabled. A third category provides services to the elderly, including those with disabilities. Schooling is provided for free to all Iranians until the end of secondary level. In order to care for and educate children in accordance with their age and capabilities, day care centres were established under the auspices of the Ministry of Labour and Social Affairs, as well as through other organisations. The appearance of rehabilitation was formalised in 1968 with the ratification of a law to establish the Rehabilitation Organisation, affiliated with the Ministry of Labour and Social Affairs. Of course, before that time activities in this field were carried out by the military, or the Lion and Sun Society (an organisation like the Red Cross. In the early 1980's, with the ratification of the Islamic revolution council after the victory of the Islamic revolution, the Rehabilitation Organisation was among several institutions that merged to create the Welfare Organisation. A disabled child needs proper nutritional care as much as, if not more than, a non-disabled child. Malnutrition can potentially prone a child to further morbidities, and thus imposes further suffering to the affected child, his/her family and the whole community, both emotionally and financially. However, many factors may predispose a child (disabled or non-disabled) to malnutrition even in developed countries with high health standards.

Iraq

In Iraq people with disabilities are from all genders, ages, and socioeconomic status. Many people with disabilities have limited or no access to healthcare and rehabilitation, education, skills training, and employment opportunities. During the years of war, and all the man-made disasters throughout, have further increased the number of disability, to approximately reach two-million people. Disability stands at an intersection of public health, human rights and development. During the national launch of the Global Report on Disability, that took place at Helena Rehabilitation Centre in Erbil, Iraq, the Minister of Health of the Kurdistan Regional Government. Government of Iraq represented by the Ministries of Health and their partners were committed to continuing efforts to uphold human and health rights for the estimated two million brothers and sisters living with disability. WHO is supporting the Ministry of Health to strengthen and improve its disability registration system, to ensure health systems are more inclusive and responsive to the needs of people living with disabilities.

While incremental improvements have been made with regards to Iraq's recognition of the rights of persons with disabilities (PWDs), more tools are needed to organically integrate PWDs into society so that their inclusion is sustainable, and that they are empowered to participate both socially and economically. Ten years after the United States went to war, one of the most common numbers associated with the conflict is the tally of Americans killed. According to Linda Bilmes, a Harvard University professor who's written extensively on the long-term costs of the wars, the ultimate bill for war costs comes due many decades later. A staggering 45 per cent of the 1.6 million veterans from the wars in Iraq and Afghanistan are now seeking compensation for injuries they say are service-related. That is more than double the estimate of 21 per cent who filed such claims after the Gulf War in the early 1990s.

Syria

The two and half-year conflict have made persons with disabilities extremely vulnerable to gross rights violations on a daily basis. Living in the midst of conflict is physically and emotionally distressing, but all the more so for persons with disabilities who face the same if not greater barriers in times of armed conflict. Syria is a State Party to the Convention on the Rights of Persons with Disabilities. Under Article 11 of the Convention, parties are obliged under international humanitarian and human rights law to take all necessary measures to ensure the protection and safety of persons with disabilities in situations of risk, including armed conflict. Refugees have faced extreme emotional upheaval, and the stress of being displaced is often all the greater in the case of persons with disabilities.

Prior to 2011, the number of people with disabilities was estimated at more than 500,000. Today, their needs are very important, but the current crisis makes even more difficult the work of professionals. The World Health Organisation estimates that 15 per cent of any population will be persons with disabilities. The United Nations High Commissioner for Refugees, Government of Lebanon, local actors and the wider international community are providing Syrian refugees with assistance to meet their basic needs. There may be even higher rates of disability in communities that have fled war or conflict, as people acquire new impairments from injuries and/or limited healthcare. Persons with disabilities remain one of the most vulnerable and socially excluded groups in any displaced community. Conflict can lead to physical injuries, extreme duress from witnessing traumatic events, a breakdown in health services, lack of access to proper food and safe water, and can leave children separated from families, homes and schools, sometimes for years.

In 2009, IECD launched project in order to meet their needs in continuous education and to support local association. Since 2009, IECD has worked with several Syrian associations to improve the care of children and adolescents who suffer from cerebral palsy, mental retardation or other disabilities. In Homs and Aleppo, IECD provides technical and financial support to partner organisations which continue to offer quality care to disabled children. Since 1996, the Said Foundation has been running a Syria Disability Programme with the aim of improving the lives of children with disabilities. SFD is committed to a child-focused approach that puts the needs, rights and potential of children with special needs first; that aims to built capacity from individual to organisational level; and that engages with all stakeholders in a participative, non-discriminatory, non-sectarian and non-political manner. SFD follows the National Plan for Disability as a framework for its support.

Since early 2013, Handicap International has deployed rehabilitation teams to northern Syria to provide physical therapy to the injured and disabled. The organisation has worked with injured Syrian refugees in Jordan and Lebanon since the summer of 2012. Handicap International helps hospitals and clinics care for injured refugees by supplying rehabilitation equipment and organising physical therapy sessions for patients. Displacement has a severe negative impact on the daily life of disabled and injured people, who need urgent access to health services but also long-term medical, financial and social support. The lack of psychosocial or mental healthcare is a major challenge, significantly affecting the well-being of older people but also placing an additional burden on their families.

Yemen

Yemen is located in the south-west corner of the Arabian Peninsula bordering the Arabian Sea, the Gulf of Aden, the Red Sea, the south of Saudi Arabia and the west of Oman. Today's Republic of Yemen was established with the merging of the former North and South Yemen in 1990. When individuals with different levels of functioning encounter barriers to health services, education, employment, public services, and infrastructure, they are disabled. That is, disabled in the sense that their ability to participate in economic activities and lift themselves from poverty suffers. Disability is to be understood as an interaction between human functioning and an environment which does not account for different levels of functioning. The concept of disability has in the past twenty years developed from a medical model focusing on the individual's impairment to a social model of functioning and participation, focusing on limitations in activities and restrictions in social participation.

There is no accurate information or studies on the situation of disabled people, just piecemeal and uncoordinated studies. In recent years, the government has given attention to data management on disability for programme planning and policy-making. Impairments and disabilities are due to road accidents, hereditary issues, accidents from construction work and firearms, poor medical infrastructure and medical mistakes, iodine and vitamin 'A' deficiency, poor maternal health related to malnutrition, and other environmental factors including epidemics, natural disasters, pollution, and inaccessible environments. While Yemen is not a war zone country, land mines are still causing a number of impairments, especially among the rural population.

There are a number of causes for the high prevalence of disability. One set of causes is communicable diseases such as meningitis, rubella and polio. Another set of causes includes malnutrition as well as iodine and vitamin 'A' deficiency. Malnutrition lowers resistance and exposes both mother and child to increased ill-health and potential long-term disablement. The National Disability Strategy outlines the vision, objectives and principles of a rights-based approach to disability. Yemen does not have a disability strategy but is planning to develop one with support from the World Bank. There is a disability law that guarantees rights to access social services and employment opportunities, but this is not enforced according to our informants. Under the law (61/1999) *'Concerning the care and rehabilitation of disabled persons'* disabled people are accorded all the rights due to them under the constitution. The law allocates responsibility for this sector to the Ministry of Social Affairs and Labour (MoSAL) and to the Disability Fund (DF).

The healthcare system delivers services at three levels: primary, secondary and tertiary levels. The primary level is peripheral and combines Health Units. Modern maternity care is poorly developed. Yemen still has incidents of polio. The consequences for the individual are various degrees of paralysis. There is uncertainty about the prevalence of disability as for many other poor countries. Disabled persons are considered to be vulnerable and looking after them and being kind to them is a religious duty which people will also be rewarded for. Teasing people with disabilities is forbidden. There is a story in the Quran about a blind man who called on the prophet but the prophet was busy and did not pay him much attention. A majority of the people live in villages scattered in the mountains. Village life in the rural areas is based on agriculture which produces both cash crops such as qat and crops for home consumption.

Oman

Oman is located in the farthest south-east of the Arabian Peninsula and extends between latitudes 16°40 and 26°20 north and longitudes 51°50 and 59°40 east. Its western borders are with the United Arab Emirates and the kingdom of Saudi Arabia while the Republic of Yemen lies on its southern borders. The Arabian Sea is on east borders. It overlooks two seas, the Arabian Sea and the Gulf of Oman. In the Sultanate, the collection of data about the disabled is carried by the Ministry of National Economy, Ministry of Health and the Ministry of Social Development, through Censuses, specialised surveys and administrative records. The 1993 Census was the first experience for the Sultanate with regard to collection of disability. 2003 Census adopted the definition endorsed by the United Nations in 1998 which considers the disabled as the person faced with continuous difficulties which impair his/her ability to exercise a number of activities which are appropriate to his capabilities. The Sultanate is striving to best use its human resources, seeking to secure job opportunities, increase economic growth and maintain equilibrium between supply and demand in the labour market.

To reduce unemployment and limit dependence on foreign labour, since 1988 the Government has pursued the Omanisation policy, aiming at gradually increasing the participation of qualified Omanis in the labour market with special emphasis on increasing female participation in both the public and private sectors to replace expatriate labour. The participation of Omani women in different economic sectors is one of the important and influential contributions in the Omani society. Women's participation in informal sector jobs such as handicrafts and traditional industries is becoming increasingly significant. It is very essential to consider the facilities available in the school and university complexes which have to be suitable for the needs of disabled students. There should be careful attention to the design of the classrooms that has to accommodate the type of disabilities exhibited by students who are included in the classroom. Diverse severity of the disabilities represented between the disabled students in the class might need special demands from the classroom teacher.

The Ministry of Social Development (MoSD) stipulates that two per cent of total posts in government offices should be reserved for the disabled. The rule for private sector states that any establishment with a staff of more than 50 is encouraged to hire candidates with disability. According to MoSD, there are currently 2,417 registered disabled jobseekers in the sultanate. The ministry has said that it is working to find out the total number of disabled in the country, the nature of their disabilities, their capabilities and how many of them are willing to work. Disability is still a taboo subject in the country. MoSD is carrying out a study to find out the number of disabled, their unemployment rate. Of the total 2,543 people covered under MoSD's various schemes from 2006 to 2013, 627 people with disabilities were provided jobs with the help from MoM.

Even though employers are reluctant to hire the disabled as they feel they would not do the best possible job, experts say this is not always the case. There are many jobs in both the public and private sector which can be done efficiently by a disabled person. With Oman having more than 62,000 disabled people, Oman Association for Disable (OAD) is calling for the government to set up an authority that will look into their grievances. There is a need to make offices in both the public and private sector disabled-friendly. It's just a matter of providing accessibility, as most of them get on really well without much additional support. Oman has become more disabled-friendly in recent years and the society has become much more understanding, though a structured approach to the needs of the nation's challenged population may be required, according to an official at Oman Association for the Disabled. OAD tries to participate in all local, regional and international events and seminars related to disabled people. Oman has always tried to be as disabled-friendly as possible. Random disregard for the disabled from individuals should not be misconstrued as the overall policy of Muscat or Oman. Society clearly empathises with the disabled.

Saudi Arabia

Saudi Arabia is the largest country in the Middle East occupying approximately four-fifth of the Arabian Peninsula and has a population of approximately 28,376,355. Disability is a condition or function judged to be significantly impaired relative to the usual standard of an individual or group. The term is used to refer to individual functioning, including physical impairment, sensory impairment, cognitive impairment, intellectual impairment, mental illness, and various types of chronic diseases. The Kingdom of Saudi Arabia is based on the Islamic Sharia, which emphasises human rights, and particularly person with disabilities rights to live with dignity and benefit from welfare. The Kingdom has focused on person with disability since initiation of its social and economic development plans two decades ago, with the government providing modern and appropriate welfare means for person with disabilities to help them adapt to society, the environment, and life by taking into consideration their intellectual, psychological, physical and livelihood features. Royal family members support public and private organisations and facilities for person with disabilities, and donations are raised from wealthy families in the Kingdom. Several royal foundations are quite active in terms of developing infrastructure for persons with disabilities, but the type and quality of services are not well known, as these institutions are still under development and not fully operational. Institutions for persons with disabilities are more prevalent in urban than rural areas, with an uneven distribution of facilities irrelative to persons with disabilities distribution.

The Ministry of Education operates the Noor Institute for the Blind, the Amal Institute for the Deaf and the Institute for the Intellectually Disabled. Over the last two decades, the Ministry of Health has established numerous rehabilitative services for persons with disabilities and other residents in the country. The Ministry of Education provides educational rehabilitation through educational institutions such as the Noor Institute for the Blind, Amal Institute for the Deaf and the Institute for the Mentally Retarded. The Ministry of Labour and Social Affairs has established Vocational Rehabilitation Centres for persons with disabilities. These centres focus on rehabilitation of physically or intellectually disabled persons between the ages of 15 and 45. Saudi Arabia is one of the 12 Eastern Mediterranean countries that collaborate with WHO in CBR, planning and implementing national programmes on rehabilitation.

Islam, as a divine religion is against discrimination whether based on any racial, gender, colour, or ability. In the Holy Book of Qur'an, Allah the Almighty has assured us (translation of meanings) in Surah Al-Inshirah that *"with every hardship there is relief,"* (94:5) and in Surah Al-Baqarah that *"Allah burdens not a person beyond his scope"*. In Surah Yusuf the Qur'an states, *"Truly no one despairs of Allah's soothing mercy, except those who disbelieve"*.

The number of disabled in the Kingdom has reached 720,000, roughly four per cent of the Saudi population, according to the Social Affairs representative in Madinah. The ministry spends a total amount of about SR 1.6 billion annually for the benefit of the disabled. Those rehabilitated at all centres in the country number 11,645. In all the Arab countries the needs of individuals who suffered impairments are almost ignored during implementation of development plans. If correct and adequate data of disability is collected and identified early; planners will find it easy to create projects suitable for the disabled people in future. The number of the disabled is probably far higher than the values estimated, because those who are searching for jobs are not the elderly, children, complex disabled, and never ever most of the disabled women. The topic of disability is an important societal issue. Depending upon the definition used, it is currently estimated that 3.73 per cent of the population has functional disabilities which limit their independence. In the Saudi society, the incidence of consanguineous marriages is high. As a result, the risk of disabilities associated with genetic causes is significant. Saudi society's view of people with disabilities is based on a simple notion of disability, and comprises helplessness, continuing dependence, being home-bound, low quality of life and lack of productivity. There are great opportunities in to develop new information about disabilities, particularly their nature, their incidence, and their impact on society.

United Arab Emirate

The United Arab Emirates (UAE) is a federation of seven emirates situated in the southeast of the Arabian Peninsula and bordering Oman from the east and Saudi Arabia from the west. The UAE consists of seven emirates, which are Abu Dhabi, Dubai, Sharjah, Ajman, Umm al Quwain, Ras alKhaimah and Fujairah. The capital and second largest city of the United Arab Emirates is Abu Dhabi. It is also the country's centre of political, industrial, and cultural activities.

The United Arab Emirates has been updating federal laws regarding the rights of the disabled. Since 2006, several laws have been enacted, but not all are regularly enforced. Wheelchair accessible entrances are available in most of the newer parts of Dubai. It is the older parts such as Karama, Satwa and some parts of Deira that still lack these conveniences. The Roads and Transportation Authority (RTA) has been the most active government department in including special needs considerations in buildings. The RTA announced special rates for disabled travellers using public transport. The reported rates have ranged from free travel to a 50 per cent discount. However, nothing has been implemented as of October 2010. According to UAE Federal Law No. 29 of 2006 (In Respect of the Rights of People with Special Needs), schools may not discriminate or refuse admission based on learning difficulties or special needs. Implementation of this law has been slow, but is compulsory for both private and public schools. Disabled Driver Training Course using specially adapted vehicles with hand controls for people with waist downwards disability. His Highness Lieutenant General Sheikh Saif Bin Zayed Al Nahyan, Deputy Prime Minister, Minister of Interior and Deputy Chairman of the Emirates Identity Authority, has affirmed that the attention paid by the UAE to people with disabilities has deep roots in *"our Islamic religion"* and the humanitarian approach of the UAE society, which was firmly established by the founder of the UAE and builder of its civilisation the late Sheikh Zayed Bin Sultan Al Nahyan, may Allah have mercy upon him, and was followed by President His Highness Sheikh Khalifa Bin Zayed Al Nahyan, may Allah protect him, based on his belief that people with disabilities are a significant segment of the UAE society that deserves all support, care and attention.

Dubai Government cares for people with disabilities and allocates the most convenient parking closest to buildings and ramps for them, provided they have the handicapped stickers on their cars. All stickers are free of cost with citizens, residents and tourists eligible to apply to the RTA. In case a person with disability prefers to drive his/her own car, they can enroll for a disabled driver training course from Emirates Driving Institute and obtain their own license, before applying for a special parking permit. The UAE has always been committed to providing education and careers for disabled people and integrating them into productive and social life by supporting and equipping them with new life skills. More than 800 disabled students have been placed in different schools in Abu Dhabi since 2007. There are over 800 hearing-impaired individuals in Abu Dhabi. Most parents never understand the unique care which deaf children need. Most deaf students in the UAE travel abroad for study, either to school, university or work, as they find the appropriate social and educational setting, which encourages their independence and increases their learning opportunities.

People with disabilities will receive training, job opportunities and career development under a deal between the Ministry of Social Affairs and Majid Al Futtaim Ventures. As part of the agreement, handmade goods and products by people with disabilities will be promoted at Majid Al Futtaim's retail outlets and at centres owned by the ministry. The goal of the partnership is to help integrate people with disabilities into society. The roles and rights of people with disabilities are protected under a federal law issued in 2006 and amended in 2009. More work is needs to be done to support the rights of disabled people, according to the UAE's Minister of International Cooperation and Development. Dubai is home to an estimated 5,452 disabled people of which remain out of work despite efforts by the government to root out discrimination in the job market. Data is scarce, but the cost to the government of unemployed Emiratis with disabilities is thought to be huge. CDA launched campaigns to encourage employees in the private sector to hire Emiratis with disabilities. The agency offers training and support to firms that sign up to the Elkayt scheme, and matches candidates to their recruitment needs. Some of Dubai's largest firms, including Al Rostamani Group, Al Futtaim Group and Al Ghandi motors, are enrolled in the programme. Although Dubai has a general law that safeguards the rights of people with disabilities, it stops short of forcing employers to make adjustments to the workplace to accommodate them.

The UAE Ministry of Social Affairs develops programmes for special needs rehabilitation and care, and prepares implements and supervises vocational training programmes. In addition, several government, semi-government and private entities provide services to UAE nationals and residents with special needs. The Abilities Development Centre for Special Needs has been organising the Challenge Championship for people with special needs at Al Jazira Club since 2010, in conjunction with the UAE National Day celebrations. Law No. 29/2006 to protect the rights of people with disabilities was approved by President His Highness Shaikh Khalifa Bin Zayed Al Nahyan in 2006. The Law guarantees the rights and protection in health, education, work and entrepreneurship and public services for physically challenged people. The law extends to all kinds of disability but doesn't classify disability by name, for example, autism.

UAE Government always encourages disable people for involving in sports. When people with disabilities compete on the sports field, the surge of energy that propels them forward makes them feel anything is possible. Sport, experts agree, helps the disabled to heal, grow and enjoy a new lease on life. For everyone, playing sport is a way to renew life, to invigorate the mind and body, to strengthen moral. Putting athletes with disabilities back into action is a key part of helping them to maintain their general health. Sport helps people with special needs progress and develop a great deal because it transfers them to a new stage. Sport is a common language, it creates a unified force. Ali Harzallah, the president of the Arab Union of Sports for Special Groups, says the key is to use the healthy body parts and train the disabled areas. There are a lot of disabled people who have proven themselves through sport; a lot, not just a few. According to the federal law, Article 2 guarantees the rights of the person with special needs and to provide all the services within the bounds of his abilities and capacities. The special needs may not be a reason to hinder the person with special needs from obtaining such rights and services especially in the field of welfare and social, economic, health, educational, professional, cultural and promotional services. Article 3 state guarantees for the person with special needs the equality with people without special needs and non-discrimination due to special needs in all the legislations. It also guarantees to observe the same in all the policies and programmes of economic and social development, and to take the appropriate procedures to prohibit the discrimination based on the special needs.

Ministry of Social Affairs (MSA) is one of the federal ministries and includes several departments. One of these departments is the Department of Welfare and Rehabilitation of

Persons with Disabilities (DWRPD). This department oversees and manages the affairs of persons with disabilities in the UAE, it is authorised to coordinate with federal and local departments to implement Federal Law No. 29 of 2006 (Disabilities Act). The issue of accessibility for persons with disabilities is one of the recent issues in the Arab countries and in the UAE in particular. Before the enactment of federal Law No. 29 of 2006 regarding the rights of persons with disabilities accessibility was a few of slopes or ramps built incorrectly in front of some shopping centres and other public buildings. Federal Law No. 29 of 2006 *"Regarding the Rights of Persons with Disabilities"* has significantly helped to raise public awareness of the concept and issue of accessibility in the UAE. In particular, Articles 22 and 23 of Chapter V are dedicated to mandate accessibility for persons with disabilities: Article (22): states: *"Every person with disability shall have the right to an accessible environment and to have access to everything that others have access to."* Article (23) mandates: *"The concerned bodies shall ensure coordination to set the engineering criteria and specifications for establishments and public facilities, issued by a Decision of the Cabinet, based on the recommendation of the Minister. The decision shall regulate the application of these criteria, specifications and exceptions, with regard to the qualification of establishments for the use of persons with disabilities, in order to meet their needs and ensure their safety. MSA has been also involved in publishing a set of technical manuals and accessibility checklist to help architects and designers to provide accessibility for persons with disabilities in public places such as shopping malls, hotels, airports, public parks,....... Etc.*

Jordon

The historical development of the Jordanian state is inseparable from the flight of refugees from other countries in the region, including 800,000 Palestinians who fled to Jordan from conflict in the West Bank and from the Gulf War. The Gulf War and ongoing conflict on the West Bank have impacted on the number of disabled people in the country. There has been a rise in the number of people with conflict-related impairments (especially among the refugee community), while the capacity of government and localities to respond to the needs of disabled people is under strain. There are severe shortage of specialised centres, personnel, funds and facilities to support disabled people, especially in rural areas. There is also practically no support from governmental and non-governmental bodies to disabled people who wish to live independently in the community, although the Queen Alia Fund has started to change this with a small programme to support disabled people who live in their own home through providing adaptations such as appropriate toilets and a ramp. Accordingly, impairment may be explained as an act of God, designed to test the faith of individuals and their capacity to accept that fate with gratitude and patience. This perception of disability as a test of the faith and as God's will plays a major part in shaping attitudes towards disabled people. There is evidence that Arab societies (including Jordan) have tended to treat disabled people as people with no prospects and no potential, and have viewed impairment as something shameful and as an ordeal to be endured by the family. Disabled people constitute, and/or are perceived to constitute, an inevitable and significant drain on family resources and a potential source of damage to family status.

Community-based Rehabilitation (CBR) has been put forward as one way to increase the availability of services to disabled people in developing countries. In Jordan, the eight CBR programmes - serving a total of 500 people which are currently under way or in the planning stages have been spearheaded and funded by international agencies and organisations. The International Year of Disabled Persons was the first time that thought was given to legislation as a means of improving the situation of disabled people. Jordan signed the Convention on the Rights of Persons with Disabilities on 30th March 2007, and ratified it on 31 March 2008. The Convention was then integrated in the domestic legal system through its publication in the National Gazette of Jordan. Jordan adopted the Law on Disabled People Rights (no. 31 of 2007), which repealed the previous law on entitled Persons with Disabilities Care Law (no. 12 of 1993).

Around 7.7 per cent of Jordanian households have at least one person with a disability, a report said, as the Kingdom joined other world countries in marking International Day of People with Disability. Women with disabilities suffer double discrimination and are more prone to sexual and physical abuse, sometimes in the form of medical intervention. Meanwhile, the Higher Council for the Affairs of Persons with Disabilities (HCD) said it has concluded collecting data for a study on the situation of women with disabilities in the central and northern regions and started conducting a survey on the needs of special education cadres and an assessment of social rehabilitation programmes. Jordan ratified the UN Convention on the Rights of People with Disabilities in 2008. The UN launched International Day of People with Disability to shed light on the needs and rights of over one billion people worldwide living with a form of disability. Jordan adopted a new law in 2007 to protect the rights of people with disabilities. The existing services are still insufficient, and there is a growing demand. In 2006, Handicap International launched a project to promote the rights of people with disabilities in Irbid and Kerak, in the west of the country. Another project started in 2008 in the town of Dlail to forge partnerships with local associations and to develop adapted public services to improve the participation of people with disabilities in the community.

Lebanon

Disabled people are continue to be marginalised in terms of education and employment. The lack of equal access to quality education has contributed to a situation where people with disabilities are often deprived of gaining basic knowledge and skills necessary to becoming full members of society. Under Lebanese Law, all children with disabilities have the right to attend regular schools. In terms of employment, while both private- and public-sector companies are obliged to employ specified quotas of disabled workers, the positions available often come with low wages and without health and social benefits. Strengthening the role of the parents and supporting the role of NGOs, which often replace public institutions, are key to inclusion. Out of an estimated Lebanese population of 4.5 million, an estimated ten per cent have disabilities, according to a 1990 UNDP survey.

In 2007, Lebanon signed the Convention on the Rights of Persons with Disabilities. Even earlier, in 2000, the country's Parliament passed Law 220/2000, which concerns the rights of persons with disabilities. The ministry has rendered a mere five schools accessible for persons with physical disabilities, the draft report goes on, while a great number of public schools still refuse people with disabilities. Disabled children in Lebanon have rights to education, set out in domestic laws on disability and education and in the Convention on the Rights of the Child (CRC). According to the CRC, education should help disabled children achieve social integration. Although disabled children have specially protected rights to education, international studies show that disabled people have less education and fewer qualifications than the general population. In Lebanon, most mainstream schools exclude children with disabilities. As a result, most disabled children miss out on education altogether. The minority of disabled children who get an education pay a heavy price.

Lebanese Physical Handicapped Union (LPHU) is a grassroots organisation built by and for people with disabilities. It believes that they have an important role to play in arriving at vision of society by working with people with disabilities, a population that has been traditionally marginalised. As such, their specific mission is: (a) To defend the rights of people with disabilities; more specifically to work towards their access to equal opportunities and a quality life and to ensure that their basic needs (health, education, employment, socio-economic integration, freedom of choice) are fully respected and guaranteed; (b) To eradicate marginalisation and gender discrimination from the lives of people with physical disabilities; (c) To mobilise people with physical disabilities to speak on their own behalf; and (d) To promote the spread of a culture of inclusion and right of participation.

Bahrain

Bahrain is preparing a national strategy to protect the rights of disabled and promote the inclusive development of people with disabilities through mainstreaming of services such as education, health and housing. The initiative is being spearheaded by the United Nations Development Programme in collaboration with the Social Development Ministry and Higher Committee for the Care of the Disabled. The year-long project began more than four months ago and includes conducting background studies and compiling existing data. The disability policy in Bahrain is expressed in law, in guidelines adopted by the Government and in guidelines adopted by the National Disability Council. The emphasis is on rehabilitation, anti-discrimination law, accessibility measures, individual support, and prevention. Since the adoption of the Standard Rules the Government has taken action in order to convey the message of full participation.

The rights of persons with disabilities are protected by a combination of special and general legislation. The only mechanism available in order to protect the rights of disabled persons is different societies or organisations. A national authority, local Governments, and the organisers/providers of services are reviewing the operation of accessibility standards. Sign language is used as the first language in education of deaf people. Government measures for encouraging media and other forms of public information make the services accessible. Legal provisions mandate the representatives of persons with disabilities to participate in policy-making and to work with Governmental institutions. Bahrain's Ministry of Social Development on 18th September, 2013 announced a 9.6 million Bahraini dinar ($25.7 million) plan to provide care for disabled people and people with special needs. The plan aims to cover around 99,000 disabled people in cities across the kingdom and is due to run until 2016 in co-operation with the UN Developmental Programme. The plan provides for assisting disabled people with healthcare and education and empowering them economically and socially.

Israel

The State of Israel provides services to children and adults with physical, sensory, mental health and intellectual disabilities. In recent years, Israel ratified the United Nations Convention on the Rights of People with Disabilities and legislation has been passed to promote the inclusion of people with disabilities in the community. About one million Israelis, or 25 per cent of the working-age population, have at least one disability, and almost half have more than one disability. The rates of disability are much higher for Arab-Israelis and Ethiopian-Israelis. Nearly19 per cent of the working-age population has a moderate-to-severe disability and six per cent a mild disability. Over 260,000 individuals receive some type of disability pension from the Social Security Institute, and the numbers have been growing rapidly. Another 50,000 people receive disability allowances from the Israel Defense Forces. 200,000 receive other forms of on-going income support.

There are more than one and half million handicapped people and their income is much lower than the national average, according to a report published by the Commission for Equal Rights of Persons with Disabilities at the Justice Ministry.

According to the report, 60 per cent of disabled people live on the edge of poverty and one-third of them feel lonely. The report revealed that almost no change has taken place over the past few years in the gap between Israelis suffering from disabilities and the rest of the population, despite new laws and extensive activity on the part of governmental elements and social organisations aimed at improving the situation.

Between 800,000 and one million people of prime working age suffer from disabilities, according to a report by JDC-Israel. The study found that the breakdown of disabilities among this population is 17.5 per cent physical, 9.2 per cent mental, 4.2 per cent cognitive, 4.2 per cent vision and 3.7 per cent hearing. In addition, 2.5 per cent of those with disabilities have a learning disability and 2.1 per cent suffer from a chronic illness. According to the report, about five per cent of the working-age population suffers from severe disabilities. Another 11 per cent have moderate disabilities and five per cent have light disabilities, which do not disturb their daily activities very much. About 220,000 of Israeli children have disabilities, more than half of which are learning and behavioural disabilities. According to the figures, about 80 per cent of people with disabilities have become disabled between the ages of 18 and 65. People with acquired disabilities, the report indicates, face more difficulties in maximising their rights and being recognised as disabled by the authorities.

Since the establishment of the State of Israel in 1948, there has been an intensive effort to develop a set of laws for people with disabilities. However, during the last 50 years, the Israeli Knesset (parliament) has failed to set an integrative and consistent disability policy. The major disability programmes were enacted over a period of years and reflect the varying values and pool of resources available at the time. The three major pieces of legislation for people with disabilities are the Veterans with Disabilities Law of 1959, The Work-Related Disability Law of 1954 and the General Disabilities Law of 1975. The Work-Related Disability Law provides temporary and permanent cash benefits to those injured on the job or who have contracted a work-related disease. The General Disability Law was adopted after most of the other disability programmes were already in place. It seeks to provide a guaranteed minimum income to disabled individuals who are not covered by other programmes. The first impact of disability rights in legislation is evident in the Special Education Law of 1988. This law emphasises the integration and mainstreaming of children and adolescents with special needs.

The United Nations Convention on the Rights of People with Disabilities was adopted by the UN in 2006, signed by the State of Israel in 2007 and ratified by it in 2012. The Convention sets international standards for equality, full participation, inclusion and integration in society, accessibility and autonomy of people with disabilities. The Convention applies standards to various spheres of life such as employment, education and housing. The Convention's implementation requires changes in the legislation and regulations regarding guardianship for people with disabilities and their right to independent living and independent housing in the community. Access Israel, a non-profit organisation dedicated to making Israel an accessible place for all its citizens, including those living with an array of disabilities.

Azerbaijan

Azerbaijan is a member of the UN's Convention on the Rights of Persons with Disabilities. About 4.6 per cent of the Azerbaijani population is registered as disabled or vulnerable. Azerbaijan's Ombudsman protects and promotes human rights, the rights of vulnerable children and people with disabilities. The Heydar Aliyev Foundation aims to improve the living conditions of vulnerable children and adults, as well as assist children and adults with disabilities to integrate into society and earn an income. The Union of Disabled People keeps statistics about people with disabilities, has information about their rights, as well as social projects, news and a photo gallery.

The Azerbaijani government has drafted four socio-medical rehabilitation programmes for disabled people and children. They are part of the 2012-2015 Governmental Programmes on Physical Protection of Disabled Persons, on Social Protection of Disabled Children, on the Rehabilitation of Disabled People and Children and on the Development of the Disability Criteria. The ministry aims to apply European legal and social standards on physically disabled people. These standards suggest that people of this category are able-bodied, employable and have equal rights in society. Azerbaijan, as a member of the Convention on the Rights of Persons with Disabilities, is committed to adjusting the national norms and legislation with international regulations. Over the past ten years, the disabled people's allowances have increased by 9.6 per cent. About 5,000 of the disabled people were provided with apartments and 3,000 with cars. Fourteen regions of the country have rehabilitation centres for the handicapped, where 14,000 disabled have been treated and 7,000 provided with free prosthesis and wheelchairs. Protecting the rights of the disabled in the country is in focus of civil society. Azerbaijani legislation envisions that all people should have access to information.

The Convention on the Rights of Persons with Disabilities and its Optional Protocol was adopted on 13th December, 2006 by the United Nations, and was opened for signature on 30th March, 2007. Azerbaijan ratified the Convention on the Rights of Persons with Disabilities and its Optional Protocol in January 2009, becoming one of the first countries in the region to do so. In line with the requirement under Article 31(1) of the CRPD, Azerbaijan submitted to the Committee on the Rights of Persons with Disabilities a comprehensive state party report on measures taken to give effect to its obligations under the CRPD and on the progress made in that regard within two years after the entry into force of the CRPD for Azerbaijan in January 2011. According to Article 148(2) of the Constitution of the Republic of Azerbaijan, the provisions of the Convention on the Rights of Persons with Disabilities constitute an integral part of the legislative system of the Republic of Azerbaijan. According to Article 148(2) of the Constitution of the Republic of Azerbaijan, the provisions of the Convention on the Rights of Persons with Disabilities constitute an integral part of the legislative system of the Republic of Azerbaijan.

Article 1 of the Disability Prevention and Disabled Persons (Rehabilitation and Social Protection) Act 1992 prohibits discrimination against PWD and CWD. Article 16 of the Labour Code indirectly prohibits discrimination against PWD during hiring, or a change in or termination of employment ... on the basis of other factors unrelated to the professional qualifications, job performance, or professional skills of the employees.... Article 16.2 of the Labour Code directly states that affirmative action measures for PWD shall not be considered discrimination. Article 7(1) of the Law on Individual Labour Contracts indirectly prohibits discrimination against PWD on the basis of other factors which are not related to the working qualities, results of labour, and professional skills of the employee while establishing, altering or terminating the labour relations.

Armenia

Armenia is about to introduce major changes to the way disabled benefits are assessed, so that people will be categorised according to their ability to work. Experts point to a shortage of workplaces with proper accessibility, and warn that the new classification system might be just as open to corrupt practices as the current one. The employment register currently shows 170,000 registered disabled people, of whom 90,000 are considered to be able to work to some extent.

Disability in East Asia

East Asia is the eastern sub-region of the Asian continent. More than 1.5 billion people, about 38 per cent of the population of Asia and 22 per cent or over one-fifth of all the people in the world, live in East Asia. The history of East Asia is predominantly the history of the Chinese Dynasties that dominated the region in matters of trade as well as militarily, such as the Qin and the Han Dynasties. The UN sub-region of Eastern Asia and other common definitions of East Asia contain the entirety of the People's Republic of China, Japan, North Korea, South Korea, Mongolia and Taiwan. The culture of East Asia has been influenced by the civilisation of northern China. East Asia shares a Confucian ethical philosophy, Buddhism, political and legal structures, and historically a common writing system.

People's Republic of China

In China, a disabled person is defined as one who suffers from abnormalities of loss of a certain organ or function, psychologically or physiologically, or in anatomical structure and has lost wholly or in part the ability to perform an activity in the way considered normal. The term disabled persons refers to those with visual, hearing, speech or physical disabilities, intellectual disabilities, psychiatric disabilities, multiple disabilities and/or other disabilities. China has approximately 85 million people with disabilities, according to the United Nations. Experts in the field, including professors of special education, human-rights officials and lawyers representing the disabled, say that the Chinese government, despite some progress, is not doing enough to ensure that people with disabilities have equitable access to higher education or really any education at all. At the end of 2012, more than 90,000 disabled children had no access to schooling, according to the China Disabled Persons' Federation, a quasi-government organisation. Between 2008 and 2012, only 35,000 disabled people were enrolled in mainstream higher-education institutions, the organisation said. To put that in context, nearly seven million people graduated from college in China in 2013 alone.

Nearly 83 million women and men in China or 6.3 per cent of the population had a disability in 2006. Slightly over half of this population (52 per cent) is male, and 48 per cent female. Most people with disabilities (75 per cent) live in rural areas. The Government of China has adopted and implemented a number of laws, policies standards and initiative pertaining to people with disabilities, including their right to productive and decent work. The China Constitution, enacted in 1982 and amended in 1988, 1993, 1999 and 2004, provides a general protection to people with disabilities. The Law on the Protection of Disabled Persons, enacted in 1991 and amended in 2008, safeguards the rights of people with disabilities. The Rehabilitative Medical Education Plan (1992) contains regulations on training and education of rehabilitation doctors and therapists, physiotherapists and occupational therapists. The Rules on the Employment of Disabled Persons adopted in 2007, encourage social groups and individuals to support their employment through various means, and bans discrimination. The Employment Promotion Law (2007) contains an anti-discrimination provision relating to persons with disabilities. The Regulations on Construction of Accessible Environment (2012) require local governments to construct various public facilities to accommodate disabled persons. Established in 1988, the China Disabled Persons' Federation (CDPF) is a unified organisation of/for the 85 million people with disabilities. It is a nationwide umbrella network reaching every part of the country and has been allocated responsibility for issues related to disability by the Government.

The Government has established a quota system that requires all public and private employers to reserve no less than 1.5 per cent of job opportunities for persons with disabilities, in accordance with specific regulations established by local provincial governments. Those who fail to meet the required quota must pay a fee to the Disabled Persons Employment Security Fund, which in turn supports vocational training and job-placement services for people with disabilities. The State Council Working Committee on Disabilities has been established to steer and coordinate the disability work. It is composed of 36 ministries and social groups. Social attitudes towards people with disabilities have gone through a gradual, yet fundamental change in China since then, thanks to the active advocacy of people within the disability community, as well as governmental support for disability initiatives.

A 2013 Human Rights Watch report noted that in 2008 the Chinese government ratified the United Nations Convention on the Rights of Persons with Disabilities, which calls for inclusive education at all levels. Still, the report said, the central government in Beijing has no clear and consistent strategy to achieve that goal. China's Education Ministry offered guidance on how to provide the gaokao, the college-entrance examination, in Braille or electronic form to accommodate the blind. Human Rights Watch called this an important breakthrough. The ministry also announced plans to ensure that at least 90 per cent of children with visual, hearing, and intellectual disabilities receive primary and middle school education by the end of 2016. The Constitution in China provides a general principle regarding the protection of people with disabilities, with Article 45 establishing that, *"all citizens ... have the right to material assistance from the state and society when they are old, ill or disabled."* The State develops the social relief, medical, health, and social insurance services required by Chinese citizens with disabilities for them to enjoy this right. Their Constitution also says, *"...the state and society help make arrangements for the work, livelihood and education of the blind, deaf-mute and other handicapped citizens."* The law in China places great emphasis on the importance of rehabilitation, with the government including rehabilitation in national and social development programmes. The Chinese government has both developed and supported rehabilitation programmes with the goal of mainstreaming and facilitating the participation of people with disabilities in society.

South Korea

Foreigners with a disability who are resident in South Korea are entitled to receive the same welfare benefits as Korean citizens. Practical information for people with disabilities, and application forms for the People with Disabilities Card, is available from the local district office. Each disability is allocated a grade and benefits are based on this grade. Benefits depend on the grade of the disability, as well as other circumstances, for example, a family's income and a disabled person's age. Korean law takes into account many types of disabilities for which benefits are granted. These include physical, visual, auditory, linguistic, and intellectual disabilities; brain lesion; developmental and mental disabilities; kidney, heart, respiratory, liver and facial disabilities, as well as ostomy and epilepsy. A person with severe disabilities who is unable to work receives a monthly disability pension from social welfare.

While South Korea has made the leap from poverty to rich nation in a generation, its conservative culture still largely fails to come to grips with the challenges of disability. Choi and other campaigners say the government's assessment system, which determines the access to crucial basic pensions worth up to $100 a month, as well as awarding support services such as home help, is degrading and inhumane. An official at South Korea's Ministry of Health and Welfare, which administers the benefits, says that it is aware of some of the issues and is studying the problem, although it may be moving too slowly for the country's human rights body, which is considering asking parliament to revise the system. On 2nd September, the National Human Rights Commission of Korea ruled that eliminating candidates from job applications due to mental conditions of family members is a discriminatory act.

North Korea

It is no secret that eugenics has been a core goal for many of history's most brutal dictatorships, and North Korea is no exception. So deep is the desire to eradicate any impurity from the population that no one with a handicap or disability is even permitted to live in the capital city of Pyongyang, even if that disability was acquired through injury or illness. Families with infants born handicapped or disabled are physically removed from the city and relocated to rural areas, where they are far less likely to come into contact with others or to be seen by visitors. North Korea had established their welfare system for the disabled as propaganda to ultimately attract support from foreign organisations that assist disabled people. This was deemed similar to the recent increased attention invested in North Korea's tourism industry, as it is becoming more difficult to secure foreign currency due to sanctions against North Korea from the international community.

North Korea is participating for the first time in the Paralympic Games, a possible shift for a county were disabled people have faced enforced isolation and abuse. North Korea has one of the world's worst human rights records. Activists accuse it of particularly inhumane treatment of the disabled, who number about 1.8 million, some 7.5 per cent of the population, according to the Green Tree Charity Foundation in South Korea. Those with disabilities are sent away from the capital city and particularly those with mental disability are detained in areas or camps known as 'Ward 49' with harsh and subhuman conditions. Any handicapped people have voluntarily moved to other parts of the country. North Korea systematically exiles mentally retarded and disabled people from the capital, so as not to mar its beauty. The North Korean regime reacted typically to the 1990's famine, which killed some two million North Koreans, by putting propaganda into overdrive.

North Korea signing of the Convention took place in the context of continuous modifications made to its legal system after the revision of the North Korean Constitution in April 2009. Among the changes made, Article 8 states that North Korea protects and respects human rights. Since then, it has enacted a series of human rights related regulations, such as its Law on Labour Protection (July 8, 2010) and Laws to Protect Children and Women's Rights (December 22, 2010), making clear its intention to respect or improve human rights. North Korea's signing of the Convention is particularly notable because whereas modifications in the human rights system under the Kim Jong-un regime primarily took place at the domestic level, the Convention on the Rights of Persons with Disabilities is an international law. To begin with, from a legal perspective, North Korean authorities must modify its relevant legal system in accordance with the Convention, before ratification. In June 18, 2003, North Korea passed the Democratic People's Republic of Korea Disabled People Protection Code. However, this law is far from adequate when compared to the Convention. North Korea needs to analyse the contents of the Convention in detail and modify its relevant legal system to address areas of weakness.

Japan

Japan lacks any law prohibiting discrimination against the handicapped, although advocates for the disabled are trying to change that. To be sure, Japan is in many ways one of the most sensitive and civilised societies in the world. Tokyo is one of the few major cities in the world where a blind person can ask a taxi driver the fare on the meter and count on not being cheated. Japanese society emphasises conformity, and the essence of the Japanese proverb about the nail that sticks out gets hammered down is drummed into children from the moment they set off for the first day of school. The disabled are the nails that stick out, and they complain that they get hammered. Japan, like many countries, lags behind the United States in building wheelchair ramps and elevators, although new buildings tend to have them.

With advances in medical technology and improvements in public health and nutrition, the average life span of the Japanese people has markedly increased. As the elderly population expands, the number of bedridden and senile persons who require care is growing rapidly. Welfare measures for the benefit of elderly persons are carried out on the basis of the Social Welfare Service Law for the Elderly, enacted in 1963. Provisions of the Health and Medical Service Law for the Elderly, enacted in 1982 are relevant to maintaining and protecting elderly persons' physical and mental health. Public welfare measures for handicapped persons are carried out on the basis of the Law for the Welfare of Physically Disabled Persons, enacted in 1949; the Law for the Welfare of Mentally Handicapped Persons, enacted in 1960; and the Law concerning Basic Policies for the Handicapped, enacted in 1970. These laws apply to measures for people of age 18 and ever since handicapped persons under the age of 18 are covered by provisions of the Child Welfare Law. Persons designated as physically handicapped are entitled to various public welfare services, including consultation and guidance, special rehabilitation and medical services, the replacement or repair of auxiliary equipment and devices, and accommodation in various types of rehabilitation facilities. To help disabled persons to be self-reliant in society, central and local governments provide economic assistance by purchasing items which they manufacture, and various types of activities have been devised to respond to disabled persons' needs in ways that facilitate their participation in society.

Internationally, the government of Japan signed the Convention of Rights of People with Disabilities in 2007, but it has not been ratified yet. Since the number of countries who have ratified this convention is as many as 138 (as of October 2013), the Japanese government improves various social measures for people with disabilities, and is preparing conditions so that ratification of the convention may be made. Six welfare acts, including the Public Assistant Act, Child Welfare Act, Act on Welfare of Physically Disabled Persons, Act on Welfare of Mentally Retarded Persons, Act on Social Welfare Service for Elderly, Act on Welfare of Mothers with Dependents and Widows, services are provided to people with needs of such services. The National Pension includes a scheme for adults with disabilities. It is called the Disability Basic Pension. The pensioners include the persons who obtained disabilities in his/her childhood and those who were born with disabilities. The Act for Comprehensive Welfare for Persons with Disabilities was promulgated in June 2012, and reorganised the scheme of service for people including children under 18 years old with disabilities. As there are lots of challenges for people with disabilities to be employed, vocational rehabilitation services that include vocational evaluation and guidance, work preparation support, assessment of persons with intellectual disabilities, and comprehensive employment support for persons with mental disabilities are very important.

Philippines

Of the 92.1 million household population in the country, 1,443 thousand persons or 1.57 per cent had disability, based on the 2010 Census of Population and Housing. Of the total PWD in 2010, males accounted for 50.9 per cent while females comprised 49.1 per cent. Males with disability outnumbered females in the age groups 0 to 64 years. The largest excess in the number of males was in the age group 0 to 14 years with a sex ratio of 121 males per 100 females. On the other hand, there were more females with disability than males in the age group 65 years and over.

The general public is now more open and understanding about disabilities, and many individuals, companies and civic or welfare organisations give money or in-kind donations to persons with disabilities. The National Council for the Welfare of Disabled Persons (NCWDP) is responsible for the registration of persons with disabilities in collaboration with local governments, the Department of Social Welfare and Development (DSWD), and other organisations. But the registration system has not yet been able to cover all persons with disabilities for two main reasons: (1) information on registration has not been widely disseminated, therefore many persons with disabilities do not know how to register themselves, (2) there is a lack of access to public welfare office or other public offices to which persons with disabilities could refer for assistance. Most persons with disabilities live in poverty. The National Statistics Office (NSO) conducts a population survey every five years, which includes data on disabilities. The country is still in the process of collecting reliable statistics regarding the situation of disabilities. Ambulation aids, prostheses, or thoses and orthopaedic shoes are mostly directly donated to persons with disabilities. There are currently 94 special education institutions (including The Philippine National School for the Blind, National School for the Deaf and other private institutions), 14 special education centres which are set up within existing schools, 19 boarding schools, 2 hospital schools and 4,292 special education classes in public schools.

Taiwan

Taiwan Access for All Association is a cross-disability, grassroots-organisation, founded in 2004 in Danshui Township, Taipei. It was founded by a group of people with disabilities, family members and friends of the disabled. Taiwan Access for All Association was originally only a web-based network (Accessible Life Network), which provided disability-related news and information by a small group of volunteers with and without disabilities in 2002. Taiwan Access for All Association is governed and staffed by a majority of disabled people. In Taiwan, equal opportunity policies and facilities for people with disabilities are enshrined in law. The Disabilities Rights Protection Act in Taiwan was enacted in July 2007 in compliance with the UN's Standard Rules on the Equalisation of Opportunities for Persons with Disabilities. The metro and subway (MRT), trains and Taiwan

High Speed Rail (THSR) are all accessible. New public buses in metropolitan Taipei are fully equipped for easy wheelchair access with designated areas and appropriate security belts. Most traffic lights are equipped with audible signals for the visually impaired, so that they can cross the road safely. Guide dogs travel free of charge on public transportation. The supplementary allowance for people with disabilities includes the following: Subsidies and benefits for adults; VAT rebates for adapting a home; Income tax rebates.

Mongolia

Mongolia is a large land-locked country with a total area of 1.56 million square km. There are several statistics, regarding the disability issue. According to the data from Ministry of Health and Social Welfare, there are around 1,15,000 (4.8 per cent of the total population) disabled people. Another survey (Social Welfare Centre) says, that 67,558 people with disabilities are registered to receive different kinds of social subsidies for disability and 44,800 people receive certain types of social allowance for disability. The disabled people are belonging to the poorest and most vulnerable group of the society. After transition to the market economy and budget cuts for health, social welfare and education services, all disabled people faced a huge variety of problems, having a very limited capacity for competency in a free market system. Rehabilitation services are centralised at the capital city of Ulaanbaatar. Disabled people from rural areas often can not receive them at all due to the financial difficulties connected to transportation.

Before 1989, the socialist government of Mongolia pursued a policy of institutionalising disabled people, building a network of special schools and residential care facilities. While this system addressed basic needs for disabled people, it excluded them from social and political life. Following the political and economic changes of the 1990s, this institutional framework collapsed. Due to shortages of funds and resources, special schools in rural areas were closed and social benefits for disabled children decreased dramatically. The Ministry of Education, Culture and Science, National Commission of Human Rights in Mongolia, Child's fund of United Nations, Save the Children, SIDA (International Development Agency in Sweden) and Association on Parents with Disabled children are developing together information-advertisement materials and organising trainings to change traditional tendency of community and to increase public awareness about the right, special needs, skills and opportunities of disabled children.

Many international organisations are cooperating and contributing in the field of disabled children such as Child Fund of United Nations, UNESCO, Asian Development Bank, Save the Children UK, World Vision Mongolia, SIDA, VSO, ADRA, JICE, Canada Fund and AIFO. The Ministry of Education, Culture and Science is implementing a programme *"Education for Disabled children"* with financing from International Development Agency in Sweden/SIDA. The Ministry of Education, Culture and Science has collected statistics about the children with disabilities who attend secondary schools and kindergartens. Based on the statistics it was obvious that teachers can not determine and classify who are the disabled children as there is no combination methodology and concrete concept about the disabled children.

Disability in Central Asia

Central Asia is the core region of the Asian continent and stretches from the Caspian Sea in the west to China in the east and from Afghanistan in the south to Russia in the north. The idea of Central Asia as a distinct region of the world was introduced in 1843 by the geographer Alexander von Humboldt. In modern contexts, all definitions of Central Asia include five republics of the former Soviet Union: Kazakhstan, Kyrgyzstan, Tajikistan, Turkmenistan, and Uzbekistan. Central Asia is an extremely large region of varied geography, including high passes and mountains, vast deserts, and especially treeless, grassy steppes. Central Asia has long been a strategic location merely because of its proximity to several great powers on the Eurasian landmass.

Kazakhstan

The recognition of persons as being legally disabled apparently began in the first quarter of the twentieth century, when Kazakhstan joined the Soviet Union. From 1980 through 1991, the conceptual framework for determination of disability status was set by the 1956 State Pension Law of the USSR. Disability status was defined by loss of the ability to work. The 1990 USSR Disability Law then became the basis for republican disability laws, which were enacted with similar names and identical content in Kazakhstan, Uzbekistan, Belarus, and probably other USSR republics. In the early 1990s, the economic crisis in Russia and Kazakhstan made all possible sources of income desirable for all potentially disabled persons, forcing them to apply for the disability status ignored before.

Employment of people with disabilities of working age is still a big problem. About 70 per cent of the people with disabilities, or around 400,000 people, are employable. Only 11 per cent of them (45,000 people) are employed. The low employment rate is the result of poor work of the authorised government agencies that do not inform the employers of the benefits they could get from employment of disabled people. State policy on disabled persons' protection is based on the Constitution of Kazakhstan and other legislative norms. State policy guarantees creation of social, economic, legal conditions to provide equal opportunities for life and integration to the society for the disabled persons. State carries out measures aimed to protect rights and freedoms, to ensure disability's preventive measures and to establish equal conditions for disabled people in the society.

Kazakhstan fully supports the adoption and implementation of non-discrimination legislation at the domestic level, as the Sapporo Declaration states:"*We demand that every country adopt and implement anti-discrimination legislation and policies that ensures the equalisation of opportunity for disabled people. We also recognise that non-discrimination and equality of opportunity must be intrinsic components of any human rights convention for disabled people.*" Whereas media images and stories influence thinking and establish social norms, people with disabilities have endured misrepresentation, defamation and lack of representation in the media. They are seldom seen as individuals beyond the framework of their disabilities. The legacy of demeaning, isolating, and institutionalising people with disabilities embedded negative and inaccurate beliefs and attitudes about what it means to live with a disability.

Kyrgyzstan

For decades now, parents in Kyrgyzstan whose children happen to have a disability have been routinely advised to place them into institutional care. Maternity nurses, relatives, neighbours, doctors: it seemed like the whole of society is against these children staying with their birth families. More and more staff in institutions welcomes the idea of a gradual transformation of their institutions into family support centres. The Government of Kyrgyzstan proclaims itself to be against discrimination against children with disabilities and is in favour of their inclusion into society. In the last five years, two new laws were introduced that specifically stipulate the rights of children with disabilities. While one included important changes in language to be used to refer to children with disabilities, the second new law which has been introduced on State benefits in the Kyrgyz Republic stipulates the provision of monthly social benefits for children with disabilities. Identification of children with disabilities at the level of healthcare organisations is carried out through referrals to medical institutions (hospitals). There are still various types of institutions under the supervision of various ministries, where children with disabilities are admitted according to age and type of disability. Children with disabilities have also become part of the reforms undertaken by the government in childcare system lately. Monthly benefits for children with disabilities are defined based on the medical indicators used to categorise children by different conditions and types of disability.

The Kyrgyz Republic is strongly committed to protecting the rights of disabled children. The Government of Kyrgyzstan supports the principles of social inclusion and non-discrimination against disabled children. Kyrgyzstan is a relatively young country and, like many other countries in the region, it is still shaking off the legacy of the Soviet model of care of disabled children. The UN Convention on the Rights of the Child, ratified by the government of the Kyrgyz Republic, gives every child equal rights, regardless of whether or not they are disabled. Disabled children have equal rights to a family, to participate in social activities, and to an inclusive education. According to the statistics of the Ministry of Labour and Social Development, on 1st January, 2007 there were 19,931 disabled children, approximately one per cent of the total child population. Overall governmental responsibility for disabled children is mainly delegated to various Ministries and their governmental organisations. The Ministry of Health is responsible for the registration and rehabilitation of children. According to sources in the Ministry of Labour and Social Development there are over 40 NGOs in the country working on the social integration of disabled children. Kyrgyzstan took an important step in 2006 by adopting the Children's Code, a legislative instrument calling for priority attention to be paid to child-related issues.

Kyrgyzstan legislation concerning disability consists of the Constitution, the Law on the Rights and Guarantees of Persons with Disabilities (2008), other relevant legal regulations and acts as well as international treaties. Moreover, Kyrgyzstan laws specify that ratified by the Kyrgyz parliament international treaties take precedence over the national legislative provisions. Kyrgyzstan was one of the first countries in CIS to ratify in 1994 the UN Convention on the Rights of the Child, in 1995 the UN Convention against Discrimination in Education and much more lately in 2006 to adopt The Children's Code of the Kyrgyz Republic. Article 16.2 of new 2010 Constitution of the Kyrgyz Republic states that among other listed forms of discrimination nobody can be discriminated on the basis of disability. Article 45 affirms the right of everyone to have education and articulates that general basic and secondary education in state educational establishments is obligatory and free of charge. The main legal document on disability is the law on the Rights and Guarantees of Persons with Disabilities adopted in 2008. It guarantees access to education for persons with disabilities. The state guarantees for the persons with disabilities the necessary conditions for having access to information, education and vocational training.

Tajikistan

Tajikistan is working with the Government to improve disability rehabilitation services and increase the numbers of trained rehabilitation professionals in the country. With financial support from the United States Agency for International Development (USAID), they have started a three-year project to develop a national policy, and improve the system and services for physical rehabilitation, with a focus on community-based services and human resource development. Significant numbers of children in the country have multiple impairments, including cerebral palsy and congenital anomalies, and need rehabilitation services. Other groups in need include people affected by stroke, diabetes and road traffic accidents, and older people with reduced functioning or mobility. In 2010, Tajikistan experienced a large polio outbreak affecting 712 people, mostly children. Many of these have developed impairments and need long-term physical rehabilitation care.

The total number of registered persons with disabilities is more than 164,000, according to statistics provided by Tajikistan's Ministry of Labour and Social Protection of the Population (MLSPP) in September 2012. Tajikistan remains the only Central Asian country that has not signed the CRPD. Tajikistan's new law *"On Social Protection of Persons with Disabilities"* from December 2010 represents significant progress in comparison to the 1991 law of the same title. The 2010 law states that it shall determine the legal, economic and organisational basis for ensuring the social protection of disabled persons and provide them with equal opportunities of vital activity and integration into society. Tajikistan is already a state party to more than 60 international conventions. Under these conventions, Tajikistan has obligations regarding children with disabilities, women with disabilities and landmine survivors. Accession to the CRPD will synergise the implementation of national laws and responsibilities under other international conventions. To improve disability services, the Tajikistan government created the Disability Coordination Council in early 2012.

According to Tajikistan law no. 458 on Social Protection of the Disabled in the Republic of Tajikistan (Law); a disabled person is defined as a person with physical, intellectual or mental abnormality. Despite Tajik legislation aimed at supporting and offering privileges to persons with disabilities, not all have been able to benefit from their rights or gain these privileges. Taking into consideration this reality, the government has recently worked out and approved social protection reform and relevant programmes. Tajikistan is currently undergoing transition from socialism to a market economy and in the process of carrying out social welfare reform. Disability prevention is a major strategic objective, as the level of disability or number of persons with disabilities is perceived as important indicators of the level of health of the overall population. Prior to 1992, persons with disabilities received free medical rehabilitation at a special physiological clinic in the city of Khujand based on a decision by the Special Medical Checking Commission of policlinics. The lack of wheelchairs is a problem. There are a few organisations that carry out the vocational rehabilitation programme. The international organisation, ORA International, conducts a range of activities aimed to help persons with disabilities adapt to boarding schools by teaching sewing, shoemaking, joinery and knitting. Community-based Rehabilitation is an effective way to activate disability-related activities.

Turkmenistan

Deaf and Blind Society of Turkmenistan (DBS) with the support of the United Nations Development Programme, teaches people with disabilities basic literacy and how to function outdoors. From 2005 to 2009, the programme helped give more than 220 visually and hearing-impaired individuals a new start in life. About 80 per cent of graduates got jobs: some people from the provinces set up their own private businesses at home, while others work for DBS. UNDP has helped DBS train sign-language interpreters to support DBS efforts in training the hearing impaired, including children. It bought minibuses, as well as computer equipment to produce audio books.

Joint project of UNDP and Turkmen Society of blind and deaf persons (TSB and TSDP) is aimed at social integration of women with disability. Besides special trainings, the training visits to the ministries, social organisations, meetings with representatives of mass media, with women – leaders, lawyers, workers of culture, education, and medical doctors are organised for them. They will share with their experience in professional career. Turkmenistan became the first country in the Central Asia, which acceded to the Convention on rights of disabled persons in September 2008 and ratified the Facultative Protocol to it in 2010. Being based on previous experience of co-operation, the Representative office of UN Development Programme in Turkmenistan in 2012 announced new project, which common goal is further advancement of social integration of people with disabilities and creation of contacts between TSB and TSDP, state institutions, law enforcement agencies, private sector and international organisations.

Uzbekistan

The Law on Social Security of Disabled People in the Republic of Uzbekistan, Article 1 defines a person with disability as one who is in need of aid because he/she has physical or mental problems. Daily activities such as moving, orientation, speech, behavioural control, and/or work on one's own are completely or partly limited. There are 327,199 Persons with Disabilities, which makes up 1.33 per cent of the total population of the country. Among them, 80,711 were newly registered in 2000. The Constitution and other acts of the Republic of Uzbekistan regulate all the personal, social, and economic rights of persons with disabilities. The central government exercises strong authority over local governments regarding persons with disabilities welfare administration. Medical treatment and rehabilitation is conducted in all medical and prevention institutions within the Ministry of Health system for all types of diseases. The social security of Persons with Disabilities is a critical task for the Government of Uzbekistan. Social security includes ensuring free access to social infrastructure. The Uzbek government perceives the need to create good work facilities for the vocational rehabilitation of persons with disabilities.

A major issue for those at the home and thousands like them across Uzbekistan is the social protection of disabled people. The Uzbek constitution provides that *"every person has the right to social support in old age, in the event of the loss of ability to work, in the event of the loss of a provider, and in other cases anticipated by law. Pensions, allowances and other forms of social assistance may not be lower than the officially established sustenance minimum."* Doctors responsible for assessing patients' capacity for work have allowed patients to be de-registered as disabled because they *'no longer have any permanent disability'*. According to the UNICEF, the number of children registered as disabled increased from 70,000 in 1996 to 125,000 in 2005. They are cut off from their families and community from an early age, often segregated in large facilities and special schools. Almost 20000 disabled children are currently in institutions for disabled. Indeed, Uzbekistan is the first CIS country that adopted a law on social protection of people with disabilities, as well as a state programme on the rehabilitation of people with disabilities. Work is also underway in the country in terms of inclusive education and promotion of the right of children to live in a family environment.

Disability in South-East Asia

Southeast Asia is a sub-region of Asia, consisting of the countries that are geographically south of China, east of India, west of New Guinea and north of Australia. Very little is known about Southeast Asian religious beliefs and practices before the advent of Indian merchants and religious influences from the 2nd century BCE onwards. Western influence started to enter in the 16th century, with the arrival of the Portuguese and Spanish in Maluku and the Philippines. The vast majority of Southeast Asia falls within the warm, humid tropics, and its climate generally can be characterised as monsoonal. Even prior to the penetration of European interests, Southeast Asia was a critical part of the world trading system.

Indonesia

Indonesia has in 1999 ratified the Discrimination (Employment and Occupation) Convention 1958 (No. 111). Nevertheless, it has yet to ratify the Vocational Rehabilitation and Employment (Disabled persons) Convention (No. 159). In October 2011, Indonesia ratified the UN Convention on the Rights of People with Disabilities (UNCRPD). The ratification of the UN convention, which promotes the equal treatment of disabled people, is an important step towards improving rights for disabled people. People with disabilities are recognised as among the most vulnerable groups, facing discrimination in access to education, skills training and employment. PROPEL-Indonesia aims at to support the addressing of gaps in policy and legislative protection on employment and training of persons with disability to ensure they are consistent with international standards.

Handicap International launched its operations in Indonesia in January 2005, when it provided victims of the tsunami in Aceh province with physiotherapy services, psychological assistance and financial support in order to help survivors rebuild their lives. The organisation now works in a wider variety of fields via its office in Yogyakarta. The Government of Indonesia and non-governmental organisations provide health, education and other social services for persons with disabilities. However, many projects and facilities are concentrated in the larger cities. Education facilities for persons with disabilities provide rehabilitation and compulsory education. Persons with disabilities frequently face obstacles when seeking job opportunities. Ministry of Manpower of Indonesia has taken the initiative to implement measures to promote the placement of persons with disabilities in the work force. Sensitivity to the use of disability-related terminology remains an issue as seen in the use of terminology such as handicap and mentally handicapped. The major approach Indonesia takes to prevent disabilities is through strengthening the health system and services including immunisation, nutrition programmes and the referral system. According to the UN report, the provision of rehabilitation services within Indonesia begun in 1950 and has strengthened ever since due in part to the National Development Plan, as well as regional and international movements on rehabilitation services. In 1996, the Social, Home Affairs, Education and Culture, as well as the Religion Ministries decided to provide financial aid to children with disabilities and transportation to schools for children living in remote areas or so that they could attend boarding schools.

UN Convention on the Rights of Persons with Disabilities (2006) and its Optional Protocol is the most achieved international legal instrument on disability. Indonesia ratified the UN Convention in November 2011. ILO Convention No. 159 and Recommendation No. 168 also regulate rights of persons with disabilities. The Government of Indonesia is yet to ratify this ILO Convention. Business cases indicate that workers with disabilities make productive employees and often perform better than non-disabled workers with regard to attendance, work safety and job retention. In order to assure effectiveness and productivity of workers with disabilities, it is important that the company conducts a job analysis. This will give valuable information to the person with disability and ensure him/her that he/she will perform the tasks in the best way. For an improved productivity and a pleasant work environment good communication and friendly relationships among staff are necessary. With supports from the United Nations Partnership on the Rights of People with Disabilities (UNPRPD) and in collaboration with various stakeholders including ILO and UNFPA, the event counted with the participation of Disabled People Organisations from several regions of Indonesia.

Malaysia

There are 445,006 people with disabilities registered as of 2012. However, as registration is voluntary, it is not reflective of the real numbers in the country. Malaysia's has taken an important step to protect the rights of people with disabilities by ratifying the Convention on the Rights of Persons with Disabilities in 2010.

The Government has adopted the Persons with Disabilities Act 2008 and provides social protection services in areas such as health, rehabilitation and education for children with disabilities guided by the National Policy for Persons with Disabilities and the National Plan of Action for Persons with Disabilities. Despite the establishment of the Persons with Disabilities Act in 2008, the law is still not fully enforced. Basic facilities for the disabled in buildings and other amenities are still lacking. More has to be done to raise awareness of the rights of the disabled community and the problems that they face in their daily lives. The Persons with Disabilities Act of 2008 states that disabled people should be treated equally with access to public services and facilities. Further, the law noted that the government and pertinent providers should make necessary improvements in ensuring availability to services for the disabled.

In Malaysia, the government has shown its commitment towards improving the quality of life among its population of people with disabilities, by signing the Proclamation on Full Participation and Equality of People with Disabilities in the Asia and Pacific Region, on May 16, 1994. On February 25, 1998 the Cabinet approved the establishment of the National Coordinating Body known as the National Advisory and Consultative Council for People with Disabilities, to replace the National Implementation Committee for the well-being of the Disabled, which had been formed on August 30, 1990. A number of national social welfare and social service policies secure the rights of the disabled people. The National Welfare Policy 1990 aims to create a stable and secure society, self-reliance, equalisation of opportunities, fostering the spirit of mutual help, and support towards enhancing the caring culture. The National Social Policy 2003 emphasises to enhance and ensure that persons with disabilities enjoy equal rights and full participation in the Malaysian society. The Policy focuses on 15 priority areas namely, advocacy, health, rehabilitation, education, employment, personal safety and social protection, support services, social development, human resource, participation, research and development, housing, children and women disability, and accessibility. The objectives of the National Policy for Persons with Disabilities 2007 are to achieve social integrity and stability, national fortitude and well-being for a progressive and established Malaysian society.

Thailand

Nearly two million women and men, or approximately three per cent of the population, have a disability. A majority of people with disabilities live in rural areas. The Government of Thailand has adopted and implemented a number of laws, Cabinet resolutions, regulations and policies pertaining to people with disabilities, including their right to productive and decent work and to basic services, workers' compensation, social security and entrepreneurship development. The Thai Constitution, adopted in 1997 and amended in 2007, contains anti-discrimination provisions based on physical or health conditions and guarantees accessibility to social welfare and services for persons with disabilities. The Declaration on Rights for People with Disabilities, approved and signed by the former Prime Minister, is a pledge made by the people of Thailand to persons with disabilities. It is now used as a reference in the provision of services for people with disabilities.

More than 90 per cent of Thais are Buddhist. In the teachings of Buddhism, disability is an outcome of a vice that a person had in his/her previous life. On the other hand, Buddhism teaches to have mercy on the weak. Thailand experienced a serious economic crisis in 1997. Large numbers of employees were laid off and persons with disabilities were no exception. Disability-related organisations have appealed to the government to set elevators in all stations, and succeeded in obtaining a government promise to do so within the next five years. The Ministry of Education designated 1999 as the year of education for disabled persons and laid down several plans to enlarge educational opportunities for persons with disabilities through the promotion of integrated education in regular schools and the improvement of special education.

Thailand had been actively involved in the drafting of the Convention on the Rights of Persons with Disabilities since the beginning through its active participation in the CRPD Ad-hoc Drafting Committee. The Royal Thai Government has consistently developed disability policies aimed at improving the quality of life of persons with disabilities and enhancing their dignity. According to the 2007 National Statistics Office data, Thailand has 1.9 million persons with disabilities, consisting of about

2.9 per cent of the entire population (63 million persons). Thailand's commitment to the disability movement is demonstrated at the highest level. The Prime Minister chairs the National Committee for the Empowerment of Persons with Disabilities, which has the authority to formulate policies and regulations as stipulated by law. A sub-committee has been set up in every province of the country to implement policies and enhance the protection of disabled persons at the local level. Accordingly, the Government has issued a regulation which requires that every registered person with a disability is entitled to a Disabilities Allowance of 500 Baht per month. In 2010, approximately 440,400 persons with disabilities were provided with such an allowance. Moreover, those persons who are over 60 years old are also entitled to an Old Age Allowance of 500 Baht per month, in addition to the Disabilities Allowance.

The prevalence of people with intellectual disability is approximately one per cent of the population. The population of Thailand is about 67 million with a growth rate of approximately 1.79 per cent per annum. In 1974, Ministry of Public Health reformed the service system integration as comprehensive services, prevention, promotion, treatment, and rehabilitation for physical, mental, and intellectual disorders. In 1979, Ministry of Public Health applied the Primary Health Care (PHC) strategies to develop the Intellectual Disability (ID) services in term of mental health element by training village health volunteers, ten persons from each tambon (7,255 tambons), to search for cases of psychosis, mental retardation / intellectual disability, and epilepsy. The department of special training for disability including Intellectual Disability under Ministry of Education provided three schools for children with intellectual disabilities and also built up many special schools for people with intellectual disabilities. Education Law clarified that all children must have compulsory education for nine years which also includes the ID children, if they are able to learn.

In Thai culture, especially in the rural area, Intellectual Disability children and adults are taken care by their families and stay in their own homes. The Disabled Persons Promotion and Development Life Quality Act came into force on 18th September, 2007. It repeals and replaces similar legislation passed in 1991. The Act establishes a National Commission for Promotion and Development of Disabled Persons Life Quality (the Commission). This authority has power to draft master plans for these purposes, to issue regulations, to cancel or prohibit any act which discriminates against disabled persons, to consider support of any public or private sector activities concerning the disabled, to specify standards or to certify organisations for the disabled, and other matters. Unfair discrimination of the disabled by policies, rules, regulations or procedure by a public authority, private organisation or private individual, is made illegal. Unfair discrimination includes any act or omission, not directly intended to discriminate, but the result of which causes a disabled person to lose rights or benefits which a person should receive by virtue of being disabled. A fund for the promotion and development of the life quality of the disabled is to be established, to protect and develop the quality of life of the disabled, to provide assistance, rehabilitation, education and employment of the disabled.

The National Health Security Office has recently announced its plans under the White Canes project to provide training for more than 68,000 blind people nationwide to help them to live independently. The course which lasts for 120 hours will teach skills to facilitate as much as independence as possible, or to teach a level of functionality that requires the minimum of assistance for the blind. From the National Statistics Office 2009 Survey, 64.8 per cent of persons with disabilities over 15 and 45.5 per cent over 60 were unemployed. The number of persons with disabilities who were employed is 35.2 per cent. Most of the employed persons worked in the agricultural and fisheries sectors, which accounted for 19.4 per cent of the total. On 22th June, 2010, the Government approved the draft Ministerial Regulation which increases the proportion of disabled persons from 200:1 to 100:1 and requires the annual contribution to the Fund to be an amount equal to the minimum wage a disabled worker would have been paid. The Royal Thai Government also provides entrepreneurship loans from the Rehabilitation of Disabled Persons Fund as investment fund with five years repayment term with no interest rate. The Constitution of the Kingdom of Thailand B.E 2550 (2007) states that a person shall enjoy an equal right to receive education for the duration of not less than 12 years, which shall be provided by the State, and be of the requisite quality standard, and without charge. The indigent, the disabled, persons of infirmity or persons suffering from a specific state of difficulty shall be accorded the right under paragraph one, and be entitled to such support from the State so as to enable them to receive education comparable to that received by other person.

Myanmar

In Myanmar, the concept of person with disabilities generally refers to a person with physical or intellectual disability. Most citizens in Myanmar are Buddhists and according to their belief, persons with disabilities have done something wrong in their past lives which have resulted in their disability. Public awareness activities, considered to be the focal point for the successful implementation of disability-related programmes, have been planned for the long-term. Ministries concerned with disability, especially the Ministry of Health and the Ministry of Social Welfare, Relief and Resettlement, together with NGOs, have worked towards creating awareness through various activities, special programmes, advertisements and the presentation of daily activities of special schools on television. The law on Rehabilitation and Employment of persons with disabilities was first enacted in 1958. For the time being, the existing law is being reviewed in preparation for the fourth draft law for persons with disabilities, which is being prepared to provide more disability-related services and programmes.

The Ministry of Health has a programme for early detection, intervention and management of disabilities. Immunisation, prenatal care, health education and information on the care of newborn babies are part of the programme. Immunisation has been implemented to prevent polio and other debilitating diseases. Considerable progress has been made on rehabilitation through hospital-based rehabilitation services, community-based rehabilitation and the production of low-cost technical aids. The Myanmar Disabled Sports Federation was formed in 1989 with the aim of promoting sports activities, which can eventually promote self-confidence and self-reliance in persons with disabilities. The social and vocational rehabilitation sector is supervised by the Department of Social Welfare (DSW). National Rehabilitation Hospital provides training for nurses, physiotherapists and technicians for assistive device etc. In terms of International NGOs, there are some activities focused on disabilities. For example, World Vision International has cooperated in the medical treatment and rehabilitation of the hearing impaired with the Eyes, Ears, Nose and Throat (EENT) Hospital. JICA has provided training opportunities in Japan for persons with disabilities, disability-related personnel or administrators.

Government of the Republic of the Union of Myanmar, newly elected in October 2010, has already initiated ensuring the rights of people with disabilities, at the national level through the international level. The Myanmar government signed the Bali Declaration on Inclusive Development for People with Disabilities on 17th November, 2011, and the Convention for Rights of Person with Disabilities on 7th December, 2011. People in Myanmar think about disability in a traditional way. A family will usually regard a disabled person as a burden. And often a disabled person can feel like a burden because he or she doesn't have a chance to lead a productive life. Government-funded facilities for the disabled are limited. For a nation of 56 million people, there is just one school for disabled children, one vocational training centre for adults, and one rehabilitation centre - all in the commercial capital Yangon. The disabled make up around 2.3 per cent of the population, or some 1.3 million people, according to government figures. Stigma and lack of mobility hamper them in their efforts to get a good education and a job. They are isolated and excluded from society. As children they cannot go to school; as adults they have little or no income because it is almost impossible for them to get employment. The Education Ministry's policy is to provide opportunities for disabled children in ordinary schools, but problems remain.

Vietnam

Vietnam has one of the world's highest rates of people living with disability per capita. According to the 2009 national census almost eight per cent of the country's population had a disability, although more recent statistics from the World Health Organisation estimated the figure to be approximately 15 per cent. A vast majority of people with disabilities in Vietnam, or 75 per cent, live in rural areas and attend school at rates far below those of non-disabled persons. The Government of Vietnam has adopted and implemented a number of laws, policies, standards and initiatives pertaining to people with disabilities, including their right to productive and decent work. The Constitution of the Socialist Republic of Vietnam was adopted in 1992 and amended in 2001 by the National Assembly. The protection of people with disabilities is enshrined in Articles 59 and 67. The Vietnam National Law on Disability (2010) includes the establishment of the inter-agency National Coordinating Council on Disability (NCCD), the enactment of the barrier-free access code, standards for public construction and for public transport, and several disability inclusion provisions in the Vocational Training Law. Vietnam also works to achieve targets set in a new Asian and Pacific Decade of Persons with Disabilities for the period 2013 to 2022. Make the Right Real, the new decade, launched in November 2012, aims to promote the full realisation of the rights of persons with disabilities, including through the ratification and implementation of the UN Convention on the Rights of Persons with Disabilities in the Asia-Pacific region. Vietnam has a large disabled population due to war and the disease, poverty, and low quality and use of formal healthcare resulting from its low income country status.

In 1998, the National Ordinance on People with Disabilities Act was passed by the Vietnamese National Assembly, which put into place a series of initiatives which sought to advance the rights and interests of people with disabilities. The Ministry of Labour Invalids and Social Affairs (MOLISA) oversees the protection of the rights of people with disabilities and the implementation of protective legislation. The National Action Plan to Support with Disabilities (2012-2020) is currently working on issues such as improving accessibility to public buildings and transportation, early intervention, inclusive education, and medical and legal services. It also aims to provide vocational training and employment for 250,000 people with disabilities.

Lao People's Democratic Republic

The mountainous topography of Lao PDR, lack of transportation and communication infrastructure and inadequate budget has created difficulties in the provision of educational, health, immunisation and rehabilitation services for persons with disabilities. There is a lack of human resources directed at assisting persons with disabilities in becoming self-sufficient and raising their capacity to contribute to national social and economic development and security. Publicity campaigns on the prevention of disability, rehabilitation and promotion of equal rights have been carried out. Individual government ministries have their own programmes for the prevention, identification and early intervention of disabilities. There are still cases where parents hide the existence of children with disabilities, as they think disability is a curse or an embarrassment to the family, or they do not think treatment or rehabilitation is warranted for their children with disabilities. Provincial rehabilitation services are provided through 18 provincial hospitals under the NCMR because NCMR is responsible for persons with disabilities at the village and community level. The National Centre for Medical Rehabilitation (NCMR), which was established in 1962, is subordinate to the Ministry of Health. The centre was originally established as a prosthetic centre, but has provided disability-related services since 1975. The Ministry of Labour and Social Welfare manages 12 villages/hostels for persons with disabilities. There are currently no formal vocational training or rehabilitation facilities specifically for persons with disabilities.

Established in 2001, the Lao Disabled People's Association (LDPA) is a membership-based organisation for people with disability advocating disability rights and providing services to members based on their needs. The LDPA is one of the few officially recognised non-profit associations in Lao PDR. The LDPA creates strong partnerships with government and non-government organisations at local, national, regional and international levels. Due to the lack of availability of professional healthcare in provincial Laos, and the financial costs involved, many people in Laos do not receive healthcare treatment when necessary. This can include sexual, reproductive and maternal healthcare, which contributes to disability, and the treatment of illness or injury, which also contribute to disability. Poverty is widely recognised to be both a cause and a consequence of disability. People with disabilities are less likely to be employed, and likely to be paid less for the same work, which means that overall people with disabilities are much more likely to fall below the poverty line. On the one hand, lack of education and skills means that a disabled person is less employable whilst on the other hand negative attitudes, particularly about productivity, and lack of access to transport and buildings, means that overall work and employment for people with disabilities remains a major challenge.

In Laos, Australia is supporting a Catholic Relief Services pilot project to train schools and communities to help children with disability to access and participate in education. Australia expects to draw on experiences from the pilot to help the Government of Lao to develop a disability-specific module in training packages for teachers, school principals and village education committees. The Government of Lao PDR does not have a written policy on disability. In 1995, though, it ratified the Proclamation of the Asian and Pacific Decade of Disabled Persons, thus committing itself to working towards the goal of assuring full participation and equality of people with disabilities in society. In this context, the Government has announced its intention to strengthen its co-operation with international organisations and NGOs in order to promote the development of people with disabilities in Lao PDR. Under the Lao constitution, people with disabilities, like other citizens, have the right to equality before the law. No specific legislation has been introduced to date to guarantee this right. In 1993, a government decree provided for the education of deaf and blind children, and a school was established in the National Medical Rehabilitation Centre in Vientiane as a first step in its implementation. In 1995, a Compulsory Education Act was introduced, making attendance at and completion of primary school obligatory for all. Schools throughout the country are now obliged to accept children with disabilities and the number of disabled children in school has increased. There are approximately 10,000 war veterans in Lao PDR. The Government provides some services to disabled war veterans through the Department of War Veterans. The policy has been to establish government-run villages, where disabled ex-soldiers and their families live. The National Medical Rehabilitation Centre (NMRC) was set up in 1964 under Ministry for Health, to provide physical rehabilitation services and supply prostheses. The centre also provides training to health professionals. It is reported that the centre has also been involved in the establishment of a village or villages for disabled civilians, similar to those set up for disabled war veterans.

The Government of Lao PDR has adopted a number of laws and policies pertaining to people with disabilities, including their right to decent and productive work and access to basic services. Under the Constitution all citizens are equal before the law. This can be interpreted as meaning that people with disabilities have the same rights as other citizens. Decree on Social Security Scheme for Corporate Employees, 2000, regulates allowances for work accidents and professional diseases and long-term allowances for permanent losses of working ability. Responsibility for disability-related policies and services lies with several ministries, including the Ministry of Labour and Social Welfare, with its Department of Veterans' Affairs, the Ministry of Public Health, and the Ministry of Education. The NCDP, chaired by a representative of the Ministry of Labour and Social Welfare, coordinates efforts to promote the full participation of disabled Laotians. Community-based Rehabilitation is a strategy within community development for the rehabilitation, equalisation of opportunities and social integration of all people with disabilities and their families, using existing structures within the community. Lao PDR also works to achieve targets set in the Biwako Millennium Framework for Action and Biwako plus Five towards an Inclusive, Barrier-free and Rights-based Society for Persons with Disabilities in Asia and Pacific.

People with disabilities have limited access to training and employment-related services. The situation of people with disabilities needs to be viewed in the broader context of the country's least developed country status, with its widespread poverty, low level of educational and skills training opportunities and limited healthcare provision. The current vacuum in vocational training and employment-related services for disabled people should be tackled in a three-pronged approach, catering for the requirements of people with disabilities of working age, many of whom have had little or no education; the needs of disabled school-leavers; and the requirements.

Cambodia

The recent turbulent history of Cambodia has left the legacy of a high number of persons with disabilities of all ages and conditions. Health and social services as well as educational facilities have been destroyed, and there are no financial means or the human resources to cope with the overwhelming needs of disabled persons. Rehabilitation services are still limited, especially services that address the needs of children and women with disabilities. More than 85 per cent of Cambodians practice Buddhism. People believe in Karma: Committing good, receives good; Committing bad, receives bad. In Buddhist theory or teachings, disability is the outcome of a bad deed that a person committed in his/her previous life. A major factor restricting the full participation and equality of opportunities of persons with disabilities is the prevalence of perceptions and practices that prevent them from functioning as full members of society. Skills training, income generation and job placement are important factors for vocational rehabilitation of persons with disabilities. In Cambodia persons with disabilities typically come from the poorest segments of society.

Persons with disabilities are one of the most vulnerable groups as there is limited access to education, skills/vocational training, job placement, income generation opportunities, and other social services. Cambodia's physical environment contains many obstacles for persons with disabilities. The majority of public building entrances and exits are inaccessible to persons with disabilities. The lack of basic health.care, malnutrition, bad hygiene, and poverty are also regarded as serious causes of disabilities. Recently, disabilities caused by traffic accidents have been increasing especially in Phnom Penh due to the rapid and uncontrolled increase in the number of vehicles and motorcycles as well as weak enforcement of traffic laws. Although efforts have been undertaken to promote Education for All including children with disabilities, educational opportunity for adults with disabilities is still minimal. Persons with disabilities experience a lack of accessibility, appropriate support, and encouragement from their families and community.

Estimates of people with disabilities in Cambodia vary significantly. According to the 2004 Census of the National Institute of Statistics, nearly five per cent of the country's population is disabled. The Government of Cambodia has adopted and implemented a number of laws, Cabinet resolutions, regulations and policies pertaining to people with disabilities, including their right to productive and decent work. Law on the Protection and the Promotion of the Rights of People with Disabilities (2009) provides for the right of people with disabilities to be employed without discrimination in the public and private sectors. It requires an employer, who employs more than a certain number of full-time employees, to employ a proportional number of full-time disabled people. It further requires that reasonable accommodation be made at the workplace. Policy on Education for Children with Disabilities (2008) and its Master Plan (2009), aims to ensure the equal rights of all children with disabilities to an equal education with other children. Circular on Improving the Quality Standard for Vocational Training Centres (2008), provides guidelines for the provision of vocational training services and job placement. Cambodia also works to achieve targets set in the Biwako Millennium Framework for Action and Biwako plus Five towards an Inclusive, Barrier-free and Rights-based Society for Persons with Disabilities in Asia and Pacific. Both form regional policy guidelines for the Asian and Pacific Decade of Disabled Persons, which has been extended to 2012.

Handicap International's goal in Cambodia is to support a better future for people with disabilities and to take action to prevent the causes of disability. In 1982, Handicap International's story began in a commitment made by a group of French doctors to help disabled Cambodian refugees living in the vast Khao Dang refugee camp across the border in northern Thailand. CDPO is a movement of Cambodians with disabilities and was established in September 1994. Cambodian Disabled Peoples Organisation (CDPO) is a membership-based, non-governmental federation of disabled people's organisations which legitimately claims to be the organisation representing disabled people. It exists to develop networks of people with disabilities so as to support, protect, serve and promote their rights, achievement, and interests, in order to bring about their fuller participation and equality in society.

Brunei Darussalam

Brunei Darussalam, the Government of His Majesty the Sultan and Yang Di-Pertuan of Brunei Darussalam is strongly committed in ensuring that matters related to people with disabilities, comprising 1.06 per cent of the Sultanate's total population, are given high priority in national agendas. Brunei Darussalam has signed the Convention of the Rights of Persons with Disabilities in 2007 and is currently working towards its ratification. Currently, several policies and programmes are already in place. For instance, financial assistance is extended to people with disabilities under the Old Age and Disability Pensions Act 1954, and micro-credit finance facilities are also available without the need for collateral or a guarantor, to those who wish to embark on income generating project. Brunei Darussalam's strong commitment is also reflected in the establishment of a Special Committee on Persons with Disabilities and the Elderly in 2008 under the purview of the National Council on Social Issues. The Strategic Framework includes a specific chapter that focuses on ASEAN's work in promoting and improving the welfare of persons with disabilities, with activities that aimed to promote network collaboration, inclusive for people with disabilities in ASEAN member state. Poverty and disability have proven to function together in a vicious cycle with each exacerbating the debilitating effects of the other due to poor living conditions, malnutrition and lack of access to healthcare and education.

At present, the Ministry of Home Affairs provides job seeking services for unemployed citizens through a dedicated agency in promoting employment. On the other hand, both the Ministry of Culture, Youth and Sports and the Ministry of Health are providing services which are related to capacity building and promoting employability of vulnerable people. The Employment Order 2009, which came into operation on 3rd September, 2009, is the main legislation governing the terms and conditions of employment in Brunei Darusalam. Since 1954, the Department of Community Development (DCD) has administered social welfare programmes by providing welfare benefits in cash and in kind to the elderly and persons with disability. It also provides rehabilitation and counseling services as well as assistance to the vulnerable in acquiring employment and small business setup to gain self-reliance. As part of the providing elders and persons with disability, the Department of Community Development, Ministry of Culture, Youth and Sports have introduced the Self-Reliance Scheme to its welfare recipients in June 2006. This microfinancing scheme provides seed capital to initiate or expand small scale businesses with exemption of interests, administrative charges, guarantor requirements and collateral. Realising that human resources are the most valuable asset and key to its future, Brunei Darussalam puts priority on the social welfare and development of its people including women, children and older persons.

Brunei Darussalam is a signatory to the Convention on the Rights of Persons with Disabilities in its effort to further promote the rights of PWDs in Brunei Darussalam. A National Committee / Task Force were set up to oversee this Convention led by the Community Development Department. There are various legislations / policies that ensure welfare for all. Special Committee on Disabled and Elderly are established under the National Council on Social Issues. The committee formulates policies and implementations with regards to the disabled and elderly. Although there are regulations and legislation regarding the vulnerable people especially the old age and disabled people in terms of welfare provisions there are still gaps that exist.

Singapore

The employment opportunities for the disabled have increased in the last two decades because of strong economic development. Since the establishment of Bizlink Centre in 1986, a more concerted effort has emerged to assess and place disabled for employment. Despite the improved prospects for employment of the disabled, the number of disabled who have been placed in jobs has not grown significantly. Generally many people including potential employers are still prejudiced against the disabled who are often stereotyped as incapable and have no abilities to manage work. Such an orthodox perception is still prevalent. The number of actual disabled individuals is four per cent of its population and that is by the traditional approach; many of whom fall squarely within the main categories of physical impairment, vision impairment, hearing impairment and intellectual impairment. At present, the disabled are supported by about 186 organisations including special schools and voluntary welfare organisations. Of the 186, only 11 provide some form of sports to the disabled and almost all cater to persons of a specific disability only. The Singapore Disability Sports Council is the only organisation which reaches across all disability groups, offering a wide range of sports at both elite and non-elite levels. It is, in fact, Singapore's national disability sports organisation.

In 1980, a small group of persons with disabilities, with the help of about 100 volunteers, decided to set up an organisation of persons with disabilities for persons with disabilities. This was motivated by the belief that to further the cause of the disability movement one must engage persons with disabilities in that process, thereby empowering those with disabilities to have a voice of their own. Singapore's own Disabled People's Association was not officially registered until 28th April, 1986. DPA provides a unique service, that of being the only organisation that advocates for all persons with disabilities. Since then there have been significant advances towards making Singapore a more inclusive and accessible society. In 2007, the then Ministry of Community Development, Youth and Sports (now Ministry of Social and Family Development) announced the Enabling Master Plan 2007-2011 and this was then followed up by the Enabling Master Plan 2012-2016. DPA has worked with the Government to ensure that persons with disabilities are involved in policy formation and implementation. The Disabled People's Association of Singapore is responsible for research and providing resources, information and support on all matters affecting disabled people: transport, equipment, employment, entertainment, shopping and independent living. It runs assistance schemes for people and their families.

East Timor

East Timor as a new country is facing a number of challenges. Following East Timor's independence, the country is undergoing significant changes while everything needs to start from zero. There are many issues that affect education and the broader economic development. It is estimated that there are at least 48,243 persons with disabilities. The Ministry of Health reports 2,064 persons are presently under its treatment for mental disabilities, although the most recent census results indicate there are approximately 13,308 persons with mental disabilities in the country. There are an estimated 29,488 persons with visual impairments and 17,672 persons with hearing impairments. The Ministry of Social Solidarity provides some social assistance to combat poverty among persons with disabilities in the form of a monthly disability allowance for persons determined by government assessment to be unable to work due to a severe disability. The lack of rails, ramps or alternative entrances were common obstacles to accessibility. Irrigation moats built around the perimeter of buildings frequently prevented access. Raised entrances to control flooding, navigated by high steps, were particularly unmanageable for persons with disabilities. The International Covenant on Economic, Social and Cultural Rights, which Timor-Leste has ratified, provides for the right of all persons to participate in cultural life. Article 30 of the CRPD further guarantees this right. To date, Timor-Leste has taken the most noticeable action on this right.

Timor-Leste has ratified seven core human rights treaties that encompass the promotion and protection of rights of persons with disabilities. Among those treaties, the Convention on the Rights of the Child stipulates specific obligations for States to protect the rights of persons with disabilities that are binding in Timor-Leste. Timor-Leste's Constitution explicitly provides for non-discrimination and equal treatment for persons with mental or physical disabilities. The Penal Code classifies the mistreatment of a person with a disability by a caretaker as a crime punishable by up to six years' imprisonment. Timor-Leste has not signed the Convention on the Rights of Persons with Disabilities. Although it is not a signatory to the treaty, Timor-Leste has already begun to implement measures to address some key aspects of disability rights, while in other areas much greater attention is needed. To date the most significant policy accomplishment regarding persons with disabilities is the Ministry of Social Solidarity's establishment in 2010 of the National Strategy for Community Based Rehabilitation, in line with principles and guidelines set by the World Health Organisation, the International Labour Organisation, UNESCO and the Convention on the Rights of Persons with Disabilities.

Handicap International's goal in East Timor is to champion the rights of people with disabilities and ensure more children with disabilities can attend school. As East Timor emerges from years of conflict, people with disabilities, particularly women and girls with disabilities are amongst the most vulnerable in society. At present, only limited information about the situation for people with disabilities in the country is available. Handicap International has launched a new project in East Timor, where it aims to enhance the skills of people working in the disability sector.

Conclusion

Disability is a universal element in the human condition to which no one is immune. Unrecognised as a problem for development, the condition of being disabled is at the bottom of the development agenda. Government of Bangladesh is now very conscious and become proactive on the need for appropriate policies, laws and plans for the education, training and rehabilitation of the PWDs (Persons with Disabilities). Acquiring accurate data on the prevalence of disability in Nepal is a difficult task for different reasons, including the lack of a common understanding how to define disability and the stigma associated with it. Census 2001 of India has revealed that over 21 million people in India as suffering from one or the other kind of disability. This is equivalent to 2.1 per cent of the population. Among the total disabled in the country, 12.6 million are males and 9.3 million are females. According to the Population and Housing Census of Bhutan, the number of disabled persons is 21,894, representing 3.4 per cent of the country's total population. Ninety five per cent of children with disabilities in Afghanistan do not attend schools due to inaccessible environment. The level of literacy rate for adults and children with disabilities is very low because of the less attention and lack of literacy education facilities in the country. Poverty and disability are closely linked and have detrimental impact on the level of inclusion in society and its overall development. From social perspective, both poverty, and disability are product of capitalist development.

Disabled people are often found among the poorest of the poor and in a developing country like Sri Lanka; disabled people face discrimination at every level of society. In Iraq people with disabilities are from all genders, ages, and socioeconomic status. Many people with disabilities have limited or no access to healthcare and rehabilitation, education, skills training, and employment opportunities. The two and a half-year conflict in Syria have made persons with disabilities extremely vulnerable to gross rights violations on a daily basis. In Yemen, there are a number of causes for the high prevalence of disability. One set of causes is communicable diseases such as meningitis, rubella and polio. The number of disabled in the Kingdom has reached 7,20,000, roughly four per cent of the Saudi population. The United Arab Emirates has been updating federal laws regarding the rights of the disabled. Since 2006, several laws have been enacted, but not all are regularly enforced. The disability policy in Bahrain is expressed in law, in guidelines adopted by the Government and in guidelines adopted by the National Disability Council. There are more than one and half million handicapped people living in Israel and their income is much lower than the national average.

Nearly 83 million women and men in China or 6.3 per cent of the population had a disability in 2006. The Kyrgyz Republic is strongly committed to protecting the rights of disabled children. The Government of Kyrgyzstan supports the principles of social inclusion and non-discrimination against disabled children. Kyrgyzstan is a relatively young country. The total number of registered persons with disabilities in Tajikistan is more than 164,000. There are 445,006 people with disabilities registered in Malaysia as of 2012. Nearly two million women and men, or approximately three per cent of the population in Thailand, have a disability. Vietnam has one of the world's highest rates of people living with disability per capita. According to the 2009 national census almost eight per cent of the country's population had a disability, although more recent statistics from the World Health Organisation estimated the figure to be approximately 15 per cent.

Selected Books

1. Anne Digby, and David Wright (2002). *From Idiocy to Mental Deficiency: Historical Perspectives on People with Learning Disabilities,* Taylor and Francis.
2. Benedicte Ingstad and Susan Reynolds Whyte (1995). *Disability and Culture,* University of California Press.
3. Christopher M. Bell (2011). *Blackness and Disability: Critical Examinations and Cultural Interventions,* LIT Verlag Münster.
4. Colin Barnes and Geof Mercer (2010). *Exploring Disability,* Polity
5. Dan Goodley (2010). *Disability Studies: An Interdisciplinary Introduction,* SAGE.
6. David Wright, Anne Digby, and Digby Anne (1996). *From Idiocy to Mental Deficiency: Historical Perspectives on People with Learning Disabilities,* illustrated.
7. Gary L. Albrecht, Katherine D. Seelman, and Michael Bury (2001). *Handbook of Disability Studies.* SAGE Publications.
8. Gary L. Albrecht, Katherine D. Seelman, Michael Bury (2001). *Handbook of Disability Studies,* SAGE Publications.
9. Geoffrey Dale Arnott (2011). *The Disability Support Worker,* Pearson Education Australia.
10. Graham Pullin (2009). *Design Meets Disability,* MIT Press.
11. Hayley Fitzgerald (2008). *Disability and Youth Sport,* Taylor and Francis.

12. Henri-Jacques Stiker (1999). *A History of Disability*, University of Michigan Press.
13. Jane Seale (2006). *E-Learning and Disability in Higher Education: Accessibility Research and Practice*, Taylor and Francis.
14. Karen P. DePauw, and Susan J. Gavron (2005). *Disability Sport*, Human Kinetics.
15. Lennard J. Davis (1995). *Enforcing Normalcy: Disability, Deafness, and the Body*, Verso.
16. Lennard J. Davis (2006). *The Disability Studies Reader*, Taylor and Francis.
17. Lennard J. Davis (2013). *The Disability Studies Reader*, Routledge.
18. Mairian Corker and Tom Shakespeare (2002). *Disability/ Postmodernity: Embodying Disability Theory*, Bloomsbury Academic.
19. Mairian Corker, and Tom Shakespeare (2002). *Disability - Postmodernity: Embodying Disability Theory*, Continuum Publ.
20. Martha Craven Nussbaum (2006). *Frontiers of Justice: Disability, Nationality, Species Membership*, Harvard University Press.
21. Paul K. Longmore (2003). *Why I Burned My Book and Other Essays on Disability*, Temple University Press.
22. Rob Imrie (1996). *Disability and the City: International Perspectives*, SAGE.
23. Robert McRuer and Anna Mollow (2012). *Sex and Disability*, Duke University Press.
24. Robert McRuer (2006). *Crip Theory: Cultural Signs of Queerness and Disability*, NYU Press.
25. Sharon N. Barnartt (2010). *Disability as a Fluid State*, Emerald Group Publishing.
26. Shelley Lynn Tremain (2005). *Foucault and the Government of Disability*, University of Michigan Press.
27. Simi Linton (1998). *Claiming Disability: Knowledge and Identity*, NYU Press.
28. Soren V. Randall (2006). *Learning disabilities: new research*, Nova Science Publishers.
29. Steven D. Edwards (2005). *Disability: definitions, value and identity*, Radcliffe Publishing.
30. Tobin Siebers (2008). *Disability Theory*, University of Michigan Press.
31. Tom Shakespeare (1998). *Disability Reader: Social Science Perspectives*, Bloomsbury.

4

Disable People in India

"When the sun shall be folded up; and when the stars shall fall; and when the mountains shall be made to pass away; and when the camels ten months gone with young shall be neglected; and when the seas shall boil; and when the souls shall be joined again to their bodies; and when the girl who hath been buried alive shall be asked for what crime she was put to death; and when the books shall be laid open; and when the heavens shall be removed; and when hell shall burn fiercely; and when paradise shall be brought near: every soul shall know what it hath wrought."

–The Quran

Introduction

India is a country in South Asia. It is the seventh-largest country by area, the second-most populous country with over 1.2 billion people, and the most populous democracy in the world. The Indian economy is the world's tenth-largest by nominal GDP and third-largest by purchasing power parity. Following market-based economic reforms in 1991, India became one of the fastest-growing major economies. India is a federation with a parliamentary system governed under the Constitution of India, which serves as the country's supreme legal document. It is a constitutional republic and representative democracy, in which majority rule is tempered by minority rights protected by law.

Federalism in India defines the power distribution between the federal government and the states.

In India there are various government ministry working for welfare of labour. The responsibility of the Ministry of Labour and Employment is to protect and safeguard the interests of workers in general and those who constitute the poor, deprived and disadvantaged sections of the society in particular, with due regard to creating a healthy work environment for higher production and productivity and to develop and coordinate vocational skill training and employment services. The Ministry of Personnel, Public Grievances and Pensions is a coordinating agency of the Central Government in personnel matters, especially in respect of issues concerning recruitment, training, career development, staff welfare and post retirement dispensation. Ministry of Urban Employment and Poverty Alleviation is the apex authority at the national level to formulate policies, sponsor and support programmes, coordinate the activities of various Central Ministries, State Governments and other nodal authorities and monitor the programmes concerning all the issues of urban employment, poverty and housing in the country.

Ministry of Commerce and Industry formulates and implements the Foreign Trade Policy, responsible for matters relating to multilateral and bilateral commercial relations, state trading, export promotion measures and development and regulation of certain export oriented industries and commodities. Ministry of Micro, Small and Medium Enterprises formulation and implementation of policies and programmes/projects/schemes is undertaken by the Ministry with the assistance of its attached office, public sector enterprise, statutory bodies and autonomous organisations. The Ministry of Rural Development implements schemes for generation of self-employment and wage employment, provision of housing and minor irrigation assets to rural poor, social assistance to the destitute and Rural Roads.

Estimation of Disability in India

The history of collection of data on disability/ infirmity dates back to the inception of modern Indian Census in 1872. The questionnaire of the 1872 Census included questions not only on physically and mentally infirm but also persons affected by leprosy. Collection of information on infirmities in each of the successive decadal censuses continued till 1931. No attempt was made to collect information on disability through census of 1951, 1961, 1971. Since 1981 had been proclaimed as the "International Year for the Disabled", it resulted in inclusion of a question on disability during censuses the world over and India was no exception to it. However, the question on only three broad categories of physical disabilities, viz. `Totally Blind', `Totally Dumb' and `Totally Crippled', was canvassed during the House listing Operations of 1981 Census.

In India, the disability sector in general estimates that four to five per cent of the population is disabled. The Planning Commission recognises this figure as five per cent. A report by the World Bank states that while estimates vary, there is growing evidence that persons with disability are around 40-80 million, which constitute between four to eight per cent of India's population. Both Census 2001 and NSS round of 2002 estimate lower incidence of disability in the country. The Census of India showed that the prevalence of disability in India was 2.2 per cent translating into 21.9 million affected individuals, 12.6 million are males and 9.3 million females. Employment rates of persons with disability vary with geographical location (urban or rural), gender, education, and type of disability. According to 2011 Census of India, 68 per cent of India lives in rural areas. Therefore, in the overall population, the number of disabled is proportionately higher in rural areas, accentuated by general poverty considerations and poor access to health services.

As per Census (2001) findings, where not more than one type of disability was recorded for each PWD, about half of them were found to have visual disability, more than a-fourth had movement disability, about ten per cent were having mental disability, seven per cent had speech disability and six per cent were with hearing disability. In rural India, the prevalence of disability was much higher (2.21 per cent) as compared to that in its urban counterpart (1.93 per cent). Again, among males, the prevalence of disability (2.37 per cent) was significantly higher than that among females (1.87 per cent). Among the major states the prevalence of disability (percentage of disabled in total population) was relatively much higher in J & K (3 per cent), Orissa (2.8 per cent), Kerala (2.7 per cent), Tamil Nadu and H.P. (2.6 per cent each) while it was quite low in Maharashtra (1.6 per cent), Jharkhand, Punjab and Delhi

(1.7 per cent each), Karnataka and Andhra Pradesh (1.8 per cent each) etc. More than half of the disabled were of age less than 30 and only one-fourth of disabled persons were of age 50 or more. This is of serious concern as most of the disabled persons were found to be very young. The proportions vary marginally across different sets of population categories.

According to conservative estimates, approximately six per cent of India's population is disabled. And if we go by what the U.N. officials or various other experts say, the figure could very well be in double digits. After all, Australia does admit officially that 18 per cent of their population is affected by one form of disability or the other. United Kingdom's disabled population is estimated at 14.2 per cent, whereas in the United States, it is nine per cent. Rajiv Gandhi was a man of vision. When he became Prime Minister of India, he recognised disability as a core issue. He appointed a high-powered committee under the chairmanship of Justice Baharul Islam. The committee gave its report in 1988 but before anything very concrete could materialise, Rajiv Gandhi went out of power in 1989. The Congress government under P.V. Narasimha Rao picked up the issue from where it had got left and to keep a long story short, *'The Persons with Disabilities (Equal Opportunities, Protection of Rights and Full Participation) Act, 1995'* was passed by the Indian Parliament in December of 1995. It was notified on 7th February, 1996 and thus, it became the law of the land.

National Sample Survey Organisation has been conducting comprehensive nation-wide large scale sample surveys on disability almost once in ten years. According to the survey estimates, in 2002, there were 18.5 million disabled persons in the country and they formed about 1.8 per cent of total population. Again out of them 10.63 per cent suffered from more than one type of the disabilities. The types of disability covered were (i) mental disability in the form of (a) mental retardation or (b) mental illness, (ii) visual disability in the form of (a) blindness or (b) low vision, (iii) hearing disability, (iv) speech disability, and (v) locomotor disability. In the latest NSS survey on disability, the proportion of disabled persons in the population was found to be relatively high (more than 2 per cent) in H.P (2.6 per cent), Orissa (2.5 per cent), Kerala (2.2 per cent), and Punjab (2 per cent) while it was significantly low in Delhi (0.6 per cent), Assam

(1.0 per cent), Jharkhand (1.2 per cent), Rajasthan (1.5 per cent) etc. The first comprehensive survey on physical disability was carried out in NSS 36th round (July –December, 1981) and its follow-up survey in NSS 47th round (July – December, 1991). As per the latest NSSO Disability Survey (July to December 2002) report, the number of disabled persons in the country was estimated to be 18.5 million, who formed about 1.8 per cent of the total population. On the other hand Population Census 2001 found 21.9 million of PWD in India (about 2.13 per cent of total population).

The country's disabled population has increased by 22.4 per cent between 2001 and 2011. The number of disabled, which was 2.19 crore in 2001, rose in 2011 to 2.68 crore—1.5 crore males and 1.18 crore females. Rural areas have more disabled people than urban areas. In Maharashtra, Andhra Pradesh, Odisha, Jammu and Kashmir and Sikkim, the disabled account for 2.5 per cent of the total population, while Tamil Nadu and Assam are among those where the disabled population is less than 1.75 per cent of the total population, says the 2011 Census on the disabled. The growth rate of disabled population is more in urban areas and among urban females. The decadal growth in urban areas is 48.2 per cent and 55 per cent among urban females. Among scheduled castes it is 2.45 per cent. Most of the disabled are those with movement disability. According to the census, 20.3 per cent of the disabled are movement disabled followed by hearing impaired (18.9 per cent) and visually impaired (18.8 per cent). Nearly 5.6 per cent of the disabled population is mentally challenged, a classification introduced in the 2011 census. Road and industrial accidents rendered many movement disabled in 2001-11. Earlier, polio was the major cause for disability but after its eradication from various states, the main cause of movement disability is accidents. Lifestyle disorders also led to many becoming hearing and visually disabled.

Disability is not a charity issue. It is a developmental concern and unfortunately it does not figure in the government's scheme of things and that is really unfortunate. It is a matter that agitates a vast mast majority of people with mental and physical disabilities in India who face discrimination and stigma on a daily basis. They have been campaigning for a new disability rights bill which will have a bearing on their lives. According to government data on disability from the year 2011, there are over 26 million disabled people in India, whose population has increased by over 22 per cent over the past decade. Activists place the figure at anywhere between 60 and 70 million people.

Reasons of Disability in India

India is a vast country with variable social, cultural, geographical and economic background. Polio, communicable and congenital diseases are still major problems adding to the number of disabled. In addition rapid industrialisation, mechanisation of farming and increase in vehicular traffic has increased the number of accidents. Evaluation of disability so far being followed in the country is based on parameters of certain development countries. Even these parameters are not adequate. With different social milieu, economic factors, extended family system, low literacy rate, habits/A.D.L. and lack of statutory provisions for social security India has to develop its own parameters to evaluate the disabilities.

The most dramatic is the reduction in polio, though the almost total elimination of new leprosy cases in official statistics is also an important achievement. A large proportion of disabilities in India are preventable, including disabilities that arise in the circumstances surrounding birth, including maternal conditions, from malnutrition, and from causes such as traffic accidents or workplace injuries. The many causes of disability, and the unclear genesis of some disabilities, make it difficult to define comprehensively the scope of interventions and public policies that impact the level and nature of disability in India. While coverage of polio has progressed remarkably, there appears to have been an overall decline in immunisation rates at the national level, with the most serious decline evidenced in the north-eastern states. The Centres for Disease Control report that in India there were 135 polio cases with onset of paralysis in 2004, and for 2005, India reported only 66 polio cases with onset of paralysis for the year: mostly in Bihar and UP. This compares to several thousand cases per year as recently as 1998, and much higher rates previously.

National Skill Development Mission

Government of India has launched the National Skill Development Mission with an outlay of Rs. 22800 crores in the

Eleventh Plan. The target is to skill 500 million youth in five to seven years. The rationale is to create a pool of trained and skilled workforce, sufficient to meet domestic requirements of a growing economy, with surpluses to cater to the skill deficits in other ageing economies, thereby effectively leveraging India's competitive advantage and harnessing India's demographic dividend. The Directorate General of Employment and Training (DGET) functions as the executive arm of the Ministry and is responsible for the management of all vocational skilling initiatives.

International Standards and Conventions in India

India has ratified the United Nations Convention on the Rights of Persons with Disability (UNCRPD) in 2007. Article 27 of UNCRPD *"recognises the right of persons with disability to work, on an equal basis with others; this includes the opportunity to gain a living by work freely chosen or accepted in the labour market and work environment that is open, inclusive and accessible to persons with disability"*. India has not ratified ILO Convention 159, which concerns Vocational Rehabilitation and Employment (Disabled Persons) Convention. This convention has been ratified by more than 80 countries. The Convention requests ratifying states to set out a policy on vocational rehabilitation and employment of disabled persons in the open labour market. The Convention of Rights of Persons with Disabilities and the Biwako Millennium Framework for Action and Biwako plus Five (ESCAP 2003) reflect a shift from a medical to social model of disability. In the medical model, individuals with certain physical, intellectual, psychological and mental conditions (impairment) are regarded as pathologic or abnormal; it is simply the abnormality conditions themselves that are the cause of all restrictions of activities.

The UN Convention on the Rights of Persons with Disabilities represents a huge step forward for the promotion of access to services for people with disabilities in all contexts and environments. It does so using a holistic and integral approach: both through articles related to different kinds of services and through cross-cutting principles, involving all relevant stakeholders. The role of international relief and development actors is fully acknowledged in this Convention, which sets out the obligations applicable to their actions. This is of particular importance in countries and contexts that can be characterised as challenging environments, where the roles and responsibilities of these actors can be crucial in ensuring access to services for large parts of the population. The United Nations' Convention on the Rights of Persons with Disabilities has helped here by introducing an international standard for disability rights, and specifically mentions situations of risk in its Article 11, and international co-operation in its Article 32. Its provisions require governments to ensure that international co-operation [...] is inclusive of and accessible to persons with disabilities.

Birth registration (Articles 12, 18) is critical for children with disabilities, who are disproportionately affected by registration refusals, which constitutes a denial of citizenship and consequently a denial of access to basic services such as healthcare and education. Persons with disabilities are to be included in the general education system, with access to free and compulsory primary education, secondary and tertiary education as well as vocational training and lifelong learning opportunities. Individual support and reasonable accommodation should be provided when necessary. Persons with disabilities should have access to health services that are gender-sensitive, including health-related rehabilitation. Support services play a key role in making the environment and communication accessible to persons with disabilities.

The Ottawa Charter, agreed at the First International Conference on Health Promotion, Ottawa, Canada, in November 1986, defines health promotion as the process of enabling people to increase control over, and to improve, their health. To reach a state of complete physical, mental and social well being, an individual or group must be able to identify and realise aspirations, satisfy needs, and change or cope with the environment. Health is seen as a resource for everyday life, not the objective of living. Health is a positive concept emphasising social and personal resources, as well as physical capacities. The same Charter recognises that the fundamental conditions and resources for health are peace, shelter, education, food, income, a stable ecosystem, sustainable resources, social justice and equity. Improvement in health requires secure foundation in these basic prerequisites.

The Convention on the Rights of Persons with Disabilities and its Optional Protocol were adopted on 13th December, 2006 at the United Nations Headquarters in New York, and were opened for signature on 30th March, 2007. It is the first comprehensive human rights treaty of the 21st century and is the first human rights convention to be open for signature by regional integration organisations. The Convention entered into force on 3rd May, 2008. The Convention marks a paradigm shift in attitudes and approaches to persons with disabilities. The Convention is intended as a human rights instrument with an explicit, social development dimension.

The Disability and Vulnerability Focal Point (DVFP) is a mechanism developed by Handicap International to ensure the basic and specific needs of vulnerable and disabled persons are met with an efficient and multidimensional response. The DVFP is a temporary facility set up in an affected community to identify and assess needs, supply services and refer patients. Based on a simple structure and mobile teams, the DFVP makes it possible to assess needs on a permanent basis, wherever the DFVP is located. It is capable of providing a range of responses. These include health, protection, non-food items, but also specialist support, such as rehabilitation or other services. The DVFP also provides partners with information and raises their awareness of disability.

Government Efforts and Employment

In India, government departments and public sector enterprises have been important employers of disabled people. Whilst government initiated the policy of three per cent reservation of jobs for persons with disability in 1977, the reservation was only in the lower ranking jobs (C andD categories). However, with India adopting the Disability Act of 1995, the reservation was extended to higher ranking (A and B) categories. Other measures adopted by Government of India include establishment of National Institutes like the National Institute for Visually Handicapped, Dehradun; National Institute of Orthopedically Handicapped, Calcutta; National Institute of Mentally Handicapped, Hyderabad and National Institute of Hearing Impaired, Mumbai. These are information, documentation and rehabilitation centres. Most of the posts are reserved for orthopedically handicapped persons and even these posts do not get filled as the persons with disability are not trained to pass the written tests and interviews. In the case of posts which are reserved for visually impaired and hearing impaired people, most of the posts remain unfilled for many years.

The Eleventh Plan states, *"The backlog of vacancies for persons with disability continues to be large, both at the centre and the states. This backlog should be cleared in a time-bound manner and in a campaign mode"*. Two main reasons for the low representations of persons with disability in the government jobs and public sector are: (a) inadequate job identification process, (b) limited coverage of disability categories. The system of job identification is arbitrary. Companies typically have several concerns and doubts, which prevent them from hiring persons with disability. While some companies are employing the disabled, the work has still not been mainstreamed. While non-profit agencies have been in the training space for a long time, most of them are in the traditional farm and non-farm sector. With an open economy and rise of the service sector, some of these training agencies have shifted focus to newer opportunities like telecom, automobile sector etc. The Government of India has reserved three per cent vacancies against identified posts in Group 'C' and Group 'D' for persons with disabilities. The categories of persons with disability benefited by this scheme are the visual impaired, the hearing impaired and the orthopedically impaired on one per cent reservation for each category in the Central Government services, Public Sector Banks and Government Undertakings. NTPC is the largest Indian state owned energy provider. It addresses the issue of disability through two institutional set ups. One is the Corporate CSR group and the other is the NTPC Foundation the focus is on health, education and employment of persons with disability.

A Central Sector Scheme of providing one lakh jobs per annum to the persons with disabilities, with a proposed outlay of Rs. 1800 crore, during the Eleventh Plan was announced in the Union Budget 2006-07. Under the Scheme, the Government will make payment of the employer's contribution to the Employees Provident Fund and Employees State Insurance for the first three years, as an incentive, in return of employment of persons with disabilities with monthly wage up to Rs. 25,000 per month. Provision of Rs. 16 crore for four years for making adequate publicity of the scheme has also been approved. Self-Employment was considered as the most suitable or as the only option available for disabled people in India for a very long time and the focus of most NGOs was to prepare people for self-employment. Self-Employment is certainly an important option for people in general across socio-economic levels, including people with disabilities.

Under India's Disability Act (1995), a person with a disability is anyone who suffers at least 40 per cent impairment from a medical issue such as blindness, low vision, leprosy, hearing problems, locomotor disability, mental retardation or mental illness. To qualify for benefits, a Disability Certificate is required. Any person who qualifies and is resident in India can apply for one. They are granted by a doctor affiliated to a government notified hospital after an examination. The certificate is issued by the Commissioner for Disabilities. Children with disabilities have the right to free education up to the age of 18. They also qualify for transport benefits, scholarships and free uniforms, books and teaching materials. Disabled people are entitled to concessions for train travel for themselves and one accompanying person by presenting their Disability Certificate. There are separate reservation counters for disabled people at railway stations. Wheelchairs are also available. There are special carriages on most trains for disabled people. Public transportation for people in wheelchairs can be a challenge. New metro systems in cities such as New Delhi and Bangalore have lifts and ramps, but buses are not adapted for wheelchair users. Parking spaces reserved for disabled people are rare.

Under the Disabilities Act of India, children with disabilities have the right to free education until they reach the age of eighteen in schools that are integrated, or in special, schools. Children with disabilities have the right to appropriate transportation, removal of architectural barriers, as well as the restructuring of curriculum and modifications in the examination system. Scholarships, uniforms, books, and teaching materials are all provided to children with disabilities for free in India. Parents of children with disabilities are required to obtain a disability certificate in order to access the facilities mentioned above; they can obtain this certificate from their nearest government hospital, where an Identity Card from the, 'Office of the Commissioner for Disabilities,' will issue it. People in rural areas can obtain this Identity Card from their Block Development Officer's Office (BDO). India's Persons with Disabilities Act has a set of policies and concessions in place for people with disabilities, yet does not include non-negotiable rights. People with disabilities are not able to claim accessibility features as a matter of right in India. The Ministry of Statistics and Programme Implementation (MOS & PI) is the apex body in developing standards and definitions for collecting the statistical data on various subjects. It was observed that there were variations in estimates of disability as obtained from NSSO 2002 Survey and Census 2001. The MOSandPI constituted a Technical Advisory Committee (TAC) on Disability statistics to review the conceptual framework and definitions for the measurement of disability and to examine the reasons of variations in the estimates of disability as obtained from NSSO 2002 survey and Census 2001.

Role of Supreme Court of India

The Supreme Court ruled in favour of three per cent reservation for differently-disabled candidates in civil services, not only at the stage of their appointments but also for departmental promotions. Giving a level-playing field to more than four crore people with disabilities in India, the apex court held that the Centre, states and Union Territories were obligated to implement the rules of reservation for this class in the matters of appointment, selection, direct recruitment, deputation and also for promotions. It asked the Centre to show a big heart and give the differently-abled people their due in all central and state government jobs. A bench led by Chief Justice of India R.M. Lodha reiterated its earlier verdict that the principle of not exceeding 50 per cent reservation would not be applicable while granting quota for differently-abled people. The bench expressed its displeasure at the government seeking to adopt a hyper-technical approach, as its counsel pressed that three per cent reservation could be given only at the stage of appointment but not for promotion. The Persons with Disabilities Act provides for three per cent quota for the differently-abled people.

The bench, however, told the Additional Solicitor General that the objective of the reservation policy, as envisaged by Parliament, was unequivocal that the differently-abled people must get the benefits without technical impediments. "*Once Parliament prescribes for reservation in appointments, it will cover direct recruitment, promotion and even deputation. Our experience tells us that it is one legislation that has never been effectively implemented. In any case, it is a beneficial legislation and you should interpret in a manner so that they get the benefits,*" said the bench. The three per cent reservation, as clarified by the apex court judgment, is to the extent of one per cent each for the blind, hearing and speech impaired, and persons suffering from locomotor disability or cerebral palsy.

Some of the Landmark Judgments

Deaf Employees Welfare Association v Union of India

This petition was filed seeking a Writ of Mandamus directing the Central and State governments to grant equal transport allowance to its government employees suffering from hearing impairment as what was being given to blind and other disabled government employees. The allowance given to the hearing impaired employees was significantly lower than the allowance granted to other employees with disabilities. The Supreme Court allowed the petition and directed the Respondents to grant transport allowance to speech and hearing impaired persons also on par with blind and orthopaedically disabled government employees. The court held that *"there cannot be further discrimination between a person with disability of 'blindness' and a person with disability of 'hearing impairment'. Such discrimination has not been envisaged under the Disabilities Act."* It held that equality of law and equal protection of law afforded to all persons with disabilities while participating in government functions. The court held that the dignity of persons with hearing impairments must be protected by the state.

Kritika Purohit and Anr. Vs. State of Maharashtra and Ors

The petitioner was a visually impaired student who sought admission to the course in Bachelor of Physiotherapy but was not permitted to apply for the same. The petitioner contended that although the post of a physiotherapist was considered to be suitable for blind persons, the denial of courses in physiotherapy for blind persons ran counter to Section 39 of the PWD Act and that the respondents were obliged to make all accommodations for the Petitioner in conformity with Article 24(2) of the CRPD. The court also noted the petitioner's reliance on the circular of the Mumbai University in mandating that resources should be made available to visually impaired student to allow them to complete their courses. In view of these materials, the court observed that the respondents had shown a negative attitude towards persons with disabilities and *"have not cared to consider the object underlying the provisions of Disabilities Act, 1995"*. Therefore, by an interim order dated 2nd August, 2010, it directed the Commissioner of Disabilities to consider all the materials and make suitable instructions to the respondents for making necessary arrangements for admission of visually challenged students. It also directed that the petitioner should be provisionally admitted for the course and should be provided with resources for translation of the material to braille.

Manjunatha vs. Government of Karnataka and Ors

In this case, the petitioner, who was completely blind sought to apply for the B. Ed. Course under the government quota of seats in Karnataka. However, he was denied admission by reason of the condition that persons with disability greater than 75 per cent would not be eligible for admission. The announcement issued by the respondent permitted applications from persons with disability but restricted it to such applicants who had a disability exceeding 40 per cent but below 75 per cent. The Karnataka High Court allowed the petition by holding that such a provision in the announcement ran counter to the PWD.

Ritesh Sinha vs. State of Haryana

In this case, an important interim order was passed by the High Court of Punjab and Haryana and the matter is still pending. The petitioner was a person with locomotor disability and was appointed as a clerk by the District and Sessions Judge, Karnal in the post reserved for physically disabled persons. Thereafter his services were terminated due to his inability to perform the duties as a clerk who was expected to write the office notes and maintain records in his own hands.

Bhagwan Dass and Anr vs. Punjab State Electricity Board

In this case, the Appellant was an Assistant Lineman in the Respondent Board. During his service, he became totally blind and the Respondent failed to accommodate him in an alternative post as per Section 47 of the PWD Act and terminated his service. Therefore the appellant approached the High Court of Punjab and Haryana against the termination of his service. The high court dismissed the petition and the Appellant appealed to the Supreme Court.

Conclusion

The country's disabled population has increased by 22.4 per cent between 2001 and 2011. The number of disabled, which was 2.19 crore in 2001, rose in 2011 to 2.68 crore. India has ratified the United Nations Convention on the Rights of persons with disability in 2007. In India, government departments and public sector enterprises have been important employers of disabled people. Whilst government initiated the policy of three per cent reservation of jobs for persons with disability in 1977, the reservation was only in the lower ranking jobs (C andD categories). However, with India adopting the Disability Act of 1995, the reservation was extended to higher ranking (A and B) categories. Other measures adopted by Government of India include establishment of National Institutes like the National Institute for Visually Handicapped, Dehradun; National Institute of Orthopedically Handicapped, Calcutta; National Institute of Mentally Handicapped, Hyderabad and National Institute of Hearing Impaired, Mumbai. Under India's Disability Act (1995), a person with a disability is anyone who suffers at least 40 per cent impairment from a medical issue such as blindness, low vision, leprosy, hearing problems, locomotor disability, mental retardation or mental illness.

Under the Disabilities Act of India, children with disabilities have the right to free education until they reach the age of eighteen in schools that are integrated, or in special, schools. Children with disabilities have the right to appropriate transportation, removal of architectural barriers, as well as the restructuring of curriculum and modifications in the examination system. Scholarships, uniforms, books, and teaching materials are all provided to children with disabilities for free in India. Parents of children with disabilities in India are required to obtain a disability certificate in order to access the facilities.

Selected Books

1. Anne Digby, and David Wright (2002). *From Idiocy to Mental Deficiency: Historical Perspectives on People with Learning Disabilities,* Taylor and Francis.
2. Benedicte Ingstad and Susan Reynolds Whyte (1995). *Disability and Culture,* University of California Press.
3. Christopher M. Bell (2011). *Blackness and Disability: Critical Examinations and Cultural Interventions,* LIT Verlag Münster.

4. Colin Barnes and Geof Mercer (2010). *Exploring Disability*, Polity.
5. Dan Goodley (2010). *Disability Studies: An Interdisciplinary Introduction*, SAGE.
6. David Wright, Anne Digby, and Digby Anne (1996). *From Idiocy to Mental Deficiency: Historical Perspectives on People with Learning Disabilities*, illustrated.
7. Gary L. Albrecht, Katherine D. Seelman, and Michael Bury (2001). *Handbook of Disability Studies*. SAGE Publications.
8. Gary L. Albrecht, Katherine D. Seelman, Michael Bury (2001). *Handbook of Disability Studies*, SAGE Publications.
9. Geoffrey Dale Arnott (2011). *The Disability Support Worker*, Pearson Education Australia.
10. Graham Pullin (2009). *Design Meets Disability*, MIT Press.
11. Hayley Fitzgerald (2008). *Disability and Youth Sport*, Taylor and Francis.
12. Henri-Jacques Stiker (1999). *A History of Disability*, University of Michigan Press.
13. Jane Seale (2006). *E-Learning and Disability in Higher Education: Accessibility Research and Practice*, Taylor and Francis.
14. Karen P. DePauw, and Susan J. Gavron (2005). *Disability Sport*, Human Kinetics.
15. Lennard J. Davis (1995). *Enforcing Normalcy: Disability, Deafness, and the Body*, Verso.
16. Lennard J. Davis (2006). *The Disability Studies Reader*, Taylor and Francis.
17. Lennard J. Davis (2013). *The Disability Studies Reader*, Routledge.
18. Mairian Corker and Tom Shakespeare (2002). *Disability/Postmodernity: Embodying Disability Theory*, Bloomsbury Academic.
19. Mairian Corker and Tom Shakespeare (2002). *Disability - Postmodernity: Embodying Disability Theory*, Continuum Publ.
20. Martha Craven Nussbaum (2006). *Frontiers of Justice: Disability, Nationality, Species Membership*, Harvard University Press.
21. Paul K. Longmore (2003). *Why I Burned My Book and Other Essays on Disability*, Temple University Press.
22. Rob Imrie (1996). *Disability and the City: International Perspectives*, SAGE.
23. Robert McRuer and Anna Mollow (2012). *Sex and Disability*, Duke University Press.

24. Robert McRuer (2006). *Crip Theory: Cultural Signs of Queerness and Disability,* NYU Press.
25. Sharon N. Barnartt (2010). *Disability as a Fluid State,* Emerald Group Publishing.
26. Shelley Lynn Tremain (2005). *Foucault and the Government of Disability,* University of Michigan Press.
27. Simi Linton (1998). *Claiming Disability: Knowledge and Identity,* NYU Press.
28. Soren V. Randall (2006). *Learning disabilities: new research,* Nova Science Publishers.
29. Steven D. Edwards (2005). *Disability: definitions, value and identity,* Radcliffe Publishing.
30. Tobin Siebers (2008). *Disability Theory,* University of Michigan Press.
31. Tom Shakespeare (1998). *Disability Reader: Social Science Perspectives,* Bloomsbury.
32. See https://www.goodreads.com/work/quotes/632609.

5

Challenges of Disable People

"Part of the problem with the word 'disabilities' is that it immediately suggests an inability to see or hear or walk or do other things that many of us take for granted. But what of people who can't feel? Or talk about their feelings? Or manage their feelings in constructive ways? What of people who aren't able to form close and strong relationships? And people who cannot find fulfillment in their lives, or those who have lost hope, who live in disappointment and bitterness and find in life no joy, no love? These, it seems to me, are the real disabilities."

–Fred Rogers

Introduction

Equalisation of opportunities for marginalised people has been on the world agenda for the past two decades. The first decade was the women is decade (1975 to 1985) and the second, was the decade for people with disabilities (1983-1992). Testing for discrimination against persons with disabilities is particularly challenging because different types of disabilities call for different testing strategies and because of the potential importance of capturing not only differential treatment but also denial of reasonable accommodation or reasonable modification. Violence and abuse are serious problems for persons with disabilities, who are at greater risk than non-disabled persons. Historically, individuals with disabilities have not been considered reliable reporters of abuse nor have they been given the chance to be self-directed in many domains of their life. Violence against women with disabilities has received far greater attention than has violence against men with disabilities. Disability is believed to be the consequence of an impairment that may be physical, cognitive, mental, sensory, emotional, developmental, or some combination of these. Disabilities are an umbrella term, covering impairments, activity limitations, and participation restrictions. An individual may also qualify as disabled if he/she has had impairment in the past or is seen as disabled based on a personal or group standard or norm. Such impairments may include physical, sensory, and cognitive or developmental disabilities. Mental disorders and various types of chronic disease may also qualify as disabilities.

From the Solomon Islands to Sweden, disabled people have been organising and campaigning for equal rights and citizenship. Local, national and international organisations controlled by disabled people lead the struggle to make the world a less disabling place. People with learning disabilities are amongst the most socially excluded and vulnerable groups. Very few have jobs, live in their own homes or have real choice over who cares for them. Many have few friends outside their families and those paid to care for them. Their voices are rarely heard in public. Visual impairment represents a continuum, from very poor vision, to people who can see light but no shapes, to people who have no perception of light at all. Low vision is defined as vision that is between 20/40 and 20/200 after correction. The barriers in the society can be mainly classified into two: the environmental and attitudinal barriers. The major environmental barriers are of two types: Architectural and Communication. Lack of information is another major barrier faced by Disabled People.

The first-ever world report on disabilities highlights the barriers facing millions of handicapped people living on this planet and ways to overcome them. More than a billion people on earth live with some kind of disability. That's 15 per cent of the population and their numbers are growing. Many face tremendous barriers in education, healthcare, transportation, jobs ... even having their voices heard. The fallout, according to the new study; people with disabilities are likely to have poorer health outcomes, lower educational achievements, less participation in the economy and higher poverty rates. There is a significant dearth of research on the prevalence and consequences of disabilities among youth. The data that does exist shows that young people with disabilities face many more challenges than their non-disabled peers. In addition, they may also have to cope with challenges linked to gender, poverty, ethnicity or sexuality. Young people with disabilities are among the poorest and most marginalised of the world's youth. Estimates suggest that there are between 180 and 220 million youth with disabilities worldwide, and nearly 80 per cent of them live in developing countries. People with disabilities of working age are two times as likely to be unemployed as those without disabilities. When people with disabilities are employed, they are more likely to be working part-time and for significantly lower wages, especially women with disabilities.

People with disabilities already use the Internet and other types of technologies at levels that are below those of the rest of the population. People with various abilities clearly face various challenges when accessing the Internet. People who experience visual impairments may face challenges due to a lack of compatibility of Web content with the screen reader they use, a software application that provides computer-synthesised speech output of items appearing on the screen, as well as equivalent text provided in the back-end code. People who experience motor impairments, such a limited or no use of their hands or fingers, may face barriers due to a cluttered layout, links and buttons that are too small, as well as other important navigability considerations such as requiring the use of a pointing device,

that may make entire functions and sites unusable for them. While the range of potential barriers to people who experience disabilities in the online environment is extensive, there are ways to develop and implement technologies so they are included. There are known and achievable ways to address the access barriers mentioned challenge. Challenging behaviour used to be described as 'problem behaviour' or 'difficult behaviour' or 'socially unacceptable behaviour'. But in recent years, the term challenging behaviour reflects the fact that some of the behaviours are a challenge to professionals, teachers and parents. Persons with disabilities may face challenges because of the physical or mental limitations. But the attitudes of other people may also create barriers. Understanding this social aspect of disability is essential. Protection for persons with mental disabilities deserves special attention. These persons have the same rights as persons with any other kind of disability. They may have trouble expressing them or even identifying that they have a disability. A new report from Human Rights Watch looks at discrimination in China's education system toward children with disabilities. According to the report, 28 per cent of disabled children are not receiving compulsory education, and 40 per cent are illiterate. Children who do go to school are often not provided extra resources they need to participate effectively.

Types of Abuse

Individuals with disabilities experience forms of violence and abuse similar to those without disabilities, such as physical injury, sexual assault, emotional trauma, and financial abuse. Mistreatment comes in many forms and may have more severe consequences for people with disabilities. Men and women with disabilities have described common and unique personal barriers to managing abuse. Another complex issue for men and women with disabilities is addressing abuse when the perpetrator is a family member or a friend who also provides personal assistance. Social service providers and healthcare personnel may not fully understand the unique situations that place individuals with disabilities at increased risk for abuse and mistreatment or may not be aware of the system barriers that make addressing abuse particularly complex. Men and women with disabilities consistently highlight barriers to violence prevention and management that are inherent in the way disability services are designed and implemented.

Children with physical or learning disabilities are more vulnerable to the full range of mental health disorders and the additional social, family and emotional stresses of everyday life. As young people with learning disabilities move into adulthood, to ensure continuity of care and support for the young person and their family; and to provide equality of opportunity in order to enable as many disabled young people as possible to participate in education, training or employment. Disabled young people and their families often find the transition to adulthood both stressful and difficult. For many, there has been a lack of co-ordination between the relevant agencies and little involvement from the young person. Some young people are not transferred from children's to adult services with adequate healthcare plans, which results in their exclusion from adult services.

The greatest problem that handicapped children face is their actual physical/mental disabilities. Because of the physical limitations children with disabilities live with, their plane of social existence is compromised. They are limited in extracurricular activities depending on their specific issues. Socially handicapped children feel isolated because of these invisible boundaries that are cast about them. There are a number of emotional conflicts that arise because of a child's handicap. This occurs not only for the child but for his family and close relatives. One of the most visible problems that children with disabilities have has their behavioural issues. There are a variety of causes for the destructive, reticent or unmotivated behaviour children might exhibit. Children with physical and mental disabilities experience personal limitations in the social, psychological and economic spheres, some of which can be alleviated with parental, community and governmental support. Most children are naturally social and keenly aware of ostracism. Disabled children stand out as different, and may become targets for ridicule, bullying and mockery. Children are remarkably resilient, but the psychological effects of physical and mental disability can be lasting and subtle. In stable families with adequate incomes, children may be shielded from the immediate economic effects of a physical or psychological condition.

Having a handicapped child born into a family and grow into adulthood is one of the most stressful experiences a family can endure. Parental reactions to the realisation that their child is exceptional usually include shock, depression, guilt, anger, sadness, and anxiety. Individuals handle each of these feelings differently and may stay in certain stages longer than others. A number of practical problems may make living with a handicapped child especially demanding. For example, there may be financial strain to provide necessary medical expenses, special equipment, possibly special schools and caretakers in the parents absent. Physical handicaps may cause various degrees of weaknesses and in co-ordination of the limbs which may affect mobility, posture and manual dexterity. Other physical problems such as heart diseases may cause poor exercise tolerance and low level of physical fitness. Cerebral palsy, late stage of muscular dystrophy and facial burns may affect the pupils' ability in verbal communication. On top of this, their non-verbal communication may also be affected because these conditions may limit their facial expression and ability in signing.

Parents of children with disabilities face great sadness, fear, worry and more from loved ones and even family members, regarding their little angels with eyes of spite, concern and even disbelief they are really disabled at the time. When a parent first discovers their baby or child has a disability, they do not stop to even think about the costs and how it will affect the family in the long run. All they can think about is how to help their child. Families can find themselves isolated from their support circles (family and friends) when dealing with a child that has special needs or disabilities. Many families stop socialising when they discover they have a child with special needs, out of fear for how that child and they will be received by the public and those around them that matter to them, how their child will be loved while they learn to deal with the issues at hand. The greatest problem of physically handicapped people is that they are to depend on others to lead normal life, though many modern devices have been invented to make their life easier. The government has arranged seat reservation in bus, trains and cost of tickets subsidised for physically impaired persons. The persons with visibility impaired, are to toil hard, while crossing roads or negotiating public transportation. However, these persons have amply proved in various jobs that they are equally competent in comparison to normal persons, if they are provided with necessary support.

Lack of Appropriate Communication

The lack of appropriate communication remains the biggest hindrance to PWDs accessing health services, even when they have HIV/AIDS. This is followed by the fact that many physically impaired PWDs cannot access health services either because they have no wheelchairs or they cannot easily navigate their wheel chairs at health centres. Lack of money raises the issue of poverty, which is prevalent in the disability community and affects their ability to access necessary care and treatment of HIV/AIDS. Persons with disabilities are confronted with the same difficulties as any displaced person, when fleeing in dangerous situations, in temporary accommodations or in situations of repatriation or resettlement.

Persons with disabilities experienced a multitude of barriers when trying to access health services, the most common of which was being unable to afford the transport costs to get to the health centres which may be up to six miles away from their home. Transport was reported to be more expensive for reasons related to their disability. Persons with disabilities reaching the Health Centres reported many difficulties in actually accessing services as a result of inaccessible infrastructure and negative behaviours by staff.

Visually disabled and partially sighted people need to use medicines like their sighted counterparts for many diseases and health conditions. Some are parents and need to give medicines to their children. Those who live separately without the assistance of sighted relatives need to administer medicines by themselves for these purposes. Visually disabled or partially sighted people are potentially more likely to have unsafe practices related to medicine use.

Refugees

The situation for many persons living with disabilities in the Middle East is challenging, in particular when it comes to effect change in their respective countries, and especially with regard to national Governments. The problem is compounded for the numerous persons with disabilities who live as refugees, outside of the normal protection and policy framework put into place by the government of the country in which they reside. Palestinian refugees in Lebanon are highly dependent on the United Nations Relief and Works Agency as a key provider of social services such as education, healthcare and social protection services. As a result of the difficulties experienced in accessing health services, persons with disabilities in rural areas tended to go to health centres as a last resort or not at all. Some would use locally available alternatives, such as herbs.

Lack of Education

Lack of education is a key concern for most disabled young people in the developing world. In many countries, children with disabilities are considered to be incapable of learning, no matter what their disability is. Often a disabled child is considered a distraction to other students and simply sent home. School buildings are routinely built with stairs, or far from community centres, making them inaccessible to those with mobility impairments. Lack of trained teachers, appropriate teaching materials and an unwillingness to include disabled children in the regular classroom limits access to education for millions of blind and intellectually disabled children as well as those with mental health difficulties. The social isolation, poverty and discrimination faced by children with disabilities also sets upon interconnected pattern of problems. In developed nations there exist extensive educational systems for most children with disabilities through late adolescence. Some nations integrate these adolescents into general classrooms. Others provide specialised classes and training in social and job skills to help in the transition to adulthood. These programmes have varying degrees of success.

Lack of Employment

Employment rates of disabled youth are rarely tracked in developing countries. Unemployment among disabled young women in all societies, averages 50 per cent higher than unemployment among comparably educated disabled young men, (which itself is double that of their non-disabled male peers). There are an increasing number of programmes that address the specific needs of young people with disabilities, organised by government agencies, private voluntary organisations, religious organisations and community groups. However, globally the number of such programmes remains small. People with disabilities are facing unnecessary extra difficulties when trying to tackle debt problems because creditors are failing to recognise their specific needs.

People with mental health problems or learning disabilities have worse physical health and die younger than the general population, conclude a major investigation by the Disability Rights Commission of Great Britain. Its 18 month investigation into primary care services took evidence from health professionals, policy-makers, and disabled people and analysed eight million medical records. The findings showed that:

(a) People with mental health problems (including schizophrenia, bipolar disorder, and depression) have higher rates of obesity, smoking, heart disease, diabetes, respiratory disease, and stroke than the general population.

(b) People with bipolar disorder or schizophrenia have higher rates of hypertension and breast cancer, and those with schizophrenia are almost twice as likely to have bowel cancer.

(c) People with learning disabilities have higher rates of obesity and respiratory disease, and

(d) People with mental health problems or learning disabilities are likely to die younger than other people, and those with mental health problems are more than twice as likely to have strokes or coronary heart disease before the age of 55.

All disabled people living and working in Netherlands can apply for support maintaining an active social life and taking care of themselves. Special care needs are provided by government programmes. Examples are adapting a house for wheelchair-use or long-term, regular professional care. Dutch law ensures that persons with disabilities have the same rights (and duties) as others in the fields of education, housing, public transport and the labour market. The government encourages people with disabilities to be as independent as possible. In order to achieve this, a large number of measures have been taken to enable the disabled to participate in society on an equal basis with others.

One of the specific aspects of the disability service sector is the need for both specialised services and accessible mainstream services at community level. People with disabilities have the same fundamental right to access mainstream services in the community (education, health-care, employment, social services and social protection) as any other citizen. Experience tends to show that the main factors determining access to services for people with disabilities can be grouped into three main categories, according to whether they are related to the organisation of the services system at local or national level (planning, funding, monitoring, continuous improvement), to the internal management of the services or to the attitudes of users and the population with regard to these service. The quality of access to services by disabled people can not be dissociated from the quality of the services themselves. If the service is well-planned, managed and monitored, the number of people using or asking for it will increase. The quality of services for people with disabilities is a comprehensive approach that can be applied to very different socioeconomic settings.

People with learning disabilities should be fully involved in the decision-making processes that affect their lives. This applies to decisions on day to day matters such as choice of activities, operational matters such as staff selection and strategic matters such as changes to eligibility criteria. People with learning disabilities may need specialist equipment because they also have a physical disability or sensory impairment. Assistive technology can increase their control, choice and independence through improving cognitive and social functioning. Most people with learning disabilities have greater health needs than the rest of the population. They are more likely to experience mental illness and are more prone to chronic health problems, epilepsy, and physical and sensory disabilities. An increasing number of young people with severe and profound disabilities have complex health needs.

Disabilities of all types affect employees and can pose various mental or physical challenges. In many situations, a disability may impact the amount of time it takes for an employee to complete a task or get from one part of a facility to another. Some disabilities may be known while others remain unknown to an employer. According the Americans with Disabilities Act (ADA) employees with disabilities can continue to work without fear of losing their jobs. The ADA disallows discrimination against otherwise qualified individuals in an employment setting because of mental or physical disabilities. People with disabilities as a minority population are perhaps the most diverse minority on planet Earth. Basic accommodation is a challenge people with disabilities face in the workplace. The needs are almost always very basic and inexpensive ones, yet some employers continue to believe the accommodations a person with disabilities needs are expensive. Introducing people with disabilities into the workplace and allowing them to both meet and work with experience employees can not only help them feel welcome; it presents them with the potential to learn from experienced employees. Employers need to find ways to permit workers with disabilities to transition comfortably into working environments.

Nearly twenty-two years after the passage of the Americans with Disabilities Act and thirty-nine years after the passage of the Rehabilitation Act of 1973, two of the most significant disability employment-related pieces legislation in American history, people with disabilities continues to be employed at much lower levels than people without disabilities/the general population. According to the most recent data from the Department of Labour's Bureau of Labour Statistics (April 2012), people with disabilities had a 20.3 per cent labour force participation rate compared to 69.1 per cent for their non-disabled peers, and people with disabilities had an unemployment rate of 12.5 per cent compared to 7.6 per cent for their non-disabled peers. Many employers miss out on the talents and capabilities of qualified candidates who live with disabilities, simply because they assume that accommodation is a burden for reasons that don't bear out in reality. People with disabilities and disfigurements have to work harder than non-disabled people to get their foot on the career ladder. The government's Office for Disability Issues reported that in 2011 the employment rate among people with disabilities was 48.8 per cent, compared to 77.5 per cent among those without. Employers broadly interpret disability as covering multiple and diverse conditions ranging in severity from mild to severe. They tend to classify disability as either physical or mental/psychological. Several employers explicitly noted that having disability does not automatically discount people from being successful at their jobs.

Conclusion

Young people with disabilities are among the poorest and most marginalised of the world's youth. Estimates suggest that there are between 180 and 220 million youth with disabilities worldwide, and nearly 80 per cent of them live in developing countries. People with disabilities of working age are two times as likely to be unemployed as those without disabilities. Individuals with disabilities experience forms of violence and abuse similar to those without disabilities, such as physical injury, sexual assault, emotional trauma, and financial abuse. Mistreatment comes in many forms and may have more severe consequences for people with disabilities. Children with physical or learning disabilities are more vulnerable to the full range of mental health disorders and the additional social, family and emotional stresses of everyday life. The greatest problem that handicapped children face is their actual physical/mental disabilities. Because of the physical limitations children with disabilities live with, their plane of social existence is compromised. They are limited in extracurricular activities depending on their specific issues. Parents of children with disabilities face great sadness, fear, worry and more from loved ones and even family members, regarding their little angels with eyes of spite, concern and even disbelief they are really disabled at the time.

The lack of appropriate communication remains the biggest hindrance to PWDs accessing health services, even when they have HIV/AIDS. Lack of education is a key concern for most disabled young people in the developing world. In many countries, children with disabilities are considered to be incapable of learning, no matter what their disability is. Employment rates of disabled youth are rarely tracked in developing countries. Unemployment among disabled young women is common in all societies.

Selected Books

1. Anne Digby, and David Wright (2002). *From Idiocy to Mental Deficiency: Historical Perspectives on People with Learning Disabilities,* Taylor and Francis.
2. Benedicte Ingstad and Susan Reynolds Whyte (1995). *Disability and Culture,* University of California Press.
3. Christopher M. Bell (2011). *Blackness and Disability: Critical Examinations and Cultural Interventions,* LIT Verlag Münster.
4. Colin Barnes and Geof Mercer (2010). *Exploring Disability,* Polity.
5. Dan Goodley (2010). *Disability Studies: An Interdisciplinary Introduction,* SAGE.
6. David Wright, Anne Digby, and Digby Anne (1996). *From Idiocy to Mental Deficiency: Historical Perspectives on People with Learning Disabilities,* illustrated.
7. Gary L. Albrecht, Katherine D. Seelman, and Michael Bury (2001). *Handbook of Disability Studies.* SAGE Publications.
8. Gary L. Albrecht, Katherine D. Seelman, Michael Bury (2001). *Handbook of Disability Studies,* SAGE Publications.
9. Geoffrey Dale Arnott (2011). *The Disability Support Worker,* Pearson Education Australia.

10. Graham Pullin (2009). *Design Meets Disability,* MIT Press.
11. Hayley Fitzgerald (2008). *Disability and Youth Sport,* Taylor and Francis.
12. Henri-Jacques Stiker (1999). *A History of Disability,* University of Michigan Press.
13. Jane Seale (2006). *E-Learning and Disability in Higher Education: Accessibility Research and Practice,* Taylor and Francis.
14. Karen P. DePauw, and Susan J. Gavron (2005). *Disability Sport,* Human Kinetics.
15. Lennard J. Davis (1995). *Enforcing Normalcy: Disability, Deafness, and the Body,* Verso.
16. Lennard J. Davis (2006). *The Disability Studies Reader,* Taylor and Francis.
17. Lennard J. Davis (2013). *The Disability Studies Reader,* Routledge.
18. Mairian Corker and Tom Shakespeare (2002). *Disability/ Postmodernity: Embodying Disability Theory,* Bloomsbury Academic.
19. Mairian Corker, and Tom Shakespeare (2002). *Disability - Postmodernity: Embodying Disability Theory,* Continuum Publ.
20. Martha Craven Nussbaum (2006). *Frontiers of Justice: Disability, Nationality, Species Membership,* Harvard University Press.
21. Paul K. Longmore (2003). *Why I Burned My Book and Other Essays on Disability,* Temple University Press.
22. Rob Imrie (1996). *Disability and the City: International Perspectives,* SAGE.
23. Robert McRuer and Anna Mollow (2012). *Sex and Disability,* Duke University Press.
24. Robert McRuer (2006). *Crip Theory: Cultural Signs of Queerness and Disability,* NYU Press.
25. Sharon N. Barnartt (2010). *Disability as a Fluid State,* Emerald Group Publishing.
26. Shelley Lynn Tremain (2005). *Foucault and the Government of Disability,* University of Michigan Press.
27. Simi Linton (1998). *Claiming Disability: Knowledge and Identity,* NYU Press.
28. Soren V. Randall (2006). *Learning disabilities: new research,* Nova Science Publishers.
29. Steven D. Edwards (2005). *Disability: definitions, value and identity,* Radcliffe Publishing.
30. Tobin Siebers (2008). *Disability Theory,* University of Michigan Press.
31. Tom Shakespeare (1998). *Disability Reader: Social Science Perspectives,* Bloomsbury.

6

Assistance to Disable People

"Dreams are like living things; they can grow, they can suffer disabilities, they can have deficiency diseases and they can also die off when they meet unfavourable and favourable conditions respectively." **-Israelmore Ayivor**

Introduction

God created men and women to build life together and to complete one another all lifelong. Islam opened the door to women to wade through all the fields of struggle in life side by side with men, supporting each other, helping, and completing one another. Women bear the brunt of frustrations of a difficult world that their husbands face whether as anger or alcoholism, even as they endure in the very same world. A male dominated government is not stupid to make special schemes for women. If it hopes to develop the country, the money must go in the hands of the person improving the conditions. A woman with an income means a well fed child. An educated woman means a better income, better planned families, awareness of health, a hope of greater ability for the next generation. Human beings, by nature, structure their social relationships in order to assist each other to attain the necessities of life and to enhance the quality of their lifestyles. During the historical development of societies, this has taken many forms, with different groups at different times dominating the shape, meaning and accessibility of social assistance.

In most western societies, people don't starve, they get educated and have sufficient healthcare to reach an old age. The problem of rising poverty and socio-economic gaps is one of the main problems that western societies face today, and western governments have failed to tackle through financial assistance. Governments solve large problems by general means, but the problem of poverty is individual, the government doesn't have the ability to solve the problem at the personal case by case level that leads people out of poverty. Perhaps the most striking example of that is looking at women's role in the workplace. Women are more likely than men to work in professional occupations rather than in occupations like construction or transportation. They are much less likely to be employed in higher paying job groups such as the computer and engineering fields than their male counterparts.

Disability Certificate

Disability certificates are necessary for different purposes such as availing benefits related to education, employment or various Government scheme applicable for disable persons. Government is updating its functionality and accuracy in every field; on these lines Government expects that the benefits and rights available for disables should be provisioned to real disables. For this purpose Government has launched this certification system and is expected that malpractices will be eliminated by the use of this system. The Department of Health and Family Welfare, Government of NCT of Delhi has been issuing Disability Certificates to the Persons with Disabilities from last many years. The Disability Certificates are issued by the Notified Government Hospitals.

The doctor may be called upon to testify as an expert witness in the court of justice. The expert witness is legally bound to declare his knowledge of the case and express his opinions. Effects of disability are physical, social, psychological and vocational, since the total disability is not purely a medical condition, medical man should evaluate the Permanent Physical Impairment rather than total disability. Physical impairment evaluation certificate is to be issued only by Medical Doctors who are registered under the 1st schedule of M.C.I. Act, 1956. Aggregate of permanent physical impairment should not exceed more than 100 per cent.

The institute issues the disability certificates to persons with locomotor or multiple handicaps (major component being locomotor handicap only). The applicant has to fill an application form, submit the required address proof, age proof, may be required to submit five passport size good quality photographs. All the old relevant treatment record along with investigation reports- blood tests reports, X-rays, MRI etc should be available at the time of application. The applicants are screened by one of the doctors and if found suitable for issuing a disability certificate his personal information's are collected and entered in the proforma on the computer. After that the person is referred for required assessment in physiotherapy, occupational and/or speech therapy departments or advised further investigations or consultations, if required. Once these assessments completed, the person is given date for assessment by the board and issual of the Certificate.

Schemes for Disable People

It has been the constant endeavour of the Government to provide the disabled persons with aids/appliance at minimum costs. The requirement for providing of aids/appliances, which are essential for the social, economic and vocational rehabilitation of the disabled persons, has come into sharp focus, particularly after the enactment of the Persons with Disabilities (Equal Opportunities, Protection of Rights and Full Participation) Act, 1995, which came into force in 1996. The Scheme aims at helping the disabled persons by bringing suitable, durable, scientifically-manufactured, modern, standard aids and appliances within their reach. The estimates, according to 58th Sample Survey conducted by NSSO in 2002, indicate that there are about 18.04 million persons with various types of disabilities in the country. The Scheme will be implemented through the Implementing Agencies. The Scheme shall also include under its ambit, medical/surgical correction and intervention, which is essential prior to fitment of aids and appliances. The cost could range from Rs. 500 for hearing and speech impaired to Rs. 1,000 for visually disabled and Rs. 3,000 for orthopaedically disabled. A person with disabilities fulfilling following conditions would be eligible for assistance under ADIP Scheme through authorised agencies:

1. He/she should be an Indian citizen of any age.
2. Should be certified by a Registered Medical Practitioner that he/she is disabled and fit to use prescribed aid/appliance.
3. Person who is employed/self-employed or getting pension and whose monthly income from all sources does not exceed Rs. 10,000 per month.
4. In case of dependents, the income of parents/guardians should not exceed Rs. 10,000 per month.
5. Persons who have not received assistance from the Government, local bodies and Non-Official Organisations during the last three years for the same purpose.
6. However, for children below 12 years of age this limit would be one year.

The Indian Law and Disability

The Constitution of India premised on the principle of social justice and human rights. The Preamble, the Directive Principles of State Policy and the Fundamental Rights enshrined in the Constitution stand testimony to the commitment of the State to its people. These provisions envisage a very positive role for the State in the upliftment of the status of disadvantaged groups. Article 46 stipulates that, *"The State shall promote with special care the educational and economic interests of the weaker sections of the people, and, in particular, of the Scheduled Castes and the Scheduled Tribes, and shall protect them from social injustice and all forms of exploitation."* The Disability Rights Commission will play an important role in helping individuals enforce their rights under the Disability Discrimination Act. A group is being set up to advise the Commission on issues relating to people with learning disabilities. Effective advocacy can transform the lives of people with learning disabilities by enabling them to express their wishes and aspirations and make real choices. Advocacy helps people put forward their views and play an active part in planning and designing services which are responsive to their needs. The Government's long-term aim is to have a range of independent advocacy services available in each area so that people with learning disabilities can choose the one which best meets their needs.

The Disability Rights Initiative provides legal aid, takes up high-impact public interest litigation, provides access to the legal system and campaigns to improve facilities for persons with all types of disabilities. It engages in out-of-court advocacy and has initiated extensive work on law reform for people with disabilities. This stems from the obligation of the state to bring all its laws, policies and rules in conformity with the UN Convention on Rights of Persons with Disabilities, which has been signed and ratified by India. According to the 2001 census, 2.1 per cent of India's population has some form of disability. People with disabilities have to apply for certificates to avail of government entitlements. These are granted after a medical officer examines the person in question and grants percentage points for various enumerated disabilities. If the percentage crosses 40 per cent, the person is granted a certificate of disability. Over the last two decades, the protection of persons with disabilities was made mandatory with the passing of certain legislations including the PWD Act (1995) and the Mental Health Act (1987). Employment, education and creating a non-discriminating environment for all persons with disabilities were some of the rights that are given special attention here. It is known that other general legislations also contain provisions that deal with persons with disabilities within the ambit of that law. However, these provisions are not necessarily sensitive. Thus, protection against abuse, social security, custody of children, provision of basic needs such as shelter within the family and marital home are issues that still need to be adequately addressed.

The Ministry of Social Justice and Empowerment of the Government of India has been holding national consultative meetings on proposed amendments to the Persons with Disabilities Equal Opportunities, Protection of Rights and Full Participation Act (PWD Act). To the delight of disability groups, India ratified the UN Convention on the Rights of Persons with Disabilities (Disability Convention) in October 2007. This Convention marks a formal shift from the archaic medical model to the social model, and promotes the rights of people living with disabilities. Article 1 encapsulates the overall objective of the Convention which is *"to promote, protect and ensure the full and equal enjoyment of all human rights and fundamental freedoms by all persons with disabilities, and to promote respect for their inherent dignity."* The Convention recognises that persons with disability are right-holders instead of passive recipients of government schemes. In contrast, the PWD Act has a different foundation. The PWD Act was enacted in order to implement the Proclamation on the Full Participation and Equality of People with Disabilities, an instrument that did not expressly recognise rights, but laid emphasis on the need to eliminate physical and social barriers so as to promote the participation of people living with disabilities. The PWD Act, thus, does not internalise any of the core principles that form the bedrock of the Disability Convention.

The PWD Act adopts a narrow definition of disability and confines it to *"blindness; low vision; leprosy-cured; hearing impairment; locomotor disability; mental retardation; and mental illness"*. As opposed to this, the Disability Convention recognises that disability is an evolving concept and avoids listing specific conditions and severities and broadly casts persons with disabilities to *"include those who have long-term physical, mental, intellectual or sensory impairments which in interaction with various barriers may hinder their full and effective participation in society on an equal basis with others."* The core human rights principles stated in Article 3 of the Disability Convention are respect for inherent dignity and individual autonomy; non-discrimination, full and effective participation and inclusion; respect for difference; equality of opportunity; accessibility, gender equality; respect for the evolving capacity of children with disabilities and their right to preserve their identities. These general principles have been well etched in several provisions of the Convention.

Persons with Disabilities (Equal Opportunities, Protection of Rights and Full Participation) Act, 1995

The provisions contained in the Persons with Disability (Equal Opportunities, Protection of Rights and Full Participation) Act, 1995, imposes several obligations on the Central and State Governments for taking up various measures to ensure equal participation of people with disabilities in all walks of life. Section 25(a) of the Act specifically mentions that *"within the limits of their economic capacity and development, the appropriate Governments and the local authorities, with a view to preventing the occurrence of disabilities, shall – undertake or cause to be undertaken surveys, investigations and research concerning the cause of occurrence of disabilities"*. The Act, which catalogues the rights of people with disabilities in India, was passed by the Parliament of India on

December 12, 1995, and notified on February 7, 1996. The Act was a landmark in that, for the first time, it stated that people with disabilities had the right to equal opportunities and full participation and that these rights would be protected by the law. The Act is arranged in three distinct parts: Part I comprises Chapter 1-4 dealing with the administrative arrangement for implementation. Part II comprises Chapter 5-11 dealing with the substantive rights and corelated obligations. Part III provides a mechanism for the monitoring of the Act in the Centre and States. Chapter 12 establishes the office of the Chief Commissioner and State Commissioners for person with disabilities. The objectives of the act are:

1. To spell out the responsibility of the State towards the prevention of disabilities. Protection of rights, provision of medical care, education, training, employment and rehabilitation of persons with disabilities.
2. To create a barrier-free environment for disabled persons.
3. To remove any discrimination against disabled people in the sharing of developed benefits for non-disabled persons.
4. To counteract any situation of abuse and the exploitation of disabled persons.
5. To lay down strategies for the development of comprehensive programmes services and the equalisation of opportunities for disabled persons.
6. To make special provisions for the integration of persons with disabilities into social mainstream.

The Central Government shall by notification constitute a body to be known as the Central Coordination Committee to exercise the powers conferred on, and to perform the functions assigned to it, under this Act. 2. The office of the Member of the Central Coordination Committee shall not disqualify its holder for being chosen as or for being a Member of either House of Parliament. The appropriate Government may, by notification require that from such date as may be specified by notification the employer in every establishment shall furnish such information or return as may be prescribed in relation to vacancies appointed for persons with disability have occurred or are about to occur in that establishment to such Special Employment Exchange as may be prescribed and the establishment shall thereupon comply with such requisition. Any person authorised by the Special Employment Exchange in writing, shall have access to any relevant record or document in the possession of any establishment and may enter at reasonable time and premises where he believes such record or document to be, and inspect or take copies of relevant records or documents or ask any questions necessary for obtaining any information.

All Government educational institutions and other educational institutions receiving aid from the Government shall reserve not less than three per cent seats for persons with disabilities. The appropriate Governments and local authorities shall reserve not less than three per cent in all poverty alleviation schemes for the benefit of persons with disabilities. The appropriate Governments and the local authorities shall, within the limits of their economic capacity and development, provide incentives to employers both in public and private sectors to ensure that at least five per cent. Of their work force is composed of persons with disabilities. The appropriate Governments shall by notification make schemes to provide aids and appliances to persons with disabilities. The appropriate Governments shall provide financial assistance to universities other institutions of higher learning professional bodies and non-governmental research units or institutions, for undertaking research for special education, rehabilitation and manpower development. The State Government shall appoint any authority as it deems fit to be a competent authority for the purposes of this Act. No person to establish or maintain an institution for persons with disabilities except in accordance with a certificate of registration. Save as otherwise provided under this Act, no person shall establish or maintain any institution for persons with disabilities except under and in accordance with a certificate of registration issued in this behalf by the competent authority.

Appointment of Chief Commissioner for persons with disabilities: (1) The Central Government may, by notification appoint a Chief Commissioner for persons with disabilities for the purposes of this Act. A person shall not be qualified for appointment as the Chief Commissioner unless he has special knowledge or practical experience in respect of matters relating to rehabilitation. The salary and allowances payable to and other terms and conditions of service (including pension, gratuity and other retirement benefits) of the Chief Commissioner shall be such as may be prescribed by the Central Government. The Central Government shall determine the nature and categories of officers and other employees required to assist the Chief Commissioner in the discharge of his functions and provide the Chief Commissioner with such officers and other employees as it thinks fit. Establishments in the transport sector shall, within the limits of their economic capacity and development for the benefit of persons with disabilities, take special measures to: (a) adapt rail compartments, buses, vessels and aircrafts in such a way as to permit easy access to such persons; (b) adapt toilets in rail compartments, vessels, aircrafts and waiting rooms in such a way as to permit the wheel chair users to use them conveniently. The appropriate Governments and the local authorities shall, within the limits of their economics capacity and development provide for: (a) ramps in public buildings; (b) adaptation of toilets for wheel chair users; (c) braille symbols and auditory signals in elevators or lifts; (d) ramps in hospitals, primary health centres and other medical care and rehabilitation institutions.

The Office of the Commissioner for Persons with Disabilities was established as an Independent Statutory Authority under section 60 of the Persons with Disabilities (Equal Opportunities, Protection of Rights and Full Participation) Act, 1995. Independent office of the Commissioner for Persons with Disabilities started functioning in Delhi from August, 2009 till then the Department of Social Welfare was looking after the functions of Commissioner for Persons with Disabilities. In Delhi, there is a provision of one Commissioner for Persons with Disabilities with one Deputy Commissioner and other supporting staff. Where in any recruitment year any vacancy under Section 33, cannot be filled up due to non-availability of a suitable person with disability or, for any other sufficient reason, such vacancy shall be carried forward in the succeeding recruitment year and if in the succeeding recruitment year also suitable person with disability is not available, it may first be filled by interchange among the three categories and only when there is no person with disability available for the post in that year the employer shall fill up the vacancy by appointment of a person, other than a person with disability. The Commissioner for Persons with Disabilities is broadly responsible to:

- co-ordinate with departments of the Government of National Capital Territory of Delhi for the programmes and schemes for the benefit of persons with disabilities;
- monitor the utilisation of funds disbursed by the Government of National Capital Territory of Delhi;
- take step to safeguard the rights and facilities made available to persons with disabilities;
- to take up the matter with appropriate authorities looking into the complaints with respect to matters relating to deprivation of rights of persons with disabilities and non-implementation of laws, rules, bye-laws, regulations, executive orders, guidelines or instructions made or issued by the appropriate Governments and the local authorities for the welfare the protection of rights of persons with disabilities.

The Commissioner for Persons with Disabilities is vested with the powers of Civil Court under the Code of Criminal Procedure, 1973 and every proceeding before the Commissioner for Persons with Disabilities is a judicial proceeding within the meaning of sections 193 and 228 of the Indian Penal Code (45 of 1860). Further, there is also an Office of the Chief Commissioner for Persons with Disabilities (CCD) under Government of India which looks after issues of Persons with Disabilities concerning at Government of India level and its organisations.

The Rehabilitation Council of India Act 1992

The Rehabilitation Council of India was set up by the Government of India in 1986, initially as a society to regulate and standardise training policies and programmes in the field of rehabilitation of persons with disabilities. The urgent need for minimum standards was felt as the majority of persons engaged in education; vocational training and counselling of persons with disabilities were not professionally qualified. Poor academic and training standards adversely affect the chances of disabled succeeding in the world of work. The Rehabilitation Council of India regulates training standards for sixteen categories of rehabilitation workers. The Council is proactively promoting training and research initiatives utilising experience of specialised as well as mainstream academic institutions. The Rehabilitation Council of India was set up as a registered society in 1986.

However, it was soon found that a society could not ensure proper standardisation and acceptance of the standards by other organisations. The Parliament enacted Rehabilitation Council of India become a Statutory Body on 22nd June, 1993. The RCI Act was amended by the Parliament in 2000 to work it more broadly. The Act casts norms responsibility on the Council. It also prescribes that any one delivering services to people with disability, with out processing qualifications recognised by RCI, could be prosecuted. The Council has the twin responsibility of standardising and regulating the training of personnel and professionals in the field of Rehabilitation and Special Education.

The Rehabilitation Council of India was set up as a registered society in 1986. On September, 1992 the RCI Act was enacted by Parliament and it became a Statutory Body on 22nd June, 1993. The Act was amended by Parliament in 2000 to make it more broad based. The mandate given to RCI is to regulate and monitor services given to persons with disability, to standardise syllabi and to maintain a Central Rehabilitation Register of all qualified professionals and personnel working in the field of Rehabilitation and Special Education. The Act also prescribes punitive action against unqualified persons delivering services to persons with disability. The Chairperson or a member shall hold an office for a term of two years from the date of his appointment or until his successor shall have been duly appointed whichever is longer. A casual vacancy in the Council shall be filled in accordance with the provisions of Section 3 and the person so appointed shall hold office only for the remainder of the term for which the member in whose place he was appointed would have held that office. The Council shall meet at least once in each year at such time and place as may be appointed by the Council and shall observe such rules of procedure in the transaction of business at a meeting as may be presented. The Chairperson or, if for any reason, he is unable to attend the meeting of the council, any member elected by the members present from amongst themselves at the meeting shall preside at the meeting.

All questions which come up before any meeting of the Council shall be decided by a majority of votes of the members present and voting and in the event of equality of votes, the Chairperson, or in his absence, the person presiding shall have a second or casting vote. The Council shall constitute from amongst its members an Executive Committee and such other committee for general or special purposes as the Council deems necessary to carry out the purposes of this Act. The Central Government shall appoint the Member-Secretary of the Member Council to exercise such powers and perform such duties under the direction of the Council as may be prescribed or as may be delegated to him by the Chairperson. The Council shall, with the previous sanction of the Central Government employ such officers and other employees as it deems necessary to carry out the purpose of this Act. The Council shall, with the previous sanction of the Central Government fix the allowances to be paid to the Chairperson and other members and determine the conditions of services of the Member-Secretary, officers and other employees of the Council.

The Council may enter into negotiation with the authority in any country outside India for settling of a scheme or reciprocity for the recognition of qualifications, and the pursuance of any such scheme, the Central Government may, by notification amend the schedule so as to include therein any qualification which the Council has decided should be recognised and by such notification may also direct that an entry shall be made in the last column of the schedule declaring that it shall be the recognised qualification only when granted after a specified date. Every university or institution in India which grants a recognised qualification shall furnish such information as the Council may from time to time, require as to the courses of study and examinations to be undergone in order to obtain such qualification, as to the ages at which such courses of study and examinations are required to be undergone and such qualification is conferred and generally as to the requisites for obtaining such qualification.

The Council shall appoint such member of Inspector as it may deem requisite to inspect any University or Institution where education for practicing as rehabilitation professional is given or to attend any examination held by any University or Institution for the purpose of recommending to the Central Government recognition of qualifications granted by that University or Institution as recognised rehabilitation qualifications. The Council may appoint such number. Visitors as it may deem requisite to inspect any University or institution wherein education for rehabilitation professional is given or attend any examination for the purpose of granting recognised rehabilitation qualifications. The Council may prescribed the minimum standards of education required for granting recognised rehabilitation qualification by Universities or institutions in India. The Council may prescribe standards of professional conduct and etiquette and a code of ethics for rehabilitation professionals.

Every rule and every regulation made under this Act shall be laid as soon as may be after it is made, before each House of Parliament, while it is in session for a total period of thirty days which may be comprised in one session or in two or more successive sessions and if, before the expiry of the session immediately following the session or the successive session aforesaid, both Houses agree in making any modification in the rule or regulation or both Houses agree that the rule or regulation should not be made, the rule or regulation shall thereafter have effect only in such modified form or be of no effect, as the case may be; so, however that any such modification or annulment shall be without prejudice to the validity of anything previously done under that rule or regulation.

The National Trust for Welfare of Persons with Autism, Cerebral Palsy, Mental Retardation and Multiple Disabilities Act 1999

The enactment of the National Trust for Welfare of Persons with Autism, Cerebral Palsy, Mental Retardation and Multiple Disabilities Act, 1999 (referred to as the National Trust Act) aims to fulfil a common demand of families seeking reliable arrangement for their severely disabled wards. The National Trust Act mandates the creation of a Local Level Committee (LLC) comprising District Magistrate along with one representative from a registered organisation and one person with a disability. The Act also lays down duties of the legal guardian who has to furnish periodic returns to the LLC about the assets of the ward and their disposal in his hands. The National Trust for Welfare of Persons with Autism, Cerebral Palsy, Mental Retardation and Multiple Disabilities Act, 1999 provides for a law relating to certain specified disabilities. Clause (j) of Section 2 of that Act defines a person with disability to mean a person suffering from any of the conditions relating to autism, cerebral palsy, mental retardation or a combination of any two or more of such conditions and includes a person suffering from severe multiple disabilities. This Act empowers a Local Level Committee to appoint a guardian, to a person with disabilities, who shall have the care of the person and property of the disabled person.

With effect from such date as the Central Government may, by notification, appoint there shall be constituted, for the purposes of this Act, a body by the name of the National Trust for Welfare of Persons with Autism, Cerebral Palsy, Mental Retardation and Multiple Disabilities, which shall be a body corporate by the name aforesaid, having perpetual succession and a common seal, with power, subject to the provisions of this Act, to acquire, hold and dispose of property, both movable and immovable, and to contract, and shall, by the said name, sue or be sued. The general superintendence, direction and management of the affairs and business of the Trust shall vest in a Board which may exercise all powers and do all acts and things which may be exercised or done by the Trust. The head office of the Trust shall be at New Delhi and the Board may, with the previous approval of the Central Government, establish offices at other places in India.

The Chairperson or a Member shall hold office for a term of three years from the date of his appointment or until his successor shall have been duly appointed, whichever is longer. Before appointing any person as the Chairperson or a Member, the Central Government shall satisfy itself that the person does not and will not, have any such financial or other interest as is likely to affect prejudicially his function as such member. The Board shall meet at least once in three months at such time and place as may be determined by the Board by regulations and shall observe such rules of procedure in the transaction of business at a meeting as may be prescribed. The Chairperson, if for any reason is unable to attend the meeting of the Board, any member elected by the Members present from amongst themselves at the meeting, shall preside at the meeting. The Chairperson may resign his office by writing under his hand addressed to the Central Government: Provided that the Chairperson shall continue in office until the appointment of his successor is made by the Central Government. The Central Government shall appoint the Chief Executive Officer to exercise such powers and perform such duties under the direction of the Board as may be prescribed or as may be delegated to him by the Chairperson.

All questions considered at a meeting shall be decided by a majority of votes of the members present and voting and in the event of equality of votes, the Chairperson or in his absence, the member presiding at the meeting, as the case may be, shall have a second or casting vote. The funds of the Trust shall be deposited in a nationalised bank and operated by any two of the three signatories nominated by the Board, one of the three being the Chief Executive Officer. The Comptroller and Auditor General of India and any other person appointed by him in connection with the audit of the accounts of the Trust shall have the same rights, privileges and authority in connection with such audit as the Comptroller and Auditor General of India has in connection with the audit of Government accounts and in particular, shall have the right to demand the production of books of account, connected vouchers and other documents and papers and to inspect the offices of the Trust. The accounts of the Trust as certified by the Comptroller and Auditor General of India or any other person appointed by him in this behalf, together with the audit report thereon, shall be forwarded by the 31st December every year to the Central Government, and that Government shall cause the same to be laid before each House of Parliament.

The Mental Health Act, 1987

The Indian Lunacy Act, 1912 has no relevance today because our medical science is rapidly growing and advanced. Mental illness is now not incurable and it can be cured with proper and timely diagnosis. The society's mood is also changed and the person now realised that no stigma should be attached to such type of diseases. The experience of the working of Indian Lunacy Act, 1912 (4 of 1912) has revealed that it has become outmoded. With the rapid advance of medical science and the understanding of the nature of malady, it has become necessary to have fresh legislation with provisions for treatment of mentally ill persons in accordance with the new approach. The Mental Health Act, 1987 was aimed at to consolidate and amend the law relating to treatment and care of mentally ill persons regarding their property and matter connected therewith. The Act has been divided into six chapters dealing with different matters. It deals with the establishment of Central and State authorities for mental health services, their appointments, their functions, the psychiatric hospitals and nursing homes, their establishment, admission to such institution of mentally ill person has been elaborately provided in the Act. The Mental Health Bill comes into an Act after passing by both the Houses of Parliament and has received the assent of the President on 22nd May, 1987 and it is known as the Mental Health Act, 1987.

MHA (1987) came into force in 1993, replacing the Indian Lunacy Act, 1912. It is divided into ten chapters consisting of 98 sections. Rights of patients with mental illness undermined can be brought forward by adding rights of the persons with mental illness in the preamble of MHA (1987). In the current MHA (1987) the review processes or appeal processes for mentally ill patients are far from realistic. Hence, it can be said that the procedure prescribed by the MHA (1987) for involuntary admission and treatment can be considered as arbitrary and unreasonable. Unfortunately, there are no guidelines or provisions under MHA (1987) for emergency crisis intervention to help families caring for a mentally ill family member. MHA (1987) is silent regarding the consent for treatment, and the method to be adopted when a severely ill patient refuses well established treatments like medication or modified electroconvulsive therapy.

The Central Government shall establish an authority for mental health with such designation as it may deem fit. The State Government shall establish an authority for mental with such designation as it may deem fit. The Central Government may, in any part of India, or the state government may, within the limits of its jurisdiction, established or maintain psychiatric hospitals or psychiatric nursing homes for the admission, and care of mentally ill persons at such places as it thinks fit; and separate psychiatric hospitals and psychiatric nursing homes may be established. Every person, who holds, at the commencement of this Act, a valid license authorising that person to establish or maintain any psychiatric hospital or psychiatric nursing home, shall, if the said person intends to establish or continue the maintenance of such hospital or nursing home after the expiry of the period referred to in Clause (a) of the proviso to sub-section (1) of Sec. 6, make at least one month before the expiry of such period, an application to the licensing authority for the grant of a fresh license for the establishment or maintenance of such hospital or nursing home, as the case may be.

The Mental Health Act, 1987 provides for a law relating to the treatment and care of mentally ill persons and to make better provision with respect to their property and affairs. According to the said Act, mentally ill person means a person who is in need of treatment by reason of any mental disorder other than mental retardation. Sections 53 and 54 of this Act provide for the appointment of guardians for mentally ill persons and in certain cases, managers in respect of their property. The prescribed appointing authorities are the district courts and collectors of districts under the Mental Health Act, 1987.

The Rights of Persons with Disabilities Bill, 2014

The Rights of Persons with Disabilities Bill, 2014 was introduced in the Rajya Sabha on February 7, 2013 by the Minister of Social Justice and Empowerment, Mr Mallikarjun Kharge. The Bill repeals the Persons with Disabilities (Equal Opportunities Protection of Rights and Full Participation) Act, 1995. Disability is defined to include 19 conditions such as: autism; low vision and blindness; cerebral palsy; deaf blindness; haemophilia; hearing impairment; leprosy; intellectual disability; mental illness; muscular dystrophy; multiple sclerosis; learning disability; speech and language disability; sickle cell disease; thalassemia; chronic neurological conditions; and multiple disability. Persons with benchmark disabilities are defined as those with at least 40 per cent of any of the above specified disabilities.

The Bill states that persons with disabilities shall have the right to equality and shall not be discriminated against on grounds of their disability. Rights of disabled persons include protection from inhuman treatment and equal protection and safety in situations of risk, armed conflict, humanitarian emergencies and natural disasters. The Bill provides for the access to inclusive education, vocational training and self-employment of disabled persons. All government institutions of higher education and those getting aid from the government are required to reserve at least five per cent of seats for persons with benchmark disabilities. The central and state governments have to identify posts in establishments under them to be reserved for persons with benchmark disabilities. At least five per cent of the vacancies are to be filled by persons or class of persons with at least 40 per cent of any of the disabilities. Of this, one per cent shall be reserved for persons with (i) blindness and low vision; (ii) hearing and speech impairment; (iii) locomotors disability; (iv) autism, intellectual disability and mental illness; and (v) multiple disabilities. The Bill provides that the reservation has to be computed on the basis of total number of vacancies in the strength of a cadre. The government may exempt any establishment from this provision. The Bill provides that if a district court finds that a mentally ill person is not capable of taking care of himself or of taking legally binding decisions, it may order guardianship to the person. The nature of such guardianship is also specified. The central and state governments are required to establish a National and State Commissions for Persons with Disabilities, respectively.

This Bill who seeks to replace the Persons with Disabilities (Equal Opportunities, Protection of Rights and Full Participation) Act, 1995, attempts to bring India in line with the 21 century understanding of the rights of persons with disabilities as captured in the UN Convention on the Rights of Persons with Disabilities ratified by India. This version of the Bill is the last in a series of versions that were made public by the Ministry over the last two years. This new clause provides that reservation for persons with disabilities shall be only for the specific posts that are expressly identified by the concerned authority. Thus, even if a person is able to do the work required for a particular post, he will be ineligible unless it is specifically reserved. This is highly controversial and violates UNCRPD principles since it presumes, wrongly, that persons with disabilities can only perform some jobs or tasks. This provision must be deleted.

Government introduced the Rights of Persons with Disabilities Bill in Rajya Sabha, seeking to increase reservation for disabled persons in public sector jobs from existing three per cent to five per cent and reserve seat for them in higher educational institutions. At present, the reservation for the disabled is only three per cent in the ratio of one per cent each for the physically, visually and hearing-impaired persons. The new Bill, if passed by the Parliament, will extend the quota by two per cent, covering two new additional categories - mentally disabled and people with multiple disabilities. The proposed legislation divides the broad categories into various sub-categories, seeking to include as many types of disabilities as possible. It includes sickle cell disease, thalassemia and muscular dystrophy besides autism, spectrum disorder, blindness, cerebral palsy, chronic neurological conditions, mental illness and multiple disabilities. The Bill, introduced by the Union Minister for Social

Justice and Empowerment Mallikarjun Kharge, also provides for setting up National Commission for Persons with Disabilities, which will have statutory powers besides establishing a dedicated National Fund for Persons with Disabilities. The proposed legislation is expected to bring more clarity in defining disability. Anyone suffering 40 per cent disability or more will continue to be defined as a 'person with disability'. Besides making provisions to prevent people with disabilities from harassment while getting disability certificates, the proposal legislation also provides for stringent punitive measures under which anyone violating the provisions could face from six months to five years of imprisonment and a fine from Rs. 10,000 to five lakhs. The government had in December (2003) decided to replace the Persons with Disabilities (Equal Opportunity Protection of Rights and Full Participation) Act of 1995 with the new Bill. It maintained that the proposed legislation is in consonance with the United Nations Convention on Rights of Persons with Disabilities, which India had signed in 2007. Various Disabled Rights Groups had protested against the Bill in its current form, saying the provisions were not in tune with the norms of UN convention. The groups had identified 20 shortcomings and suggested amendments in the Bill.

Hundreds of disabled people staged a protest demanding the passage of the Disability Rights Bill in the ongoing parliament session, after the Rajya Sabha was adjourned for the second day since the introduction of the Bill. Despite the assurances given by the political leaders not to politicise the matter, leaders in the Rajya Sabha are not letting the house discuss the bill at all. Members of the disabled community have been protesting and lobbying to get the bills passed. There are about 70 million disabled people in India. More than 80 per cent of the disabled in the country live in villages and remain unemployed and hapless throughout their lives because of the lack of opportunities from the government. If the Disability Rights Bill gets clearance in parliament with the amendments suggested by the rights groups, then avenues for disabled people in education and employment will open up.

The eagerly awaited bill, which is still pending in parliament, seeks to expand the definition of disability from the current seven categories to 19 to include sickle cell disease, thalassemia and muscular dystrophy besides autism spectrum disorder, blindness, cerebral palsy, chronic neurological conditions and mental illness. In addition, the bill seeks to increase jobs for disabled persons in the public sector from the current three to five per cent and reserve seats for them in higher educational institutions. Furthermore, it will also require all recognised educational institutions to be inclusive and provide reasonable accommodation. Though the campaigners had hoped the bill would be passed in this past session of parliament, if failed to do so. Now it is unclear how long they will have to wait, but it is expected they will have to rely on the next government after May, 2014, elections. If the bill is passed, the national disability commission will be expected not just to draw up guidelines but also have the powers to enforce them and levy hefty fines for those violating the new deal. India ratified the UN Convention on the Rights of Persons with Disabilities in October 2007. The convention marked a formal shift from the archaic medical model to the social model, and promotes the rights of people living with disabilities.

International Human Rights Law

International human rights law provides a powerful, but often neglected, tool to advance the rights and freedoms of persons with mental disabilities. International law may seem marginal or unimportant in developed countries with democratic and constitutional systems of their own. Yet, even democracies often resist making reforms to mental health law and policy, and domestic courts do not always compel the changes necessary to improve the rights and welfare of persons with mental disabilities. International human rights law is important in the context of mental health because of two fundamental ideas unique to global protection of rights and freedoms. First, human rights law is the only source of law that legitimises international scrutiny of mental health policies and practices within a sovereign country. Second, international human rights law provides fundamental protections that cannot be taken away by the ordinary political process. The human rights movement solidified the inherent rights and freedoms of individuals by recognising these rights under international law and piercing the veil of national sovereignty to hold states accountable for violations. Human rights, afford all persons fundamental rights and freedoms and place duties on government to respect them. Rather than focusing on personal obligations, classic understandings of human rights centre around a government's duty to respect rights and freedoms.

There are three legal instruments which make up the International Bill of Human Rights. These are the Universal Declaration of Human Rights, passed by the General Assembly of the United Nations in 1948, the International Covenant on Civil and Political Rights (ICCPR), and the International Covenant on Economic, Social and Cultural Rights (ICESCR), both adopted in 1966. Many experts believe that a new human rights convention on the theme of disability is necessary to give status, authority and visibility to disability rights that cannot be achieved through the process of interpretations and refinement of the existing treaties and Standard Rules. In response to a continued advocacy for a specific disability convention, in December 2001 the UN General Assembly passed a resolution establishing an Ad Hoc Committee *"to consider proposals for a comprehensive and integral international convention to promote and protect the rights and dignity of persons with disabilities, based on the holistic approach in the work done in the field of social development, human rights and non-discrimination"*.

The Disability Rights Movement

Unlike other movements like Feminism or Lesbian Movements which have distinct agendas of either gender justice or the right to sexual orientation, the Disability Rights Movement does not have systematic path. Disability Rights Movement even in the West has a very recent origin and tries to draw strength from the traditional legal order rather than by critiquing or deconstructing it. The Disability Rights Movement in India and in Third World countries is discursive and disorganised and there is no written document to trace its origin. Actually in India the Disability Rights Movement has been launched by NGOs and a large number of NGOs have mushroomed all over the country. Until 1995 there was no law that even defined discrimination against people with disabilities. It is only with the 'Persons with Disabilities Act,' passed in 1995 that discrimination specifically against persons with disabilities came under the purview of the law. The Ministry of Social Welfare was largely concerned with problems of persons with disability and with providing them privileges.

Large numbers of voluntary organisations are operating in India, especially for the welfare of person with disabilities. Sincere and dedicated efforts on the part of government and voluntary organisations have resulted in high level of literacy among person with disabilities and increased awareness among persons with disabilities and their parents about their rights and capabilities. But the dark side is that, many of voluntary organisations believe on charity model. These organisations are not professionally managed. Disability movement in India has succeeded in changing the approach towards disability from moral model to charity model but limited has been achieved in the direction of human rights model. Collective efforts on the part of person with disabilities, their advocates, voluntary organisations, government and society at large are required to create real world where abilities and disabilities are not seen on the basis of physical or mental impairment but disability is seen as diverse abilities.

International Disability Rights Monitor

The International Disability Rights Monitor (IDRM) is an international grass-roots research project designed to document and assess the status of people living with disabilities worldwide. It represents an ongoing collaboration between the Centre for International Rehabilitation (CIR) and many international and national disability groups. The IDRM is the world's only systematic international shadow monitoring report focusing on disability rights. The mission of the International Disability Rights Monitor (IDRM) project is to promote the full inclusion and participation of people with disabilities in society and to advance the use of international humanitarian law in ensuring that the rights of people with disabilities are respected and enforced.

Prevention of Disability

A large proportion of disabilities in India are preventable, including disabilities that arise in the circumstances surrounding birth, including maternal conditions, from malnutrition, and from causes such as traffic accidents or workplace injuries.

Immunisation Programmes

The goal of the Immunisation Programme is to reduce and ultimately eliminate the incidence of vaccine preventable diseases by working in conjunction with public and private healthcare providers throughout the state. Accomplishing this goal will require achieving and maintaining high vaccination coverage levels, improving vaccination strategies among under vaccinated populations, prompt reporting and thorough investigation of suspected cases and rapid institution of disease control measures. The Immunisation Programme develops strategies to ensure that the children and adults of the Commonwealth are appropriately immunised and have access to vaccines. Vaccinations are incredibly important, because immunisation doesn't just protect you; it also protects everyone around you. When you get vaccinated against a disease, you build up your immune system, making you stronger and more resistant to that disease. India has long had vertical programmes that address comprehensive immunisation according to international norms of the Universal Programme for Immunisation. Immunisation affects mortality, morbidity and disability. Measles in particular is associated with blindness, and other vaccine preventable illnesses predispose infants and children to other diseases which may in turn cause long-term disability.

National Health Policy (2002) is directed towards achieving an acceptable, affordable and sustainable standard of health through an appropriate health system. Provision of universal immunisation of children against vaccine preventable diseases is one of the major goals under this policy. Country developed a comprehensive Multi Year Strategic Plan for Immunisation in 2005 with an addendum in 2010 to achieve these targets of improving access and utilisation of immunisation in the country. The Government of India procures and supplies all UIP vaccines along with diluents to all states. In addition to vaccines, syringes of different capacities, are also procured centrally and supplied to states. The process involves vaccines and logistics forecasting, scheduling, ensuring supplies as per need, and so on. Disposal of immunisation waste is strictly as per Central Pollution Control Board (CPCB) guidelines for biomedical waste disposal. The principles followed are segregation of waste at source (at the session site), transportation to the PHC or CHC, treatment of sharps and potentially biohazard us plastic waste, disposal of sharps in sharp pits and treated plastic waste through proper recycling.

The Immunisation Programme runs due to the coordinated efforts of different cadres of health staff working in the states at different levels (states, districts, PHCs and CHCs). The Government of India has enhanced the training capacity for cold chain technicians by setting up the National Cold Chain and Vaccine Management Resource Centre (NCCVMRC) at National Institute of Health and Family Welfare (NIHFW), New Delhi and also the National Cold Chain Training Centre (NCCTC) at State Health Transport Organisation (SHTO), Pune, and Maharashtra. There is a remarkable achievement, particularly considering the fact that in 2009 India accounted for nearly half of the total number of polio cases globally and there were an estimated two lakh cases of polio every year in the country in the year 1978.

Polio Eradication

Polio is a crippling and potentially fatal infectious disease. There is no cure, but there are safe and effective vaccines. The strategy to eradicate polio is based on preventing infection by immunising every child until transmission stops and the world is polio-free. Polio (poliomyelitis) is a highly infectious disease caused by a virus. It invades the nervous system and can cause irreversible paralysis in a matter of hours. Polio is spread through person-to-person contact. When a child is infected with wild polio-virus, the virus enters the body through the mouth and multiplies in the intestine. Young children who are not yet toilet-trained are a ready source of transmission, regardless of their environment. Polio can be spread when food or drink is contaminated by faces. There is also evidence that flies can passively transfer polio-virus from faeces to food. There is no cure for polio, only treatment to alleviate the symptoms. Heat and physical therapy is used to stimulate the muscles and antispasmodic drugs are given to relax the muscles. While this can improve mobility, it cannot reverse permanent polio paralysis.

Polio remains endemic in three countries – Afghanistan, Nigeria and Pakistan. Until polio-virus transmission is interrupted in these countries, all countries remain at risk of importation of polio, especially in the 'polio-virus importation belt' of countries from West Africa to the Horn of Africa. The Global Polio Eradication Initiative (GPEI) is financed by a wide range of public and private donors, who help meet the costs of the Initiative's eradication activities. The requirements for 2013-18 are projected to be approximately $ 5.5 billion. Over $ 11 billion has been invested in the Global Polio Eradication Initiative since its launch in 1988. These contributions have reduced the incidence of polio by 99 per cent and laid the foundations for an infrastructure to be used beyond polio eradication. The Centers for Disease Control report that in India there were 135 polio cases with onset of paralysis in 2004, and for 2005, India reported only 66 polio cases with onset of paralysis for the year: mostly in Bihar and UP. With respect to disability, the story of recent years has positive elements as well, perhaps the most high profile being progress against polio through the Pulse Polio Immunisation campaign (PPI).

The Global Polio Eradication Initiative (GPEI) has driven a 99 per cent reduction in polio cases during the last two decades, from nearly 350,000 cases in 1988 to fewer than 1,500 in 2010. Improved vaccines and immunisation programmes have spurred the decline. The discovery of an effective polio vaccine by Jonas Salk in 1955 gave the world hope against this terrible disease. Salk's inactivated polio vaccine (IPV), along with Albert Sabin's oral polio vaccine (OPV) discovery in 1963, have been key factors in global immunisation efforts, bringing us closer than ever to complete eradication of polio.

India has not reported any case of polio since a two-year old girl got polio paralysis on 13th January, 2011 in Howrah district of West Bengal. India's victory over polio paves the way for polio-free certification of the South East Asia region of WHO. India overcame huge challenges, with a strong commitment that matched $ 2 billion allocation over the years to stop polio. Implementing innovative strategies, the programme reaches an incredible 99 per cent coverage in polio campaigns, ensuring every child; even in the remotest corner of the country is protected against polio. India introduced the oral polio vaccine in 1985 in the Universal Immunisation Programme in the backdrop of over 200,000 cases of polio annually (as per estimates of the Indian Academy of Pediatrics). In 1995, the first national polio immunisation campaign was held; since then two national and multiple sub-national campaigns are rolled out every year for children up to five years of age. In each national polio campaign, 2.3 million lakh vaccinators, led by 1,55,000 supervisors, visit 209 million households to immunise 170 million children up to the age of five years.

India has reached a major landmark by not reporting a polio case for nearly three years. This has brought the entire Southeast Asia region of WHO closer to polio-free certification. In 2012, India was taken off the global list of polio-endemic countries which reduced to three. With the certification of the Southeast Asia region now, four of the six WHO regions will become polio-free, leaving only WHO's African region and East Mediterranean region to be certified. India's polio-free status has demonstrated that global eradication of polio is an achievable goal. Best practices and lessons learned from India's initiative are being applied by polio-endemic countries like Nigeria, Afghanistan and Pakistan. The programme now serves as a model for health programmes globally - it's demonstrated that it's possible to achieve ambitious health goals through high vaccination coverage, even in areas with weak health systems. WHO, in collaboration with the government of India, established the 'National Polio Surveillance Project' (NPSP) in 1997 to provide technical support in key areas of surveillance for polio and mass vaccination campaigns. Over the years, NPSP's role expanded to include additional areas such as routine immunisation, polio-free certification and end-game strategy. Cross-cutting areas include evidence generation, research and immunisation monitoring, programme strategy development, capacity building of government staff, accreditation of laboratories and providing timely feedback to government for action at all levels. Mass awareness was created by banners, posters, hoardings and engaging celebrities through television and radio. Newspaper advertisements in local languages also created awareness. Vaccinators were trained to enhance their interpersonal skills, so they could mobilise communities better.

National Blindness Control Programme

The NBCP was started in 1982 and is one of the largest disability prevention programmes. It undertakes activities like general eye care, cataract surgery, correction of refractive errors, etc. The NBCP, like other vertical programmes functions at the apex through a National Programme Management Cell in MoH, State Ophthalmic Cells, tertiary Regional Institutes of Ophthalmology and Eye Hospitals, and at the district level through District Blindness Control Society and District/Sub-District Hospitals. The objectives of the programme are: (1) To reduce the backlog of blindness through identification and treatment of the blind; (2) To develop comprehensive eye care facilities in every district; (3) To develop human resources for providing eye care services; (4) To improve quality of service delivery to the affected population; (5) To secure participation of voluntary organisations/private practitioners in eye care; (6) To enhance community awareness on eye care; (7) To provide best possible treatment for curable blindness available in the district/region; and (8) To set up the mechanism for referral coordination and feedback between organisations dedicated to prevention, treatment and rehabilitation. The NPCB funds are released by Government of India (GOI) to State Blindness Control Society or State Health and Family Welfare Society based on the Annual Action Plan submitted. The Cabinet Committee on Economic Affairs (CCEA), the highest body constituted by the Parliament of India, has endorsed and approved a budget of INR 12,500 (twelve thousand and five hundred) million for the XI five-year plan (2007-12) period.

At the national level, a National Programme Management Cell has been established in the Directorate General of Health Services (DGHS), Department of Health in the Ministry of Health and Family Welfare. It has two wings viz: the Technical Wing in the DGHS which deals with the ophthalmic section and the Administrative Wing that deals with blindness control section. At the State level, each State has an Ophthalmology Cell in respective Directorate of Health Services devoted to the programme implementation and monitoring. Gradually the process of setting up of a State Blindness Control Society in each State has been initiated. At the district level, District Blindness Control Society (DBCS) has been established in almost, all the district. The National Programme for Control of Blindness has made efforts to foster inter-sectoral coordination, partnership with professional bodies, private sector and NGOs, co-ordination with donor agencies and involvement of community. Constitution of District Blindness Control Society in each district of the country has been undertaken with the prime objective of ensuring multi-sectoral approach to blindness control where besides health sector, education, welfare, media and revenue sectors are involved in various activities.

Reduction in the backlog of the blind person by active screening of population above 50 years, organising screening eye camp and transporting operable cases to eye care facilities. Development of eye care services and improvement in quality of eye care by training of personnel, supply of high tech equipments, are strengthening follow up services and monitoring of services. To make eye care comprehensive, besides cataract surgeries other Intra Ocular Surgical operations for treatment of Glaucoma, Diabetic Retinopathy etc. may also be provided free of cost to the poor patients through governments as well as qualified non-government organisations. Corneal Blindness is important as it mostly occurs in children and productive adult age. Effective intervention may lead to substantial reduction in corneal blindness and decreased demand of corneal transplantation. Common causes of corneal blindness are due to Vitamin - A deficiency infection, injury and malnutrition. Donated eyes need to be removed within six hours of death of the individual. Eye removal procedure takes 10 to 15 minutes. Donated eyes are to be preserved in specific solutions stored in eye banks and utilised for transplantation at cornea grafting centres within 72 hours.

National Leprosy Eradication Programme

Leprosy is one of the world's oldest and most dreaded diseases that have tormented humans throughout history, leaving lasting impressions on religion, literature and art. In addition to the physical effects of the diseases, patients have also suffered severe social stigma and ostracism from their families, communities, and even health professionals to such an extent that leprosy has been known since ancient times as the death before death. In the past two decades, marked success of combined efforts from the World Health Organisation, local governments, health professionals, and non-governmental organisations (NGOs) in identifying patients with leprosy and providing effective treatment to them has resulted in near elimination of leprosy. The origin of leprosy has always been a matter of uncertainty and an Indian or African origin for the disease has often been assumed based on historical sources that support an initial spread of the disease from Asia to Europe by the armies of Alexander the Great after 400 BC.

Unfortunately, social stigma, alienation, and violence against sufferers of leprosy are attitudes that have continued through the ages up to the 20th century and these still exist, though in a diluted form. One of the first advances away from the age of superstition into the modern scientific era occurred in response to the last endemic wave of leprosy in Europe, which peaked in Norway in the mid-1800s, when approximately 3,000 cases were reported. The WHO Steering Committee on Chemotherapy of Mycobacterial Diseases recommended that the search for new drugs and new drug regimens should continue to consolidate efforts towards the goal of elimination of leprosy, improved patient compliance, develop alternate agents against dapsone/ clofazimine/rifampicin resistant bacilli, kill persistent bacilli more efficiently and to develop supervised/supervisable regimens (short) for prevention of drug resistance. The Ministry of Health and Family Welfare and Ministry of Social Justice and Empowerment, GOI are expanding rehabilitation services to the persons with disabilities. For example, Ministry of Health and Family Welfare is under the process of establishing physical medicine and rehabilitation department in medical colleges and regional hospitals. The most striking trend in global leprosy in recent years is the decreased prevalence in India. India's contribution to the global leprosy burden has declined from 73 to 54 per cent of the total newly detected leprosy cases over these years.

The World Health Assembly in May 1991 adopted a resolution for global leprosy elimination as a public health problem by the year 2000. After the declaration of the global elimination, a target was reset for the remaining 15 countries to achieve elimination at the national level by the end of December, 2005. India was one of these countries. The National Health Policy of India 2002 also set the goal of leprosy elimination in India by the end of year 2005. Modified Leprosy Elimination Campaign (MLEC) approach was first started in India during 1997-1998 with the objective to increase mass awareness about leprosy in the general population, to give training to the General Health Service (GHS) personnel who were not involved for leprosy service delivery so far and to detect the hidden leprosy cases in all the States/ UTs and to put them under Multiple Drug Therapy (MDT). Subsequently four more MLECs were conducted with excellent results. The National Leprosy Eradication Programme has achieved its principal goal of leprosy elimination as a public health problem at the National level, which was doubtful in the minds of many experts about five years back. During the process of elimination, the National Programme achieved a number of benefits for the suffering leprosy patients and the community. When the performance of the National Leprosy Eradication Programme (NLEP) was assessed in 1997, it was found that some states were lagging behind, although the progress was satisfactory at the national level.

Direct Payments

Direct payments give local councils power to offer people money to pay for the support they have been assessed as needing in lieu of providing the services direct. Direct payments are highly effective in enabling people with learning disabilities to gain greater control over their lives, because they can choose how they want their support needs met. The success of direct payments for people with learning disabilities depends on good support services. Most local councils operate support schemes, but often these are focused on the types of support people with physical disabilities may need. Schemes must be accessible to people with learning disabilities, so that they too have the right support to manage a direct payment and remain in control.

Conclusion

In the last twenty years, a number of statutes relating to the disability sector have been enacted. The major laws dealing with disability are the Mental Health Act, 1987, The Rehabilitation Council of India Act, 1992, the Persons with Disabilities (Equal Opportunities, Protection of Rights and Full Participation) Act, 1995, and The National Trust for Welfare of Persons with Autism, Cerebral Palsy, Mental Retardation and Multiple Disabilities Act, 1999. With the passing of these laws there are a plethora of provisions for protection, care, treatment, rehabilitation, security and empowerment for persons with different disabilities. These laws help effect a change in the way society looks at disability. But unfortunately, these laws are not being implemented properly in the North East region with even the awareness level remaining low, as the study reveals. The situation with regard to implementation of Persons with Disabilities Act is quite dismal in most States. The authorities have failed to give full effect to the statutory mandate of identification and reservation of jobs for persons with disabilities. The process for issuing disability certificates needs to be regularised and simplified. Most public buildings and facilities are not accessible. There is scant awareness among the police and administration about their responsibilities towards the mentally ill.

Selected Books

1. Benedicte Ingstad and Susan Reynolds Whyte (1995). *Disability and Culture,* University of California Press.
2. Christopher M. Bell (2011). *Blackness and Disability: Critical Examinations and Cultural Interventions,* LIT Verlag Münster.
3. Geoffrey Dale Arnott (2011). *The Disability Support Worker,* Pearson Education Australia.
4. Graham Pullin (2009). *Design Meets Disability,* MIT Press.
5. Hayley Fitzgerald (2008). *Disability and Youth Sport,* Taylor and Francis.
6. Henri-Jacques Stiker (1999). *A History of Disability,* University of Michigan Press.
7. Jane Seale (2006). *E-Learning and Disability in Higher Education: Accessibility Research and Practice,* Taylor and Francis.
8. Karen P. DePauw, and Susan J. Gavron (2005). *Disability Sport,* Human Kinetics.
9. Lennard J. Davis (1995). *Enforcing Normalcy: Disability, Deafness, and the Body,* Verso.
10. Lennard J. Davis (2006). *The Disability Studies Reader,* Taylor and Francis.
11. Robert McRuer and Anna Mollow (2012). Sex and Disability, Duke University Press.
12. Robert McRuer (2006). Crip Theory: Cultural Signs of Queerness and Disability, NYU Press.
13. Sharon N. Barnartt (2010). Disability as a Fluid State, Emerald Group Publishing.
14. Shelley Lynn Tremain (2005). Foucault and the Government of Disability, University of Michigan Press.
15. Simi Linton (1998). Claiming Disability: Knowledge and Identity, NYU Press.
16. Soren V. Randall (2006). Learning disabilities: new research, Nova Science Publishers.

7

Conclusion and Recommendations

Disability is the umbrella term for impairments, activity limitations and participation restrictions, referring to the negative aspects of the interaction between an individual and that individual's contextual factors. Everyone in the world, male or female, rich or poor, educated or non-educated, married or unmarried, should have equality in human right. Intellectual disability is a global phenomenon which needs a global perspective. Everyone should have an equalised opportunity to have an access to care, education, vocation, socialisation, etc. by a global team for a global struggle. The Millennium Development Goals established a unifying set of developmental objectives for the global community. Around 15 per cent of the world's population, or estimated one billion people, live with disabilities. They are the world's largest minority. Unemployment among the persons with disabilities is as high as 80 per cent in some countries. Often employers assume that persons with disabilities are unable to work. The World Bank estimates that 20 per cent of the world's poorest people have some kind of disability, and tend to be regarded in their own communities as the most disadvantaged. Statistics show a steady increase in these numbers. Persons with disabilities face a lot of challenges and are sometimes abused both in the developed and developing countries. People with disabilities in developing countries in Africa face many limitations, despite the proclamation of the UN Decade of Disabled Persons. Their human rights receive little or no respect, the general development programmes do not take into account the needs of disabled people or their participation in programmes, disabled people have little or no access to services offered to other citizens, they are unable to take decisions concerning their own future, and they are generally poor, living at the bottom of the social scale.

The Academic Network of European Disability experts were established by the European Commission in 2008 to provide scientific support and advice for its disability policy Unit. In particular, the activities of the Network will support the future development of the EU Disability Action Plan and practical implementation of the United Nations Convention on the Rights of Disabled People. In Sweden 1.5 million people are disabling. The Disabled Peoples Organisation is an umbrella organisation of associations for people with disabilities in Denmark. In 2007, 25.6 thousand persons of working age were for the first time recognised as disabled in Lithuania. There are ten million disable people in Britain. There are five million disabled people living in France, two million of who are less mobile. There are reportedly more than 165,000 disabled people in Moldova, roughly five per cent of the population. In Slovenia it has been estimated that between 160,000 and 170,000 people are disabled.

About 3.8 million Canadians reported having a disability in 2012. About 56.7 million people i.e., 19 per cent of the population had a disability in 2010 in USA. Mentally and physically disabled children and adults in Mexico continue to live in abusive and squalid conditions in many orphanages and mental health facilities throughout the country. The situation of persons with multiple disabilities, many of them presenting mental disability is blurred in Guatemala. According to the household survey, the total population of Honduras is estimated to be 66,97,916 people. From 1960 to 1990, the interior regions of Nicaragua were the site of prolonged and violent political revolution. The conflicts resulted in an increased number of persons with disabilities throughout the country. Disabled people's organisations estimate that 15 per cent of the population has some form of disability in Argentina. Brazil is one of the largest countries in the region, and thus has a large population of people with disabilities i.e., 14 per cent of the populations had some kind of disability. Just under one in five Australians (18.5 per cent or 4.0 million persons) reported having a disability in 2009. In each South Asian country, at least ten per cent of the population lives with a disability. Disability and poverty are intricately linked. Disability causes poverty and poverty exacerbates disability people with disabilities are among the poorest and most vulnerable.

Disability is a universal element in the human condition to which no one is immune. Unrecognised as a problem for development, the condition of being disabled is at the bottom of the development agenda. Government of Bangladesh is now very conscious and become proactive on the need for appropriate policies, laws and plans for the education, training and rehabilitation of the PWDs (Persons with Disabilities). Acquiring accurate data on the prevalence of disability in Nepal is a difficult task for different reasons, including the lack of a common understanding how to define disability and the stigma associated with it. Census 2001 of India has revealed that over 21 million people in India as suffering from one or the other kind of disability. This is equivalent to 2.1 per cent of the population. Among the total disabled in the country, 12.6 million are males and 9.3 million are females. According to the Population and Housing Census of Bhutan, the number of disabled persons is 21,894, representing 3.4 per cent of the country's total population. Ninety five per cent of children with disabilities in Afghanistan do not attend schools due to inaccessible environment. The level of literacy rate for adults and children with disabilities is very low because of the less attention and lack of literacy education facilities in the country. Poverty and disability are closely linked and have detrimental impact on the level of inclusion in society and its overall development. From social perspective, both poverty, and disability are product of capitalist development.

Disabled people are often found among the poorest of the poor and in a developing country like Sri Lanka; disabled people face discrimination at every level of society. In Iraq people with disabilities are from all genders, ages, and socioeconomic status. Many people with disabilities have limited or no access to healthcare and rehabilitation, education, skills training, and employment opportunities. The two and a half-year conflict in Syria have made persons with disabilities extremely vulnerable to gross rights violations on a daily basis. In Yemen, there are a number of causes for the high prevalence of disability. One set of causes is communicable diseases such as meningitis, rubella and polio. The number of disabled in the Kingdom of Saudi Arabia has reached 720,000, roughly four per cent of the population. The United Arab Emirates has been updating federal laws regarding the rights of the disabled. Since 2006, several laws have been enacted, but not all are regularly enforced. The disability policy in Bahrain is expressed in law, in guidelines adopted by the Government and in guidelines adopted by the National Disability Council. There are more than one and half million handicapped people living in Israel and their income is much lower than the national average. Nearly 83 million women and men in China or 6.3 per cent of the population had a disability in 2006. The Kyrgyz Republic is strongly committed to protecting the rights of disabled children. The Government of Kyrgyzstan supports the principles of social inclusion and non-discrimination against disabled children. Kyrgyzstan is a relatively young country. The total number of registered persons with disabilities in Tajikistan is more than 164,000. There are 445,006 people with disabilities registered in Malaysia as of 2012. Nearly two million women and men, or approximately three per cent of the population in Thailand, have a disability. Vietnam has one of the world's highest rates of people living with disability per capita. According to the 2009 national census almost eight per cent of the country's population had a disability, although more recent statistics from the World Health Organisation estimated the figure to be approximately 15 per cent.

The disabled population in India has increased by 22.4 per cent between 2001 and 2011. The number of disabled, which was 2.19 crore in 2001, rose in 2011 to 2.68 crore i.e., 1.5 crore males and 1.18 crore females. India has ratified the United Nations Convention on the Rights of persons with disability in 2007. In India, government departments and public sector enterprises have been important employers of disabled people. Whilst government initiated the policy of three per cent reservation of jobs for persons with disability in 1977, the reservation was only in the lower ranking jobs (C and D categories). However, with India adopting the Disability Act of 1995, the reservation was extended to higher ranking (A and B) categories. Other measures adopted by Government of India include establishment of National Institutes like the National Institute for Visually Handicapped, Dehradun; National Institute of Orthopedically Handicapped, Calcutta; National Institute of Mentally Handicapped, Hyderabad and National Institute of Hearing Impaired, Mumbai. Under India's Disability Act (1995), a person with a disability is anyone who suffers at least 40 per cent impairment from a medical issue such as blindness, low vision, leprosy, hearing problems, locomotors disability, mental retardation or mental illness.

Under the Disabilities Act of India, children with disabilities have the right to free education until they reach the age of eighteen in schools that are integrated, or in special, schools. Children with disabilities have the right to appropriate transportation, removal of architectural barriers, as well as the restructuring of curriculum and modifications in the examination system. Scholarships, uniforms, books, and teaching materials are all provided to children with disabilities for free in India. Parents of children with disabilities in India are required to obtain a disability certificate in order to access the facilities.

Young people with disabilities are among the poorest and most marginalised of the world's youth. Estimates suggest that there are between 180 and 220 million youth with disabilities worldwide, and nearly 80 per cent of them live in developing countries. People with disabilities of working age are two times as likely to be unemployed as those without disabilities. Individuals with disabilities experience forms of violence and abuse similar to those without disabilities, such as physical injury, sexual assault, emotional trauma, and financial abuse. Mistreatment comes in many forms and may have more severe consequences for people with disabilities. Children with physical or learning disabilities are more vulnerable to the full range of mental health disorders and the additional social, family and emotional stresses of everyday life. The greatest problem that handicapped children face is their actual physical/mental disabilities. Because of the physical limitations children with disabilities live with their plane of social existence is compromised. They are limited in extracurricular activities depending on their specific issues. Parents of children with disabilities face great sadness, fear, worry and more from loved ones and even family members, regarding their little angels with eyes of spite, concern and even disbelief they are really disabled at the time.

The lack of appropriate communication remains the biggest hindrance to PWDs accessing health services, even when they have HIV/AIDS. Lack of education is a key concern for most disabled young people in the developing world. In many countries, children with disabilities are considered to be incapable of learning, no matter what their disability is. Employment rates of disabled youth are rarely tracked in developing countries. In the last twenty years, a number of statutes relating to the disability sector have been enacted. The major laws in India dealing with disability are: The Mental Health Act, 1987, The Rehabilitation Council of India Act, 1992, The Persons with Disabilities (Equal Opportunities, Protection of Rights and Full Participation) Act, 1995, and The National Trust for Welfare of Persons with Autism, Cerebral Palsy, Mental Retardation and Multiple Disabilities Act, 1999. With the passing of these laws there are a plethora of provisions for protection, care, treatment, rehabilitation, security and empowerment for persons with different disabilities. These laws also help effect a change in the way society looks at disability. But unfortunately, these laws are not being implemented properly in the North East region with even the awareness level remaining low, as the study reveals. The situation with regard to implementation of Persons with Disabilities Act is quite dismal in most States. The authorities have also failed to give full effect to the statutory mandate of identification and reservation of jobs for persons with disabilities. The process for issuing disability certificates needs to be regularised and simplified. Most public buildings and facilities are not accessible. There is scant awareness among the police and administration about their responsibilities towards the mentally ill.

Bibliography

1. 10 *majorly successful people with disabilities,* Retrieved from http:/ www.huffingtonpost.com/2013/10/22/famous-people-with-disabilities_n_4142930.html
2. 2 per cent jobs quota for disabled in Oman should be implemented better: Association, Retrieved from http:// www.muscatdaily. com/Archive/Oman/2-job-quota-for-disabled-in-Oman-should-be-implemented-better-Association-2xer
3. 2000 *GAM: Disabled Children in Mainstream Schools,* Retrieved from http://www.unicef.org/evaldatabase/index_14290.html
4. 2014 *UNHCR country operations profile - Central African Republic,* Retrieved from http://www.unhcr.org/pages/49e45c156.html
5. 2014 UNHCR regional operations profile - East and Horn of Africa, Retrieved from http://www.unhcr.org/pages/49e4838e6.html
6. *7.3 million Severely disabled persons were living in Germany,* Retrieved from https://www.destatis.de/EN/FactsFigures/SocietyState/Health/DisabledPersons/Current.html
7. *7.7 per cent of households have at least one person with disability (2013),* Retrieved from http://jordantimes.com/77-of-households-have-at-least-one-person-with-disability
8. *A Recent History of the Disability Rights Movement in El Salvador,* Retrieved from http://upsidedownworld.org/main/el-salvador-archives-74/1384-a-recent-history-of-the-disability-rights-movement
9. *A review of the situation of disabled people and the welfare system in Greece (2009),* Retrieved from http://www.travors.eu/down load_material/subhABOUT%20TRAVORS/ENglish%20site/backgroundreport_greece.pdf

10. *A review of the situation of people with disabilities in Estonia* (2009), Retrieved from http://www.travors.eu/download_material/subhABOUT%20TRAVORS/ENglish%20site/backgroundreport_estonia.pdf
11. *A special school for children with intellectual disabilities in Cotonou, Benin;* See more at: http://en.handiplanet-echanges.info/Members/ime—cotonou_539/a-special-school-for-children-with-intellectual-en#sthash.U3UVstKY.dpuf
12. *A US–Iran Dialogue on Law, Policy, and Advocacy,* Reprieved from http://www.stimson.org/images/uploads/researchpdfs/Iran_and_America_A_Dialogue_on_Disability.pdf
13. A.M. Golam Haider, *Employment Situation of People with Disabilities in Bangladesh,* Retrieved from http://www.disabilityrightsfund.org/files/employment_ situation_of_ people_with_disabilities_in_bangladesh.pdf
14. *Access to services for persons with disabilities in challenging environments* (2010), Retrieved from http://www.handicap-international.fr/fileadmin/documents/publications/AccessToServicesAmman.pdf
15. *Accor web site,* http://www.accor.com
16. *Action programme for persons with disability* 2007-2013, Retrieved from http://www.mddsz.gov.si/fileadmin/mddsz.gov.si/pageuploads/dokumenti__pdf/api_07_13_en.pdf
17. *Activities addressing rights of persons with disabilities: A baseline assessment* (2010), Retrieved from http://www.hrcm.org.mv/publications/otherreports/DisabilityReport13April2010.pdf
18. *ADD in Sudan,* Retrieved from http://www.add.org.uk/sudan
19. Addressing Safety Challenges for Disabled Workers, Retrieved from http://ehstoday.com/safety/addressing-safety-challenges-disabled-workers
20. Adsmantia Pollis (2010), A new universalism, Adsmantia Pollis and Peter Schwab (Eds), *Human Rights: New Perspectives,* Viva Books, New Delhi, p. 10.
21. *Advancing the Cause of Disability Rights in Lao PDR,* Retrieved from http://www.powerinternational.org/Disability-Rights-in-Lao-PDR.html
22. *Advocating for People with Disability in Cameroon,* Retrieved from http://www.coeworld.org/family/cameroon/advocating-people-disability-cameroon
23. Afghanistan disability report: UNICEF, Retrieved from http://www.unicef.org/media/files/PreliminaryfindingsAfghanistandisabilityreport.pdf

24. *Afghanistan: Disability deprives children of education,* Retrieved from http://www.irinnews.org/report/81016/afghanistan-disability-deprives-children-of-education
25. *Afghanistan: Disabled people have tough time, lack education, jobs,* Retrieved from http://www.irinnews.org/report/75645/afghanistan-disabled-people-have-tough-time-lack-education-jobs
26. Africa (2014), Retrieved from http://en.wikipedia.org/wiki/Africa
27. *Africa's disabled cursed by apathy and abuse,* Retrieved from http://www.aljazeera.com/indepth/features/2013/09/2013922121017135639.html
28. Ai-Gul S. Seitenova and Charles M. Becker (2008), *Disability in Kazakhstan: An Evaluation of Official Data,* Retrieved from http://siteresources.worldbank.org/SOCIALPROTECTION/Resources/SP-Discussion-papers/Disability-DP/0802.pdf.
29. Akhila Mol, *Complete Information on the Rights of a Disabled Person in India,* Retrieved from http://www.preservearticles.com/201101233658/complete-information-on-the-rights-of-a-disabled-person-in-india.html
30. Akhter Hussain, *Report on Women with Disabilities in Bangladesh,* Retrieved from http://wwda.org.au/wp-content/uploads/2013/12/bangladeshwwd1.pdf.
31. Alok Kumar Gupta and Nidhi Mathur (2008), Disabled in Kashmir and their human rights, Sudhir Kr. Singh and A. Kachhap (Eds), *Disability, citizenship and social exclusion,* First edition, Anamika Publishers and Distributors (P) Ltd, New Delhi, pp. 108-162.
32. *Americans with Disabilities Act of* 1990 *(2012),* Detailed available at http://en.wikipedia.org/wiki/Americans_with_ Disabilities_Act_of_1990.
33. Amit Rahul (2008), Disability, citizenship and social exclusion, Sudhir Kr. Singh and A. Kachhap (Eds), *Disability, citizenship and social exclusion,* First edition, Anamika Publishers and Distributors (P) Ltd, New Delhi, p. 30.
34. Andrew K Dube (2005), *Participation of disabled people in the PRSP/PEAP process in Uganda,* Retrieved from http://r4d.dfid.gov.uk/pdf/outputs/disability/policyproject_uganda_prsp.pdf.
35. Angelo D. Marra, *Brief outlook on provisions concerning disability in Italy and methods to enforce law,* Retrieved from http://disability-studies.leeds.ac.uk/files/library/marra-Laws-and-Enforcement.pdf.

36. *Angola,* Retrieved from http://www.handicap-international.org.uk/where_we_work/africa/angola.
37. Anil Bhat (2008), *Disabilities and human rights of security personnel in Northwest India*, Sudhir Kr. Singh and A. Kachhap (Eds), Disability, citizenship and social exclusion, First edition, Anamika Publishers and Distributors (P) Ltd, New Delhi, p. 54.
38. Anne Digby, and David Wright (2002). *From Idiocy to Mental Deficiency: Historical Perspectives on People with Learning Disabilities,* United Kingdom: Taylor and Francis.
39. Arie Rimmerman (2005), Israel's Equal Rights for Persons with Disabilities Law: Current Status and Future Directions, *Disability Studies Quarterly,* Fall 2005, Volume 25, No. 4, Retrieved from http://dsq-sds.org/article/view/626/803.
40. *Armenia Reforms Disability Rules,* Retrieved from http://iwpr.net/report-news/armenia-reforms-disability-rules.
41. Asia (2014), Retrieved from http://en.wikipedia.org/wiki/Asia
42. *Asia and the Pacific, Proceedings of the meeting,* Bangkok, 6 July 2005, http://www.ilo.org/skills/what/pubs/lang—en/docName—WCMS_143518/index.htm.
43. *Asia faces five challenges for its economic future* (2014), Retrieved from http://www.imf.org/external/pubs/ft/survey/so/2014/res052914a.htm.
44. *Asia*, Retrieved from http://www.ipcc.ch/pdf/assessment-report/ar4/wg2/ar4-wg2-chapter10.pdf.
45. *Asia: Challenges of stability and growth,* Retrieved from http://www.imf.org/external/np/seminars/eng/2012/korea/
46. *Assessment of the Situation of Children with Disabilities in Kyrgyzstan,* Retrieved from http://www.ceecis.org/ccc/publications/Assessment_of_the_situation_of_children_with_disabilities_in_Kyrgyzstan_2008_ENG.pdf.
47. *Associations and Facilities for the Disabled in Bali,* See http://bali.angloinfo.com/information/healthcare/people-with-disabilities/
48. *Australian Bureau of Statistics, Retrieved from* http://www.disabled-world.com/disability/statistics/disability-statistics-australia.php.
49. *Australian network of disability, states and facts,* Retrieved from http://www.and.org.au/pages/disability-statistics.html
50. *Austria: The Austrian Federal Government's Disability Concept (1993).* Follow this and additional works at: http://digitalcommons.ilr.cornell.edu/gladnetcollect
51. B. Zinamider, *NGO report with the evaluation of the Asian-Pacific Decade activities,* Retrieved from http://www.dinf.ne.jp/doc/english/intl/02rnn/mongolia_e.html

52. B.R. Alamelu (2008), Human rights and disability feminism, Sudhir Kr. Singh and A. Kachhap (Eds), *Disability, citizenship and social exclusion*, First edition, Anamika Publishers and Distributors (P) Ltd, New Delhi, p. 62.
53. Badhte Kadam, *Imphal by SS Manipur* (November 14, 2011), Detailed available at http://kanglaonline.com/2011/11/badhte-kadam-imphal-by-ssmanipur/
54. *Bahrain in move to protect rights of disabled* (2010), Retrieved from http://www.tradearabia.com/news/HEAL_190873.html
55. *Bahrain plan to provide education, healthcare for disabled* (2013), Retrieved from http://al-shorfa.com/en_GB/articles/meii/newsbriefs/2013/09/19/newsbrief-10
56. *Bahrain*, Retrieved from http://www.independentliving.org/standardrules/UN_Answers/Bahrain.html
57. Baker, E., Wang, M., and Walberg, H. (1994). *The effects of inclusion on learning. Educational Leadership* 52, 33-35.
58. Balal Idrees and Rehan Ilyas, Discrimination and stigmatisation of physically disable people student in a general educational environment in Pakistan: a case study, *Academic Research International*, Vol. 2, No. 2, March 2012, pp. 622-623, Retrieved from http://www.savap.org.pk/journals/ARInt./Vol.2(2)/2012(2.2-69).pdf
59. Banerji, M. and Dailey, R.A. (1995). A study of the effects of an inclusion model on students with specific learning disabilities. *Journal of Learning Disabilities* 28(8), 511-522.
60. *Bangladesh*, Disabled Development Trust-BDDT, See http://www.bddt.org/
61. Barbara Kolucki, *Creating a "Disability-Friendly" Childhood Development Programme in the Maldives*, Retrieved from http://www.disabilityworld.org/05-06_01/children/maldives.shtml
62. Barbara Murray (1998), *People with Disabilities in Lao PDR Training for Employment and Income Generation: Key Issues and Potential Strategies*. Follow this and additional works at: http://digitalcommons.ilr.cornell.edu/gladnetcollect
63. Barbara Rose Johnston (2010), Human environmental rights, Adsmantia Pollis and Peter Schwab (Eds), *Human Rights: New Perspectives*, Viva Books, New Delhi, p. 95.
64. Baume, P. and Kay, K. (1995) *Working Solution: Report of the Strategic Review of the Commonwealth Disability Services Programme*, Canberra: Australian Government Publishing Service.
65. *Being disabled in Algeria* (2014), Retrieved from http://vivalalgerie.wordpress.com/2013/03/14/being-disabled-in-algeria/

66. *Being disabled in Guatemala and the story of Paula García,* Retrieved from http://www.teamaroundthechild.com/allnews/developmentsintreatment/461-being-disabled-in-guatemala-and-the-story-of-paula-garcia.html

67. *Belize,* Retrieved from http://www.cirnetwork.org/idrm/reports/americas/countries/belize.html

68. Benedicte Ingstad and Susan Reynolds Whyte (1995). *Disability and Culture,* California (USA): University of California Press.

69. Benedicte Ingstad and Lisbet Grut (2007), *See me, and do not forget me People with disabilities in Kenya,* Retrieved from http://siteresources.worldbank.org/DISABILITY/Resources/Regions/Africa/LCKenya2.pdf

70. *Better services for people with disabilities in Tajikistan,* Retrieved from http://www.euro.who.int/en/countries/tajikistan/news/news/2013/11/better-services-for-people-with-disabilities-in-tajikistan

71. Bhekie Jele, *Swaziland Federation Organisation of Disabled People Develops Women's Programme,* Retrieved from http://www.disabilityworld.org/09-10_02/women/swaziland.shtml

72. *Bhutan* 2013*: Human rights report,* Retrieved from http://www.state.gov/documents/organisation/220601.pdf

73. Biswajeet Saikia (2008), Disability and skill development in India, Sudhir Kr. Singh and A. Kachhap (Eds), *Disability, citizenship and social exclusion,* First edition, Anamika Publishers and Distributors (P) Ltd, New Delhi, p. 136.

74. *Blind Education and Rehabilitation Development Organisation,* See http://www.berdo-bd.org/

75. Boyce, W (2000) Adaptation of Community Based Rehabilitation in Areas of Armed Conflict, *Asia Pacific Disability Rehabilitation Journal,* Vol 11, No 1, 2000.

76. *Brief overview: Kyrgyzstan legislation and access to education for children with intellectual and other disabilities,* Retrieved from http://kelechekplus.kg/files/2011/12/Overview-of-KG-legislation_education_27sep10.pdf

77. *Brunei Darussalam country report, The 9th ASEAN and JAPAN High Level Officials Meeting on Caring Societies,* Retrieved from http://www.mhlw.go.jp/bunya/kokusaigyomu/asean/2011/dl/Brunei_CountryReport.pdf

78. *Brunei to ensure people with disabilities given high priority in national agendas* (2013), Retrieved from http://globalaccessibilitynews.com/2013/12/13/brunei-to-ensure-people-with-disabilities-given-high-priority-in-national-agendas/

79. Bupinder Zutshi, *Disability Status in India: Case Study of Delhi Metropolitan Region,* Detailed available at http://www.disabilityindia.org/StatusBookFrame.cfm

80. Bupinder Zutshi, *Disability Status in India: Case Study of Delhi Metropolitan Region*, Detailed available at http://www.disabilityindia.org/StatusBookFrame.cfm
81. *Burkina Faso*, Retrieved from http://www.handicap-international.org.uk/where_we_work/africa/burkina_faso
82. *Burundi*, Retrieved from http://www.handicap-international.org.uk/where_we_work/africa/burundi
83. *Cambodian Disable Peoples Organisation*, Retrieved from http://www.dpi.org/NationalCambodia
84. Canada: Immigration and Refugee Board of Canada, *Libya: Situation of disabled persons (2002-June 2004)*, 21 June 2004, LBY42752.E, available at: http://www.refworld.org/docid/41501c2d15.html
85. *Canadians in Context - People with Disabilities*, Retrieved From http://www4.rhdcc.gc.ca/indicator.jsp?andindicatorid=40
86. *Canadians in Context - People with Disabilities*, Retrieved from http://www4.hrsdc.gc.ca/.3ndic.1t.4r@-eng.jsp?iid=40
87. *Cape Verde: Children with disabilities may now benefit from social pension*, Retrieved from http://www.ilo.org/public/portugue/region/eurpro/lisbon/html/portugal_cips_eng3_pt.htm
88. Carrefour Group 2009 Sustainability Report.
89. *Carrefour web site*, http://www.carrefour.com
90. *Census of people of disabilities in Rwanda*, Retrieved from http://uphls.org/IMG/pdf/REPORT_CENSUS_PWD_01Janv11.pdf
91. *Census of population with disabilities in Rwanda*, Retrieved from http://uphls.org/IMG/pdf/REPORT_ CENSUS_ PWD_01Janv11.pdf
92. *Centre for Disability in Development*, Retrieved from http://www.cdd.org.bd/
93. *Challenges faced by People with Disabilities (PWDs) in Utilising HIV/AIDS Communication and Related Health Services in Uganda*, Retrieved from http://www.africacampaign.info/uploads/media/add_reporton_hivaidsand_disability_01.pdf
94. *Challenges from Disabled People*, Retrieved from http://disability-studies.leeds.ac.uk/files/library/stone-chapter-2.pdf
95. *Challenging convention in Burkina Faso*, Retrieved from http://www.theguardian.com/global-development-professionals-network/2013/jun/10/challenging-convention-burkina-faso
96. Chamari L Weeraratnea, Sharmika T Opathaa, Chamith T Rosa, *Challenges faced by visually disabled people in use of medicines, self-adopted coping strategies and medicine-related mishaps*, Retrieved from http://www.searo.who.int/publications/journals/seajph/whoseajphv1i3p256.pdf?ua=1

97. *Changing attitudes towards people with disabilities*, Retrieved from http://www.unicef.org/disabilities/index_66543.html

98. Chapter 2, *Attitude towards disability and people with disabilities*, Retrieved from http://siteresources.worldbank.org/INDIAEXTN/Resources/295583-1171456325808/Chapter02.pdf

99. Chapter 2, *Attitude towards disability and people with disabilities*, Retrieved from http://siteresources.worldbank.org/INDIAEXTN/Resources/295583-1171456325808/Chapter02.pdf

100. Chapter 3: *The Status of People with Disabilities in Bolivia*, Retrieved from http://drpi.research.yorku.ca/LatinAmerica/resources/BoliviaRep/Chapter3

101. Chapter 3: *The Status of People with Disabilities in Bolivia*, Retrieved from http://drpi.research.yorku.ca/LatinAmerica/resources/BoliviaRep/Chapter3

102. Chapter 8 *Policy for People with Disabilities, Social Security in Japan* 2014, Retrieved from http://www.ipss.go.jp/s-info/e/ssj2014/pdf/08_SSJ2014.pdf

103. *Child Health and Disability Team (CHAD)*, Retrieved from http://www.boroughofpoole.com/communities-and-people/children-and-family-care/child-health-and-disability-team/

104. *Child protection*, Retrieved from http://unicef.kz/en/services/child_welfare/?sid=312g4fq0n61i1b1ouend1egd62

105. *Children of Guinea-Bissau: Realising Children's Rights in Guinea-Bissau*, Retrieved from http://www.humanium.org/en/guinea-bissau/

106. *Children of Liberia: Realising Children's Rights in Liberia*, Retrieved from http://www.humanium.org/en/liberia/

107. *Children with Disabilities in Tajikistan: A Situational Analysis Report*, Retrieved from http://www.unicef.org/tajikistan/Article_3_Children_with_disabilities.pdf

108. *Children with Special Education Needs in Kazakhstan, Kyrgyzstan, and Tajikistan*, Retrieved from http://www.opensocietyfoundations.org/publications/children-special-education-needs-kazakhstan-kyrgyzstan-and-tajikistan

109. *Chile's Inclusive Hiring Integrates Disabled People Into ARAMARK Workforce* , Retrieved from http://www.enriching liveseveryday.com/EmployeeAdvocacy/ARAMARK ChileHandicapped PeopleProgram.aspx

110. Chris Adams (2013), *Millions went to war in Iraq, Afghanistan, leaving many with lifelong scars*, Retrieved from http://www.mcclatchydc.com/2013/03/14/185880/millions-went-to-war-in-iraq-afghanistan.html#storylink=cpy

111. Chris Joseph, *The Advantages of Hiring Disabled People in a Company*, Retrieved from http://smallbusiness.chron.com/advantages-hiring-disabled-people-company-11233.html
112. Christopher M. Bell (2011). *Blackness and Disability: Critical Examinations and Cultural Interventions*, Munster: LIT Verlag Munster.
113. Cole (2006), *Disabled people face difficulties in accessing primary care*, Retrieved from http://www.ncbi.nlm.nih.gov/pmc/articles/PMC1569976/
114. Colin Barnes and Geof Mercer (2010). *Exploring Disability*, Cambridge: Polity.
115. *Complete national overview – Cyprus*, Retrieved from, http://www.european-agency.org/country-information/cyprus/national-overview/complete-national-overview
116. *Condemned to beg? Forging new futures for Senegal's disabled population*, Retrieved from http://www.theguardian.com/global-development-professionals-network/2013/jun/10/new-futures-for-senegal-disabled
117. Connelly, F.M. and Clandinin, D.J. (1990). Stories of experience and narrative inquiry. *Educational Researcher* 19(5), 2-14.
118. Copenhagen Declaration and Programme of action adopted by the World Summit for Social Development.
119. *Corporates in Oman should keep disabled in mind: Haider Jawad Sultan Al Lawati* (2014), Retrieved from http://wap.shabiba.com/news/39158/Article-%E2%80%98Corporates-in-Oman-should-keep-disabled-in-mind%E2%80%99
120. Council Directive 2000/78/EC of 27 Nov. 2000 establishing a general framework for equal treatment in employment and occupation. OJL 303, 2 Dec. 2000, pp. 16-22.
121. *Country Profile on Disabilities Kingdom of Thailand*, Retrieved from http://siteresources.worldbank.org/DISABILITY/Resources/Regions/East-Asia-Pacific/JICA_Thailand.1.pdf
122. *Country Profile on Disabilities Tajikistan*, Retrieved from http://siteresources.worldbank.org/DISABILITY/Resources/Regions/ECA/JICA_Tajikistan.pdf
123. *Country Profile on Disability Federal Democratic Republic of Ethiopia*, Retrieved from http://siteresources.worldbank.org/DISABILITY/Resources/Regions/Africa/JICA_Ethiopia.pdf
124. *Country profile on disability Islamic Republic of Pakistan* (2002), Retrieved from http://siteresources.worldbank.org/DISABILITY/Resources/Regions/South%20Asia/JICA_Pakistan.pdf

125. *Country Profile on Disability Kingdom of Cambodia,* Retrieved from http://siteresources.worldbank.org/DISABILITY/Resources/Regions/East-Asia-Pacific/JICA_Camboida.pdf

126. *Country Profile on disability Kingdom of Nepal (2002),* Retrieved from http://siteresources.worldbank.org/DISABILITY/Resources/Regions/South%20Asia/JICA_Nepal.1.pdf

127. *Country Profile on Disability Kingdom of Saudi Arabia (2002),* Retrieved from http://siteresources.worldbank.org/DISABILITY/Resources/Regions/MENA/JICA_Saudi_Arabia.pdf

128. *Country Profile on Disability Lao People's Democratic Republic,* Retrieved from http://gwweb.jica.go.jp/km/FSubject0601.nsf/3b8a2d403517ae4549256f2d002e1dcc/54a619bb76fd92034925727d0008246b/$FILE/LaoPDR(2002).pdf

129. *Country Profile on Disability People's Republic of Bangladesh,* Retrieved from http://siteresources.worldbank.org/DISABILITY/Resources/Regions/South%20Asia/JICA_Bangladesh.pdf

130. *Country Profile on Disability Republic of Honduras (2002),* Retrieved from http://siteresources.worldbank.org/DISABILITY/Resources/Regions/LAC/JICA_Honduras.pdf

131. *Country Profile on Disability Republic of Indonesia (2002),* Retrieved from http://siteresources.worldbank.org/DISABILITY/Resources/Regions/East-Asia-Pacific/JICA_Indonesia.pdf

132. *Country Profile on Disability Republic of Uzbekistan,* Retrieved from http://siteresources.worldbank.org/DISABILITY/Resources/Regions/ECA/JICA_Uzbekistan.pdf

133. *Country Profile on Disability the Republic of the Philippines,* Retrieved from http://siteresources.worldbank.org/DISABILITY/Resources/Regions/East-Asia-Pacific/JICA_Philippine.pdf

134. *Country Profile on Disability Union of Myanmar,* Retrieved from http://siteresources.worldbank.org/DISABILITY/Resources/Regions/East-Asia-Pacific/JICA_Myanmar.pdf

135. *Country Profile on Disability: Kingdom of Saudi Arabia (2002),* Retrieved from http://digitalcommons.ilr.cornell.edu/cgi/viewcontent.cgi?article=1233andcontext=gladnetcollect

136. *Country Profile on Disability: Republic of Honduras.* Retrieved from http://siteresources.worldbank.org/DISABILITY/Resources/Regions/LAC/JICA_Honduras.pdf

137. D'Alonzo, B.J., Giordano, G. and Vanleeuwen, D.M. (1997). *Perceptions by teachers about the benefits and liabilities of inclusion, Preventing School Failure* 42(1), 4-10.

138. Dan Goodley (2010), *Disability Studies: An Interdisciplinary Introduction*, New Delhi: SAGE.
139. David Wright, Anne Digby and Digby Anne (1996). *From Idiocy to Mental Deficiency: Historical Perspectives on People with Learning Disabilities*, London: illustrated.
140. *Deaf Enabled Foundation*, See http://def.org.in/about-def/history.html
141. Decent Work Country Programme 2010-13: Sultanate of Oman, Retrieved from http://www.ilo.org/public/english/bureau/programme/dwcp/download/oman.pdf
142. *Declaration on the Rights of Disabled Persons*, UNGA Res. 3447 of 9 Dec. 1975.
143. *Defining Impairment and Disability*, Retrieved from http://disability-studies.leeds.ac.uk/files/library/Northern-Officers-Group-defining-impairment-and-disability.pdf
144. *Delta Holding, web site*, http://www.deltaholding.rs
145. *Democratic Republic of Congo*, Retrieved from http://www.spinalcord.org/resource-centre/askus/index. php?pg=kb.pageandid=1595
146. Depouy, L. *Human Rights and Disabled Persons*. New York: United Nations, 1993, p. 20.
147. Despouy, L. (1993), *Human Rights and Disabled Persons*,United Nations Centre for Human Rights, Geneva.
148. *Developing Accessibility for persons with Disability in Public Places and Transport*, Retrieved from http://ud2014.se/wp-content/uploads/submissions/ud2014_submission_26.pdf
149. *Development and Ability Organisation (DAO)*, Retrieved from http://www.daoafghanistan.org/adu.htm
150. *Dimension of Disability in India*, chapter 4, Retrieved from http://mospi.nic.in/Mospi_New/upload/disablity_ india_statistical_data_11mar2011/Chapter%204-Dimension_Disability.pdf
151. *Disabilities in Asia-Pacific*, Retrieved from http://www.unescobkk.org/education/inclusive-education/what-is-inclusive-education/disabilities-in-asia-pacific/
152. *Disabilities in Somalia - Disability Action Network*, Retrieved from http://www.disabled-world.com/news/asia/disability-somalia.php
153. *Disabilities in Sri Lanka*, Retrieved from http://www.prithipura.org/page.php?area_id=1andpage_id=5
154. *Disability* (2012), Detailed available at http://www.who.int/topics/disabilities/en/
155. *Disability* (2014), Retrieved from http://en.wikipedia.org/wiki/Disability

156. *Disability and employment* (2013), Retrieved from http://www.un.org/disabilities/documents/toolaction/employmentfs.pdf
157. *Disability and Employment in Argentina: The Right to Be Exploited?* See https://nacla.org/news/disability-and-employment-argentina-right-be-exploited
158. *Disability and Health News India*, Retrieved from http://www.disabled-world.com/news/asia/india/
159. *Disability and HIV/AIDS*, Retrieved from http://www.un.org/disabilities/default.asp?id=1560
160. *Disability and poverty in developing countries: A snapshot from the world health survey* (2011), Retrieved from http://siteresources.worldbank.org/SOCIALPROTECTION/Resources/SP-Discussion-papers/Disability-DP/1109.pdf
161. *Disability and sports*, Retrieved from http://www.un.org/disabilities/default.asp?id=1563
162. *Disability Australia*, 2009, Retrieved from http://www.abs.gov.au/ausstats/abs@.nsf/Lookup/4446.0main+features42009
163. *Disability expectations: Investing in a better life, a stronger Australia*, Retrieved from http://www.pwc.com.au/industry/government/assets/disability-in-australia.pdf
164. *Disability framework in Pakistan*, Retrieved from http://www.sightsavers.net/in_depth/policy_and_research/social_inclusion/13173_ Disability%20Framework %20in%20Pakistan.pdf
165. *Disability framework in Pakistan*, Retrieved from http://www.sightsavers.org/in_depth/policy_and_research/social_inclusion/13173_Disability%20Framework%20in%20Pakistan.pdf
166. *Disability in Afghanistan: Taking a Capabilities Approach to look at Research Challenges and Policy Implications*, Retrieved from http://www.ucl.ac.uk/lc-ccr/lccstaff/jean-francois-trani/HDCAconf0905.pdf
167. *Disability in Africa Region*, Retrieved from http://web.worldbank.org/WBSITE/EXTERNAL/TOPICS/EXTSOCIALPROTECTION/EXTDISABILITY/0,,contentMDK:20183406~menuPK:417328~pagePK:148956~piPK:216618~theSitePK:282699,00.html
168. *Disability in America Info graphic*, Retrieved from http://www.disabled-world.com/disability/statistics/american-disability.php
169. *Disability in Burkina Faso*, Retrieved from http://www.hs-b.org/index.php/en/about-us/disability-in-burkina-faso

170. *Disability in India (2012),* Detailed available at http://www.ccdisabilities.nic.in/page.php
171. *Disability in Lesotho,* Retrieved from http://www.lnfod.org.ls/disability-in-lesotho.html
172. *Disability in Nigeria,* Retrieved from http://www.awapo.org/specialneeds.html
173. *Disability in Sri Lanka,* Retrieved from http://www.ecsatlanka.org/govpolicy
174. *Disability in the Southeast Asia Region,* 2013, Retrieved from http://www.searo.who.int/entity/disabilities_injury_rehabilitation/topics/disability_factsheet.pdf
175. *Disability in the Workplace: Company Practices (2010),* Retrieved from http://www.ilo.org/wcmsp5/groups/public/@ed_emp/@ifp_skills/documents/publication/wcms_150658.pdf
176. *Disability in the Workplace: Company Practices,* Working Paper No 3, Retrieved from http://www.ilo.org/wcmsp5/groups/public/@ed_emp/@ifp_skills/documents/publication/wcms_150658.pdf
177. *Disability in the Workplace: Employers' Organisations and Business Networks (2011),* Retrieved from http://ilo.org/skills/pubs/WCMS_167204/lang—en/index.htm
178. *Disability in Vietnam,* Retrieved from http://www.agentorangerecord.com/images/uploads/resources/studies/Disability,%20poverty%20and%20social%20 protection%20in%20Viet%20Nam.pdf
179. *Disability Inclusion in the Syrian Refugee Response in Lebanon (2013),* Retrieved from http://reliefweb.int/sites/reliefweb.int/files/resources/Disability_Inclusion_in_the_Syrian_Refugee_Response _in_Lebanon.pdf
180. *Disability Inclusion in the Syrian Refugee Response in Lebanon,* Retrieved from http://usicd.wordpress.com/2013/09/06/disability-inclusion-in-the-syrian-refugee-response-in-lebanon/
181. *Disability Information Statistics and News from Central America and Mexico,* Retrieved from http://www.disabled-world.com/news/central-america/
182. *Disability is still a barrier to employment in Oman: experts,* Retrieved from http://www.muscatdaily.com/Archive/Oman/Disability-is-still-a-barrier-to-employment-in-Oman-Experts-1y85
183. *Disability issues in Sweden,* Retrieved from http://www.government.se/sb/d/15473/a/183502
184. *Disability Law and Access to Rights,* Retrieved from http://www.disabilityindia.co.in/Disability-Law-and-Access-to-Rights/disabilitylawandrights.php

185. *Disability News Information and Statistics from Countries in South America,* Retrieved from http://www.disabled-world.com/news/south-america/

186. *Disability News Information and Statistics from Countries in South America,* Retrieved from http://www.disabled-world.com/news/south-america/

187. *Disability news: India,* Retrieved from http://www.disabled-world.com/news/asia/india/

188. *Disability policies audit in Namibia, Swaziland, Malawi and Mozambique,* Retrieved from https://www.ucl.ac.uk/lc-ccr/downloads/DISABILITY_POLICY_AUDIT_RESEARCH_FINAL_ REPORT.pdf

189. *Disability policy audit in Namibia, Swaziland, Malawi and Mozambique: Final Report* 2008, Retrieved from http://www.ucl.ac.uk/lc-ccr/downloads/DISABILITY_POLICY_AUDIT_ RESEARCH_FINAL_REPORT.pdf

190. Disability policy in Nepal, Retrieved from http://mend.org.nz/Policy_paper_Nepal_disability.pdf

191. Disability prevention and rehabilitation (DPR) and life style related diseases programme, Retrieved from http://www.health.gov.bt/doph/ncdd/dprLsrd.pdf

192. *Disability Rights and the Road to Legal Reform,* Retrieved from http://archive.thedailystar.net/forum/2011/December/disability.htm

193. *Disability Rights International's Work in Turkey,* Retrieve from http://www.disabilityrightsintl.org/work/country-projects/turkey/

194. Disability rights law manual, Retrieved from http://www.blast.org.bd/content/publications/flier-eng.pdf

195. *Disability rights movements,* Retrieved from http://en.wikipedia.org/wiki/Disability_rights_movement

196. Disability rights, Retrieved from http://www.hrln.org/hrln/disability-rights.html

197. Disability Scoping Study for DFID Uganda (2009), Retrieved from http://www.ucl.ac.uk/lc-ccr/downloads/06052009_Disability_Scoping_Study_Uganda.pdf

198. *Disability Situation and Impact of ADD work in Bangladesh* (2003). Retrieved from http://www.independentliving.org/docs6/uddin200309.html

199. Disability situation in Ghana, Retrieved from http://www.gfdgh.org/disability%20situation%20in%20ghana.html

200. Disability Support and Services in Australia, Retrieved from http://www.aph.gov.au/About_Parliament/Parliamentary_

Departments/Parliamentary_Library/Publications_Archive/archive/disability

201. Disability, natural disasters and emergency situations, Retrieved from http://www.un.org/disabilities/default.asp?id=1546
202. Disability, Retrieved from http://fpd.gsfc.nasa.gov/diversity/Disabililties_Info.pdf
203. *Disable persons association in Bhutan's*, Retrieved from http://dpab.org.bt/about-us/dpab-history/#.Uz91QjtQHFw
204. *Disable persons welfare*, Retrieved from http://www.rgfindia.com/dpw.htm
205. *Disabled Canadians still face staggering barriers to success, report warns*, Retrieved from http://www.theglobeandmail.com/news/national/disabled-canadians-still-face-staggering-barriers-to-success-report-warns/article16944376/
206. *Disabled child*, Retrieved from http://www.btl.gov.il/English%20Homepage/Benefits/Disabledchild/Pages/default.aspx
207. *Disabled Children in the Republic of Kazakhstan*, Retrieved from http://www.open-heart-centre.ru/howwework/childrenwithdisabilities/disabeldchildreninrk.html
208. *Disabled in North Korea Confined to Homes, Expelled From Capital*, Retrieved from http://www.rfa.org/english/korea/nkorea_disabled-20070613.html
209. Disabled Moroccans struggle for integration, Retrieved from http://magharebia.com/en_GB/articles/awi/reportage/2008/04/25/reportage-01
210. *Disabled Moroccans struggle for integration*, Retrieved from http://magharebia.com/en_GB/articles/awi/reportage/2008/04/25/reportage-01
211. Disabled people, Retrieved from http://censusindia.gov.in/(S(5124esqnp2s1urebwn3he455))/Census_And_You/disabled_population.aspx
212. Disabled people's rights in Venezuela, Retrieved from http://embavenez.co.uk/sites/embavenez.co.uk/files/factsheets/Disabled_people_rights_in_Venezuela.pdf
213. *Disabled people's rights in Venezuela*, Retrieved from http://embavenez.co.uk/sites/embavenez.co.uk/files/factsheets/Disabled_people_rights_in_Venezuela.pdf
214. Disabled peoples association, Retrieved from http://www.dpa.org.sg/?page_id=42
215. Disabled peoples organisations and community based rehabilitation in Africa, Retrieved from http://www.dinf.ne.jp/doc/english/asia/resource/apdrj/z13jo0100/z13jo0112.html

216. *Disabled People's Rights,* Detailed available at http://hcdg.org/disabilityrights.htm
217. *Disabled Persons in India, NSS 58tth round, (July – December* 2002), Retrieved from http://mospi.nic.in/rept%20_%20pubn/485_final.pdf
218. *Disabled Person's Parking Card,* Retrieved from http://www.citizensinformation.ie/en/travel_and_recreation/traffic_and_parking/disabled_persons_parking_card.html
219. Discrimination (Employment and Occupation) Convention (No. 111), 1958; Discrimination (Employment and Occupation) Recommendation (No. 111), 1958.
220. *Discrimination at Work in Asia,* Retrieved from http://www.ilo.org/declaration/info/factsheets/WCMS_DECL_FS_89_EN/lang—en/index.htm
221. Dorothy Watson and Brian Nolan (2011), *A Social Portrait of People with Disabilities in Ireland,* Retrieved from http://www.socialinclusion.ie/documents/2011-09-21_SocPortraitPWDReportforWebsite.pdf
222. *Dow web site,* Retrieved from http://www.dow.com
223. Dr Federico Montero, *Legislation on Disability: The Costa Rican Experience,* Retrieved from http://www.independentliving.org/docs1/hr12.html
224. Dr G.P.S. Dhillon and Dr B.N. Barkakaty, National Leprosy Eradication Programme in India: achievements and deficiencies, Health Administrator, Vol. XVIII, Number 2: 4-7.
225. Dr Jaturong Boonyarattanasoontorn, Dr Thipaporn Portawin and Somsak Nakalajarn, Situation of Disabled Persons in Thailand and the 3rd National Disabled Persons' Life Quality Development Plan (AD 2007-2011), Retrieved from http://swhcu.net/km/mk-articles/sw-km/89-situation-of-disabled-persons-in-thailand.html
226. Dr Paul Ackerman, Dr Mary S. Thormann and Dr Sharmin Huq (2005), *Assessment of Educational Needs of Disabled Children in Bangladesh,* Retrieved from http://www.beps.net/publications/bangladesh_disabled_children_report040605.pdf
227. Dr S. Vasoo, *Singapore: employment opportunities for disabled people,* See http://www.disabilityworld.org/01-03_04/employment/singapore.shtml
228. *Driving for people with disabilities,* Retrieved from http://www.dubai.ae/en/Lists/Articles/DispForm.aspx?ID=51andcategory=Citizens
229. Eduardo Joly (2009), *Disability and Employment in Argentina: The Right to Be Exploited?* Retrieved from http://nacla.org/news/disability-and-employment-argentina-right-be-exploited

230. Eduardo Joly (2009), *Disability and Employment in Argentina: The Right to Be Exploited?* Retrieved from https://nacla.org/files/04202007_1.pdf

231. Educators for Inclusive Programmes: A Call for Professional Unification. *Early Childhood Education Journal* 25(2), 137-139.

232. *Egypt's Visually Disabled People Plead for Improvement,* Retrieved from http://dar.aucegypt.edu/bitstream/handle/10526/3299/JRMC-460%20Final%20Audio%20Documentary%20Final%20Script.pdf? sequence=2

233. *El Salvador,* Retrieved from http://www.state.gov/documents/organisation/160164.pdf

234. Elizabeth Parks, *Holly Williams, and Jason Parks* (2011), A Sociolinguistic Profile of the Deaf People of Panama, Retrieved from http://www-01.sil.org/silesr/2011/silesr2011-031.pdf

235. Elizabeth Parks, Holly Williams, and Jason Parks (2011): *A Sociolinguistic Profile of the Deaf People of Panama,* Retrieved from http://www-01.sil.org/SILESR/2011/silesr2011-031.pdf

236. Elsheikh, A.S., Alqurashi A.M. (2013), Disabled Future in the Kingdom of Saudi Arabia, *IOSR Journal of Humanities and Social Science,* Volume 16, Issue 1, pp. 68-71.

237. Employability: A resource guide on disability for employers in Asia and the Pacific, 2007.

238. *Employing persons with disability: Guideline for Employers,* Retrieved from http://betterwork.org/indonesia/wp-content/uploads/20130201_Employing-Persons-with-Disabilities-Guideline_English_Final4.pdf

239. Employment (Transition from War to Peace) Recommendation No. 71, 1944.

240. *Employment and Disabled Persons,* Detailed available at http://www.dnis.org/Employment.pdf

241. *Employment disable people in Ukraine,* Retrieved from http://www.undp.org/content/undp/en/home/ourwork/povertyreduction/projects_and_initiatives/projects_ukraine/

242. *Employment of Disable peoples in India* (2009), Detailed available at http://www.dnis.org/Employment.pdf

243. *Employment of People with Disabilities: The Impact of Legislation (East Africa),* Retrieved from http://www.ilo.org/wcmsp5/groups/public/@ed_emp/@ifp_skills/documents/publication/wcms_107841.pdf

244. Employment of Persons with Disabilities in Public Sectors in India Emerging Issues and Trends: An Evaluation Study with Special Reference to Persons with Disabilities Act (1995), *Society*

for Disability and Rehabilitation Studies, Detailed available at http://planningcommission.nic.in/reports/sereport/ser/ser_pdp1206.pdf

245. *Employment of Persons with Disabilities,* Retrieved from http://www.paycheck.pk/main/labour-laws/illness-work/employing-disabled-person
246. *Employment Rights of disabled women in India: A Study of Compliance and Impact of the Persons with Disabilities Act with Special Reference to UP,* Rajasthan, Bihar, Maharashtra and Tamil Nadu.
247. *Employment Service Convention (No. 88),* 1948; Employment Service Recommendation (No. 83) 1948.
248. *Employment-related services for persons with disabilities,* Retrieved from http://wadhwani-foundation.org/wp-content/themes/wadhwani-new/img/ond/2008-Planning-commission-report-on-PwD-Employment.pdf
249. *Employment-related services for persons with disabilities,* Retrieved from http://wadhwani-foundation.org/wp-content/themes/wadhwani-new/img/ond/2008-Planning-commission-report-on-PwD-Employment.pdf
250. *Empowering People with Disabilities for Rural Development,* Retrieved from http://www.ilo.org/employment/units/rural-development/WCMS_159006/lang—en/index.htm
251. *Empowering People with Disabilities for Rural Development,* Retrieved from http://www.ilo.org/employment/units/rural-development/WCMS_159006/lang—en/index.htm
252. *Enabling and Mobilising Afghan Disabled (2014),* Retrieved from http://www.cbm.org/programmes/Enabling-Mobilising-Afghan-Disabled-299720.php
253. *Ernst and Young web site,* Retrieved from www.ey.com
254. *Escaping stigma and negligence: people with disability in Sierra Leone,* Retrieved from http://siteresources.worldbank.org/DISABILITY/Resources/News—Events/463933-1184017167861/3975400-1229373211417/SL_PWD_Policy_Note_Jan7.pdf
255. *Ethiopia,* Retrieved from http://www.handicap-international.org.uk/where_we_work/africa/ethiopia
256. *Ethiopia: Finding space for people with disabilities on HIV agenda,* Retrieved from http://www.irinnews.org/report/95032/ethiopia-finding-space-for-people-with-disabilities-on-hiv-agenda
257. European Social Charter (Revised), Strasbourg, 3 May 1996. Any references in the above text are to the 1996 version.

258. Evaluation of Norwegian support to promote the rights of persons with disabilities: The Nepal country report (2012). *Mainstreaming disability in the new development paradigm – Nepal.*
259. *Everyday life (2014),* Retrieved from http://en.wikipedia.org/wiki/Everyday_life
260. *Example of inclusive education in Nepal,* Retrieved from http://www.unicef.org/rosa/InclusiveNep.pdf
261. *Examples of inclusive education,* Retrieved from http://www.unicef.org/rosa/InclusiveNep.pdf
262. *Facilities for Disabled,* Detailed available at http://jakemp.nic.in/schemes/scheme7.htm
263. *Facilities for People with Disabilities in Dubai,* Retrieved from http://dubai.angloinfo.com/information/healthcare/people-with-disabilities/
264. *Facilities for People with Disabilities in Dubai,* Retrieved from http://dubai.angloinfo.com/information/healthcare/people-with-disabilities/
265. *Facts on People with Disabilities in China,* Retrieved from http://www.ilo.org/wcmsp5/groups/public/—asia/—ro-bangkok/—ilo-beijing/documents/publication/wcms_142315.pdf
266. Factsheet on Persons with Disabilities, Retrieved from http://www.un.org/disabilities/default.asp?id=18
267. *FAPED - Angolan Federation of the Association of People with Disabilities,* Retrieved from http://r4d.dfid.gov.uk/PDF/Outputs/SAFOD/AngolaSRPcountryReportEngish.pdf
268. *Fast Retailing CSR Report* 2010, http://www.fastretailing.com/eng/csr/report/pdf/csr2010_e.pdf
269. *Fast Retailing web site,* http://www.fastretailing.com
270. Felix Silwimba, *Possibilities of Independent Living of persons with disabilities in Africa,* Detailed available at http://www.independentliving.org/toolsforpower/tools5.html
271. *FIIAPP cooperates to educational insertion of disabled people in Tunisia (2014),* Retrieved from http://thediplomatinspain.com/en/fiiapp-cooperates-to-educational-insertion-of-disabled-people-in-tunisia/
272. *Filipino employers' attitudes toward persons with disabilities,* Retrieved from http://business.inquirer.net/104615/filipino-employers-attitudes-toward-persons-with-disabilities
273. *First ever Special Trainee Programme in Pakistan* (2010). Retrieved from http://www.step.org.pk/
274. Foo Gaik Sim (1999), *Integrated women and girls with disabilities into mainstream vocational training: A practical guide,* Retrieved from http://www.ilo.org/wcmsp5/groups/public/—ed_emp/—ifp_skills/documents/publication/wcms_107918.pdf

275. *Food security challenges in Asia,* Retrieved from http://www.adb.org/documents/food-security-challenges-asia

276. For a detailed discussion see Samoy, E. and Waterplas, L., Sheltered Employment in the European Community, Commission of the European Union, Brussels, 1992; Samoy, E. and Waterplas, L., Sheltered Employment in five member states of the Council of Europe: Austria, Finland, Norway, Sweden and Switzerland. Council of Europe, 997; Thornton P., and Lunt, N., Employment Policies for Disabled People in Eighteen Countries: A Review, Social Policy Research Unit, University of York, 1997.

277. *For a more detailed description and discussion,* See Degener and Quinn, op. cit., p. 60 et seq.

278. For detailed suggestions on placement strategies and practices see (1) Murray B. and Heron R., Placement of

279. For example, Degener and Quinn, op. cit., refer to the Standard Rules as 'a compensatory alternative' (p. 18).

280. Four bog challenges of Asia in 2014: HSBC, Retrieved from http://www.cnbc.com/id/101302526#.

281. *Frequently Asked Questions on Equal Opportunity,* Retrieved from http://www.civilrights.org/equal-opportunity/faq.html

282. Fuchs, D. and Fuchs, L. (1995). *What's special about special education? Phi Delta Kappan* 76, 522-530.

283. *Funding crisis means UKDPC will go volunteer-only within days,* Retrieved from http://disabilitynewsservice.com/2013/06/funding-crisis-means-ukdpc-will-go-volunteer-only-within-days/

284. Futures Stolen: Barriers to Education for Children with Disabilities in Nepal, Retrieved from http://www.hrw.org/sites/default/files/reports/nepal0811ForWebUpload.pdf

285. G.M. Monawar Hosain, David Atkinson, and Peter Underwood (2002), Impact of Disability on Quality of Life of Rural Disabled People in Bangladesh, *J Health Popul Nutr* 2002 Dec. 20(4): 297-305.

286. *Gabon comes to the aid of Disabled People,* Retrieved from http://en.gabonews.com/headlines-reader-en/items/gabon-comes-to-the-aid-of-disabled-people.html

287. Galina Solodunova, *Children with disabilities in Kyrgyzstan: from shut-in care to respect in society,* Retrieved from http://www.unicef.org/kyrgyzstan/reallives_25437.html

288. Gargiulo, R.M.; Sluder, L.C.; and Streitenberger, D. (1997). Preparing Early Childhood.

289. Gary Craig (2008), Social justice in a multicultural society: experience from the UK, Santap Sanhari Mishra and Azmal

Hussain (Eds), *Conceptualising social justice, Social justice; Concepts and country experience,* The ICFAI University Press, Hyderabad.

290. Gary L. Albrecht, Katherine D. Seelman, and Michael Bury (2001). *Handbook of Disability Studies,* New Delhi: SAGE Publications.
291. Gary L. Albrecht, Katherine D. Seelman, Michael Bury (2001). *Handbook of Disability Studies,* New Delhi: SAGE Publications.
292. *General situation of people with disabilities in Albania,* Retrieved from http://www.beyondbarriers.org/?q=node/8
293. Geoffrey Dale Arnott (2011). *The Disability Support Worker,* Pearson Education Australia.
294. Germany –ANED country profile, Retrieved from http://www.disability-europe.net/content/aned/media/Germany%20-%20ANED%20country%20profile.pdf
295. *Ghanaians ban 'spirit child' killing,* Retrieved from http://www.bbc.com/news/world-africa-22335634
296. Giangreco, M. F. and Putnam, J.W. (1991). *Supporting the education of students with severe disabilities in regular education environments. In Critical issues in the lives of people with severe disabilities,* ed. M.H. Meyer, C.A. Peck, and L. Brown, 245-270. Baltimore: Paul H. Brookes.
297. *Global development voices: Living with disabilities,* Retrieved from http://www.theguardian.com/global-development/2011/dec/15/disability-voices-development
298. *Global polio eradication initiatives,* Retrieved from http://www.polioeradication.org/
299. *Government Action on Disability Policy A Global Survey Part II - Government Replies as Country Profiles Eritrea,* Retrieved from http://www.independentliving.org/standardrules/UN_Answers/Eritrea.html
300. Government Action on Disability Policy: A Global Survey: Part II - Government Replies as Country Profiles: Bahrain, Retrieved from http://www.independentliving.org/standardrules/UN_Answers/Bahrain.html
301. *Government Initiatives,* Detailed available at http://www.disabilityindia.org/djgovinitiativesnov07B.cfm
302. Graham Pullin (2009). *Design Meets Disability,* Cambridge: MIT Press.
303. Grundfos Sustainability Report 2009.
304. Grundfos web site, http://grundfos.com
305. *Guide to disability rights in India,* Retrieved from http://www.1800wheelchair.ca/news/post/disability-rights-in-canada.aspx

306. Hala Khalaf (2011), *UAE Government moves to encourage more sport for disabled people,* Retrieved from http://www.thenational.ae/news/uae-news/uae-government-moves-to-encourage-more-sport-for-disabled-people
307. *Handicap International,* Retrieved from http://www.handicap-international.org.uk/where_we_work/asia/afghanistan
308. *Handicap International: Algeria,* Retrieved from http://www.handicap-international.org.uk/where_we_work/africa/algeria
309. *Handicap International: Indonesia,* Retrieved from http://www.handicap-international.org.uk/where_we_work/asia/indonesia
310. *Handicap international: Injured and disabled people forgotten in 'highly disabling' Syria crisis,* Retrieved from http://www.handicap-international.org.uk/resources/latest_news/emergencies/20131203-injured-disabled-people-forgotten-highly-disabling-syria-crisis
311. *Handicap International: Jordon,* Retrieved from http://www.handicap-international.org.uk/where_we_work/middle_east/jordan
312. *Handicap International: Mali,* Retrieved from http://www.handicap-international.org.uk/where_we_work/africa/mali
313. *Handicap International: Sierra Leone,* Retrieved from http://www.handicap-international.org.uk/where_we_work/africa/sierra_leone
314. *Handicap International: Syria,* Retrieved from http://www.handicap-international.us/syria
315. *Handicap International; Angola,* Retrieved from http://www.handicap-international.org.uk/where_we_work/africa/angola
316. *Handicap International-Sri Lanka* Retrieved from http://www.handicap-international.us/sri_lanka
317. *Handicap Solidaire Burkina's* Overview, Retrieved from http://www.linkedin.com/in/hsburkina
318. Hangzhou, China (2007), *Regional Preparatory Workshop on Inclusive Education East-Asia,* Retrieved from http://www.ibe.unesco.org/fileadmin/user_upload/Inclusive_Education/Reports/hangzhou_07/mongolia_ inclusion_07.pdf
319. Hans-Joachim Heintze (2007), On the relationship between human rights law protection and international humanitarian law, V.B. Malleswari (Ed), *Human Rights: International Perspectives,* The ICFAI University Press, Hyderabad, p. 164.

320. Harry, B., Allen, N. and McLaughlin, M. (1995). *Communication versus Compliance: African-American Parents' Involvement in Special Education. Exceptional Children* 61(4), 17-21.

321. Hayes Brown (2014), Report: Syria's disabled refugees find themselves doubly victimised, Retrieved from http://thinkprogress.org/world/2014/04/09/3424570/report-syria-disabilities/

322. Hayley Fitzgerald (2008). *Disability and Youth Sport*, United Kingdom: Taylor and Francis.

323. Heba Hagrass, Definitions of Disability and Disability Policy in Egypt, Retrieved from http://disability-studies.leeds.ac.uk/files/library/Barnes-emw-Chapter-10.pdf

324. Heba Hagrass, *Definitions of Disability and Disability Policy in Egypt*, Retrieved from http://disability-studies.leeds.ac.uk/files/library/Barnes-emw-Chapter-10.pdf

325. Henri-Jacques Stiker (1999). *A History of Disability*, Ann Arbor: University of Michigan Press.

326. Henry Enns, *The Role of Organisations of Disabled People: A Disabled Peoples' International Discussion Paper*, Retrieved from http://www.independentliving.org/docs5/Role of Org Dis People.html

327. History of life on Earth (2014), Retrieved from http://www.bbc.co.uk/nature/history_of_the_earth

328. History of the Earth (2014), Retrieved from http://en.wikipedia.org/wiki/History_of_the_Earth

329. *Honda CSR Report* 2009, http://world.honda.com/CSR/pdf/2009/e_csr09_all.pdf

330. *Honda web site*, http://world.honda.com

331. Honduras, Retrieved from http://www.cirnetwork.org/idrm/reports/americas/countries/honduras.html

332. *Hong Kong has a long way to go on disabled rights and attitudes*, Retrieved from http://www.scmp.com/comment/insight-opinion/article/1371189/hong-kong-has-long-way-go-disabled-rights-and-attitudes

333. *How aid is changing disabled people's lives in Uganda*, Retrieved from http://www.channel4.com/news/aid-ade-adepitan-uganda-millennium-development-goals

334. *How Long Will Life Survive on Earth?*, Retrieved from http://www.universetoday.com/25367/how-long-will-life-survive-on-earth/

335. *How to include the disability issues in disaster management: Following floods* 2004 *in Bangladesh*, Retrieved from http://www.handicap-

international.fr/bibliographie-handicap/5CooperationInternationale /contextes_urgence/HIDisaster.pdf

336. *Human (2012)*, Detailed available at http://en.wikipedia.org/wiki/Human
337. Human (2014), Retrieved from http://en.wikipedia.org/wiki/Human
338. *Human Brain Power Demystified (Oct 15, 2009)*, Retrieved from http://www.slideshare.net/secretofmindpower/human-brain-power-demystified
339. Human Resources Development Convention (No. 142), 1975.
340. *Human rights of disabled persons*, Retrieved from http://www.cidh.org/countryrep/brazil-eng/chaper%2010%20.htm
341. Human rights of the people with disability in Nicaragua (2006), Japan International Cooperation Agency (JICA), Costa Rica office, National Council of rehabilitation (CONARE), Nicaragua.
342. I.B. Sareen, National Programme for control of blindness, Health and Population: Perspectives and Issues 24(2): 99-108, 2001.
343. IBM 2008 Corporate Responsibility Report.
344. IBM Human Ability and Accessibility Center, http://ibm.com/able
345. IBM web site, http://www.ibm.com
346. Ibrahim Amin Alqaryouti, Inclusion the Disabled Students in Higher Education in Oman, *International Journal for Cross-Disciplinary Subjects in Education (IJCDSE)*, Volume 1, Issue 4, December 2010, pp. 216-220.
347. *Identical crisis (2006)*. Retrieved from http://www.theguardian.com/society/2006/nov/29/socialcare.guardiansociety supplement
348. ILC. Eighty-eighth Session, Geneva, 2000, Conclusions concerning human resources training and development.
349. ILO Human Resources Development Convention (No. 142), 1975.
350. ILO Unlocking potential: A multinational corporation roundtable on disability and employment.
351. ILO; Women swell ranks of working poor, in World of Work, No. 17, Sep.-Oct. 1996, ILO Geneva.
352. Immunisation Programme, Retrieved from http://www.idph.state.ia.us/ImmTb/immunisation.aspx
353. *Improving Education for Children with Disabilities in Kyrgyzstan*, Retrieved from http://www.opensocietyfoundations.org/voices/improving-education-children-disabilities-kyrgyzstan
354. *In Burma, Children with Disabilities Struggle to Access Schools*, Retrieved from http://www.irrawaddy.org/feature/burmas-disabled-children-struggle-access-schools.html

355. In focus: disability rights in India, Retrieved from http://www.bond.org.uk/in-focus-disability-rights-in-bangladesh

356. *In the Democratic Republic of the Congo, a wheelchair makes Meshak more mobile,* Retrieved from http://www.unicef.org/infobycountry/drcongo_69513.html

357. Inception Report on Intellectually Disabled in Egypt (2005), Retrieved from http://www.jldd.jp/gtid/countryreport/Ms_Abdel_Malek_Yvette.pdf

358. *Including persons with disabilities in National Statistics,* Retrieved from http://www.cbm.org/article/downloads/82788/Including_persons_with_disabilities_in_national_statistics_Morocco.pdf

359. *Inclusion of children with disabilities in Tajikistan,* Retrieved from http://ec.europa.eu/europeaid/documents/case-studies/tajikistan_social-cohesion_disability_en.pdf

360. Inclusion of People with Disabilities in Cambodia, Retrieved from http://www.ilo.org/wcmsp5/groups/public/@ed_emp/@ifp_skills/documents/publication/wcms_115096.pdf

361. *Inclusion of People with Disabilities in Cambodia,* Retrieved from http://www.ilo.org/wcmsp5/groups/public/@ed_emp/@ifp_skills/documents/publication/wcms_115096.pdf

362. *Inclusion of People with Disabilities in China,* Retrieved from http://www.ilo.org/wcmsp5/groups/public/—ed_emp/—ifp_skills/documents/publication/wcms_112380.pdf

363. Inclusion of People with Disabilities in Ethiopia, Retrieved from http://www.ilo.org/wcmsp5/groups/public/@ed_emp/@ifp_skills/documents/publication/wcms_112299.pdf

364. *Inclusion of People with Disabilities in Ethiopia,* Retrieved from http://www.ilo.org/wcmsp5/groups/public/@ed_emp/@ifp_skills/documents/publication/wcms_112299.pdf

365. *Inclusion of People with Disabilities in Kenya,* Retrieved from http://www.ilo.org/wcmsp5/groups/public/—ed_emp/—ifp_skills/documents/publication/wcms_115097.pdf

366. *Inclusion of People with Disabilities in Kenya,* Retrieved from http://www.ilo.org/wcmsp5/groups/public/@ed_emp/@ifp_skills/documents/publication/wcms_115097.pdf

367. Inclusion of People with Disabilities in Lao People's Democratic Republic, Retrieved from http://www.ilo.org/wcmsp5/groups/public/@ed_emp/@ifp_skills/documents/publication/wcms_115098.pdf

368. *Inclusion of People with Disabilities in Lao People's Democratic Republic,* Retrieved from http://www.ilo.org/wcmsp5/groups/public/@ed_emp/@ifp_skills/documents/publication/wcms_115098.pdf

369. *Inclusion of People with Disabilities in Paraguay,* Retrieved from https://www.devex.com/projects/grants/inclusion-of-people-with-disabilities-in-paraguay/2763
370. Inclusion of People with Disabilities in Thailand, Retrieved from http://www.ilo.org/wcmsp5/groups/public/@ed_emp/@ifp_skills/documents/publication/wcms_112307.pdf
371. *Inclusion of People with Disabilities in Thailand,* Retrieved from http://www.ilo.org/wcmsp5/groups/public/@ed_emp/@ifp_skills/documents/publication/wcms_112307.pdf
372. Inclusion of People with Disabilities in the United Republic of Tanzania, Retrieved from http://www.ilo.org/wcmsp5/groups/public/@ed_emp/@ifp_skills/documents/publication/wcms_111461.pdf
373. Inclusion of People with Disabilities in Uganda, Retrieved from http://www.ilo.org/wcmsp5/groups/public/@ed_emp/@ifp_skills/documents/publication/wcms_115099.pdf
374. *Inclusion of People with Disabilities in Uganda,* Retrieved from http://www.ilo.org/wcmsp5/groups/public/@ed_emp/@ifp_skills/documents/publication/wcms_115099.pdf
375. Inclusion of People with Disabilities in Vietnam, Retrieved from http://www.ilo.org/wcmsp5/groups/public/—ed_emp/—ifp_skills/documents/publication/wcms_112407.pdf
376. *Inclusion of People with Disabilities in Zambia,* Retrieved from http://www.ilo.org/wcmsp5/groups/public/—ed_emp/-ifp_skills/documents/publication/wcms_115100.pdf
377. *Inclusive Education and Parents' Involvement in Mongolia,* Retrieved from http://www.eenet.org.uk/resources/eenet_newsletter/news8/page4.php
378. *Inclusive education in Pakistan: Experiences and lessons learned from the engage projects,* Retrieved from http://unesco.org.pk/education/icfe/resources/res30.pdf
379. *Increased Discrimination towards Persons with Disability in Ghana-VODEC,* Retrieved from http://news.peacefmonline.com/pages/social/201311/180980.php
380. *India (2014),* Retrieved from http://en.wikipedia.org/wiki/India
381. *India needs new legislation on Disability Rights,* Retrieved from http://infochangeindia.org/disabilities/analysis/india-needs-new-legislation-on-disability-rights.html
382. *India to provide Artificial Limbs to* 1000 *People in Afghanistan (2014),* Retrieved from http://www.ndtv.com/article/india/india-to-provide-artificial-limbs-to-1000-people-in-afghanistan-526246

383. India Today (2002). *This minority is Invisible,* Retrieved from http://indiatogether.org/health/opinions/jabidi1.htm

384. *Indian Disability Laws - an obsolete picture* (2008), Detailed available at http://www.dpiap.org/resources/pdf/DPbriefnoCLRA_11_05_16.pdf

385. *Indian Disability Laws - an obsolete picture* (2008), Retrieved from http://www.dpiap.org/resources/pdf/DPbriefnoCLRA_11_05_16.pdf

386. *Indian disabled fight for new legislation,* Retrieved from http://www.dw.de/indias-disabled-fight-for-new-legislation/a-17458169

387. *Information for countries: Bulgaria,* Retrieved from http://www.euroblind.org/convention/article-27—work-and-employment/nr/121

388. Ingrid Lewis (2009), *Education for Disabled People in Ethiopia and Rwanda,* Retrieved from http://datatopics.worldbank.org/hnp/files/edstats/ETHgmrpap09.pdf

389. *Integrated Telefónica Accessibility Plan,* www.telefonica.es/accessible

390. *International Covenant on Economic, Social and Cultural Rights,* adopted by G.A. Resolution 2200A (xxi) of 16 Dec. 1966.

391. *International Day of Persons with Disabilities* 2011, Retrieved from http://www.stat.si/eng/novica_prikazi.aspx?id=4382

392. *International Disability Rights Monitor (IDRM) Publications* - - Compendium – Iran, Retrieved from http://www.ideanet.org/content.cfm?id=5B5D7F

393. *International Disability Rights Monitor (IDRM) Publications* - - Compendium – Mexico, Retrieved from http://www.ideanet.org/content.cfm?id=585970andsearchIT=1

394. International Disability Rights Monitor (IDRM) Publications - - IDRM - Nicaragua 2004, Retrieved from http://www.ideanet.org/content.cfm?id=585971

395. International Disability Rights Monitor (IDRM) Publications - - IDRM - Brazil 2004, Retrieved from http://www.ideanet.org/content.cfm?id=535D

396. International Disability Rights Monitor (IDRM) Publications - - IDRM - Uruguay 2004, Retrieved from http://www.ideanet.org/content.cfm?id=5B5F70

397. *International Disability Rights Monitor (IDRM) Publications* - - IDRM - Argentina 2004, Retrieved from http://www.ideanet.org/content.cfm?id=525B

398. *International Disability Rights Monitor (IDRM) Publications* - - IDRM - Peru 2004, Retrieved from http://www.ideanet.org/content.cfm?id=5b5c7e

399. *International Disability Rights Monitor (IDRM) Publications* - - IDRM - Uruguay 2004, Retrieved from http://www.ideanet.org/content.cfm?id=5B5F70

400. *International Disability Rights Monitor (IDRM) Publications* - - IDRM - Chile 2004, Retrieved from http://www.ideanet.org/content.cfm?id=535F

401. *International Disability Rights Monitor,* Retrieved from http://www.idrmnet.org/

402. *International Labour Office (ILO),* See http://www.ilo.org/skills/what/pubs/lang]]en/doc Name]]

403. International Labour Organisation in his working paper three i.e. Disability in workplace: company practices which published in 2010 discuss details about the situation of disable persons in various companies.

404. *Iraq,* Retrieved from http://www.handicap-international.org.uk/where_we_work/middle_east/iraq

405. *Iraq: giving disabled people a chance to resume a normal life,* Retrieved from http://www.icrc.org/eng/resources/documents/update/2011/iraq-update-2011-10-20.htm

406. Irene Caselli (2013). *The law that empowered Ecuador's disabled.*

407. *Is 'disability' still a dirty word in Japan?* Retrieved from http://www.japantimes.co.jp/life/2006/08/27/to-be-sorted/is-disability-still-a-dirty-word-in-japan/#.U0AsDDtQHFw

408. Ivory Coast / Liberia: Hundreds of thousands will be at risk for months without urgent humanitarian international effort, warn aid agencies.

409. Jali Carino (2007), Indigenous peoples, human rights and poverty, V.B. Malleswari (Ed), *Human Rights: International Perspectives,* The ICFAI University Press, Hyderabad, p. 38.

410. Jane Seale (2006). *E-Learning and Disability in Higher Education: Accessibility Research and Practice,* United Kingdom: Taylor and Francis.

411. Javed Abidi (2002), *India Together*, Detailed available at http://www.indiatogether.org/health/opinions/jabidi1.htm

412. Jean-François Trani and Betsy VanLeit (2010), *Increasing inclusion of persons with disabilities: reflections from disability research using the ICF in Afghanistan and Cambodia*, Retrieved from http://asksource.ids.ac.uk/cf/keylists/..%5Cdisplay%5Cbibliodisplay.cfm?ID=34720andtopic=disandSearch=QL_DISSTAT05 and display=full

413. Jean-François Trani and Betsy VanLeit (2010), *Leonard Cheshire Disability and Inclusive Development Centre, Increasing inclusion of persons with disabilities: reflections from disability research using the*

ICF in Afghanistan and Cambodia, Retrieved from http://www.ucl.ac.uk/lc-ccr/centrepublications/workingpapers/WP11_Increasing_inclusion_of_persons_with_disabilities.pdf

414. Jennifer Tennant, *Disability, employment, and income: are Iraq/Afghanistan-era U.S. veterans unique*, Retrieved from http://www.bls.gov/opub/mlr/2012/08/art1full.pdf
415. *Joanne Bladd* (2010), Prejudice hampers effort to get UAE's disabled into work, Retrieved from http://www. arabianbusiness.com/prejudice-hampers-effort-get-uae-s-disabled-into-work-308220.html#.VCiuQztQHFw
416. Job-seekers with Disabilities and (2) Heron R and Murray B, Assisting Disabled Persons in Finding Employment – A Practical Guide, ILO, 1999 and 1997 resp.
417. Joshi SK, Disability in Nepal, *Kathmandu University Medical Journal* (2004) Vol. 2, No. 1 pp. 1-5.
418. Juan E. Mendez and Javier Mariezcurrena (2010), The consolidation of democracy and human rights in Latin America, Adsmantia Pollis and Peter Schwab (Eds), *Human rights: New perspectives*, Viva Books, New Delhi, p. 169.
419. Kachhal (2008), People with different abilities, Sudhir Kr. Singh and A. Kachhap (Eds), *Disability, citizenship and social exclusion*, First edition, Anamika Publishers and Distributors (P) Ltd, New Delhi, p. 44.
420. Karen P. DePauw, and Susan J. Gavron (2005). *Disability Sport*, United States: Human Kinetics.
421. Kasnitz, D. (2001), 'Life Event Histories and the US Independent Living Movement', in M. Priestley (ed.), *Disability and Life Course: Global Perspectives*, Cambridge University Press, Cambridge, pp. 67-78.
422. Kenya National Survey for Persons with Disabilities: Main Report-National Coordinating Agency for Population and Development *and* Kenya National Bureau of Statistics.
423. *Kenya National Survey for Persons with Disabilities: Reports* (2008). Retrieved from http://www.afri-can.org/CBR%20Information/KNSPWD%20Prelim%20Report%20-%20Revised.pdf
424. *Kerala State Handicapped Persons' Welfare Corporation*, Retrieved from http://kerala.gov.in/index.php?option=com_ contentand view =articleandid= 3443andItemid=2507
425. Ketaki Bardalai (2008), Status of implementation of disability legislation in North-East region, Sudhir Kr. Singh and A. Kachhap (Eds), *Disability, citizenship and social exclusion*, First edition, Anamika Publishers and Distributors (P) Ltd, New Delhi, pp. 73-87.

426. Khandaker Jahurul Alam (2009). *Bangladesh and Persons with Disabilities*, Retrieved from http://www.hurights.or.jp/archives/focus/section2/2009/03/bangladesh-and-persons-with-disabilities.html

427. King, I. (2003). *Examining middle school inclusion classrooms through the lens of learner-centreed principles, Theory into Practice* 42(2), 151-157.

428. Kishor Bhanushali (2007), *Changing Face of Disability Movement: From Charity to Empowerment*, Retrieved from http://www.handicap-international.fr/bibliographie-handicap/6SocieteCivile/Autonomisation/Changing_Face_of_Disability_Movement_From_Charity_to_Empowerment.pdf

429. *Knol: A Unit of Knowledge*, http://knol.google.com/k/uniqlo]managemant]performance#

430. *KSA has* 720,000 *disabled* (2012), Retrieved from http://www.arabnews.com/ksa-has-720000-disabled

431. *Kurumba Maldives-Disable children*, Retrieved from http://www.kurumba.com/uploads/wysiwyg/factsheets/Disabled_Persons.pdf

432. *Kuwaiti parliament Okays disability rights act*, Retrieved from http://www.kuna.net.kw/ArticleDetails.aspx?id=2059296andlanguage=en

433. *Kyobo web site*, http://www.kyobo.co.kr

434. *Kyrgyzstan Must Respect Promise to Disabled*, Retrieved from http://www.eurasianet.org/node/64262

435. *Kyrgyzstan*, Retrieved from http://www.unicef.org/ceecis/KY_Cbountry_profile_eng_29July_FINALproofed.pdf

436. Lara Farrar (2014), *In Chinese Schools, Disabled Get Shortchanged*, Retrieved from http://www.nytimes.com/2014/05/19/world/asia/in-chinese-schools-disabled-get-shortchanged.html?_r=0

437. Larissa Hotra (2008), Retrieved from http://upsidedownworld.org/main/el-salvador-archives-74/1384-a-recent-history-of-the-disability-rights-movement-in-el-salvador

438. *Latest disability situations in Bangladesh*, Retrieved from http://swidbd.wordpress.com/about/disability-situation/

439. *Latest U.S. Disability Statistics and Facts*, Retrieved from http://www.disabled-world.com/disability/statistics/census-figures.php

440. *Latvia –ANEd country profile*, Retrieved from http://www.disability-europe.net/content/aned/media/Latvia%20ANED%20country%20profile.pdf

441. Laurie E. Powers and Mary Oschwald, *Violence and abuse against people with disabilities: Experiences, barriers, and prevention*

strategies, Retrieved from http://www.phinational.org/sites/phinational.org/files/clearinghouse/Abuseand ViolenceBrief%203-7-04.pdf

442. *Law on people with disabilities 'far from being implemented* (2013), Retrieved from http://www.dailystar.com.lb/News/Local-News/2013/Apr-03/212361-law-on-people-with-disabilities-far-from-being-implemented.ashx#axzz3EfJvY0ac
443. Lawrence O. Gostin and Lance Gable (2004), *The Human Rights of Persons with Mental Disabilities: A Global Perspective on the Application of Human Rights Principles to Mental Health,* Retrieved from http://scholarship.law.georgetown.edu/facpub/98
444. *Lebanese Physical Handicapped Union,* Retrieved from http://daleel-madani.org/profile/lebanese-physical-handicapped-union
445. *Lebanon: Disabled remain marginalised, study finds* (2006), Retrieved from http://www.irinnews.org/report/26050/lebanon-disabled-remain-marginalised-study-finds
446. *Lebanon: Disabled remain marginalised, study finds,* Retrieved from http://www.irinnews.org/report/26050/lebanon-disabled-remain-marginalised-study-finds
447. Lee Kyu-Chang, *North Korea Signs the Convention on the Rights of Persons with Disabilities: Meaning and the Tasks,* Retrieved from http://www.kinu.or.kr/upload/neoboard/DATA01/co13-19(E).pdf
448. *Legal Assistance Center for People with Disabilities,* Retrieved from http://www.americanbar.org/advocacy/rule_of_law/where_we_work/europe_eurasia/moldova/news/news_moldova_judiciary_assessment_reports_0110.html
449. *Legislation on Disability: The Costa Rican Experience,* Retrieved from http://www.independentliving.org/docs1/hr12.html
450. Lennard J. Davis (1995). *Enforcing Normalcy: Disability, Deafness, and the Body,* London: Verso.
451. Lennard J. Davis (2006). *The Disability Studies Reader,* United Kingdom: Taylor and Francis.
452. *Leprosy Mission World,* Retrieved from http://www.leprosymission.org/chad.html
453. *Let's help disabled people fulfill their potential,* Retrieved from http://www.theguardian.com/commentisfree/2013/sep/21/disabled-people-potential-australia-byrne
454. *Liberia Christian Handicapped Organisation,* Retrieved from https://www.globalgiving.org/pfil/6973/projdoc.pdf
455. *Liberia,* Retrieved from http://www.handicap-international.org.uk/where_we_work/africa/liberia

456. *Life for people with disabilities in Russia is getting better* (2014), Retrieved from http://rbth.com/society/2014/05/17/life_for_people_ with_disabilities_in_russia_ is_getting_better_36725.html

457. *Lithuania –ANED country profile*, Retrieved from http://www.disability-europe.net/content/aned/media/Lithuania%20-%20ANED%20country%20profile.pdf

458. *Livelihood opportunities for person in disability*, Retrieved from http://www.undp.org/content/dam/india/docs/pub-povertyreduction/livelihood-opportunities-for-persons-with-disabilities.pdf

459. *Living with a disability in Yemen*, See http://siteresources.worldbank.org/DISABILITY/Resources/Regions/Africa/LCYemen.pdf

460. *Loas*, Retrieved from http://www.handicap-international.org.uk/where_we_work/asia/laos

461. *Looking the Other Way: Disability in Yemen*, Retrieved from http://www.escwa.un.org/divisions/div_editor/Download.asp?table_name=divisions_otherandfield_name=IDandFileID=1155

462. *Looking the Other Way: Disability in Yemen*, Retrieved from http://www.escwa.un.org/divisions/div_editor/Download.asp?table_name=divisions_otherandfield_name=IDandFileID=1155

463. Luis Fernando Astorga Gatjens, *Panama: Opportunities Expand for Disabled Persons to Obtain Employment*, Retrieved from http://www.disabilityworld.org/06-08_03/employment/panama.shtml

464. *Luxembourg–ANED country profile*, Retrieved from http://www.disability-europe.net/content/aned/media/Luxembourg%20-%20ANED%20country%20profile.pdf

465. M. Rezaul Islam, Rights of the People with Disabilities and Social Exclusion in Malaysia, *International Journal of Social Science and Humanity*, Vol. 5, No. 2, February 2015, Retrieved from http://www.ijssh.org/papers/447-H10019.pdf

466. Maher S. Al-Jadid, Disability in Saudi Arabia, *Saudi Med J* 2013; Vol. 34 (5) 4, pp. 453-459, Retrieved from http://smj.psmmc.med.sa/index.php/smj/article/viewFile/712/518

467. *Mainstreaming disability in disaster risk reduction: a training manual* (2009), Retrieved from http://www.handicap-international.fr/fileadmin/documents/publications/DisasterRiskReduc.pdf

468. Mairian Corker and Tom Shakespeare (2002). *Disability/Postmodernity: Embodying Disability Theory*, New York: Bloomsbury Academic.

469. Mairian Corker and Tom Shakespeare. *Disability - Postmodernity: Embodying Disability Theory*, United Kingdom: Continuum Publication.

470. Majid Turmusani, *Afghanistan: New Comprehensive National Disability Policy*, Retrieved from http://www.disabilityworld.org/01-03_04/gov/afghanistan.shtml

471. Majid Turmusani, *Disability Policy and Provision in Jordan: A critical perspective*, Retrieved from http://disability-studies.leeds.ac.uk/files/library/stone-chapter-12.pdf

472. *Malaysia needs to do more for people with disabilities, advocates say*, Retrieved from http://khabarsoutheastasia.com/en_GB/articles/apwi/articles/features/2013/02/27/feature-03

473. Malene Kamp Jensen (2013), *Children with disabilities among Syria's most vulnerable*, Retrieved from http://www.unicef.org/mena/media_8277.html

474. *Mali - Support to heavily disabled children in Bamako*, Retrieved from http://www.croix-rouge.mc/home/what-we-do/international-action/development/mali-support-to-heavily-disabled-children-in-bamako/

475. *Mali: Disabled seek jobs, not charity*, Retrieved from http://www.irinnews.org/report/90808/mali-disabled-seek-jobs-not-charity

476. *Mali: Disabled seek jobs, not charity*, Retrieved from Mali: Disabled seek jobs, not charity

477. Manpower 2009 Corporate Social Responsibility Update: People and Purpose.

478. *Manpower web site*, http://manpower.com

479. *Manual of disability statistics* (2012), Retrieved from http://wadhwani-foundation.org/wp-content/themes/wadhwani-new/img/ond/Disability_Manual_19mar12.pdf

480. *Manuals for doctors to evaluate permanent physical impairment*, Retrieved from http://archive.india.gov.in/allimpfrms/alldocs/12097.pdf

481. Margery Austin Turner, Carla Herbig, Deborah Kaye, Julie Fenderson and Diane Levy (2005), *Against person with disabilities: Barriers at Every Step*, Retrieved from http://www.hud.gov/offices/fheo/library/dss-download.pdf

482. Marks and Spencer, *Plan A: Doing the right thing, our Plan A commitments* 2010]2015.

483. Marks and Spencer Employee Handbook.

484. *Marks and Spencer web site*, http://www.marksandspencer.com

485. Marks and Spencer, *How we do business report* 2009: *Doing the right thing.*

486. Martha Craven Nussbaum (2006). *Frontiers of Justice: Disability, Nationality, Species Membership,* Cambridge: Harvard University Press.

487. Matthew W. Brault (2012), *Americans with Disabilities:* 2010, Retrieved from http://www.census.gov/prod/2012pubs/p70-131.pdf

488. *Mauritania's handicapped children ostracised by families and society,* Retrieved from http://english.alarabiya.net/articles/2012/10/07/242416.html

489. Medical Examination of Young Persons (Industry) Convention (No. 77), 1946; Medical Examination of Young Persons (Non-Industrial Occupations) Convention (No. 78), 1946; Medical Examination of Young Persons Recommendation (No. 79), 1946.

490. Meera Shenoy (2011). *Persons with disability and Indian labour market: Challenges and opportunities,* Retrieved from http://www.ilo.org/wcmsp5/groups/public/—asia/—ro-bangkok/—sro-new_delhi/documents/publication/wcms_229259.pdf

491. Mental Health Act (1987): Need for a paradigm shift from custodial to community care, *Indian J Med Res* 133, March 2011, pp. 246-249.

492. *Mental health and development,* Retrieved from http://www.un.org/disabilities/default.asp?id=1545

493. *Mental illness via-a-vis the persons with disabilities act in the Kerala context,* Sasisekhar Menon, Sel.Gr.Assistant, High Court of Kerala, Detailed available at http://kja.nic.in/article/MENTALILLNESS.pdf

494. *Mexico Bans Discrimination against the Disabled,* Retrieved from http://latino.foxnews.com/latino/lifestyle/2011/05/29/mexico-bans-discrimination-disabled/

495. Michael Freeman (2010), Liberal democracy and minority rights, Adsmantia Pollis and Peter Schwab (Eds), *Human rights: New perspectives,* Viva Books, New Delhi, p. 31.

496. Michael Reisch (2008), Social justice and multiculturalism: persistent tensions in the history of US social welfare and social work, Santap Sanhari Mishra and Azmal Hussain (Eds), *Conceptualising social justice, Social justice; Concepts and country experience,* The ICFAI University Press, Hyderabad.

497. Microsoft Corporate Citizenship Report 2010.

498. Microsoft web site, http://www.microsoft.com

499. *Millennium Development Goals (MDGs),* Retrieved from http://www.un.org/disabilities/default.asp?id=1470

500. *Ministry of Health of Iraq/WHO launch Global Report on Disability: Iraq:* Retrieved from http://www.emro.who.int/irq/iraq-news/

ministry-of-health-of-iraqwho-launch-global-report-on-disability.html

501. *Ministry of social justice and empowerment, About us-brief history,* Retrieved from http://socialjustice.nic.in/breif.php

502. Mirza, A. Tareen, L. L. Davidson and A. Rahman, Community management of intellectual disabilities in Pakistan: a mixed methods study, Journal of Intellectual Disability Research, volume 53 part 6 pp 559–570 June 2009.

503. *Mizoram: An inconvenience for disabled persons (May* 16-31, 2009), Detailed available at http://nenanews.com/ANE%20May%2016-31,09/Health.htm

504. *Mizoram: An inconvenience for disabled persons (May* 16-31, 2009), Detailed available at http://nenanews.com/ANE%20May%2016-31,09/Health.htm

505. Moldova Moves to Protect the Rights of People with Mental Disabilities, Retrieved from http://www.opensocietyfoundations.org/press-releases/moldova-moves-protect-rights-people-mental-disabilities

506. *Mongolia: Ulaanbaatar Grapples with Challenge of Equal Access for Disabled,* Retrieved from http://www.eurasianet.org/node/64555

507. Moon, M. and Griffin, S. Supported Employment Service Delivery Models in Wehman, P., and Moon, M. (Eds), *Vocational Rehabilitation and Supported Employment*. Paul H. Brooks Publishing Company: Baltimore MD, 1988

508. Most of 800,000 People with Disabilities in Afghanistan are Uneducated and Unemployed, Retrieved from http://www.khaama.com/most-of-800000-people-with-disabilities-in-afghanistan-are-uneducated-and-unemployed-7854325

509. Mourad Mansour, *Employers' Attitudes and Concerns about the Employment of Disabled People,* Retrieved from http://www.wbiconpro.com/32.Mourad-.pdf

510. *Movement for the Intellectually Disabled of Singapore,* Retrieved from http://www.minds.org.sg/

511. MphasiS Limited Annual Report 2009.

512. MphasiS web site, http://www.mphasis.com

513. *Myanmar: Disabled battle stigma, lack of funds,* Retrieved from http://www.irinnews.org/report/85020/myanmar-disabled-battle-stigma-lack-of-funds

514. *National Blindness Control Programme,* Retrieved from http://health.uk.gov.in/pages/display/84-national-blindness-control-programme

515. *National Council for Persons with Disabilities*, Retrieved from http://ncpwd.go.ke/
516. *National Handicapped Finance and Development Corporation, Schemes*, Retrieved from http://socialjustice.nic.in/nhfdcnew.php
517. National Inquiry into Employment and Disability: Issues Paper 1, Retrieved from https://www.humanrights.gov.au/publications/national-inquiry-employment-and-disability-issues-paper-1
518. *National Inquiry into Employment and Disability: Issues* Paper 1, Retrieved from http://www.humanrights.gov.au/publications/national-inquiry-employment-and-disability-issues-paper-1
519. *National Policy for Persons with Disabilities*, Ministry of Social Justice and Empowerment, Government of India, No.3-1/1993-DD.III, Detailed available at http://www.disabilityindia.org/nationalpolicyfordisable.cfm
520. National policy of disability in Sri Lanka (2003), Retrieved from http://www.unicef.org/srilanka/disability_policy_(1).pdf
521. National Policy on Care for People with Disability, Retrieved from http://www.gov.bw/en/Citizens/Sub-Audiences/People-with-Disabilities-/National-Policy-on-Care-for-People-with-Disabilities/
522. *National Union of Disabled Persons of Uganda NUDIPU*, Retrieved from http://abilis.fi/index.php?option=com_contentandview=articleandid=85andItemid=331andlang=en
523. *Nearly 90% of people with disabilities in Kazakhstan unemployed – prosecutor general's office*, Retrieved from http://www.interfax.kz/?lang=engandint_id=expert_opinionsandnews_id=6379
524. Neil Merrett (2012), *NGOs cite lack of regulation as a key barrier to Maldivian disability rights*, Retrieved from http://minivannews.com/society/ngos-cite-lack-of-regulation-as-a-key-barrier-to-maldivian-disability-rights-40596
525. *Nepal Integrated Blind Development Association*, See http://www.nibda.org.np/client/index.php
526. *Nepal Society of the Disabled*, Retrieved from http://www.nsd.org.np/files/aboutus.htm
527. Nidhi Singal (2008), *Forgotten Youth: Disability and Development in India*, Retrieved from http://recoup.educ.cam.ac.uk/publications/WP14-NS.pdf
528. Nidhi Singal (2008), *Forgotten Youth: Disability and Development in India, Research Consortium on Educational Outcomes and Poverty*, Retrieved from http://recoup.educ.cam.ac.uk/publications/WP14-NS.pdf

529. Nidhi Singal (2008), *Forgotten Youth: Disability and Development in India*, Detailed available at http://recoup.educ.cam.ac.uk/publications/WP14-NS.pdf
530. *Nigar Orujova, Government promotes social integration of disabled people*, Retrieved from http://www.azernews.az/azerbaijan/42766.html
531. *Niger: Educating disabled children*, Retrieved from http://www.irinnews.org/report/86343/niger-educating-disabled-children
532. *Nigeria: Enabling the Disabled*, Retrieved from http://allafrica.com/stories/201212050255.html
533. Nina Shapiro (2012), *The Implications of Sociocultural Perceptions of Disability in Rural Highland Guatemalan Towns*, Retrieved from https://apps.carleton.edu/curricular/ocs/guatemala/assets/Shapiro___Final_Paper.pdf
534. *No progress for disable people*, Retrieved from http://americamagazine.org/issue/761/signs/no-progress-disabled-people
535. Nokia Code of Conduct.
536. Nokia Sustainability Report 2009.
537. Nokia web site, http://www.nokia.com
538. Nora Ellen Groce and Parul Bakshi (2009), *Illiteracy among Adults with Disabilities in the Developing World: An Unexplored Area of Concern, Leonard Cheshire Disability and Inclusive Development Centre*, Retrieved from http://www.ucl.ac.uk/lc-ccr/centrepublications/workingpapers/WP09_Illiteracy_among_Adults_with_Disabilities_in_the_Developing_World_-_An_Unexplored_Area_of_Concern.pdf
539. Nora Ellen Groce and Parul Bakshi (2009), *Illiteracy among Adults with Disabilities in the Developing World: An Unexplored Area of Concern*, Retrieved from http://asksource.ids.ac.uk/cf/keylists/..%5Cdisplay%5Cbibliodisplay.cfm?ID =34721andtopic= edu andsearch=QL_LLEd12anddisplay=full
540. Nora Ellen Groce, Adolescents and youth with disability: issues and challenges, *Asia Pacific Disability Rehabilitation Journal*, Retrieved from http://eprints.ucl.ac.uk/15132/1/15132.pdf
541. *North Africa* (2014), Retrieved from http://en.wikipedia.org/wiki/North_Africa
542. *North Korea makes Paralympics debut. Does it signal a shift?* Retrieved from http://www.csmonitor.com/World/Asia-Pacific/2012/0829/North-Korea-makes-Paralympics-debut.-Does-it-signal-a-shift

543. *Notes from the field: We can't forget about Chad*, Retrieved from http://www.care-international.org/news/stories-and-blogs/emergency-response/chad-we-cannot-forget-chad.aspx
544. O'Reilly (2003), *The right to decent work of persons with disabilities*, Retrieved from http://digitalcommons.ilr.cornell.edu/cgi/viewcontent.cgi?article=1177andcontext=gladnetcollect
545. O'Reilly (2003), *The right to decent work of persons with disabilities*, Retrieved from http://www.ilo.org/public/english/region/eurpro/moscow/info/publ/right_dw_pd.pdf
546. *OECD says financial incentives would help Luxembourg to increase workforce participation*, Retrieved from http://www.oecd.org/els/emp/39790004.pdf
547. Office of Disability (1995), Review of the Disability Task Force, Commonwealth Department of Human Services and Health, Canberra: Australian Government Publishing Service.
548. Oliver, M. and Barnes, C. (1998), *Disabled People and Social Policy: From Exclusion to Inclusion*, Longman, London.
549. *One billion people disabled, first global report finds*, Retrieved from http://www.theguardian.com/society/2011/jun/09/billion-people-disabled-report
550. *Only 6,789 disabled persons in Pakistan, says government (April 24, 2009)*, Daily Times, Detailed available at http://www.dailytimes.com.pk/default.asp? page=2009% 5C04%5 C24%5 Cstory_24-4-2009_pg7_13
551. *Only 9% of disabled persons in Chile are employed*, Retrieved from http://www.ilovechile.cl/2010/12/09/only-9-of-disabled-persons-in-chile-are-employed/14411
552. *Opening the world to disabled people*, Retrieved from http://www.unicef.org/zimbabwe/media_13118.html
553. *Opportunity of Intellectual Disabled People in Thailand*, Retrieved from http://www.jldd.jp/gtid/acmr_18/pdf/1.pdf
554. *Organisational action (2014)*, Retrieved from http://www.aoad-af.org/
555. *Outcast Status Worsens Pain of Japan's Disabled*, Retrieved from http://www.nytimes.com/1996/04/07/world/outcast-status-worsens-pain-of-japan-s-disabled html
556. *Pakistan (2014)*, Retrieved from http://www.spinalcord.org/resource-centre/askus/index.php?pg=kb.pageandid=1628
557. *Pakistan Society for the Rehabilitation of the Disabled*, Retrieved from http://www.psrd.org.pk/index.php/component/content/article/2-uncategorised/25-welcome-to-psrdpdf
558. *Pakistan: UNESCO Country Programming Document* 2013-2017, Retrieved from http://unesco.org.pk/documents/2013/PAKISTAN_CPD.pdf

559. Paul K. Longmore (2003). *Why I Burned My Book and Other Essays on Disability*, Philadelphia: Temple University Press.

560. *Paula Campos Pinto: Family, disability and social policy in Portugal: Where are we at, and where do we want to go?* Retrieved from http://revista.aps.pt/cms/files/artigos_pdf/ART4dc4205994c60.pdf

561. *People* (2012), Detailed available at http://en.wikipedia.org/wiki/People

562. *People with Different Abilities*, Retrieved from http://unami.unmissions.org/default.aspx? ctl=Detailsan dtabid=2790 andmid=5079andItemID=816849

563. *People With Disabilities*, Retrieved from http://seoul.angloinfo.com/information/healthcare/people-with-disabilities/

564. *People with disabilities have equal rights*, Retrieved from http://www.radiomiraya.org/index.php/south-sudan-news/8829-people-with-disabilities-have-equal-rights#gsc.tab=0

565. People with Disabilities in Costa Rica, Retrieved from http://costarica.angloinfo.com/information/healthcare/people-with-disabilities/

566. *People with Disabilities in Costa Rica*, Retrieved from http://costarica.angloinfo.com/information/healthcare/people-with-disabilities/

567. *People with Disabilities in Germany*, Retrieved from http://germany.angloinfo.com/healthcare/people-with-disabilities/

568. *People with Disabilities in India*, Retrieved from http://india.angloinfo.com/healthcare/people-with-disabilities/

569. *People with disabilities in India: From commitments to outcomes* (2007), Detailed available at http://www.eldis.org/assets/Docs/55120.html

570. *People with disabilities in India: From commitments to outcomes*, Retrieved from http://siteresources.worldbank.org/INDIAEXTN/Resources/295583-1171456325808/DISABILITYREPORTFINALNOV2007.pdf

571. *People with Disabilities in Israel Facts and Figures*, Retrieved from http://brookdale.jdc.org.il/_Uploads/dbsAttachedFiles/FACTS_FIGURES2014.pdf

572. *People with Disabilities in Israel: Progress and Challenges* (2012), Retrieved from http://brookdale.jdc.org.il/_Uploads/dbsAttachedFiles/MJB-Data-Snapshot—Disabilities-in-Israel-October-2012(1).pdf

573. *People with Disabilities in Panama*, Retrieved from http://panamacity.angloinfo.com/information/healthcare/people-with-disabilities/

574. *People with Disabilities in Russia,* Retrieved from http://russia.angloinfo.com/healthcare/people-with-disabilities/

575. *People with Disabilities in Saudi Arabia,* Retrieved from http://saudiarabia.angloinfo.com/healthcare/people-with-disabilities/

576. *People with Disabilities in Thailand,* Retrieved from http://thailand.angloinfo.com/healthcare/people-with-disabilities/

577. *People with disabilities want Venezuelan revolution to continue: 'We need even more of a voice',* Retrieved from http://rabble.ca/news/2013/04/people-disabilities-want-venezuelan-revolution-to-continue-we-need-even-more-voice

578. *People With Disabilities,* Retrieved from http://madrid.angloinfo.com/information/healthcare/people-with-disabilities/

579. *People With Disabilities,* Retrieved from http://malaysia.angloinfo.com/healthcare/people-with-disabilities/

580. *People With Disabilities,* Retrieved from http://qatar.angloinfo.com/healthcare/people-with-disabilities/

581. *People With Disabilities,* Retrieved from http://seoul.angloinfo.com/information/healthcare/people-with-disabilities/

582. *People With Disabilities,* Retrieved From http://taipei.angloinfo.com/information/healthcare/people-with-disabilities/

583. *People with Disabilities,* Retrieved from http://vietnam.angloinfo.com/healthcare/people-with-disabilities/

584. *People with Disabilities: Azerbaijan,* Retrieved from http://azerbaijan.angloinfo.com/healthcare/people-with-disabilities/

585. *People With Disabilities: Belgium,* Retrieved from http://brussels.angloinfo.com/information/healthcare/people-with-disabilities/

586. *People With Disabilities: Denmark,* Retrieved from http://copenhagen.angloinfo.com/information/healthcare/people-with-disabilities/

587. *Periodic Report of Burkina Faso to the African Commission on Human and Peoples' Rights relative to the African Charter on Human and Peoples' Rights covering the Period* 2003-2009, Retrieved from http://www.achpr.org/files/sessions/49th/state-reports/3rd-2004-2006/staterep3_burkinafaso_2010_eng.pdf

588. *Personal life* (2014), Retrieved from http://en.wikipedia.org/wiki/Personal_life

589. *Persons with disabilities 'forgotten victims' of Syrian conflict – UN committee,* Retrieved from http://www.un.org/apps/news/story.asp?NewsID=45871#.VCgmYTtQHFw

590. *Persons with disabilities 'forgotten victims' of Syrian conflict – UN committee,* Retrieved from http://www.un.org/apps/news/story.asp/story.asp?NewsID=45871andCr=syriaandCr1=#.Uz-EJDtQHFw

591. *Persons with Disabilities Act,* 2011 *Working Draft (9February,* 2011 *version),* Prepared by Centre for Disability Studies, NALSAR University of Law, Hyderabad, India.

592. Persons with Disability in the Philippines (Results from the 2010 Census), Retrieved from http://web0.psa.gov.ph/content/persons-disability-philippines-results-2010-census

593. *Persons with Disability in the Philippines (Results from the* 2010 *Census),* Retrieved from http://www.census.gov.ph/content/persons-disability-philippines-results-2010-census

594. Peter Juviler (2010), Political community and human rights in postcommunist Russia, Adsmantia Pollis and Peter Schwab (Eds), *Human rights: New perspectives,* Viva Books, New Delhi, p. 116.

595. Peter Schwab and Adamantia Pollis (2010), Globalisation's impact on human rights, Adsmantia Pollis and Peter Schwab (Eds), *Human Rights: New Perspectives,* Viva Books, New Delhi, p. 221.

596. *Policy for the disabled in France* (2007), Retrieved from http://www.ambafrance-eau.org/IMG/disabled.pdf

597. *Polio eradication,* Retrieved from http://ghstrat.com/issues/polio

598. Polio eradication, Retrieved from http://www.unicef.org/india/health_3729.htm

599. Pooya Alaedini, *Training and Employment of People with Disabilities: People with Disabilities: Iran* 2003, Retrieved from http://www.ilo.org/wcmsp5/groups/public/—asia/—ro bangkok/documents/publication/wcms_113195.pdf

600. Position Statement – Disability and PRS in Liberia.

601. *Poverty and disable people in development context: examples from Jordon and Afghanistan,* Retrieved from http://r4d.dfid.gov.uk/pdf/outputs/chronicpoverty_rc/turmusani.pdf

602. Precious Sango, *Visible but Invisible: People living with disability in Nigeria,* Retrieved from http://books2africa.org/visible-but-invisible-people-living-with-disability-in-nigeria/

603. *Prevalence estimates of physical disability in Bahrain—a household survey,* Retrieved from http://www.ncbi.nlm.nih.gov/pubmed/2527840

604. *Prevalence of disability in South Africa,* Retrieved from http://www.statssa.gov.za/census01/html/Disability.pdf

605. *Prevalence of disability in South Africa: Census* 2001, Retrieved from http://www.statssa.gov.za/census01/html/Disability.pdf

606. *Problems faced by families with disabled children*, Retrieved from http://jpshaw.hubpages.com/hub/Problems-faced-by-families-with-disabled-children

607. *Problems of Handicapped Children (2014)*, Read more : http://www.ehow.com/info_8123088_problems-handicapped-children.html

608. *Proceedings of the Expert Group Meeting on Inclusion of People with Disabilities in Vocational Training: 14–16 February* 2006, Retrieved from http://www.ilo.org/wcmsp5/groups/public/@ed_emp/@ifp_skills/documents/meetingdocument/wcms_107915.pdf

609. Professor E. Azinge and Dr Chinyere Ani, *The Rights of Persons in Disability*, Retrieved from http://www.nials-nigeria.org/Editedbookcovers/THE%20RIGHTS% 20OF% 20PERSONS%20WITH%20DISABILITIES.pdf

610. *Profile of people with disabilities in Brazil*, Retrieved from http://www.cps.fgv.br/ibrecps/nw/Profile_of_ people_disabilities.pdf

611. Prokriti Nokrek, Md. Arafat Alam and Muzzafar Ahmed (2013), *Livelihood challenges for extremely poor disabled people in the southwest coastal region of Bangladesh*, Retrieved from http://r4d.dfid.gov.uk/PDF/Outputs/EEP/Shiree-WP12.pdf

612. *Promoting awareness and recognition of people with disabilities*, Retrieved from http://www.undp.org/content/kuwait/en/home/ourwork/humandevelopment/successstories/promoting-awareness-and-recognition-of-persons-with-disabilities/

613. *Promoting Rights and Opportunities for People with Disabilities in Employment*, Retrieved from http://www.ilo.org/jakarta/whatwedo/projects/WCMS_183300/lang—en/index.htm

614. *Promoting Rights and Opportunities for People with Disabilities in Employment ...*, Retrieved from http://www.ilo.org/jakarta/whatwedo/projects/WCMS_183300/lang—en/index.htm

615. *Promoting the Employability and Employment of People with Disabilities through Effective Legislation (PEPDEL)*, Retrieved from http://www.ilo.org/asia/whatwedo/projects/WCMS_112558/lang—en/index.htm

616. Ramesh Madan (2008), Encountering disability, Sudhir Kr. Singh and A. Kachhap (Eds), *Disability, citizenship and social exclusion*, First edition, Anamika Publishers and Distributors (P) Ltd, New Delhi, p. 180.

617. Rapley, C. (2003) Reconsidering the disability Dimension in Development Cooperation Activities; building national capacities for full participation and equality, Regional Workshop towards

a Comprehensive and Integral International Convention on Protection and Promotion of the Rights and Dignity of Persons with Disabilities, October 14-17, UNESCAP, Bangkok.

618. Rashed Al Mahmud Titumir and Jakir Hossain (2005), *Disability in Bangladesh: Prevalence, knowledge, attitudes and practices*, Retrieved from http://unnayan.org/reports/Disability%20Prevalence%20and%20KAP%20Study.pdf

619. Raymond Ceccotto, *Report on the employment of disabled people in European countries: Luxembourg*, Retrieved from http://www.disability-europe.net/content/aned/media/LU%20employment%20report.pdf

620. Raymond Lang, Nora Groce, Maria Kett, Jean-Francois Trani and Nicki Bailey (2009), *The Potential Impact of the Global Economic Downturn on People with Disabilities in Developing Countries*, Retrieved from http://www.ucl.ac.uk/lc-ccr/centrepublications/workingpapers/WP08_ Impact_ of_the_Global_ Economic_Downturn.pdf

621. Raymond Lang, Nora Groce, Maria Kett, Jean-Francois Trani and Nicki Bailey (2009), *The Potential Impact of the Global Economic Downturn on People with Disabilities in Developing Countries*, Leonard Cheshire Disability and Inclusive Development Centre, Retrieved from

622. *Realising inclusive education for children with disabilities in Lesotho*, Retrieved from http://africlaw.com/2013/07/15/realising-inclusive-education-for-children-with-disabilities-in-lesotho/

623. Recommendation (No. 22) *concerning the minimum scale of workmen's compensation*, 1925.

624. Reeta Bagchi (2008), Women and Disability in India, Sudhir Kr. Singh and A. Kachhap (Eds), *Disability, citizenship and social exclusion*, First edition, Anamika Publishers and Distributors (P) Ltd, New Delhi, p. 199.

625. Reeta Bagchi (2008), Women with disability and human rights in North-west India, Sudhir Kr. Singh and A. Kachhap (Eds), *Disability, citizenship and social exclusion*, First edition, Anamika Publishers and Distributors (P) Ltd, New Delhi, p. 186.

626. *Rehabilitation and Disabilities*, Retrieved from http://www.emro.who.int/irq/programmes/rehabilitation-disabilities.html

627. *Rehabilitation and Disabilities: Iraq*, Retrieved from http://www.emro.who.int/irq/programmes/rehabilitation-disabilities. html

628. *Rehabilitation and integration of people with disabilities: policy and legislation*, Retrieved from http://www.coe.int/t/e/social_cohesion/soc-sp/7th%20edition %20legislation %20e% 20in%20color.pdf

629. *Removing Barriers for the Disabled in Libya,* Retrieved from https://internationalmedicalcorps.org/sslpage.aspx?pid=2476#.VCpKKjtQHFw

630. *Removing Barriers for the Disabled in Libya,* Retrieved from https://internationalmedicalcorps.org/sslpage.aspx?pid=2476#. U0A2gjtQHFw

631. *Report on the employment of disabled people in European countries,* Retrieved from http://www.disability-europe.net/content/aned/media/DK%20-%20ANED% 202009% 20Employment %20Report%20Final.pdf

632. Report on the employment of disabled people in European countries, *Academic Network of European Disability experts,* Retrieved from http://www.disability-europe.net/content/aned/media/IS%20Employment%20report.pdf

633. *Report on the employment of disabled people in European countries,* Retrieved from http://www.disability-europe.net/content/aned/media/BE%20employment%20report.pdf

634. *Report on the Rights of persons with disabilities in Timor-Leste,* Retrieved from http://www.ohchr.org/Documents/Issues/Disability/UNHR_Report2011_en_resize.pdf

635. Report to the Commission, Feb. 2000.

636. *Report: Disabled people in Israel poor, lonely,* Retrieved from http://www.ynetnews.com/articles/0,7340,L-3813210,00.html

637. Republic of Guinea-Bissau: NGOs Alternative Report on the Implementation of the United Nations Child Rights Convention in Guinea-Bissau.

638. Republic of Moldova Center for Legal Assistance for Persons with Disabilities, Retrieved from http://lib.ohchr.org/HRBodies/UPR/Documents/session12/MD/CLAPD-CenterLegalAssistancePersonsDisabilities-eng.pdf

639. Resolution concerning Vocational Rehabilitation and Social Reintegration of Disabled or Handicapped.

640. Resolution concerning Vocational Rehabilitation of Disabled Persons, 1965 ICCPR, Article 2.

641. Revised by Nepal Government in 2006, Retrieved from http://rcrdnepa.files.wordpress.com/2010/09/definition-and-classification-of-disability-in-nepal_english.pdf

642. Reykhan Muminova, Advocacy for Persons with Disabilities in Tajikistan, Retrieved from http://www.jmu.edu/cisr/journal/16.3/sr/muminova.shtml

643. Rich Deem (2008), *Man, Created in the Image of God: How Mankind is Unique among All Other Creatures on Earth,* Retrieved from http://www.godandscience.org/evolution/imageofgod.html

644. *Rights of Disabled Persons and Japan*, Retrieved from http://www.hurights.or.jp/archives/focus/section2/2002/09/rights-of-disabled-persons-and-japan.html
645. *Rights of Disabled Persons and Japan*, Retrieved from http://www.hurights.or.jp/archives/focus/section2/2002/09/rights-of-disabled-persons-and-japan.htm
646. *Rights of People with Intellectual Disabilities: Access to Education and Employment: Estonia*, Retrieved from http://www.opensocietyfoundations.org/sites/default/files/estonia_2005_0.pdf
647. *Rights of People with Intellectual Disabilities: Hungary*, Retrieved from http://www.opensocietyfoundations.org/sites/default/files/hungary_0.pdf
648. *Rights of Persons with Disabilities in Accessing the Justice System*, Retrieved from http://www.chr.gov.ph/MAIN%20PAGES/about%20hr/advisories/pdf_files/FINAL%20full PWD report.pdf
649. Rob Imrie (1996). *Disability and the City: International Perspectives*, New Delhi: SAGE.
650. Robert McRuer and Anna Mollow (2012), *Sex and Disability*, Durham: Duke University Press.
651. Robert McRuer (2006), *Crip Theory: Cultural Signs of Queerness and Disability*, New York: NYU Press.
652. Roger S. Clark (2010), How international human rights law affects domestic law, Adsmantia Pollis and Peter Schwab (Eds), *Human rights: New perspectives*, Viva Books, New Delhi, p. 185.
653. Roland Moes and Tom Dominique (2010), *Luxembourg experience on preventing work incapacity*.
654. *Royal Government of Bhutan, Ministry of Education, National Policy on Special Educational Needs*, Retrieved from http://www.education.gov.bt/documents/10180/12859/Final-Draft-SEN-Policy-2012.pdf/2bd136d1-71af-41d7-8819-a2d177e75049?version=1.0
655. *Rural poverty approaches policies and strategies in Chad*, Retrieved from http://www.ruralpovertyportal.org/en/country/approaches/tags/chad
656. *Rwanda*, Retrieved from http://www.handicap-international.org.uk/where_we_work/africa/rwanda
657. *Rwanda: People with disabilities left out of condom campaign*, Retrieved from http://www.irinnews.org/report/88761/rwanda-people-with-disabilities-left-out-of-condom-campaign
658. *Rwanda: People with disabilities left out of condom campaign*, Retrieved from http://www.irinnews.org/report/88761/rwanda-people-with-disabilities-left-out-of-condom-campaign

659. Ryhor Astapenia (2013), *People With Disabilities In Belarus: Struggling With Barriers*, Retrieved from http://belarusdigest.com/story/people-disabilities-belarus-struggling-barriers-14561

660. S.Firat, *People with disability in Turkey, Information Technologies, Management and Society*, 2010, Volume 3, No. 2, 51-54.

661. Sabelo J. Ndlovu-Gatsheni (2007), Giving Africa voice within global governance: oral history, human rights and the United Nations human rights council, V.B Malleswari (Ed), *Human Rights: International Perspectives*, The ICFAI University Press, Hyderabad, p. 166.

662. Salah I. Al-Gain , *Sami S. Al- Abdulwahab, Issues and obstacles in disability research in Saudi Arabia*, Retrieved from http://english.aifo.it/disability/apdrj/apdrj102/arabia.pdf

663. Salai Vanni Bawi, *Understanding the challenges of disability in Myanmar*, Retrieved from http://www.burmalibrary.org/docs13/Understanding_the_Challenges_of_ Disability_ in_ Myanmar-red.pdf

664. Samsung Electro Mechanics Citizenship Report 2010,

665. *Samsung Electro Mechanics web site*,See http://sem.samsung.co.kr

666. Sanga Dorji, and Patricia Solomon (2009), Attitudes and health professionals towards persons with disability in Bhutan, *Asia Pacific Disability Rehabilitation Journal*, Volume 20, No. 2, Retrieved from http://english.aifo.it/disability/apdrj/apdrj209/professional_attitudes_dorji_solomon.pdf

667. Sanjoy Pandey (2007), Institutional approach to human rights protection: Indian Experience, V.B Malleswari (Ed), *Human Rights: International Perspectives*, The ICFAI University Press, Hyderabad, p. 217.

668. Santap Sanhari Mishra and Azmal Hussain (2008), *Conceptualising social justice, Social justice; Concepts and country experience*, The ICFAI University Press, Hyderabad, p. 3.

669. Santosh Arora (2008), Human rights and special need children, Sudhir Kr. Singh and A. Kachhap (Eds), *Disability, citizenship and social exclusion*, First edition, Anamika Publishers and Distributors (P) Ltd, New Delhi, p.100.

670. Sara Sabry (2014), *Insufficient statistics about the number of special needs people in the UAE, officials say*, Retrieved from http://gulfnews.com/news/gulf/uae/general/insufficient-statistics-about-the-number-of-special-needs-people-in-the-uae-officials-say-1.1308332

671. Sarah Safra Pallak Lebbe (2010), *Right to Development for Disabled People: A Sri Lankan case study*, Retrieved from http://

www.cmb.ac.lk/fgs/images/stories/reserch_pub/page2/master_in_human_rights/Sarah%20 Safra%20 Pallak%20 Lebbe.pdf

672. *Saudi looks to put* 100,000 *disabled people in jobs*, Retrieved from http://www.arabianbusiness.com/saudi-looks-put-100-000-disabled-people-in-jobs-490450.htm
673. Scant help for South Sudan's disabled, Retrieved from http://www.irinnews.org/report/97496/scant-help-for-south-sudan-s-disabled
674. *Scant help for South Sudan's disabled*, Retrieved from http://www.irinnews.org/fr/report/97496/scant-help-for-south-sudan-s-disabled
675. Scheme for assistance to disable persons for purchase/fitting of AIDS/Appliances (2005), Retrieved from http://socialjustice.nic.in/pdf/adipsch.pdf
676. *Scheme for rehabilitation of Disabled person*, Retrieved from http://assam.gov.in/scheme-for-rehabilitation-of-disabled-person
677. *Schemes and Facilities provided by Central and State Government*, Retrieved from http://ayjnihh.nic.in/aw/awareness/schemes 3.html
678. *School of Hope brings education to Malian children with hearing impairments*, Retrieved from http://www.unicef.org/infoby country/mali_69546.html
679. *SDGs and disability*, Retrieved from http://www.un.org/disabilities/default.asp?id=1618
680. *Self-help organisations of disabled persons*, Retrieved from http://www.wwda.org.au/wp-content/uploads/2013/12//sho dp1.pdf
681. *Senegal: Children with disability – when stigma means abandonment*, Retrieved from http://www.irinnews.org/report/90139/senegal-children-with-disability-when-stigma-means-abandonment
682. *Serbia creating opportunities for people with disabilities*, Retrieved from http://www.undp.org/content/undp/en/home/ourwork/povertyreduction/projects_and_initiatives/serbia_creating_opportunitiesforpeoplewithdisabilities/
683. Sharifa A M AL-Shehri, *Access to dental care for persons with disabilities in Saudi Arabia*, Retrieved from http://www. shancock sltd.co.uk/download. php?op= view_articlean darticle_id=1083
684. Sharon N. Barnartt (2010). Disability as a Fluid State, Bingley: Emerald Group Publishing.
685. Shelley Lynn Tremain (2005). *Foucault and the Government of Disability*, Ann Arbor: University of Michigan Press.

686. *Sierra Leone: Disabled Persons Demand Free Health Care Package,* Retrieved from http://allafrica.com/stories/201401091249.html
687. Simi Linton (1998). *Claiming Disability: Knowledge and Identity,* New York: NYU Press.
688. *Sincere' North Korean concern for disabled questioned,* Retrieved from http://www.nknews.org/2014/06/sincere-north-korean-concern-for-disabled-questioned/
689. *Situation Assessment: People with Disabilities in Azerbaijan,* Retrieved from http://www.az.undp.org/content/dam/azerbaijan/docs/sustain_development/AZ_Disability_Report_Eng.pdf
690. Situation in Malaysia, Retrieved from http://www.unicef.org/malaysia/sowc_sowc_13-situation_in_malaysia.html
691. *Situation of disability in Ethiopia,* Retrieved from http://labspace.open.ac.uk/mod/oucontent/view.php?id= 451964 andsection=1.7
692. *Slovakia –ANED country profile,* Retrieved from http://www.disability-europe.net/content/aned/media/Slovakia%20-%20ANED%20country%20profile.pdf
693. *Sochi Games Signal Change for Russia's Disabled,* Retrieved from http://www.themoscowtimes.com/news/article/sochi-games-signal-change-for-russias-disabled/488922.html
694. *Social and Employment Policies for People with Disabilities in Spain,* Retrieved from https://campus.usal.es/~inico/investigacion/invesinico/employment.pdf
695. *Social Assistance and Rehabilitation for the Physically Vulnerable,* Retrieved from http://www.sarpv.org/whoweare
696. *Social exclusion of handicap people in Poland,* Retrieved from http://netaware.ue.katowice.pl/wp-content/uploads/2013/03/National-report-Poland-Handicapped.pdf
697. *Social issue* (2014*),* Retrieved from http://en.wikipedia.org/wiki/Social_issue
698. *Social problems,* Retrieved from http://ucpressjournals.com/journal.php?j=sp
699. Social Security (Minimum Standards) Convention (No. 102) 1952, Article 35.
700. *Social Welfare Department of Tripura,* Detailed available at http://www.mapsofindia.com/tripura/government/social-welfare-department.html
701. *Social Welfare Department of Tripura,* Detailed available at http://www.mapsofindia.com/tripura/government/social-welfare-department.html

702. *Society (2012)*, Retrieved from http://en.wikipedia.org/wiki/Society.
703. *Society of the Disabled Persons Penang*, Retrieved from http://www.disabledpersonspenang.org/
704. *Society's Attitude toward People with Disabilities Historical Perspective*, Retrieved from http://paul-burtner.dental.ufl.edu/oral-health-care-for-persons-with-disabilities/societys-attitude-toward-people-with-disabilities/
705. Sodexo 2010 Corporate Citizenship Progress Review.
706. Sodexo web site, http://www.sodexo.com
707. Soheil Moeini, The Role of NGOs as Reflected in the Social Movement of the Disabled in Iran, Retrieved from http://www.stimson.org/images/uploads/research-pdfs/The_ Role_of_Non-Governmental_Organisations.pdf
708. *Somalia: Disabled children in Somaliland "must come first*, Retrieved http://www.irinnews.org/report/89514/somalia-disabled-children-in-somaliland-must-come-first
709. *Some judgments of disability rights*, Retrieved from http://cis-india.org/accessibility/blog/summary-of-judgments-on-disability-rights#fn21
710. Sony Corporation CSR Report 2009.
711. *Sony Corporation web site*, http://www.sony.net
712. Soren V. Randall (2006). Learning disabilities: new research, New York: Nova Science Publishers.
713. *South Asia (2014)*, Retrieved from http://en.wikipedia.org/wiki/South_Asia
714. *South Asia People (2014)*, Retrieved from http://www.cotf.edu/earthinfo/sasia/SApeo.html
715. *South Korea disabled struggle to be hears*, Retrieved from http://www.abc.net.au/news/2012-10-25/an-sth-korea-disabled-struggle-for-rights/4334020
716. *South Sudan*, Retrieved from http://www.handicap-international.org.uk/where_we_work/africa/south_sudan
717. Spare a thought for disabled people (April 18, 2010), *Sunday Observer*, Detailed available at http://www.sundayobserver.lk/2010/04/18/spe08.asp
718. *Special education*, Retrieved from http://www.uaecd.org/special-education
719. *Special Needs Resources and Support in the UAE*, Retrieved from http://www.expatwoman.com/abudhabi/monthly_ abudhabi_faqs_Special_ Needs_ Resources_ and_ Support_ In_ The_UAE_9261.aspx

720. *Specific learning disability*, Retrieved from http://arksped.k12.ar.us/rules_regs_08/3.%.pdf

721. *Standing up for the rights of India's disabled people in North East*, Volume 7 Issue 4 - February 15, 2010, Detailed available at http://www.dnis.org/features.php? issue_id=4andvolume_id=7andfeatures_id=171

722. *Standing up for the rights of India's disabled people in North East*, Volume 7 Issue 4 - February 15, 2010, Detailed available at http://www.dnis.org/features.php? issue_id =4an dvolume_id =7andfeatures_id=171

723. *State of Disabled Peoples Rights in Kenya (2007) Report*, Retrieved from http://disability-studies.leeds.ac.uk/files/library/african-union-of-the-blind-Kenya-Report-2007-FINAL.pdf

724. *State of the Rights of Persons with Disabilities in Bangladesh* 2009, Disability Rights Watch Group

725. Statement by H.E. Mr. Kasit Piromya, *Minister of Foreign Affairs of Thailand at the Opening of the Second Committee of UNESCAP*, 19 October 2010, Bangkok, Retrieved from http://www.mfa.go.th/humanrights/statement/61-thailands-policy-on-persons-with-disabilities

726. *Status of Implementation of Disability Legislation in North East States of India*, Retrieved from http://www.dnis.org/features.php?issue_id=20andvolume_id=3andfeatures_id=97

727. Steven D. Edwards (2005). *Disability: definitions, value and identity*, New York: Radcliffe Publishing.

728. *Strategies for skills acquisition and work for people with disabilities in southern Africa: Synthesis report- Malawi, South Africa and Zambia (2007)*, Retrieved from http://www.ilo.org/wcmsp5/groups/public/@ed_emp/@ifp_skills/documents/publication/wcms_107784.pdf

729. *Strategies for skills acquisition and work for persons with disabilities in southern Africa (Malawi) (2007)*, Retrieved from http://www.ilo.org/wcmsp5/groups/public/—ed_emp/—ifp_skills/documents/publication/wcms_107786.pdf

730. *Sudan launches Arabic version of the World Report on Disability*, Retrieved from http://www.emro.who.int/sdn/sudan-events/disability-arabicreport-launch.html

731. *Sudan: Quick facts and local partners*, Retrieved from http://www.add.org.uk/sudan-partners

732. Sudhir Singh (2008), *Disability, employment, social mobilisation and human rights in India*, Sudhir Kr. Singh and A. Kachhap (Eds), *Disability, citizenship and social exclusion*, First edition, Anamika Publishers and Distributors (P) Ltd, New Delhi, p. 205.

733. Sunil Dogra, Tarun Narang and Bhushan Kumar, Leprosy - evolution of the path to eradication, *Indian J Med Res* 137, January 2013, pp. 15-35.

734. *Support for disable children in Sri Lanka,* Retrieved from http://www.hope-for-children.org/projects/support-for-disabled-children-in-sri-lanka/

735. *Support for people with disabilities in Ethiopia (overview),* Retrieved from http://www.inclusive-education-in-action.org/iea/index.php?menuid=25andreporeid=239

736. *Supporting Disability Centres in Countryside Mongolia,* Retrieved from http://www.sustainability.net.au/public/documents/7/207/208/Sustainability_Supporting_ Disability_ Centres_in_Countryside_Mongolia.pdf

737. *Swaziland: Disabled People 'Treated Like Animals',* Retrieved from http://allafrica.com/stories/201308210820.html

738. *Sweden's disability policy,* Retrieved from https://sweden.se/society/swedens-disability-policy/

739. *Syria crisis,* Retrieved from http://www.cbm.org/Syria-crisis-CBM-supporting-refugees-with-disabilities-429018.php

740. Syria disability programme, Retrieved from http://saidfoundation.org/syria-disability-programme

741. Taiwan Access for All Association, Retrieved from http://twaccess4all.wordpress.com/

742. Tauseef Ahmed (1993). Disabled Population in Pakistan: Disabled Statistics of Neglected People, Retrieved from http://www.sdpi.org/publications/files/W13-Disabled %20 Population%20in%20Pakistan.pdf

743. Telefónica Annual Corporate Responsibility Report.

744. Telefónica Business Principles.

745. Telefónica web site, http://www.telefonica.com

746. Telenor Group Annual Report 2009.

747. Telenor web site, http://www.telenor.com

748. Telstra Business Principles.

749. Telstra Code of Conduct, http://www.telstra.com.au/abouttelstra/download/document/persresponsibility.

750. Telstra web site, http://www.telstra.com.au

751. Telstra's Fourth Disability Action Plan.

752. *Thailand,* Retrieved from http://www.mfa.go.th/humanrights/implementation-of-un-resolutions/136-thailands-status-with-regard-to-the-convention-on-the-rights-of-persons-with-disabilities-crpd-and-the-realisation-of-the-mdgs-for-persons-with-disabilities

753. Thamarashi Wickramanayake (2013). *Rights of Persons with disabilities*, Retrieved from http://www.basl.lk/article_details.php?id=5

754. Thaneswor Gautam (2009), *Mainstreaming People with Disability in the Development of Nepal*, Retrieved from http://www.socialinclusion.org.np/new/files/Thanesh owar %20 Gautam_ 1345462481dG9a.pdf

755. *The comprehensive national disability policy in Afghanistan (2003)*, Retrieved from http://www.who.int/disabilities/policies/documents/Afghanistan.pdf

756. *The Cyprus Red Cross Home for Sick Children*, Retrieved from http://www.redcross.org.cy/cgibin/hweb?-A=130and-V=kidshome

757. *The Disabled People's Movement, A Resource Pack for Local Groups of Disabled People Published by the BCODP*, Retrieved from http://disability-studies.leeds.ac.uk/files/library/BCODP-workbook4.pdf

758. The Employment (Transition from War to Peace) Recommendation, 1944 (No. 71).

759. *The European Disability Forum*, Detailed available at http://www.edf-feph.org/

760. *The failure to implement, India Together*, Detailed available at http://www.indiatogether.org/health/disability/dact.htm

761. *The first life on earth (2014)*, Retrieved from http://paleobiology.si.edu/geotime/main/htmlversion/archean3.html

762. *The forgotten tribe: people with disabilities in Zimbabwe*, Retrieved from http://www.eldis.org/go/homeandid=33637 andtype=Document#.VCtl7DtQHFw

763. *The History of Life on Earth (2014)*, Retrieved from http://animals.about.com/od/evolution/ss/evolution_2.htm

764. *The Indian Express (Sep* 12, 2014*)*, SC clears 3% reservation for disabled in jobs, promotions, See more at: http://indianexpress.com/article/india/india-others/3-quota-must-for-disabled-in-all-govt-jobs-including-ias-supreme-court/#sthash.fnUd31uO.dpuf

765. *The labour market situation of disabled people in European countries and implementation of employment policies: a summary of evidence from country reports and research studies*, Retrieved from http://www.disability-europe.net/content/aned/media/ANED%20Task%206%20final%20report%20-%20final%20version%2017-04-09.pdf

766. *The league to support the integration of disabled people*, Retrieved from http://www.ddpuk.org/lardef.html

767. *The Leprosy Mission: Chad,* Retrieved from http://www.leprosymission.org/chad.html
768. *The Mental Health Act,* 1987, Retrieved from http://www.tnhealth.org/mha.htm
769. *The Mental Health Act,* 1987, Retrieved from http://www.wbhealth.gov.in/download/MENTAL%20 HEALTH%20ACT%201987.pdf
770. *The National Association for the Habilitation of Children and Adults with Intellectual Disabilities,* Retrieved from http://www.akimisrael.com/
771. *The National Programme for Control of Blindness in India,* Retrieved from http://www.ncbi.nlm.nih.gov/pmc/articles/PMC 3562965/
772. *The National Trust for Welfare of Persons with Autism, Cerebral Palsy, Mental Retardation and Multiple Disabilities Act,* 1999, Retrieved from http://rbi.org.in/scripts/Notification User.aspx?Id=8689andMode=0
773. The other regular supervisory body is the Conference Committee on the Application of Standards.
774. *The people of Asia (*2014*),* Retrieved from http://www.lim.ethz.ch/lehre/fruehjahrssemester/international _management/R5_HB_The_people_of_Asia.pdf
775. *The Persons with Disabilities (Equal Opportunities, Protection of Rights and Full Participation) Act,* 1995, Detailed available at http://www.ccdisabilities.nic.in/page.php
776. *The Persons with Disabilities (Equal Opportunities, Protection of Rights and Full Participation) Act,* 1995, Detailed available at http://www.rehabcouncil.nic.in/pdf/pwdact1995.pdf
777. *The plights of Burma's Disable population,* Retrieved from http://rehmonnya.org/archives/106
778. *The Rights of Disabled people in the Hashemite Kingdom of Jordan As Per the National Legislative System and International Standards,* Retrieved from http://www.nchr.org.jo/english/ModulesFiles/PublicationsFiles/Files/The%20Rights %20of% 20Disabled%20people%20in%20the %20Hashemite %20Kingdom %20of%20Jordan% 20A s%20Per% 20the%20National%20 Legislative %20.pdf
779. *The Rights of Persons with Disabilities Act,* Retrieved from http://www.who.int/disabilities/world_report/2011/chapter1.pdf
780. *The Rights of Persons with Disabilities Act,* 2011, Retrieved from http://socialjustice.nic.in/pdf/workdraftdd.pdf
781. *The Rights of Persons with Disabilities Act,* Retrieved from http://cis-india.org/accessibility/blog/rights-of-persons-with-disabilities

782. *The Rights of Persons with Disabilities Act,* Retrieved from http://cis-india.org/accessibility/blog/working-draft
783. *The Rights of Persons with Disabilities Act,* Retrieved from http://clpr.org.in/tag/persons-with-disabilities-act-2010/
784. *The Rights of Persons with Disabilities Act,* Retrieved from http://www.jagranjosh.com/current-affairs/rights-of-persons-with-disabilities-bill-2011-1387010614-1
785. *The Rights of Persons with Disabilities Act,* Retrieved from http://www.ilo.org/wcmsp5/groups/public/—asia/—ro-bangkok/—sro-new_delhi/documents/publication/wcms_229259.pdf
786. *The Rights of Persons with Disabilities Act,* Retrieved from http://kafila.org/2014/02/03/a-critqiue-of-the-draft-rights-of-persons-with-disabilities-bill-2014-amba-salelkar/
787. *The Rights of Persons with Disabilities Act,* Retrieved from http://disabilitystudiesnalsar.org/CountryReportLatest.pdf
788. Retrieved from http://www.prsindia.org/billtrack/the-right-of-persons-with-disabilities-bill-2014-3122/
789. *The situation of persons with physical, motor and mental disabilities in the Islamic Republic of Iran,* Retrieved from http://www.iranhrc.org/uploads/docs/docs_en/disability.pdf
790. *The Sunday Indian (Feb 7, 2012),* Tech gap for disabled people, Retrieved from http://www.thesundayindian.com/en/story/tech-gap-for-disabled-people/3/29662/
791. *The Times of India (Dec 1, 2011),* Disabled people cannot book rly tickets online, say officials, Retrieved from http://articles.timesofindia.indiatimes.com/2011-12-01/chennai/30462279_1_southern-railway-disabled-persons-disabled-people
792. *The Times of India (Feb 22, 2014).* Disabled upset as bill for their rights stuck, Retrieved from http://timesofindia.indiatimes.com/india/Disabled-upset-as-bill-for-their-rights-stuck/articleshow/30808854.cms
793. *The Times of India (Feb 28, 2012),* Archaic laws stop disabled from flying, Retrieved from http://articles. times of india.indiatimes.com/2012-02-28/chennai/31106943_1_ambulifts-disabled-passengers-aerobridges
794. *The Times of India (Oct 9, 2010),* Wed a disabled person, get Rs. 50,000 from state, Retrieved from http://articles. timesofindia .indiatimes.com/2010-10-09/mumbai/28244825 _1_disabled-person-scheme-bitter-pill
795. *The United Nations and indigenous persons with disabilities,* Retrieved from http://www.un.org/disabilities/default.asp?id=1605
796. Thomas C. Weiss (2010), *Overview of Disability in China,* Retrieved from http://www.disabled-world.com/news/asia/china/disability-china.php

797. *Through art to integration of disabled children,* Retrieved from http://www.unicef.org/uzbekistan/reallives_5090.html
798. *Ticket Information for Disabled People,* Retrieved from http://www.fifa.com/confederationscup/organisation/ticketing/ticket-information/accessibility-tickets/
799. *Times of India (Dec 29, 2013),* Disabled population up by 22.4% in 2001-11, Retrieved from http://timesofindia.indiatimes.com/india/Disabled-population-up-by-22-4-in-2001-11/articleshow/28072371.cms
800. *Times of India (Feb 7,* 2014), Government introduces Rights of Persons with Disabilities Bill in Rajya Sabha, Retrieved from http://timesofindia.indiatimes.com/india/Government-introduces-Rights-of-Persons-with-Disabilities-Bill-in-Rajya-Sabha/articleshow/30007941.cms
801. *Times of India (Mar 26, 2014),* India's success in polio eradication is a model to the world: Dr Nata Menabde, Retrieved from http://timesofindia.indiatimes.com/interviews/Indias-success-in-polio-eradication-is-a-model-to-the-world-Dr-Nata-Menabde/articleshow/32680701.cms
802. Tirang R Neyestani et al., Nutritional status of the Iranian children with physical disability: a cross-sectional study, *Asia Pac J Clin Nutr* 2010; 19 (2):223-230.
803. *To consolidate the vital positions,* Retrieved from http://turkmenistan.gov.tm/_eng/?id=3756
804. Tobin Siebers (2008). *Disability Theory,* Ann Arbor: University of Michigan Press.
805. Togo: *Relieving disabled children from crippling customs,* Retrieved from http://www.irinnews.org/report/95683/togo-relieving-disabled-children-from-crippling-customs
806. Tom Shakespeare (1998). *Disability Reader: Social Science Perspectives,* London: Bloomsbury.
807. Tony Powers (2008), *Recognising ability: The skills and productivity of persons with disabilities,* Retrieved from http://www.ilo.org/skills/pubs/WCMS_103984/lang—en/index.htm
808. Tony Powers (2008), *Recognising ability: The skills and productivity of persons with disabilities,* Retrieved from http://www.ilo.org/public/english/employment/download/wpaper/wp3.pdf
809. Tony Powers (2008), *Recognising ability: The skills and productivity of persons with disabilities-Literature review, Employment Sector Employment* Working Paper No. 3, Retrieved from http://www.ilo.org/public/english/employment/download/wpaper/wp3.pdf
810. Tony Powers (2008), *Recognising ability: The skills and productivity of persons with disabilities,* Retrieved from http://www.ilo.org/public/english/employment/download/wpaper/wp3.pdf

811. Towards Equal Participation of People with Disabilities in South Sudan: A Survey of the Inclusion of People with Disabilities in Civic and Social Life Juba, *Central Equatoria*, Retrieved from http://www.forcierconsulting.com/wp-content/uploads/2013/04/Towards-Equal-Participation-of-People-with-Disabilities-in-South-Sudan-for-Handicap-International.pdf
812. *Training for Disability Professionals in Syria*, Retrieved from http://www.iecd.org/en/training-for-disability-professionals/
813. *Treatment of Disabled people in India*, Retrieved from http://www.pushti-marg.net/bhagwat/disabled.htm
814. Trevor R. Parmenter (2011), Promoting training and employment opportunities for people with intellectual disabilities: *International experience*, Retrieved from http://www.ilo.org/employment/Whatwedo/Publications/WCMS_167316/lang—en/index.htm
815. Tsitsi Choruma (2006), *People with disabilities in Zimbabwe*, Retrieved from http://www.progressio.org.uk/sites/default/files/Forgotten-tribe.pdf
816. *Turkey improves rights of the disabled*, Retrieved from http://turkey.setimes.com/en_GB/articles/ses/articles/features/departments/national/2014/02/27/feature-02
817. *Two stage child disability study among children* 2-9 *years: Bhutan* 2010-11, Retrieved from http://www.nsb.gov.bt/publication/files/pub9er1152un.pdf
818. *U.N. exposes North Korea's rampant forced abortions, sterilisations, infanticide, and persecution of the disabled*, Retrieved from http://liveactionnews.org/less-than-human-north-koreas-rampant-forced-abortions-sterilisations-infanticide-and-persecution-of-the-disabled/
819. *UKDPC - United Kingdom Disabled People's Council*, Retrieved from http://www.patient.co.uk/support/ukdpc-united-kingdom-disabled-peoples-council
820. Ulas Doga Eralp (2007), The European effect and diffusion of the human rights norms in Turkey, V.B Malleswari (Ed), *Human Rights: International Perspectives*, The ICFAI University Press, Hyderabad, p.103.
821. UN (1994) The Standard Rules on Equalisation of opportunities for Persons with Disabilities. NY, UN.
822. UN Committee on Economic, Social and Cultural Rights, General Comment No. 5, 1994.
823. UN General Assembly A/Conf. 157/23, 12 July 1993.
824. *Understanding disabilities in Kazakhstan with 'more than a blog*, Retrieved from http://netprophet.tol.org/2012/04/02/understanding-disabilities-in-kazakhstan-with-more-than-a-blog/

825. *Understanding Discrimination* , Retrieved from https://www.un.org/cyberschoolbus/discrim/id_8_ud_race.asp
826. UNESCO and Kuwait conclude agreement on inclusive education for persons with disabilities, Retrieved from http://www.unesco.org/new/en/media-services/single- view/news/unesco_and_kuwait_conclude _agreement _on_inclusive_education _ for_persons_with_disabilities/back/9597/#.Uz-DETtQHFw
827. UNGA Res. 31/12.
828. UNGA Res. 3447(xxx) of 9 Dec. 1975.
829. UNGA Res. 36/77 of 8 Dec. 1981.
830. UNGA Resolution 2856 of 20 Dec. 1971.
831. *UNICEF support offers hope for children with disabilities in Somaliland,* See http://www.unicef.org/somalia/reallives_12823.html
832. *United Nations Standard Rules on the Equalisation of Opportunities for Persons with Disabilities,* Retrieved from http://www.who.int/disabilities/policies/standard_rules/en/
833. United Nations, The Standard Rules on the Equalisation of Opportunities for Persons with Disabilities, 1994.
834. Universal Declaration of Human Rights, adopted by the General Assembly on 10 Dec. 1948, Article 23.
835. *Universal Immunisation Programme,* Retrieved from http://mohfw.nic.in/WriteReadData/l892s/Immunisation_UIP.pdf
836. US Department of Labour's Office of Disability Employment Policy.
837. *Uzbekistan,* Retrieved from http://www.parus87.com/disabilities.htm
838. *Uzbekistan: New school brings children with disabilities out of their homes,* Retrieved from http://www.irinnews.org/report/34281/uzbekistan-new-school-brings-children-with-disabilities-out-of-their-homes
839. *Valuing People: A New Strategy for Learning Disability for the 21st Century,* Retrieved from https://www.gov.uk/government/uploads/system/uploads/attachment_data/file/250877/5086.pdfAndrew\
840. *Venezuela: power from the ground up,* Retrieved from http://www.disabilitynow.org.uk/article/venezuela-power-ground
841. Vienna Declaration and Programme of Action, adopted by the World Conference on Human Rights on 25.
842. Vivian Nereim (2013), UAE company to provide jobs for the disabled, Retrieved from http://www.thenational.ae/news/uae-news/uae-company-to-provide-jobs-for-the-disabled
843. Vocational Rehabilitation and Employment (Disabled Persons) Recommendation (No. 168), 1983 (emphasis added).

844. *Vocational rehabilitation and employment of disabled persons,* Retrieved from http://www.ilo.org/wcmsp5/groups/public/@ed_emp/@ifp_skills/documents/publication/wcms_103529.pdf
845. Vocational Rehabilitation Centre for Handicapped (VRCs) Under Directorate General of Employment and Training, Ministry of Labour and Employment.
846. *VSO Rwanda Disability Programme Overview,* Retrieved from http://www.vsointernational.org/Images/Rwanda-disability-overview-June-2012_tcm76-37209.pdf
847. Walgreens Outreach web site, http://WalgreensOutreach.com
848. Walgreens web site, http://www.walgreens.com
849. Wardak, A, Faiz IM, and Turmusani, M (2003). *Disability Policy Development in Afghanistan: Towards Barriers Free Society, Regional Workshop towards a Comprehensive and Integral International Convention on Protection and Promotion of the Rights and Dignity of Persons with Disabilities.* October 14-17, UNESCAP, Bangkok.
850. Wehman, P., Revell, G. and Kregel, J. Supported Employment: a decade of rapid growth and impact, in Wehman, P., Kregel, J. and West, M. (Eds) *Supported Employment Research: expanding competitive employment opportunities for persons with significant disabilities.* Rehabilitation Research and Training Centre on Supported Employment, Virginia Commonwealth University, 1997.
851. Wei Liu (2007), Impact of Living or Working Environments on Persons with Disabilities, Retrieved http://ideas.repec.org/p/unt/wpmpdd/wp-07-03.html
852. *Welfare for Disabled persons,* Detailed available at http://socialwelfaremanipur.nic.in/disable.htm
853. *Welfare: Helping the elderly, the young, and the disabled: Welfare for Older People,* Retrieved from http://web-japan.org/factsheet/en/pdf/e43_welfare.pdf
854. *West Africa* (2014), Retrieved from http://en.wikipedia.org/wiki/West_Africa
855. *Westpac Annual Review and Sustainability Report* 2009, http://westpac.onlinear2009.
856. Westpac Foundation Report 2008: The Catalyst.
857. Westpac web site, http://westpac.com.au
858. *What are human rights?* Retrieved from http://www.bihr.org.uk/sites/default/files/What%20are%20human%20rights.pdf
859. *What are human rights?,* Retrieved from http://www.ohchr.org/en/issues/pages/whatarehumanrights.aspx
860. *What Are the challenges bached by disable people?* See http://www.answers.com/Q/What_are_the_ challenges_faced_by_disabled_people

861. *What Problems Do People with Disabilities Have? and Why?*, Retrieved from http://codi.buffalo.edu/archives/computing/.making/.part2.htm
862. *Who is helping people of disability in Gaugamala?* Retrieved from http://emergepovertyfree.org/who-is-helping-people-with-disabilities-in-guatemala/
863. Wipro Sustainability Report 2008•]09, http://www.wipro.com/corporate/investors/pdffiles/
864. Wipro web site, http://www.wipro.com
865. Wolfgang Benedek (2007), Final status of Kosovo: The role of human rights and minority rights, V.B Malleswari (Ed), *Human Rights: International Perspectives*, The ICFAI University Press, Hyderabad, p.191.
866. *Women and disability*, Retrieved from http://laodisabled women.com/disability/
867. *Women and girls with disabilities*, Retrieved from http://www.un.org/disabilities/default.asp?navid=13andpid=1514
868. *Workers with Disabilities, Challenges, and Solutions*, Retrieved from http://disabilitymessage.com/disability/content/workers-disabilities-challenges-and-solutions
869. *Working towards including disabled people in society, Bolivia*, Retrieved from http://www.internationalservice.org.uk/resources/news_archive/ayninakuna_bolivia.html
870. *World Facts and Statistics on Disabilities and Disability Issues*, Retrieved from http://www.disabled-world.com/disability/statistics/
871. *World Programme of Action Concerning Disabled Persons*, Retrieved from http://www.un.org/disabilities/default.asp?id=23
872. World report on disability 2011, p. 11, Retrieved from
873. World report on disability 2011, p. 12, Retrieved from http://www.who.int/disabilities/world_report/2011/report.pdf
874. Yeatman, A. (1996). *Getting Real: The Final Report of the Review of the Commonwealth/State Disability Agreement*, Canberra: Australian Government Publishing Service.
875. *Yemen: Disability Profile*, Retrieved from http://www.disabilityworld.org/12-02_05/news/yemen.shtml
876. Yusman Kamaleri and Arne H. Eide (2011), *Living Conditions among People with Disabilities in Lesotho*, retrieved from http://www.sintef.no/uploadpages/39853/Report_Lesotho_310111.pdfbb
877. Yvette Bivigou, *Educating children with disabilities in Niger*, Retrieved from http://www.unicef.org/infobycountry/niger_61049.html
878. *Zambia: People With Disabilities Left Behind in HIV Response*, Retrieved from http://www.hrw.org/news/2014/07/15/zambia-people-disabilities-left-behind-hiv-response

879. Zehra F. Arat (2010), Women's rights in Islam: Revisiting Quranic Rights, Adsmantia Pollis and Peter Schwab (Eds), *Human rights: New perspectives*, Viva Books, New Delhi, p. 71.
880. Zhanat Zakiyeva, *Disability Rights: the View from Kazakhstan*, Retrieved from http://www.disabilityworld.org/11-12_03/gov/kazakhstan.shtml
881. *Zimbabwe: Disability is much more than a physical constraint*, Retrieved from http://www.irinnews.org/report/74038/zimbabwe-disability-is-much-more-than-a-physical-constraint
882. *Zimbabwe: People Living with Disabilities Deserve Better*, Retrieved from http://allafrica.com/stories/201312190057.html

Websites

- http://www.un.org/disabilities/documents/iasg/undg_guidance_note.pdf
- http:// research.ncl.ac.uk/sparcle/Publications files/WebVol2.pdf
- http://abilis.fi/index.php? option=com_contentandview=article andid=88and Itemid=333andlang=en
- http://careerhubs21.blogspot.in/2013/11/career-opportunity-bangladesh.html
- http://cfi-blog.org/2013/10/22/combatting-exclusion-for-persons-with-disabilities-in-india-and-mexico/
- http://disabilitystudiesnalsar.org/CountryReportLatest.pdf
- http://drpi.research.yorku.ca/AsiaPacific/resources/PhilippinesCountryRep/section2
- http://dsnuk.org/caste-discrimination/what-is-caste-discrimination/
- http://ec.europa.eu/justice/discrimination/files/cowi.final_study_report_may_2011_final_en.pdf
- http://emergepovertyfree.org/who-is-helping-people-with-disabilities-in-guatemala/
- http://gwweb.jica.go.jp/km/FSubject0601.nsf/3b8a2d403517ae4549256f2d002e1dcc/f1692 ec318 8fd28 04925 72f90 02bdfcc/$FILE/Human%2 0Rights%20of% 20the%20People%20with %20 Disability%20in%20Nicaragua.pdf
- http://hatw.org.uk/supporting-village-children-into-school-in-benin/
- http://hhrd.pk/crp/wp-content/uploads/2013/02/PWDs-Statistics-in-Pakistan-2012-2.pdf
- http://kenya.cbm.org/programmes/Association-for-the-Physically-Disabled-of-Kenya-265902.php
- http://mada.org.qa/en/about-us
- http://meg http://www.dnis.org/draftpwd12.pdf
- http://mobilityghana.org/wp/
- http://nac.nic.in/pdf/rpdb_recommendations.pdf

- http://pdf.org.pk/
- http://poradna-prava.cz/diskriminace/disabfull_it.pdf
- http://rockcentre.nbcnews.com/_news/2011/11/18/8864856-dying-and-disabled-in-honduras-in-pursuit-of-lobster-to-sell-to-us
- http://saidfoundation.org/syria-disability-programme
- http://sennet.eun.org/c/document_library/get_file?uuid=746a358e-6fb9-46fe-a4c3-da48f9d 3aad1an dgroupId =32059
- http://socialjustice.nic.in/pdf/report-pwd.pdf
- http://swedishhealthcare.se/shc-news/swedish-ideas-help-change-the-view-of-disabled-in-qatar/
- http://turkey.angloinfo.com/family/schooling-education/special-needs-education/
- http://wcd.puducherry.gov.in/Corp_Eng.html
- http://who.int/disabilities/world_report/2011/chapter5.pdf
- http://www.actionaid.org/nigeria/news/call-accelerated-action-towards-child-survival-nigeria
- http://www.add.org.uk/uganda
- http://www.afri-can.org/CBR% 20Information %20in %20Matrix /EMPOWERMENT/Disability %20and% 20integra tion %20-%20Gambian%20experience.pdf
- http://www.apcdfoundation.org/?q=content/importance-disabled-peoples-organisations
- http://www.apd-india.org/profile
- http://www.aph.gov.au/About_Parliament/Parliamentary_Departments/Parliamentary_Library/pubs/BriefingBook43p/disabilitysupport
- http://www.cbm.org/El-Salvador-268095.php
- http://www.cbmuk.org.uk/news/cbm-ensure-persons-with-disabilities-have-access-to-basis-needs-in-DRC
- http://www.ccdh.org.ma/an/bulletin-d-information/tunisian-experience-promoting-rights-disabled
- http://www.cdpo.org/?page=detailandmenu1=6andmenu2=172andctype=articleandid=172andlg=en
- http://www.childrenincrisis.org/our-work/sierra-leone
- http://www.damai.org.my/
- http://www.disabilityfunders.org/disability-stats-and-facts
- http://www.disabilityindia.co.in/useful-information/state.php#Andaman and Nicobar Island
- http://www.disabilitynewsasia.com/home-mainmenu-1/247-24000-disabled-people-in-maldives-reveals-hrcm.html
- http://www.disabilitynewsasia.com/home-mainmenu-1/393—disability-still-proves-a-barrier-to-education-in-oman.html.
- http://www.disabled-world.com/news/africa/

- http://www.dnis.org/draftpwd12.pdf
- http://www.dpa.org.sg/?page_id=42
- http://www.dpi.org/
- http://www.dpi.org/bangladesh
- http://www.dw.de/germany-makes-headway-integrating-disabled-people/a-17267162
- http://www.ecsatlanka.org/disabilitynumber\
- http://www.ecsatlanka.org/termdisability
- http://www.edencentre.org/
- http://www.edf-feph.org/
- http://www.ekta.org.in/
- http://www.eoc.sa.gov.au/eo-you/discrimination-laws/australian-laws/human-rights-and-equal-opportunity-commission-act
- http://www.euroblind.org/convention/article-24—education/nr/100
- http://www.fiadisabledtravellers.com/en/world_map/central_and_south_america/uruguay.htm
- http://www.globalgiving.org/projects/help-educate-children-with-disabilities-in-ghana/
- http://www.goethe.de/wis/bib/pro/hig/Education_and_Culture.pdf
- http://www.handicap.dk/english/about_dsi
- http://www.handicap-international.org.uk/where_we_work/africa/morocco
- http://www.handicap-international.org.uk/where_we_work/africa/tunisia
- http://www.handicap-international.org.uk/where_we_work/africa/madagascar
- http://www.handicap-international.org.uk/where_we_work/asia/cambodia
- http://www.handicap-international.us/democratic_republic_of_congo
- http://www.handicap-international.us/senegal
- http://www.humanrightscommission.vic.gov.au/index.php/the-law/equal-opportunity-act
- http://www.ilo.org/wcmsp5/groups/public/—ed_emp/—ifp_skills/documents/meetingdocument/wcms_104950.pdf
- http://www.kmk.org/fileadmin/doc/Dokumentation/Bildungswesen_en_pdfs/background.pdf
- http://www.kupukupufoundation.org/disability-in-bali/
- http://www.laodisabledwomen.com/disability/
- http://www.legallyindia.com/201402054315/Constitutional-law/nalsar-calls-to-scrap-disability-rights-bill
- http://www.make-development-inclusive.org/docsen/BehinderungEntENG.pdf

- http://www.miseast.org/en/tajikistan/enabling-children-disabilities-and-women-claim-their-human-rights
- http://www.muscatdaily.com/Archive/Oman/2-job-quota-for-disabled-in-Oman-should-be-implemented-better-Association-2xer
- http://www.ncppdsa.org.za/
- http://www.newglobalcitizens.org/foundation-for-people-with-disabilities
- http://www.nytimes.com/2005/09/30/opinion/30iht-edturkey.html?_r=0
- http://www.ohchr.org/Documents/Publications/HRDisabilityen.pdf
- http://www.ohchr.org/EN/UDHR/Documents/UDHR_Translations/eng.pdf
- http://www.pids.gov.ph/dp.php?id=5144andpubyear=2013
- http://www.planusa.org/contentmgr/showdetails.php/id/2779647
- http://www.portalangop.co.ao/angola/en_us/noticias/educacao/2013/7/31/Education-wants-more-disabled-children-school-system-2014,bafc92ca-6e8e-4e8d-9ff3-dcf78f0b6ca7.html
- http://www.punchng.com/opinion/plight-of-persons-with-disabilities-in-nigeria/
- http://www.pwd.org.au/student-section/disabled-people-s-organisations-dpos.html
- http://www.serveafghanistan.org/about/history/
- http://www.servicecanada.gc.ca/eng/lifeevents/disability.shtml
- http://www.sightsavers.org/in_depth/policy_and_research/social_inclusion/13173_Disability %20 Framework%20in%20Pakistan.pdf
- http://www.southasia.ox.ac.uk/sites/sias/files/documents/Oxford%20University%20CSASP%20-%20Work%20in%20Progress%20Paper%205%20SOCIAL%20DISCRI MINATION%20IN%20INDIA% 20A%20CASE%20FOR %20 ECONOMIC %20CITIZENSHIP.pdf
- http://www.spain.info/en_IN/reportajes/cultura_accesible_para_todos_en_espana.html
- http://www.thezimbabwean.co/news/36210/15-million-disabled-people-struggle-to-survive.html
- http://www.unicef.org/ceecis/media_21067.html
- See http://www.unicef.org/ceecis/TKM_Country_ profile_eng_29July_FINAL_proofed.pdf
- http://www.unicef.org/ceecis/UZ_Country_ profile_ eng_29July_ FINAL_proofed.pdf

- http://www.unicef.org/evaldatabase/files/GAM_ 2000_800.pdf
- http://www.unicef.org/infobycountry/kazakhstan_background.html
- http://www.unicef.org/media/files/Preliminary findings Afghanistandisabilityreport.pdf
- http://www.unicef-irc.org/publications/pdf/law_reform_crc_imp.pdf
- http://www.unwomen.org/en/news/stories/2012/7/discrimination-against-women-persists-around-the-globe-hampering-development
- See http://www.vso.nl/Images/namibia-disability-summary-mar07_tcm80-20572.pdf
- See http://www.vsointernational.org/advocacy/37550/giving-voice-to-mongolia%E2%80%99s-silent-warriors%3A-disability-advocacy-campaign
- http://www.vtmh.org.au/docs/communityprofiles/Somali%20health%20disability%20perceptions%20-%20NW%20MRC.pdf
- http://www.workbridge.co.nz/?page=1331
- http://zeenews.india.com/news/nation/india-to-have-equal-opportunity-commission_856233.html
- https://www.gov.uk/government/publications/employing-disabled-people-and-people-with-health-conditions/employing-disabled-people-and-people-with-health-conditions
- wikipedia of human rights'.
- http://censusindia.gov.in/Census_And_You/disabled_population.aspx
- http://en.wikipedia.org/wiki/Declaration_ on_the_ Rights_of_Disabled_Persons
- http://socialjustice.nic.in/nhfdcnew.php
- http://techmemore.com/microsoft-software-disabled/
- http://toostep.com/idea/60-million-people-in-india-are-disabled-how-india-can-help-t
- http://www.disabled-world.com/disability/types/
- http://www.dpi.org/lang-en/resources/details.php?page=748
- http://www.guardian.co.uk/global-development/poverty-matters/2011/jul/21/disabilities-discrimination-africa
- http://www.hreoc.gov.au/disability_rights/hr_disab/areas/Ch1%20.htm
- http://www.indialawjournal.com/volume1/issue_4/article_by_bagga.html
- http://www.leeds.ac.uk/disability-studies/archiveuk/stone/chapter%202.pdf
- http://www.pch.gc.ca/pgm/pdp-hrp/canada/abl-eng.cfm

- http://www.preservearticles.com/201101233658/complete-information-on-the-rights-of-a-disabled-person-in-india.html
- http://www.preservearticles.com/201101233658/complete-information-on-the-rights-of-a-disabled-person-in-india.html
- http://www.wateraid.org/uk/what_we_do/the_need/4719.asp
- http://corporate.marksandspencer.com/documents/specific/howwedobusiness/our_people/em
- http://corporate.marksandspencer.com/file.axd?pointerid=f3ccae91d1d348ff8f523ab8afe9d8a8
- http://files.shareholder.com/downloads/MAN/956225803x0x340338/8B7676DE-8608-4CB1-
- http://nds1.nokia.com/NOKIA_COM_1/Corporate_Responsibility/Sustainability_report_2009/pd
- http://people.brandeis.edu/~nmenon/Draft04_Disability_India.pdf
- http://plana.marksandspencer.com/media/pdf/planA-2010.pdf
- http://world.honda.com/community/report/doc/Honda-Philanthropy-2009.pdf
- http://www.accor.com/fileadmin/user_upload/Contenus_Accor/Commun/pdf/EN/ACCOR_RA2
- http://www.accor.com/uploads/static/accorbook/AccorBook-gb-2009.html
- http://www.carrefour.com/docroot/groupe/C4com/Commerce%20responsable/Publications/R
- http://www.cisco.com/web/about/ac227/csr2009/index.html
- http://www.deltaholding.rs/upload/documents/reports/CSR_REPORT_Delta_Holding.pdf
- http://www.dol.gov/odep/newfreedom/coc.htm
- http://www.dow.com/commitments/pdf/GRI_71410.pdf
- http://www.e-summit.org/conference/Advocating-for-Children-with-Disabilities.html
- http://www.grundfos.com/web/grfosweb.nsf/Grafikopslag/sustainability_report_09/$file/Susta
- http://www.ibm.com/ibm/responsibility/ibm_crr_downloads/pdf/2008_IBMCRR_FullReport.pdf
- http://www.microsoft.com/about/corporatecitizenship/en-us/our-commitments/reporting
- http://www.mid-day.com/news/2012/mar/250312-Ex-army-major-is-first-disabled-Indian-at-UN-agency.htm
- http://www.mphasis.com/pdfs/Mphasis_ Annual_ Report_ 2009.pdf
- http://www.nokia.com/NOKIA_COM_1/Corporate_Responsibility/Sidebars_new_concept/Code

- http://www.o2.com/media_files/Telefonica_business_principles_07.pdf
- http://www.socialtraders.com.au/sites/www.socialtraders.com.au/files/Westpac%20Foundatio
- http://www.sodexo.com/group_en/Images/2010-Corporate-Citizenship-Progress-
- http://www.sony.net/SonyInfo/csr/issues/report/2009/pdf/CSR2009E_all.pdf
- http://www.telefonica.com/en/annual_report/pdf/Telefonica_RC09.pdf
- http://www.telenor.com/en/resources/images/report_2009_tcm28-54140.pdf
- http://www.telstra.com.au/abouttelstra/download/document/disability-action-plan-07-09.pdf
- http://www.telstra.com.au/abouttelstra/download/document/Telstra-Business-Principles.pdf
- http://www.telstra.com.au/abouttelstra/download/document/telstra-corporate-citizenshipreport-
- https://kead.or.kr/uploads/20091120151800 Casebook_InternationalEdition_final(080325).pdf
- https://sem.samsung.co.kr/en/social/sustainability_report.html
- http://www.thisischile.cl/2010/02/chilean-disabled-people-already-have-a-national-service/?lang=en
- http://venezuelanalysis.com/news/10775
- http://www.ifes.org/Content/Multimedia/Podcasts/2012/Advocating-for-the-rights-of-Persons-with-Disabilities-in-South-East-Asia.aspx
- http://delhi.gov.in/wps/wcm/connect/doit_ocpd/DoIT_OCPD/Home/About+Us/
- http://www.odisha.gov.in/disabilityportal/
- http://www.aiipmr.gov.in/Disability_Certificates.aspx
- http://www.disabilityindia.co.in/Acts-in-Disability/The-RCI-Act.php
- http://www.government.nl/issues/health-issues/disabled-people
- http://disability.challengepost.com/
- http://everydaylife.globalpost.com/problems-facing-physically-mentally-disabled-children-15470.html
- http://www.goodreads.com/quotes/tag/disability

Index

N

O

P